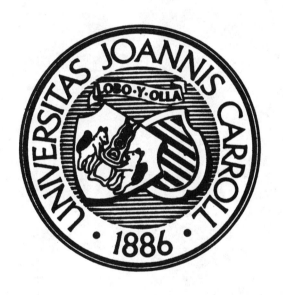

SCIENTIFIC ACADEMY

As long as Father Odenbach was around there was no lack of scientific interest at the college. He was ably assisted in this regard by Father Henry Hecken, who had been on the college staff since 1913. The return of Father Pickel in 1927 gave added strength to the interest in science. The students were anxious to work on scientific projects outside of class and in 1916 founded a scientific academy for this purpose. Prizes were awarded annually for the best treatise. Many of the students lectured to various groups around the city on their scientific activities. The academy issued a "Scientific Bulletin" and occupied space in the student publication for a number of years. Aloysius Bungart was the president of the academy in 1916 and gave talks on many subjects with some emphasis on glaciers and Indian relics.

The value of the academy seemed evident from the beginning. The *Lumina* commented that

> Where formerly there was little or nothing of a scientific nature done outside the ordinary class work, now work of a sound and truly scientific nature is being carried on; where before scientific work, if done at all, was sporadic now the work has become organized and given publicity, with the result that those ambitious of a scientific training find in the members of the academy kindred spirits in whose company they are stimulated to enthusiasm in their own respective sciences, or acquire an interest in a branch of science to which otherwise their attention would never have been attracted. In a word it has created a scientific atmosphere in the college where the slumbering coals of a taste for science are awakened and fanned into an intense interest.[115]

SOCIAL LIFE

In 1920 the Alumni broke the precedent of such stag affairs as smokers by scheduling the first dance party. Fears that it would not be a success because it was an innovation proved to be unfounded. It was attended by nearly three hundred persons and was a financial as well as a social success. The fear now was that a hall large enough for the next party could not be secured. As *The Ignatian* observed, "who doubts that stag affairs, however entertaining they may be sometimes become a bore. . . . The success of the initial plunge into high society brings a promise of more to follow."[116] It was also noted that the hall was "suitably decorated, the music fit for the Gods, the punch was as good as can be purchased these days."[117] The first ball held under the auspices of the college was held the following year on 6 April at the K of C ballroom. It, too, was a success. By 1924 there was a

Junior Prom attended by 111 couples. Still, there were complaints that the Senior Prom should have drawn more than 140 couples; the number was less than the attendance at other Jesuit college Proms in the Missouri Province.[118]

Except for the Proms, no class dances were permitted to be held under the name of the university prior to 1925. As a result, the class custom was to hold one or more dances under the name of a club which, of course, was the class itself. This was tolerated as long as the name of the university was not directly associated with the dance. In the fall of 1925 the policy was changed so that each class was to have one official dance each year.[119]

The Annual Ball of 1926 became the cause of a dispute between Bishop Schrembs and Father Boylan. The bishop said he received a complaint from a Catholic family in the city that the advertising for the Ball said it was to go until three A.M. The bishop wrote to Father Boylan saying, "I think you will agree with me that an announcement stating that dancing will be continued until three A.M. scarcely represents the Catholic ideal of Christian morality."[120]

The bishop objected to more than the three A.M. closing time for the dance; he took the occasion to review the entire question of university-sponsored dances. His informant had expressed "distinct shock" at the cut of the women's dresses and the kind of dancing at a previous Ball. The bishop instructed Father Boylan to "Kindly give this your immediate attention for I am sure that you will realize that the responsibility must rest with you."[121] The bishop said further that he knew of a public dance given under the auspices of a civic organization where women "improperly attired were asked to leave."[122] Father Boylan, therefore, was to keep strict supervision over dress and the nature of the dances.[123]

Father Boylan wrote to his Provincial, Father McMenamy, and said he had just received a *miramur* from the bishop about the Prom. Father Boylan said he had confronted Father Bracken with the three A.M. closing time, saying he had not been consulted about it. Father Boylan told his Provincial that in replying to the bishop he would "write deferentially . . . of course."[124]

It is not quite clear what Father Boylan meant by "deferentially." He apparently brought the subject up to Bishop Schrembs before the latter had said Mass one day and then had to apologize for doing it that way.[125] He then wrote at length to defend his supervision of the dances:

> I shall submit to what you expressed as your wish this morning. It will entail an outlay of money upon us, comment and disappointment in many quarters. But we can meet all of that. I have made enquiries about the affairs given here under the auspices of John Carroll within the last years, and the chaperones, prominent

Catholic ladies and gentlemen of the city, were present from start to finish at all of them. . . . We have not thus far heard of any of these balls being in a way offensive, and we are very keen on keeping our ear to the ground in these things.

It will be very easy for us to just let the young people go ahead and dance, as dance they will in any event, and withdraw our name from their doings, their dances and other affairs. But it is to keep safeguards of morality that we are trying to have these affairs conducted under our auspices. Thus far, by all accounts, according to the statements of those who were actually present, we have succeeded admirably well. I know our experience in other cities too. The dancing problem is an intricate one.

There has always been strict supervision over the ladies apparel, we leave that to prominent Catholic ladies who have chaperoned our affairs. I have been assured, that precisely in our dances there were no low backed dresses worn by the ladies. . . . I am told there are no wild goings on at all. This same lay teacher states that in our last Junior Prom liquor was not in evidence. . . .

Your lordship spoke of the dancing till three A.M. With all deference to your judgement in this matter, I must humbly resent the imputation of conniving at immorality. If the proper safeguards prevail throughout I see no change of morality to immorality between dancing before and after twelve.[126]

As a result of the bishop's objection, the original Prom arrangements were cancelled and the Prom rescheduled as an affair ending at twelve. The original plan called for the dance at the Hotel Statler to be a supper dance with Ev Jones's orchestra playing up to one o'clock and Guy Lombardo and His Royal Canadians playing from one to three A.M.[127] The revised plan called for a dinner dance ending at the required hour; the program dances after the dinner were interrupted by a singing act by Bob Hunt.[128]

Some of the "wild goings on" referred to in the correspondence between Bishop Schrembs and Father Boylan had to do with the "Charleston Menace" which was sweeping the country. The *Carroll News*, in an issue after the Prom, expressed the view that if reports about the Charleston were "credible, the present rage will leave in its path a swath of ruined buildings unequalled in extent in this country since Sherman's memorable march."[129] It was suggested that a solution might be found by placing the dance floor above a swimming pool so that when the floor collapsed the dancers might be cooled off.

On dances in general, an article in the *Carroll News* gave tongue-in-cheek support to Father Boylan's report that all of Carroll's dances were properly conducted. Moreover, a dance was "frequently the only occasion of Carroll students shaving themselves and shining their shoes."[130] Additional advantages were to be found in the opportunity of contemplating beauty at close range even though "of course, there are exceptions." Continued employment of saxophone players as well as of manufacturers of shoe polish and shaving blades were supported by such dances; the cultural values needed no discussion.[131]

Ten years later there was a rerun of the skirmish between Bishop Schrembs and a Carroll president over the hour when dances should end. The script was the same, but there were some changes in the cast; Father Rodman was now president and the students of 1936 were not as reticent as those of 1926. Rumors that the Golden Jubilee Prom of 1936 would go to three A.M. brought forth a remonstrance from Bishop Schrembs to Father Rodman:

> Some years ago I issued an order that henceforth all social events for our Catholic Collegiate Institutions must close at midnight.
>
> I am creditably informed that this rule is being violated, or that some who observe the rule are made an object of jest and ridicule on the part of those who have paid no attention to my ruling.
>
> I wish it distinctly understood that any social college affair, such as a prom, must close at midnight. Surely our people have a right to expect that our Catholic institutions will set a standard of moderation and decency.[132]

Father Rodman's reply was in the same vein as Father Boylan's had been; "I will take care that your wish is carried out. . . . I thought it was, but of course unless these things are watched continuously, abuses are apt to creep in."[133] There the resemblance to the 1926 episode ended. The matter was taken up by Father Rodman and his consultors who argued that "common practice is to the contrary, the boys find the rule rather severe."[134] It was agreed to accede to Father William Murphy's request to pay a visit to the bishop to ask for permission to present the students' argument. The visit was fruitless; Father Murphy reported that the bishop was "adamant and asked the Carroll men to help him in correcting what he thought was an abuse."[135]

The reaction of the *Carroll News* to the bishop's demands was hardly on the submissive side. An editorial entitled "Twelve Bells says the Bishop," stated that the committee for the Prom had "decided to be good little boys and abide by the rule of His Excellency." The editorial then went on to say that the committee should be praised for its willingness to go on with Prom arrangements in spite of the "peculiar rule—peculiar because it applies only to members of the collegiate circle and not to other Catholic organizations in the diocese." The editorial went on to point out that even though the Prom closed at midnight it would be no guarantee that those attending would go directly home:

> If these gentlemen insist on being night owls, nothing is going to stop them from attending the Prom and adjourning to one of those terrible dens of iniquity

which we moderns refer to as night clubs. If they attend the Prom and do not object to leaving the Prom at midnight the committee for the dance will attempt to pacify the local professors if some of the night owls wear their tuxes to the early morning classes Thursday April 16. Just attend the Prom and everyone will be happy.[136]

The bishop was not happy; an apology was demanded. In the next issue of the *Carroll News* the apology appeared in a two column box beginning at the top of the page and extending some five inches down with the heading. "Apology" in large type. After pointing out that the original editorial was addressed, not to the bishop, but to the students attending the Prom, the writer said, "Some readers of the *Carroll News* interpreted this editorial as not indicative of the true Carroll spirit—complete submission to any wish of our Bishop. We regret therefore the appearance of this editorial and offer to our Bishop and other readers our humble apology."[137] It is not clear whether the 1 April date on the issue carrying the apology bore any special significance.

ALUMNI ACTIVITIES

Increased interest in a college education meant that more students were finishing their courses. As early as 1916 the numbers in the philosophy year were increasing and the demand for more Catholic "men of learning, of deep erudition and profound scholarship" was making itself felt in the numbers attending Catholic colleges.[138] In 1921 St. Ignatius College disputed the claims of Xavier University to the title of largest enrollment in a Catholic college in the state.[139] Xavier's claim was disputed because it was discovered that the claim was based on National Catholic Welfare Council figures, which for some reason showed only 73 students at St. Ignatius whereas there were actually 142 for the year in question.

St. Ignatius alumni were still very well represented among the clergy of the diocese. Hardly an ordination class during the postwar period did not have as a majority of its members former students of St. Ignatius College. In 1918 seven out of the ten newly ordained priests were former Ignatius students, twelve out of fourteen in 1919. In 1923 twenty-one students from St. Ignatius entered the seminary, nineteen of them from the junior class, the largest number to enter in many years. Fathers Thomas C. O'Reilly, '93, and James A. McFadden, '99, were two among many of the outstanding clergy who had their early training at St. Ignatius. Both later became bishops.

Many graduates were politically oriented and so there was always a host of them running for some local office. Many also occupied various judicial offices. Frank Merrick became assistant prosecutor at the age of twenty-six. Many also went into the newspaper field. Ignatius graduates worked at each of the local papers, representing classes as far back as 1905. Former students were also represented on the *Catholic Universe* staff when Father John R. Hagan conducted an interesting and instructive Question Box. A survey of the class of 1927 showed that of the forty-two graduates, twenty-eight went into professional fields, nine into business, ten into medicine, nine into law. Three began studies for the priesthood, and one joined the Jesuits.[140]

A complaint of 1917 that St. Ignatius College was not very well known was not heard so often in later years. Yet in 1917, a reception for an important Catholic speaker arranged by a body of prominent Catholics completely ignored the St. Ignatius student orchestra in favor of one from Western Reserve.[141] The increasing number of alumni in a variety of places and positions in the city made it less likely that the university would be so ignored in the 1930s.

Although an Alumni association had existed since 1903, it was not until the 1920s that the association engaged in a more positive way to support college activities. Shortly after becoming Bishop of Cleveland, Bishop Schrembs addressed the reorganized alumni in November 1921, and urged them to keep up the same ambition they showed in their college days, to assist young men who had not the means to go to college and to give financial support to their Alma Mater.[142] Nevertheless one of the most frequently heard complaints was the need for an active Alumni association.

FACULTY CHANGE

The office of dean of men had originally been considered as a link between the faculty and student body, with emphasis on the personal development of the student. The first Jesuit to hold that office, Father Bracken, spent far more time on student activities, particularly athletics, than on the personal development of the student. In 1930 he was replaced by Father Stephen Driscoll, who emphasized that his first duty was personal relationship with the undergraduates.[143] Father Driscoll was chairman of the Committee on Student Welfare and Activities as well as chairman of the Committee on Religious Welfare. He saw his function as one of "character-building."[144] One year later Father James Quinlan succeeded Father Driscoll as dean of men. His interest was not so much in the student activities as it was in the personal problems of the student. He once said football was not his favorite sport.[145]

By 1933 a split occurred in the functions of the office of dean of men. Father Clifford LeMay came to John Carroll as student counselor dealing chiefly with spiritual and religious matters.[146] In 1943 Father William Murphy became dean of men with responsibility for nonspiritual activities.[147]

Between 1920 and 1935 the faculty expanded from nineteen to thirty-eight; the laymen increased from two to sixteen. The increase in the number of laymen stemmed not only from the inability of the Province to supply more Jesuits but also because of the departure of many Jesuits who had given long years of service to St. Ignatius College. Fathers Betten, Bracken, Haggeney, Kleist, and Winter, and Neustich, who died in 1924, and Odenbach, who died in 1933, had no equivalent replacements. Their leaving marked in a very real sense the end of an era in the university's history that could be called the "West Side Story." Father Pickel, who returned to John Carroll in 1927 after an absence of seventeen years, provided a significant link between the West Side and East Side stories. It was perhaps fitting that this should be so, since it was he who first established an East Side branch in 1907 when Loyola High School was opened.

Football Fame: The Elusive Goal, 1916–1935

Competitive sports on the intercollegiate level became widely popular in the United States during the last quarter of the nineteenth century, but not until after 1900 was there pressure on the universities to use athletics for advertising or increasing endowment revenues. St. Ignatius College was not immune to these pressures even though intercollegiate competition was not something the early Jesuit Fathers considered part of their program. Jesuit policy attempted to resist the pressure to develop intercollegiate sports. Father Rudolph Meyer, the first American-born Provincial of the Missouri Province, began his second term as Provincial in 1907 just as the Buffalo Mission became part of the Missouri Province. In an effort to put some uniformity in the burgeoning athletic programs and "to prevent the excess and moral danger to which they gradually lead," Father Meyer issued regulations to govern such programs.[1] Since it was clear that marching, calisthenics, and gymnastics would no longer suffice to provide a sound body for a sound mind, restrictions were put on the new sports to prevent them from getting out of hand. The regulations prescribed by Father Meyer required the general direction of athletics to be under a priest and not a scholastic, no overnight trips for games, and special permission for the priest who had to accompany the team on game days. No contests were to be held on Sundays, Holy days, or during Lent. "Intercollegiate contests, in general, should be discouraged rather than encouraged, and their number should be limited so far as is compatible with laudible college spirit and a moderate degree of rivalry." Uniforms were to conform to Christian modesty. Loose fitting knee pants were recommended for basketball. Shirts were to cover the upper arm. Dressing rooms were to be supervised and indoor track meets with other teams were prohibited.[2]

One of the more interesting of Father Meyer's regulations stated, "no one should be allured or admitted to any course in our Universities or Colleges, only or chiefly for the sake of forming or strengthening an athletic team."[3] Even at that early date recruiting had become a problem.

The growing athletic activity did not escape the notice of Father General Ledochowski. In 1918 according to the Missouri Province Provincial he ordered that college catalogues should not contain pictures of athletes, nor was he "pleased with the pictures of partly nude athletes that often take up considerable space in our various publications."[4] By 1932 it would seem that not much attention had been paid to all these regulations, for Father Ledochowski spoke out again. This time, the dean of the college was to be entrusted with the direction of athletics although he could delegate this office. No scholarships would be for athletics alone and there would be but one academic standard for all students. Athletes should not be recruited with financial inducements nor could a prospective athlete be placed in a preparatory program. Further reflecting the abuses of "tramp athletes" and promotional aspects of the football scene of the late 1920s, Father Ledochowski ordered that, "Schools shall stay in their own class. Small colleges shall not try to have teams capable of competing with schools manifestly beyond their class."[5] To put what he called an effective stop to lengthy trips, the Provincial's permission was now required for such trips. The Jesuits themselves were later included in similar restrictions when golf was discouraged as recreation for Jesuits. Certain concommitants of the game made it undesirable; even if golf were allowed, the golf clubs were to be the property of the Jesuit Community. It will be clear from the history of athletics at St. Ignatius College and John Carroll University that most of these restrictions appeared not to exist.

Not until 1904 did Father John Theis begin the first serious effort in the direction of a sports program at St. Ignatius College by forming an athletic association. Father Theis had been president of Canisius College from 1898 to 1901 and had attempted to convince Father General, at that time Father Luis Martin, that sports had a place in the colleges if they were kept in proper balance.[6] Not, however, until Father Furay's time, when the gymnasium which "had long been spoken of" was built, was there a serious effort at developing a full sports program.[7] Provision for an enlargement of the gymnasium of Loyola High School was also made at the same time. While the new gymnasium on the West Side was to cost between eight and ten thousand dollars, only one hundred fifty dollars was to be given for the expansion at Loyola and the students were expected to contribute a like sum.[8]

This new gymnasium replaced the original wooden college building which earlier had been converted to a makeshift gymnasium. There was a moment in the discussions of a new gymnasium when thoughts of extending the new college along West 30th Street to include the gymnasium were considered.[9] This would have proved too costly and so the plan of putting the gymnasium on Carroll Avenue was approved.[10] The new gymnasium was completed in 1914, the year in which the old gymnasium, or the original college, was torn down.[11]

Top left, Leonard H. Otting, S.J., Philosophy, 1926–27, 1933–50; *center,* Bernard S. Jablonski, Professor of French, 1932–65; *right,* Murtha Boylan, President, John Carroll University, 1925–28; *Middle left,* Aloysius Bungart, Professor of English, 1925–59; *right,* Charles M. Ryan, S.J., English and Debate, 1921–25, 1930–41; *Bottom,* Joseph A. Kiefer, S.J., Music and Classics, 1927–51

When Father Sommerhauser became president in 1915, he not only authorized the college magazine, revived the orchestra, and restored the annual play, but he also saw to it that two handball courts were built, one at the south side of the yard, the other at the east side of the yard. The project was to be financed through proceeds from plays and other activities.[12] In 1916 the clearing of the shacks behind the houses on Lorain extended the playing area of the yard.[13]

The effect on the students of the renovation of the yard and the opening of the new gymnasium was remarkable. In the fall of 1915, some two hundred students of the three hundred who had paid fees and promised to come, met in the gymnasium for a meeting of the athletic association. The account in the *Lumina* speaks for itself; as the

walls of the new gymnasium fairly rocked on their foundations, the seismograph recorded a slight quake, in the vicinity of W. 30th Street and Carroll Avenue, and close observers say that Old Mose [Cleveland] fairly wobbled on his grime stained pedestal in the public square. Do you want to know the cause of all these weird happenings? Well! "New" St. Ignatius had a rally the like of which will never again be seen or heard of in its history.

Mr. [Ormond P.] D'Haene, S.J., our new athletic director, pressed the needle, not filled with dope, but with ginger into our slothful bodies and awakened with a start those latent spirits, so that not a boy, even the wiliest, could restrain himself. Vocal chords were strained, and great orators became mere peepers in a few moments, new collars soiled and torn, were but remnants of their former selves. Stetsons became so many small and footworn doormats, and the walls echoed and reechoed with shouts of 'we will, we will' our new slogan.[14]

The cause of all the commotion was an effort to enlist the entire student body in the revived athletic association. The new officers were Albert Murphy, '16, president, and Ralph Gallagher, '18, secretary. Dan Savage, a former student and star athlete, returned as coach of whatever teams could be formed. After signing up as new members of the association, "the boys filed out like so many battle-torn warriors, smiling and glad at heart, for the victory was theirs alone."[15]

ATHLETE *VS.* STUDENT

The enthusiasm over the new gymnasium and the new spirit made basketball one of the two major sports in the years prior to and just after World War I. The "Saints," as the teams were generally called, played an eleven-game basketball schedule in 1916, winning only six against such opponents as Niagara, Canisius, Baldwin-Wallace, Kent, St. John (Toledo), Cedarville, Heidelberg, and Detroit. There were also the interclass teams forming three leagues which served as recruiting grounds for the varsity squad. Coach Dan Savage held out hope for a better season the following year as he looked over the number of returning players and new prospects. Even a change of athletic directors did not dampen spirits. D'Haene left for further studies; his successor was another scholastic, Robert Harder, who gave promise of continuing the interest in athletics.

The contrast between the attitude of athletes preparing for games and that of students preparing for class was apparently marked enough for the editor of the *Lumina*, Al Bungart, to comment at length:

> Just why athletes will do anything to make the team while students will do everything to avoid lessons, seems to be an unsolvable problem. Yet, in the former case, the reward is a mere trifle in comparison with the great good of the latter. In one case the stern exacting coach is given credit for enforcing rules; in the other the professor is regarded as a tyrant for enforcing rules in classes. When teachers lay down rules about burning the midnight oil, they are giving us the best of advice. When they assign certain difficult tasks, they are preparing our minds to prepare our positions well in the great game of life. When they insist we run around the track of Latin and Greek every night, it is to improve our mind, not theirs. And as far as delighting in the application of blue pencil liniment, the reverse in fact is true. When crippled exercise, and lame treatise, and spiked tasks, and sprained themes hobble up before their desks they are ready to give up in disgust and despair, especially is this true, when a prescription must be filled at the 'jug.' Let this time honored fallacy die a natural death. Let us look upon study as we look upon baseball practice, a necessary asset.[16]

The building of the new gymnasium certainly put an emphasis on basketball, but that sport did not immediately replace baseball. Not until 1923 did baseball fade from the sport scene for St. Ignatius. Then it was replaced by football which soon eclipsed basketball as the major sport.

BASKETBALL 1916–1923

Comparative interest in basketball and baseball might be judged by the turn-out of students for practice; in the fall of 1916, twenty-five turned out for the basketball team; in the spring fifty turned out for baseball. Lest this be taken as an indication that basketball was a second-class sport, a notation in the "Consultors' Minutes" would seem to indicate otherwise. In order to permit the Fathers to attend the evening games, it was noted that "on the day of chief basketball games, Litanies shall be before dinner scl. at 5:45 P.M. All that wish to see games shall attend spiritual exercises (points and examen) immediately after dinner instead of recreation."[17] These same minutes and the "House Diary" began to reflect the new interest in sports by noting the scores of at least the "chief games." This marked quite a change from the attitude of the "Iron Ages" where gymnastics, calisthenics, marching, and drilling were the heart of any program of physical activities.

From 1915 to 1925 the basketball schedule included such teams as Campion, Canisius, Niagara, St. John (Toledo), Hiram, Ashland, Kent, Ohio Wesleyan, Capital, Findlay, Duquesne, Baldwin-Wallace, and Western Reserve. A round of vaccinations in 1918, because of the influenza epidemic, made for a short basketball season that year. A chief complaint of the St. Ignatius boys, who were used to the space in their new gymnasium and found some other team's floors small by comparison, was the geography of the Canisius floor. After losing to Canisius in the 1916–1917 season by a 47–22 score, the *Lumina* complained:

> The basketball court at Canisius is a big handicap to any team that has been used to playing on a regulation floor or at least on a floor that is not strung with posts. Playing on a floor of that kind makes one believe that the ocean is not the only place you can get sea sick.[18]

The year 1919 marked not only the installation of new bleachers in the gymnasium at the western end, but also the completion of two tennis courts; they were used very effectively by Jack Rice, who was the District Junior Champion, and Walter Dorsey, who shared the Municipal Doubles Championship. Track replaced tennis as a team sport in 1924; by 1926 only football and basketball were left as major team sports. A brief attempt to promote a boxing team in 1920 did not succeed.

The popularity of basketball forced the addition of more bleachers in 1921. The bleachers at the west end installed in 1919 were the only real bleachers. One row of seats lined each of the other sides. Persons in these seats tended to drift toward the playing area during a game, often forcing officials to call time to get the people to move back. The installations of bleachers in the other three sides now gave the gymnasium a capacity of 1,100.

The enrollment increase in 1920 promised that the bleachers would be used. *The Ignatian* attributed the increase to Father Bracken's efforts of the previous year to get each student to return in the fall with "prototypes of themselves on their arms."[19] The potential of more students to provide better athletes was not missed. "The teams of the college are bound to derive benefit from the increased enrollment as more men will surely come out for the various varsities."[20]

Except for the addition of Creighton, Detroit, and Xavier, the basketball schedules remained much the same as they had been. Not until 1922 was success really achieved; the basketball team of 1922–1923 won twelve out of fourteen games. The victories included two over the Michigan Aggies, a team that had defeated Notre Dame, and a particularly satisfying victory over Western Reserve. The home engagement with the Michigan Aggies was played at Eagles Hall as the feature attraction of a triple bill arranged by Max Rosenblum, noted Cleveland sports promoter. The game ball of the Aggies' game was turned over to Toby Erdman, a former St. Ignatius coach, who was seriously ill.[21]

The Reserve game in March 1923 caused the most local excitement. The game was scheduled to be played on the St. Ignatius court, though efforts by local sport promoters to have the game shifted to the Public Hall were vigorously but unsuccessfully pursued. According to newspaper accounts the efforts failed because Western Reserve authorities said the move "would occasion too much confusion."[22] The game, therefore, was played as originally scheduled before an over-capacity crowd of 1,200 spectators; over one hundred were turned away. St. Ignatius had lost only to Duquesne and Ohio University; Reserve was to play Case the following week making the game an important one for the city college championship. St. Ignatius's victory over Reserve by two points, 27–25, was duly headlined in the papers. The *Plain Dealer* described the contest as a

> tale of Jim Smith and Terrible Turk [Carl Turk], captain of St. Ignatius, of how one curly headed lad, wearing the former commonplace name and another creating as much havoc as ever did a dashing Ottoman last night put on a brand of basketball that enabled their favorite college, St. Ignatius, to defeat Western Reserve cagers.[23]

Since Reserve defeated Case a week later, 30–21, St. Ignatius claimed the city championship. Reserve and St. Ignatius did not meet the following season, 1923–1924, a season which saw St. Ignatius win nine games while losing five.

BASEBALL 1915–1922

For a long period of time, baseball was able to keep pace with basketball for the students' interest. There were always good turnouts for the teams until just after World War I; then not basketball but football caused baseball's demise. Baseball schedules comprised many of the same teams as basketball but there was a little more contact with local schools including Case and Western Reserve.

Sometimes enthusiasm bubbled over into controversy, as a five-inning game with Case in 1917, in which St. Ignatius claimed a 14–1 victory. Since St. Ignatius had beaten Reserve by a 2–0 score, the Saints now claimed the city championship. The game with Case had been scheduled as a practice game but as an article in the *Plain Dealer* said, "the practice the Saints got would have gotten them into shape for a marathon race."[24] Pat Pasini, coach at Case, was irritated at the claim of city champions; he said he did not play his regulars because it was a practice game and he kept no score. Moreover, Pasini himself pitched and lobbed the ball over when St. Ignatius scored eleven times in the first inning.[25] A complicating factor was that "bad blood cropped up after the fifth inning. The St. Ignatius squad thinking it had won a victory, left the field."[26] The two teams did not meet again until 1919, when the Saints, now coached by Paddy Livingston, a former major leaguer, lost to Case by an 11 to 2 score. Prior to the defeat by Case, the Saints had beaten Western Reserve 24–7, after beating Reserve in a previous game 11–4.[27]

In 1920 the St. Ignatius team was coached by Art Brickel, '17, who had acquired a reputation as a "spitball artist" when he pitched in 1916 and 1917. The rise of football interest, which required the use of the yard for spring training left little room in the yard for baseball, which was discontinued in 1922 with no immediate prospect of resuming the sport.[28]

RISE OF FOOTBALL ENTHUSIASM 1916–1923

By replacing baseball with football, St. Ignatius College was merely following a general trend of the times in collegiate sport programs. Much of the earlier opposition to football was based on the number of injuries and deaths that resulted from the style of play in the early days of football. The situation was bad enough for President Theodore Roosevelt to call a conference at the White House in 1905 to discuss remedies. Although the president's threat to abolish football if something was not done failed to produce immediate reform, there was at least an effort to set up some standard. The period beginning around 1915 was marked by a great number of smaller colleges in Ohio and elsewhere taking up the game and the development of a variety of new tactics such as the forward pass and the "shift" popularized by Notre Dame. Jesuit colleges in this period entered the lists of colleges sponsoring football teams.

The first varsity football team at St. Ignatius College was formed in 1916 under Coach Savage. A light and comparatively green squad of "twenty blue and gold clad Richard-the-thirds stalked into the yard" from the gymnasium where they had first assembled.[29] With four regulars out with injuries the team defeated Loyola and Spencerian as well as the Alumni and lost to Baldwin-Wallace and Findlay. The following year proved to be even less successful. Coach Savage was called to military service; no replacement was made and a schedule could not be arranged.

When the SATC program was inaugurated in October 1918, the college decided not to have football. Military officials of the SATC program announced that it was not their intention to suppress football but rather to encourage it. The general effect of this announcement was that "colleges which never before went in the game are taking it up under government auspices which seems to predict a bright future for the game."[30] St. Ignatius College then planned to field a team that year but the time was too short and the end of the war in November also ended that year's football efforts. Nor was a team formed for 1919 because of "lack of heavy material."[31]

The spring of 1920 saw plans for a big football boom the following fall. Father Edward Bracken, who joined the faculty as vice-president and dean in the fall of 1919, lost no time in mobilizing what material he could find to launch a football team. He had seen brief service as a military chaplain in 1918, and had been director of athletics at St. John College, Toledo, before coming to St. Ignatius. An article in *The Ignatian*, probably inspired by Father Bracken, put the matter squarely up to the students:

> Students have reached the test of our newborn spirit of loyalty and interest in our Alma Mater. With a great deal of the novelty worn off of our recently instituted activities and mistakes made here and there or a failure met within some of our recent undertakings, giving rise to a spirit of criticism and I told you so' ism, we have now come to the crisis where we must either give up and sink back into our state of lethargy or, confident in our knowledge of the righteousness of our cause, overcome all obstacles.[32]

In May the challenge to the students was made more specific.

> The athletic management is planning a big year in football next autumn. It is doing its utmost to assure the success of putting a team in the field. . . . Now it remains for the student body to take up the task and inaugurate a regular football boom. What is needed now is good, sound, solid backing on the part of the student. . . . The matter of the team is a vital proposition but it rests solely with the students.[33]

There was little doubt that the interest in football was being pursued in earnest. The "quasi state of coma" the college had been in for a "rather long period" was about to end.[34] The ultimate purpose was to "enable St. Ignatius to take its place alongside other colleges in the line of football."[35] Some present students were expected to form the nucelus of the team, the three Catholic high schools in the city were expected to furnish good prospects, and finally, there was "a rumor afloat—and the rumor is based on sufficient evidence to give it credence—to the effect that a few well known great stars from some of the larger colleges and universities in the district will make St. Ignatius College their Alma Mater next fall."[36]

At a rally after the opening of the fall semester in 1920, Father Bracken announced there would be a football team and presented the new coach, George "Tuffy" Conn, to the students. Conn had played college football with the Oregon Aggies and was scheduled to play for the Cleveland Tigers professional football team. Conn told the students that they possessed as good a representative college team as could be found in the state and that they "may not be much on weight, but when it comes to fight and gameness nobody can beat them."[37]

The preparations for a big football year were apparently not making as much of an impression on the student body as had been hoped. An editorial on school spirit asked the students what part they were playing in putting St. Ignatius College "where it belongs and where it has deserved to belong for a long, long time."[38] The article appealed to the students to join in the efforts of the Alumni Association, which was doing all in its power "to put their Alma Mater on the map" and support the football team, "the first real college eleven that St. Ignatius has ever had."[39]

On the other hand, the same editorial expressed the fear that school spirit might be identified only with football. It warned that school spirit was not a limited thing; it "should embrace not only one branch of activities but should embrace them all"; since *The Ignatian* was a subscription paper, it was suggested that school spirit required that every student subscribe.[40]

The six-game schedule for 1920 showed a record of four victories—Hiram, Dayton, Niagara, and Ashland—against two losses—Mt. Union and St. Xavier. The 48−0 defeat by Mt. Union early in the season was forgotten by the time Niagara was defeated 3−0. A victory parade of some fifty Ignatius students marching four abreast through the downtown area continued out Euclid Avenue to East 18th Street, where the students boarded a street car that took them out to East 73rd Street. From there they walked over to Hough Avenue, where Coach Conn was living. The coach was at the time entertaining Stan Cofall, also of the Cleveland Tigers. Not to be outdone by this show of support, the coach sent out to round up some violin and banjo players who were also living in the vicinity and an impromptu musical program was arranged. The group then returned to Child's Restaurant for a midnight snack of wheatcakes; after a few more cheers the party broke up.[41]

The enthusiasm engendered by the successful season prompted St. Ignatius to claim consideration in determining the city football championship; Case had lost five of its six games and Reserve had lost all of theirs. "Why then," asked *The Ignatian*, "should we be denied to have a chance at annexing the championship. We will assert our right and if our claims go un-heeded the real College Grid championship will go unheeded this year."[42]

A suggestion that St. Ignatius meet the winner of the Case-Reserve Thanksgiving Day game was not well received by the East Siders. Neverthe-less, St. Ignatius still felt that neither Case nor Reserve could claim the city championship "until it meets Ignatius and beats them."[43] Adding insult to injury was an article in the *Plain Dealer* awarding the county football championship to Baldwin-Wallace;[44] Ignatius was not considered a con-tender for the honor since it had not played the other three teams. *The Ignatian*, quoting from sports writers of the daily papers, pointed out that the *Plain Dealer* writer probably never saw Ignatius play while the other writers who had seen the Saints considered the team "on a par" with Baldwin-Wallace.[45] One thing was certain, no matter who was awarded championship title, the stage had been set at St. Ignatius for an era of the predominance of football.

There was some fear on the part of faculty and students that emphasis on football might develop to a disproportionate point. *The Ignatian* reprinted an editorial from the newspaper of Xavier University in Cincinnati, the *Xaverian* of 1 December 1920. The editorial noted the small number of athletes in a college in proportion to the whole student body and raised the question of devoting so much energy to producing teams of high caliber. The answer was that the importance of such teams to the university should not be belittled. That almost no activity was so powerful in producing school spirit and that almost no other means, including advertising, was as useful for the school as a successful football team appeared to justify every-thing. Yet, unless there was some program in which the mass of students could participate, emphasis on athletics would not be as productive as expected.[46]

The following season, 1921, brought a measure of satisfaction in defeat-ing Baldwin-Wallace, but the season record under a new coach, "Toby" Erdman, was hardly satisfactory with but two victories against six losses. Some explanation for the poor season may be found both in a schedule that placed tougher opponents too early in the season and in the unusual number of injuries that plagued the team.

The 1921 performance of the Saints in football had made enough of an impression on Ed Bang, *Cleveland News* sports writer, to have him suggest that Case and Reserve make room for the Saints on their 1922 athletic schedules. Bang wrote:

> We see no reason why Case and Reserve should not mingle with the Catholic lads. Every now and then we are informed that the brown and white and the red and white standard bearers will meet to determine the collegiate championship of

the city in some branch of sports, but this is wrong. St. Ignatius has turned out teams that have ranked with the best produced at Case and Reserve and there is no reason why the three local colleges should not mingle on the gridiron, on the track, in the gym, engage in swimming meets and play baseball in the days to come. The Saints are willing and it wouldn't surprise us if those in charge at Case and Reserve agreed to a local athletic triumvirate.[47]

The editor of *The Ignatian* agreed, but pointed out that "efforts toward that end have proved abortive." Moreover, the two East Side schools had been unwilling to give explanations for their refusal.[48]

In the spring of 1922 an assistant football coach, Frank Burke, was hired for the fall; he was to devote most of his time to coaching the line. Burke was also to teach chemistry and mathematics. In the fall the illness of Toby Erdman forced his replacement as head coach. Isaac Martin, an experienced coach and an advocate of old style football, straight plunging, took over.

The 1922 season could be called a successful one with a record of four games won, three ties and but one loss, to Dayton by one touchdown. The victories were against Kent, St. Bonaventure, Defiance, and Wilmington; tied were Mt. Pleasant, Xavier, and Niagara. Among the stars of the team in 1922 was Carl Turk, a product of Loyola High School. Even with the honors heaped upon him, *The Ignatian* reported that, "Carl hasn't got a bit upstage. Why he would just as soon let you ride on Stanley's Steamer with him as not."[49] James "Mo" Smith, another Loyola graduate, was captain of the football team in 1922.

The turning point in the Saints' grid fortunes that season was the Xavier game. Even though the game ended in a 19–19 tie, the performance of the team gave "evidence to the assertion that the West Side of the river can now boast of a grid representative that is the equal if not the superior of those on the opposite bank."[50] The game was also seen as evidence that a "turn in the road" had been accomplished and prospects for the future were bright. Father Bracken had promised a banquet for the team if they won the Xavier game; he considered the tie just as good as a win and provided the "best meal that the Hollenden House could put out" on the Monday after the St. Bonaventure game. After the meal and "upon leaving the room a good rousing yell was given for the one who had brought Ignatius forward as it has gone—Father Bracken."[51] Further tribute was paid to Father Bracken in a "Tribute to the Men Behind the Guns" in *The Ignatian*. "The first man who is to be credited is none other than Rev. Father Bracken, who directed every activity that the team undertook . . . he was the one who made it possible to have a representative team on the field. After Father Bracken comes the illustrious manager, Kenneth Mulholland."[52]

Before the 1923 season began former Coach Toby Erdman died. Meanwhile, the college had changed its name twice. There is an amusing but probably apocryphal story, attributed to Father John Weber, '23, that when the name Cleveland University was acquired in May of 1923, new uniforms were ordered with the letter "C" on them. When the name Cleveland University was given up, in order not to waste money on discarding the uniforms, the new name had to begin with a "C," hence the name "Carroll".

The 1923 football squad was the first one to reflect large-scale recruiting efforts to supply talent. Of the squad of thirty-three, eight were from Ignatius and three from Loyola and from other local high schools, three were from Cathedral Latin, three from Lincoln, two from East Tech, one from West High, one from West Park, one from University School, and one from Willoughby. Four came from Youngstown, and one each from Pittsburgh, Boston, and Campion; two were from Little Rock, Arkansas. Only Smith and Turk were lost from the previous year's squad and nine lettermen were returning. Such teams as Baldwin-Wallace, Detroit, Carnegie Tech, and West Virginia Wesleyan were now on a schedule that also included Xavier, Dayton, Canisius, Wilmington, and Findlay. The best the team could do was to win four while losing four and tying one. There probably was some satisfaction in defeating Baldwin-Wallace 25 to 0 and achieving a scoreless tie with Detroit.

Looking back on the previous four years, the editor of *The Ignatian* in 1923 rejoiced that, "athletics were placed on a high plane of excellence; the debating team covered itself and the school with well merited renown by its victories; the Latin contest was a resounding triumph for us; in fact in every line of student endeavor, the college took great strides to the fore."[53] The only problem seemed to be that attendance at the football games was not sufficient to support "so-called big league football."[54] Crowds of seven to ten thousand were considered necessary; four to five thousand had been the average attendance.

THE 1924 FOOTBALL SEASON

The resignation of "Ike" Martin at the close of the 1923 basketball season forced another search for a coach who could handle both football and basketball. It was generally agreed that "under Martin's regime they [the teams] came out from the shadows and landed with both feet in the envied circle," and hope was expressed that a successor could be found who would go forward from the progress Martin had made.[55] By May 1924 the long-sought "Notre Dame" coach had been signed. Allen H. ("Mal") Elward, who had played end on the Notre Dame teams of 1913–1915 and also had a successful coaching record behind him, came to John Carroll in 1924. In a letter to Father Bracken, Knute Rockne recommended Mal "unreservedly" as one who "knew how to handle men."[56]

The hiring of Mal Elward sparked great enthusiasm among the students and supporters of the football team. Looking upon the 1923 season as "proof positive that the Blue and Gold 'has arrived' in the Football 'Four Hundred,' " followers of the team felt that the team, "while not over burdened with victories" had come "within striking distance" for Elward to fulfill the dream.[57]

Mal welcomed the challenge and in a letter to Carroll Boosters printed in *The Ignatian* he said:

I am coming to John Carroll with one purpose in mind, that being to give the student body, the faculty, the alumni and people of Cleveland a winning football team. . . .

You hear a lot about football systems; Notre Dame's and John Carroll's will be: perfection of fundamentals and plays, the player that never quits, and eleven men thinking all the time. These with the backing of students, faculty and alumni will give John Carroll a winner.[58]

The football camp at Vermilion, Ohio just before the beginning of classes in September was an innovation. In order to ensure the knowledge of fundamentals, thirty players led "a strenuous life," rising at 7:30 A.M. and working with short rests and meals until retiring at 10 P.M.[59] The schedule for the 1924 season was perhaps as difficult a one as had ever been arranged. The season opened 4 October with Bowling Green; then followed Canisius, Marquette, Grand Rapids, Lombard, Detroit, Wilmington, Dayton, and North Dakota. The schedule was an indication of the authorities' willingness "to continue the policy which is designed to place Carroll and Cleveland on the collegiate football map."[60]

A record of seven victories and two defeats was a respectable showing for the 1924 season. One of the two defeats was at the hands of Marquette, the other, Dayton. The Marquette loss by a 10–3 score marked the dedication of Marquette's new stadium in Milwaukee. Father Albert C. Fox, then president of Marquette and later dean at John Carroll, presided at the dedication ceremonies. The progress of the Marquette game was followed by 250 Carroll followers gathered in the gym around a canvas replica of a gridiron. A direct wire from Marquette stadium with Lambert McGannon announcing the plays made it possible to reproduce the game. The 1924 record inspired Ed Bang to suggest the need of a new stadium for the city of Cleveland because he was "certain that the time is coming when John Carroll University and Notre Dame could attract a crowd of 50,000 to 75,000 and also that a game between a Cleveland college and one of the big eastern or western schools or both east and west would tax an 80,000 stadium to its capacity."[61] The 80,000 capacity stadium was built in 1932, but it was not Cleveland college football teams that were to fill it; the eclipse of local collegiate football by professionals was not seen in Ed Bang's crystal ball.

BLUE STREAKS

The name "Saints" was used in reference to St. Ignatius College athletic teams from the earliest days. Occasionally, the teams might be referred to as the "Blue and Gold" or in later years as the "Irish," which indicated more of a Catholic than an ethnic association. The name Cleveland University and its replacement by John Carroll University in September 1923 made continued use of "Saints" inappropriate. The 1924 season was hardly under way when the sports editor of *The Ignatian* complained that the other colleges had nicknames for their teams: Marquette had its "Golden Avalanche," Yale its "Bulldogs," and Centre College its "Praying Colonels." The best that Carroll could do was to come up with "Fighting Irish" and that was already preempted by Notre Dame. The editor wondered whether among the Carroll students someone could be found to come up with a name showing originality and suitability for Carroll teams.[62] The person generally credited with christening the team with the new name, "Blue Streak," is Raymond Gibbons, '24, who followed the team on the practice field after his graduation, despite a serious illness, as long as he was able and had someone to bring him to the practice sessions. On one of these occasions he is said to have remarked about the blue-jerseyed warriors, "they're tearing around like a blue streak." At his death in October 1925, the *Carroll News* referred to him as "one of the most ardent followers of Carroll's teams and since his graduation he has kept up his interest in the Blue Streak eleven that he so aptly christened, attending every game he possibly could."[63]

The name "Blue Streak" stuck; but its use in the public press was gradual. The *Cleveland News*, for which Gibbons was still a sports writer, was naturally the first local paper to use it; others followed somewhat later. At the end of October 1924, even the *Cleveland News* was still referring to the team as the "Irish." In a story on 6 November preceding the Detroit game, Gibbons said that on "Saturday Carroll hopes to emulate Wesleyan's (Ohio) example [of beating Detroit]. If the 'blue streak' can turn the trick, . . . the local eleven will take its place among the elect football combinations of the Buckeye State."[64] This was the first public appearance of the new name. By the end of November the name was appearing in headlines;

Top left, First headline use of Blue Streak, 1924; *right,* "Mal" Elward, Football and Basketball coach, 1924–26; *Bottom left,* Frank D. Burke, Chemistry, 1921–56, First full-time layman; *right,* Edward J. Bracken, 1919–30, 1934–37

"Flyers upset Streak."[65] It is interesting to note that its early use is always in the singular; not until the 1930s does it become the plural "Blue Streaks."

The name Blue Streak was publicized elsewhere than in the daily papers. After the football banquet celebrating the success of the 1924 season, during the Blue Streak scored 260 points to its opponents' 53—the highest point score of any team in Ohio—the team was invited by the manager of the Palace Theater, Jack Royal, to be his guest at the performance of the Blue Streak of vaudeville, Rae Samuels. A "unique club" with Miss Samuels as a charter member was formed and referred to as the Blue Streak of Vaudeville and the Blue Streak of Football. After viewing Miss Samuels's performance from a special box, the team was invited on stage to initiate the new club. A return engagement in the fall of 1925 brought Miss Samuels again to Cleveland and this time she attended the Duquesne game and cheered on the "Blue Streak of Football." A writer in the *Carroll News* felt sorry for Duquesne's chance of winning; "Poor Duquesne! Saturday it will be opposed by two 'Blue Streaks'! Carroll's Blue Streak of the gridiron is a foe formidable enough to make any opponent quail, but what chance [do] they have when the 'Blue Streak of Vaudeville' is rooting against them from the stands?"[66] The answer was, not much; Carroll defeated Duquesne 33–0.

Faced with the problem of supplying replacements for the athletes lost by graduation or otherwise from the 1924 football team, the Alumni Association met in March 1925 to discuss ways of financing Carroll's determination "to give the city the kind of athletics worthy of a metropolis." Convinced that the day was "not far distant when the recognition of the public will be such as to obviate all financial worries," the Alumni proposed a one-year bank loan underwritten by the association's members. No action was taken on the proposal.[67]

UNDER THE ONE-YEAR RULE

In December 1925 came an announcement from the Ohio Athletic Conference that intercollegiate athletics would henceforth abide by a one-year rule governing eligibility of players in athletic contests. Originally intended to be binding for the 1926 football season, the rule was made immediately applicable and thus affected the 1925–1926 basketball season. Strictly speaking, John Carroll, which had always played freshmen and belonged to no conference, could have chosen not to observe the rule. The result would have been a strengthening of the negative attitude toward Carroll on the part of local and other Ohio teams who regarded the rise of John Carroll's football team with a suspicion which caused difficulty in scheduling. Because it was to Carroll's advantage to consider playing by conference rules, it was decided to put Carroll on record as observing the one-year rule immediately even though it would prevent the use of much good basketball material in the spring of 1926.[68] It would also force the football team to go with no new talent for 1926.

The 1925 football season with but two victories, Duquesne and Bethany, could hardly be considered a success. Among the seven defeats were the games with the Quantico Marines, Dayton, Detroit, Creighton, Loyola (Chicago), and Fordham. Since eight regulars played their last season in 1925, the prospects for the 1926 season did not look very bright anyway. Still, there were two victories in that year, the Quantico Marines and Adrian. The five losses were to Grove City, Creighton, Dayton, Villanova, and Lombard; there was one tie, with Detroit.

Not only had two losing seasons followed the successful 1924 one, the team was also forced to seek a new playing field. Dunn Field, the American League baseball field, later known as League Park, had been the scene of Carroll home games. Damage to the field from the football games was considered so great that games were banned there beginning in 1926. Luna Park, an amusement park where the holders of the "pink tickets" for the game were entitled to free rides on the roller coasters between halves, became the Carroll home field.[69]

In 1925 as part of an effort to shore up the sagging spirits resulting from failing football fortunes, the Carroll Union decided to ban all monograms worn by students except those earned by athletes on Carroll teams. Within a year some improvement was noticable but there were "still a large number of unofficial sweaters to be seen especially among freshmen."[70] Part of the problem was that, although Carroll athletes had been duly awarded letters and so notified, the depleted finances of the Athletic Association prevented the actual presentation of the awards.[71] Greg Conly, the 1926 football captain, was the chief organizer of the newly formed Monogram Club which was to "restore the Carroll 'C' to the dignity it deserves. Students who have been so thoughtless as to belittle the badge of their Alma Mater by flaunting all manner of foreign monograms about the college grounds would do well to cooperate with the newly organized club by recognizing the supremacy of the 'C' within the halls of Carroll."[72]

After the 1926 football season Father Bracken complained about the failure of both the students and the city to support the team. A record of four victories in seventeen games over two years is, however, hardly a record to get enthusiastic about and Father Bracken might have sought there for the reason for lack of support. Instead he pointed out that a "big college refuses to play small teams unless a satisfactory guarantee can be offered. How is it possible to make these offers when the attendance at the games will not be large enough to cover this expense?"[73] Father Bracken overlooked the performance record and urged the students to

> Let people know that there is a university in Cleveland which has a team that is a team. This means each and every student of Carroll. If each student will boost Carroll, the public and the newspapers are bound to come around and give us the necessary support and publicity and soon Carroll will be linked with Notre Dame, Dartmouth, Cornell, Michigan, Holy Cross and the rest of the big universities.[74]

VINCE REPLACES ELWARD

Father Bracken in his determination to achieve instant football success followed his own counsel and sought little or no advice from others. This approach led to Mal Elward asking to be relieved of his contract for 1927. Elward said publicly,

> I have asked for release from my contract mainly because I have had no voice in the making of the football and basketball schedules.
> The coaching game is hard enough when conditions are ideal, but I feel the responsibility is too great when your schedule is picked by someone else and your team playing out of its class almost continuously. Also, along with this condition, the drill field has been five miles from the school, making it impossible to give a player with late classes sufficient time to practice.
> Outside of this disagreement, however, relations with John Carroll have always been of the best. If my successor is able to play the proper kind of a schedule, he should be successful, for the fighting spirit of the players always has been wonderful.[75]

The *Carroll News* article on Elward's resignation carried only the fact of the resignation with no accompanying explanation.

Elward's replacement was Ralph Vince, who had played guard at Washington and Jefferson and had coached football at St. Ignatius High School since 1923 with a record of thirty victories in thirty-six games. He was expected to make changes in the style of play away from the Notre Dame style used by Elward. Over the next two years, 1927 and 1928, the football team won nine games, lost five, and tied three. The most spectacular victory was the 2–0 win over Davis-Elkins College, which in its two previous games had defeated Navy and West Virginia University. The schedules for those years were similar to previous ones with the exception of the absence of Dayton, Xavier, Detroit, and some other Jesuit colleges such as Creighton and Fordham, formerly on the schedule.

The complaint of lack of support because of poor attendance at the games was still heard. Carroll students were urged to "educate" the people of Cleveland to the fact that "they can be assured of a good football game whenever Carroll plays—no matter how big their opponents are."[76]

LOCAL COLLEGE FOOTBALL COMPETITION URGED

Ed Bang's effort in 1922 to promote a local collegiate rivalry had been ignored by Case and Reserve. One of the reasons was that Carroll did not belong to the Ohio Conference. In fact, Carroll was ignored even when it came to selecting All-Ohio teams at the end of the season. In four years of football not a single representative from a Carroll team was on any All-Ohio team. "How is it," asked the *Carroll News*, "that teams, that players, in the Conference are the only ones from which the best players are selected?" especially when such a nonconference team as Dayton was beating conference teams.[77] It was suggested that if selections were to be made only from the conference teams then the team should be called an All-Conference team, not an All-Ohio team.

The question of Carroll playing Case and Western Reserve came up once more in 1928, again prompted by the local newspapers. The *Case Tech* commented on the proposal by saying, "Consensus of student opinion on the campuses, however, seems to give such a plan the thumbs down."[78] Carroll's schedule of out-of-state teams raised questions about the Carroll program and did not entitle Carroll to recognition on equal terms with Case and Western Reserve even if the Carrol record was a good one. There were questions of "eligibility" rules, "desirability," and "natural rivalry." The subject was pursued again in the local papers in the fall of 1928 but the rumor that Carroll would play Case in 1929 turned out to be false.[79] Games with conference teams Marietta and Heidelberg were, however, scheduled for 1929. Even a victory over Heidelberg by a 20–0 score did not receive sufficient recognition by local sports writers. This failure was attributed as usual to the lack of support given by Carroll students in "talking John Carroll."[80]

One year after he became dean at John Carroll, Father Fox began to urge the development of a local athletic rivalry with Case and Western Reserve. In what was the first official statement from John Carroll on the matter, Father Fox said he saw no value in one game or an occasional game; what really develops interest is repeated annual contests. Such repetitions invite the interest of the spectator to discover which team appears superior and why. The spectator "wants to know if one institution is stronger by virtue of superior coaching, larger enrollment, or more stalwart character, and for that reason he demands an established and enduring rivalry."[81] Western Reserve's response, as reported in the *Carroll News*, was given by Dr. Frank Yocum, who said, "Instead of localizing our schedules we want to nationalize them. That is our reason for opposing a meeting with Carroll. If we started an annual game with Carroll, in addition to the one with Case, we would soon find ourselves concentrating on victory in those two games at the expense of the remainder of our schedules."[82] It seems strange that a national schedule for Carroll should be criticized while one for Reserve was desirable.

Student complaints about the kind of teams Carroll was playing began to surface in the student newspaper. It was suggested that joining the Ohio Conference would enable Carroll to play teams in its own class.[83] In 1930 Carroll promised to seek admission to the Ohio Conference and meanwhile would abide by its eligibility rules; the time for beginning the training season was a major obstacle for Carroll.

In 1930 Ray Ride became coach at Case. Ride hailed from Washington and Jefferson, Ralph Vince's Alma Mater, which made it easier for the two coaches to talk. As a result of negotiations, a two-year contract was signed with Case, the first game to be played at Van Horn field in 1931 and the second the following year in the new municipal stadium then under construction.[84] It was reported that Gordon Locke, coach at Western Reserve, had looked favorably on a game with Carroll in 1929—but had been overruled by the faculty board.[85]

It is hard to say precisely how to give credit for the breakdown of opposition to local collegiate competition. The fact that Vince and Ride had the same Alma Mater probably helped considerably. Changes of athletic directors at Carroll probably also influenced the result; in the summer of 1930 Father Bracken was reassigned to St. John College in Toledo and replaced by Father Augustine H. Bennett, who had chosen to join the Jesuits rather than pursue a professional baseball career with the Chicago Cubs. Illness overtook Father Bennett and he was advised by his physician to take an extended rest. For the second time within six weeks Carroll had a new athletic director, Father William J. Murphy. The news of Father Bracken's reassignment was the "biggest surprise to the students as well as to the alumni."[86]

In a short time Father Murphy had grasped the local situation and must be given at least some credit for scheduling the local college teams. Ray Ride played a major role in establishing what became known as the Big Four—Case, Reserve, Carroll and Baldwin-Wallace.[87] Carroll defeated Case 19–0 in the 1931 contest; lost to Reserve 8–6 in 1932; played a 0–0 tie with Baldwin-Wallace that year, and lost to Case 14–7. Not until 1933 did Carroll defeat Reserve, 7–0. That game was played at the Municipal Stadium before the largest crowd to witness a Big Four contest, 19,000 people.

FIRE, PUBLICITY, FINANCES, AND OTHER PROBLEMS

In August 1929 Luna Park burned down. The amusement park was in the hands of receivers and it was doubtful if it would be rebuilt. Carroll had already invested two thousand dollars in sodding the playing field for the fall games and was obligated to the extent of another thousand dollars for other improvements. With permission of the receiver, Carroll agreed to rebuild the stands to seat approximately six thousand people. An alumnus in the construction business, William J. Schirmer, '10, came to the aid of his Alma Mater and built the stands at cost, finishing in time for the opening football game. Carroll celebrated the occasion by overwhelming Valparaiso (Indiana) 90–0 in a game that resembled a track meet rather than a football game.

All of this sports activity coincided with the beginnings of the building campaign for the move to the Heights. Publicity was desirable but, as Father Benedict Rodman was to discover, one could not always plan what it might be. Interviewed in the fall of 1929 by Carlton K. Matson, a *Cleveland Press* editorial writer, Father Rodman had made it clear that he wanted a good football team, but he did not want it "at the price of any commercialism or weakening of academic standards in the institution."[88] The opening of training camp for football in September 1929 at Lake Stafford near Ravenna, Ohio, produced some unscheduled publicity involving both commercialism in athletics and questionable academic standards. Shortly after the camp got underway, one of the sophomore prospects, Ted Rosequist, a 1926 graduate of Central High School in Cleveland where he had been an outstanding athlete, received a mysterious letter and asked permission to return home for the weekend. What followed after Rosequist's weekend at home is a mixture of claims, counterclaims, denials, and contradictions; the only certain fact appears to be that Rosequist wanted to attend Ohio State, where he might have a chance to become an All-American, a chance he doubted he would have at Carroll, whose schedule did not attract national attention.[89] Ralph Vince charged that Rosequist was lured to Ohio State by the offer of a job from an Ohio State senior who had not been in school for more than a year. The senior claimed Rosequist had approached him, while Ohio State officials, including the coaches, denied even knowing Rosequist; how this was possible considering Rosequist's outstanding high school performance raises some question either about Ohio State's recruiting information or its disclaimer. When the dust settled on the controversy, Rosequist was not enrolled in either school.[90]

The publicity surrounding the affair was considerable. Headlines of all sizes appeared in Cleveland newspapers, most of them reflecting adversely

on Ohio State and Rosequist. The charge that Father Fox altered Rosequist's transcript was ridiculous and easy to refute. Nevertheless, Father
Rodman, who saw some good in the publicity, mentioned the affair to his
Provincial, Father O'Callaghan, in connection with a report on the 1929
campaign: "We are getting lots of publicity from the papers, especially
since Ohio State succeeded in getting our best tackle from us. This has
brought us into the limelight very much."[91]

Financial support of the football expansion plans had always been tenu-
ous. The athletic fee charged to the students was hardly sufficient to defray
increasing expenses. The Athletic Association, although ably assisted by
Alumni contributions, needed a continuous and sustaining base in order to
meet its obligations. A Boosters Club, raffles, and other means helped sus-
tain the effort. The more effort made to create new sources of finance, the
more charges of professionalism in the athletic program and the more the
line was drawn between the student and the athlete.[92] An editorial in the
Carroll News explaining the importance of Homecoming Day took the
opportunity to deny that cooperation between the Alumni Association and
the Athletic Association "has resulted in an out-and-out professionalism in
college sports."[93] In 1925 when the charges of professionalism also were
made, the consultors began to discuss athletics in rather unfavorable terms.
The Jesuit Community did, however, loan $1,500 to the Athletic Associa-
tion and expected repayment in the course of a year.[94]

Rising above all these troubles and immune from them was one sport
introduced in 1929 by Al Bungart. A group of archers, including lay faculty, gathered together under the title of "Ye Caroling Yeoman." The group
became proficient enough to be invited to appear at Public Hall at the
Sportsman's Show. This activity didn't cost any money and raised no questions of eligibility.

THREAT TO DROP FOOTBALL

In spite of Vince's reasonably good record, considering material and schedule, dissatisfaction with the performance of the teams increased among
some of the Alumni. Some Alumni still longed for a Notre Dame-style
offense and felt that the Warner system was drab and ineffective. The consultors discussed the matter and decided to let Vince resign and then appoint Thomas Yarr, a former Notre Dame player, to the post.[95] At a subsequent meeting the consultors reconsidered their decision; Vince was made
Athletic Director, relieving Father Murphy of that function, and Yarr was
given a two-year contract as coach.[96]

In the fall of 1934, the North Central Association made a report of its
visitation of the university, citing two problems: one was the lack of a de-

partment of physical education with the requisite qualified staff, and the other was a questionable method of computing grades in determining the eligibility of athletes.[97] The North Central objected to the practice of determining grade averages on the basis of the entire academic career and insisted that only the preceding semester be the basis for determining eligibility. The names of two players who had been declared ineligible were noted by the North Central visitors, although the university claimed that the names were included in a football program by "mistake." A member of the consultors reported a rumor that the North Central Association would have dropped John Carroll from the accredited list if it had not been for the intervention of Father Fox.[98]

As Father Rodman told the consultors, the Provincial had said that if football were dropped, the North Central would be unlikely to reexamine John Carroll as was planned. The North Central's insistence on a properly staffed physical education department did not suggest that the dropping of football was a real option. The consultors felt that "dropping football would mean the maintenance of an expensive department with no proper funds to pay for it."[99] Football was not dropped and the advice of Father Daniel O'Connell, Prefect of Studies of the Chicago Province, to enforce athletic regulations was accepted.[100]

The North Central Association had wrestled with the problem of enforcing regulations governing college athletics since 1902. A committee of the North Central that had been studying the problems for some time made its final report in 1933. Its recommendations were adopted by the Association and were to be used in the process of accrediting collegiate institutions. In time the various athletic conferences within the North Central also adopted the recommendations.[101] These regulations were being strictly applied at the time of the inspection of John Carroll University in 1934. For this reason the university was given two years to correct what were considered infractions of the scholarship requirements and to establish a physical education program.

The 1934 and the 1935 football and basketball seasons produced little satisfaction for those who were looking forward to athletic fame. At the end of the 1935 football season an editorial in the *Carroll News* expressed the discontent by noting a "steady decline" in athletic fortunes reaching the "absolute bottom" in 1935. The release of the coaching staff and the hiring of a new coach, Tom Conley, another Notre Dame product, was seen as evidence that the university authorities were still trying to attain the elusive goal. One encouraging note was the placing of "full power" and wider authority in the hands of the new coach. The editor of the college newspaper felt it would only be a "matter of time till John Carroll University once again ranks high on the athletic ledger of the middle west."[102] In spite of moments of glory in the succeeding years, the athletic teams never quite experienced the anticipated success. In 1951 the formation of the Presidents Athletic Conference gave some hope of building on the "success" of the 1924 season.

By 1951 the issue of recruiting practices of "big time" football in collegiate institutions had become such a problem that the North Central Association appointed a special commission to look into the matter. A new code of regulations prohibiting scholarships for athletes was adopted. The North Central, however, was not strong enough to overcome the opposition of the larger colleges and universities to the code; "the university administrators were not interested; their failure to consider how their policy affected anyone but themselves" resulted in the capitulation of the North Central to the large influential athletic associations to which the larger universities belonged. [103]

A Successful Campaign
1929–1930

Father Benedict J. Rodman became rector of the Jesuit Community and president of John Carroll University on 31 July 1928. Father Albert C. Fox, who had just finished his term as rector and president at Marquette University, became dean. The two men formed a remarkable team with wide academic experience and civic recognition that helped the university finally receive a greater measure of visibility that aided its move to the East Side. No previous president had received the public welcome that Father Rodman did. On 26 September 1928 a formal ceremony took place at the Hotel Cleveland; the speakers were City Manager William R. Hopkins, Rabbi Abba Hillel Silver of The Temple, Allard Smith, president of the Chamber of Commerce, Dr. Robert Vinson, president of Western Reserve University, and Richard J. Moriarty, president of the John Carroll Alumni. In his remarks, Vinson spoke of a community of interest which he felt the two universities shared since so many of the Carroll alumni entered the Reserve professional schools. "There can be no spirit of rivalry between the two schools," said Vinson, because of the urgent need for larger accommodations for the youth of the area. Rabbi Silver promised "whole hearted cooperation in a true spirit of fraternity"; Mr. Smith looked forward with great interest to the plans the university had for the future.[1]

Father Rodman's response was in his usual style, brief, crisp and to the point. "The day has come when the power and influence of John Carroll University should be greater, should reach out to a larger number of young men of this city and vicinity."[2] He then went on to say that the first step would be the erection of suitable buildings with a minimum capacity of one thousand students at a cost of $1,250,000. He then promised a $500,000 stadium with a seating capacity of 30,000 together with a gymnasium as soon as the civic and business interests of the city in cooperation with friends of John Carroll could bring it about; he added that education comes first but that provision must be made for sports. He made it clear that he alone was to be the spokesman for the university; he had previously cautioned the Jesuits about expressing their own opinions publicly about certain matters.[3]

Father Rodman's remarks included an assessment of present conditions on the West Side.

> To tell the honest truth I was indeed shocked when I saw the university as it is today, and the conditions surrounding it. John Carroll is widely known throughout the Middle West not only by its splendid debating teams, or by its overwhelming victories in English contests, but also by its ever keen and representative showing in the classics and other branches of learning.
>
> Remembering all this, and in all due respect to John Carroll, I was thoroughly depressed. But when I met the boys it was different. . . . They are for the most part of the type that must meet life face to face, and are out to succeed no matter what the odds might be. Chiefly, they do not comprise the wealthy class, but rather of middle class, which is a great advantage to the man himself.[4]

Students had apparently grown accustomed to the conditions that depressed Father Rodman. An article in a 1930 issue of the student newspaper noted that it was "Strange how good the old school looked until we started showing it to outsiders."[5]

A description of the conditions existing on the West Side campus in 1928 was once given by a graduate of the class of 1932, Edmund A. Smolik, who had become a respected neurosurgeon in St. Louis. He commented:

> at that time, the school consisted of the third and fourth floors of an old building with converted attic chambers on the fifth floor which housed the physical chemistry and biological departments. These overlooked an acre campus, filled with various sized cinders. On the far side of the campus was the Carroll Union building with its multiple fragmented windows. The second floor, reached by an outdoor staircase frequently in hazardous condition, housed the John Carroll *News*. In these rooms, two tables scarcely held the weight of two Woodstock typewriters. Here one could see the editor clothed in his heavy overcoat and gloves, punching out his lines.[6]

A more detailed description of the conditions on the West Side was provided for Father Rodman as the result of an inspection of the facilities by Donald Dougherty, who was to manage the revived campaign. The report, printed in the student newspaper, was a graphic description of the inadequacy of the facilities that housed both the high school and the college. There were no study halls; the students were forced to use the corridors. Recitation and lecture rooms were too few for proper scheduling. There were no professors' rooms for conferences with students and only a single room for the lay professors. That room, a rather narrow space with a window at one end and a door at the other, provided the space for the six lay faculty on the college staff. The room was too small even for that number.

It did have two distinct advantages, one for the faculty and one that the students appreciated. It made for a spirit among the lay faculty that might otherwise have been hard to achieve; this spirit in turn led to discussion, often intellectual and always heated, that caused the professors occasionally to ignore class bells. The students seemed never to have wanted to come to the room and search out a missing teacher.

There was neither a real lunchroom nor a common gathering place for recreation; Dougherty overlooked with some justification the basement quarters, the Smoke House, and the cinder and gravel yard. The number of resident students was restricted by the lack of dormitories. The investigator obviously did not wish to count Mrs. Miller's boarding house on West 29th Street as a dormitory although it housed a number of Carroll students. Some of the boarders acquired unexpected publicity very early one morning when rival bootleggers engaged in shotgun warfare. It seems there was a "beer war" on the West Side and one of the price cutters happened to be parked on West 29th when he and his car were sprayed with bullets by a passing competitor. The student newspaper noted:

> By coincidence the scene was along 'dormitory row' of John Carroll's out-of-town students, who awakened by the commotion and the blazing excitement created, demonstrated their usual alertness by dashing down in various stages of undress in time to get their pictures taken. Mervosh, Scopel, and McAnulty exploded from the house of Miller in time to form the front row of the curio seekers. O'Brien and Urbanowicz returning home from their nightly comments over hamburgers indulged in at the Greasy Spoon did the last 100 in nothing flat, in time to observe the above mentioned looking for clues among the scraps of iron and bits of wood torn by the slashing slugs of shotguns and to get in a couple of pictures (Next day the daily circulation of Cleveland's newspapers showed a distinct improvement.)[7]

Dougherty also observed that the administrative offices were inadequate; Father Fox's office was in a parlor on the first floor and his secretary's office was in with the Registrar at the other end of the long corridor. The biology lab on the fifth floor came in for merited criticism; the chemistry and physics labs were considered too small. Father Odenbach's valuable Secchi instrument was on a stair landing, hopefully to escape the fate of Ora and Labora, two statues on another landing, which were frequently sent by passing students to visit the stairwell below. A museum collected over the years was stored away for lack of proper space. There was really no chapel, St. Mary of the Assumption Church being used instead. The gymnasium was so small that Dougherty wondered at the successes of the teams that played there. An athletic field was nonexistent unless one counted nearby Edgewater Park. A final note pointed out that the Jesuits were quite poorly housed.[8]

If there was ever a man with a purpose it was Father Benedict Rodman; he knew what his assignment was at John Carroll University, and he did not allow numerous frustrations to sidetrack him. Problems in starting the new parish and the reminder of the old Buffalo Mission debt were frustrating, but never enough to cause Father Rodman to lose sight of the goal sought by rectors from the beginning of the college, a permanent establishment on the East Side. Father Rodman understood the obstacles in his way and the urgency to act as he explained to Father O'Callaghan shortly after he had made his first preparations to renew the fund drive of 1923. He and his colleagues:

> are working like dogs to make contacts and feel out the people for a new start in the spring. We have to get out there in a year or two and to do that we must start something this spring. All I have consulted agree on that and the General must be brought to see that. It is hard to revive a dead corpse. We are doing are [*sic*] best.[9]

Support in the form of sufficient funds was not the only thing that was needed. "We have nothing here to offer the boys to hold them except the faculty," declared Father Rodman, taking a hard look at the faculty's performance, which he thought in general was "wonderful."[10] He had discovered one faculty member, Father John E. Barlow, whom he thought was "angular, narrow, nagging with the lads and in our present crisis, we need just the opposite."[11] Father Rodman sought the transfer of the man in question. "I need men who can make a good impression on externs and priests, and who draw boys to them. . . . I would ask for no one's removal if it did not seem necessary."[12]

That Father Rodman kept close watch on the faculty in the ensuing years is evident from his correspondence with the Provincial. In one case he felt that the multitudinous activities Father Bracken in athletics, kept him from doing anything as dean of men; "he does nothing there and is not the man who would inspire any boy to come to me with spiritual troubles."[13]

About a year and a half later Father Rodman was still concerned about Father Bracken, this time wondering about his value to the university. Writing to the Provincial, Father Rodman said, "While I laud his spirit, I again affirm that we will never make progress with either the alumni or athletics as long as he is in charge to offend people unwittingly with his sour personality."[14] Some years earlier the same observation was made by Father Haggeney, who wrote to Father Boylan, "you know yourself how utterly impossible it is to get anything else, when you approach him on business, but a sour face and a disagreeable answer."[15]

There was at least one professor, Aloysius Bungart, a layman, who did not let external manifestations by this man obscure the real person underneath. Just as he was about to pass Father Bracken in the first floor corridor one day, the layman looked him in the eye and said, "Underneath that gruff exterior beats a heart of gold." It was one of the few occasions that the Jesuit was known to have cracked a smile.[16]

Laymen were not exempt from Father Rodman's scrutiny. Writing to Father O'Callaghan he complained, "We pay out $50,000 a year in salaries and taxes. No wonder we don't make ends meet."[17] On one occasion Father Rodman announced to the lay faculty that if things got any more difficult financially, he would let all of them go.[18]

One of Father Rodman's many frustrating moments came when certain legal matters not directly connected with the university, but under Father Rodman's jurisdiction as rector, had gotten to Rome. Answering a letter from the American Assistant, Father Rodman said, "This place has been bluffed and fooled enough in the last few years. . . . I don't think anyone realized the situation here in Cleveland except those who are here really facing the difficulties."[19]

CAMPAIGN PLANS

As part of his preparation for a new building fund campaign, Father Rodman sought to examine the building plans for the 1923 campaign. When he discovered they were nowhere to be found, Father Rodman inquired of his immediate predecessors what had become of them. Neither former rector could remember what had happened to the large painted and framed layout that represented a cost of approximately $40,000.[20] According to Father Boylan this layout was "placed in a store room beside the Treasurer's office along with other junk," and by now had probably found its way to the attic.[21] Most of the items had been disposed of and Father Boylan had no idea as to whether there were any copies of the drawings.

Father Rodman with the advice and consent of his consultors enlisted the services of Edward T. P. Graham, a Boston architect, to discuss the "ultimate plan of the university."[22] The plan submitted by Graham envisioned an administration building spacious enough for future use, a curved road plan similar to the Van Sweringen idea, division of the property into a court of education with the administration building as a terminus and school buildings on either side of the court, sufficient width of the court for growth, a dormitory group as the next large group of buildings, and finally a recreation area.[23] Graham asked for more detailed information before he would proceed to lay out the area. Father Rodman replied promptly, saying,

> Your letter and pictures received. You are chosen for architect and I beg of you to put up something memorable, serviceable and simple. Your work is fine from the drawings. I do want to have everything of service in the Administration and Faculty Building. Do you wish me to come on there sometime? Remember I want you personally to handle the work.[24]

According to a report from the campaign manager, Donald C. Dougherty, the buildings were to be adequate rather than elaborate; an administration building was to cost $1,000,000 including wings and a projection to the rear for an auditorium; the chapel was also to be in the rear; a faculty building would house fifty Jesuits at a cost of $200,000; a gymnasium would cost $400,000; and a dormitory to house one hundred students would cost $250,000. The library and science facilities were to be included in the administration building.[25] It was some time before plans were finally firmed up. In March 1930 Graham, for reasons not readily apparent, released to the university, for $20,000, his rights and interest in the plans for the buildings.[26]

In March 1929 Father Rodman announced that plans for the campaign were being prepared and that he had good reason to believe that the drive would succeed. He had consulted business interests, Catholic and non-Catholic, and had been assured of diocesan support. He felt that everyone understood that John Carroll was confronted with "an actual physical crisis" which made the move to the East Side imperative.[27] Father Rodman said his "principal concern" since coming to Cleveland had been "to renew preparations for the long postponed financing of the new John Carroll."[28] The student newspaper applauded the announcement, in which "cold facts are given to the public as to the present state of the university, a definite sketch of the new Carroll is presented, and a clear cut, methodical program of activity in carrying out the plans is indicated."[29]

One marked difference between the 1929 campaign and the 1923 campaign was its leadership and broad appeal to the city and not just the diocese; the credit for the ultimate success of the Drive has to go to Father Rodman and the men he chose to work with. Dougherty had a successful record as a fund-raiser, and committees working with him included the names of most of the prominent Clevelanders both Catholic and non-Catholic. An executive committee was composed of Monsignor McFadden, Father Rodman, George J. Arnold, J. A. Coakley, I. F. Freiburger, James J. Laughlin, Jr., Arthur H. Seibig, and Dr. F. J. Schmoldt. John J. Bernet headed the campaign committee, which included Charles E. Adams, George J. Arnold, Newton D. Baker, Samuel J. Halle, Herman R. Neff, Thomas F. Coughlin, Alfred Fritzsche, Allard Smith, Monsignor J. F. Smith, Bishop Schrembs, Robert E. Vinson, and W. G. Wilson, among many others. The Committee of Clergy was headed by Monsignor Francis T. Moran as chairman. An Alumni Campaign Council was headed by W. J. Corrigan as chairman and included A. J. Burens, C. J. Carlin, Father W. J. Manning, Father Albert J. Murphy, Joseph A. Schlitz, and T. W. Walters. A real effort had been made to enlist wide and effective support from the public. The months of activity in 1929 prior to the public campaign in January 1930 laid solid groundwork for the success of the campaign; that does not mean that there were no obstacles to be overcome or times when the best of efforts created rather than solved difficulties.

PRELIMINARY GIFTS CAMPAIGN

Critical to the success of the campaign was the contribution of the alumni as evidence that those who had graduated from the college would support it. Father Rodman was skeptical about what could be done with the alumni. Writing to Father O'Callaghan he described the alumni "As a body of men, . . . not very aggressive and certainly not very wealthy. There are no outstanding men such as I had in St. Mary's alumni. What they will do I do not know."[30] The student campaign was also critical and another question mark.

It was a pleasant surprise when just prior to the official opening of the alumni and student campaign on 18 October 1929, it was announced that the workers had collected pledges totalling $171,373, of which $41,548 had been subscribed by the students.[31] By the end of the campaign on 30 October the total amount was $213,000 "with more to come."[32] By 2 December the total amount had reached $255,000.

Bishop Schrembs gave frequent speeches in support of the campaign, many of which were lengthy and tended to review the history of the Jesuit order before getting to the point. No one could question the depth of the bishop's sincerity or commitment; he meant it when he said in a letter to Father Rodman, "I want you to know that I will leave nothing undone to help you in the upbuilding of the Greater John Carroll University."[33] The bishop's talk opening the campaign was printed and distributed throughout the diocese. It recounted the services of the Jesuits to the diocese over the previous forty years and concluded, "Surely, then, it is but right and proper that they receive at this time our whole-hearted and generous support."[34] A similar letter addressed to the clergy of the diocese noted that a

large number of the clergy of this diocese received their early ecclesiastical training at the hands of the Jesuit Fathers and many, no doubt, owe their vocations to the influence of their splendid teaching and example. . . . I feel confident that in appealing to you to lend every aid in your power to this great and important work, I am but answering the call of your own hearts.[35]

A point stressed by Bishop Schrembs in one of his talks to the priests was that the Jesuits are not "foreign":

> Don't say this is a foreign institution, I heard that the other day. Pray why is it foreign? Aren't these Jesuits with us as our own? The fact that Father Smith or Father Jones, or whatever their names may be, comes from St. Louis doesn't make them foreigners. They come to this diocese to labor here for this diocese. They labor in it just as whole-heartedly as I; just as whole-heartedly as every priest who was ever born in this diocese and the result of their labor stays here; it does not go off.[36]

After noting that the Jesuits take no money out of the diocese "except a very small pittance" to educate for replacements, the bishop went on to say,

> The Jesuits came here because they were called. They did not inject themselves upon the diocese of Cleveland: they did not obtrude themselves upon the diocese of Cleveland. It was the bishop of the diocese of Cleveland, realizing that he needed willing hands and clever heads, that he went almost on his knees to the Jesuit provincial, and asked him to send them here. . . . and he considered it a great privilege when they accepted and came.[37]

Although the bishop engaged in a bit of historical exaggeration as to how the Jesuits came to Cleveland, it is clear that the Germanicity label of the early years still persisted in many minds, but the bishop avoided direct reference to the German background for obvious reasons.

In spite of the bishop's pleas, the parish campaign had the same problems that were encountered in the 1923 campaign. There were some places outside of the Greater Cleveland area where for a variety of reasons it did not seem possible to conduct campaigns; in those places it was decided to work through a special committee canvassing some of the more likely prospects.[38] In late November there was a meeting to which fifty-two parish priests were invited; twenty-six said they would come.[39] Consensus of those attending was that $500,000 would have to come from the parishes if the campaign was to succeed and that the present method of campaigning was not working. It was recommended that the amount be proportioned as a diocesan assessment.[40] Many pastors objected to this idea and suggested other ways of obtaining funds.

Monsignor Gilbert P. Jennings, pastor of St. Agnes parish, speaking for the clergy committee, maintained "the plan adopted by the priests at their meeting and which was approved by the Right Reverend Bishop, and which has been read before the priests of the diocese, cannot be changed without upsetting the whole work of our committee."[41] The alternate plan was to allow each pastor to do whatever he intended to do in whatever way he say fit. The sum to be raised for each parish was to equal three times the normal diocesan assessment.[42] The problem seems never to have been satisfactorily resolved and was further complicated by the bishop's gift of a Memorial Chapel, supported by pledges of the priests, to the university in November. Father Hubert LeBlond took over the direction of the Parish campaign in January 1930 but the problem of parish support remained much as it had been in the 1923 campaign.

Reporting to Father O'Callaghan as the preliminary gifts campaign developed, Father Rodman wrote,

> What visiting this took you can conceive yourself. Some refused, others still have me waiting, but we have them wondering anyway. The publicity has been fine so far, the papers are with us. The men on these committees are no slouches either. If I can get one big donation from a non-Catholic, the things [*sic*] is assured, for they will all follow the lead of the prominent man. Pray hard for it will mean the making or unmaking of this place.[43]

Father Rodman closed this report with the following: "It gets fearfully tiresome sometimes. . . . This thing of meeting men and talking to them keeps you on your toes all the time and you get exhausted from it."[44]

In order to ease his burden somewhat, Father Rodman began using one of the students as a chauffeur to drive him around on his visits. A Franklin automobile had been donated by his friends for the purpose. Father Rodman also managed to break his routine of visiting prospects by occasional trips to the Jesuit property on the lake at Vermilion where he loved to walk along the shore line. Yet there was a time when he thought that this property ought to be sold because "it is doing us no good whatever. . . . The only valuable part about it is the lake property."[45] The ninety-two acre property was worth about $757 an acre but had a $70,000 mortgage on it.[46]

The story of the preliminary campaign would not be complete without mentioning an episode early in the campaign that illustrates Father Rodman's desire to leave no stone unturned in his search for funds. It may also indicate other things such as the desperation Father Rodman felt in those early days. It seems that a group of wealthy and reputable Chicago businessmen had an investment scheme called the Drake Estate that promised good returns. Father Rodman had somehow gotten wind of this venture and wrote to Father O'Callaghan asking him what he knew of it. Father O'Callaghan was less than reassuring:

All that I know about the Drake estate is what I got from Fr. [Frank] Mayer, who as you no doubt found is simply sold one hundred percent on the deal. He is convinced that the thing is going to come out all right, and that if it does, all those who participated in the affair are to be rewarded in a handsome way. He has given me some of the contracts—the gifts from some of his friends. To be candid with you, I really don't know what to advise you about this matter. His [Fr. Mayer's] brothers who are said to be hard headed business men are enthusiastic according to Frank. But they are business men, and accordingly would readily take a chance on a plunge like this. They would not be worried much by the failure of the scheme.[47]

Father Rodman apparently did talk to others about the investment for he wrote just two days after receiving Father O'Callaghan's letter that he had gotten "three or four friends to invest in the Drake Estate and to divide with us if anything comes of it. The House has nothing to put into it."[48] The scheme seems to have failed without any of the hoped-for results.

The campaign pace speeded up a bit in the fall of 1929. Reporting again to Father O'Callaghan, Father Rodman announced that "things are getting interesting. The bishop gave another ferverino at the second meeting of the Parish chairmen last night. It will make you feel fine to know that to date we have $500,000. Remember also that the Preliminary Gifts Committee has been working only ten days. The organization is going along splendidly."[49]

One minor tiff took place between the two men largely responsible for the campaign's success. Both Father Rodman and John J. Bernet were tough and competitive when it came to business. Since Father Rodman was chairman of the Executive Committee he thought he had a right to call a meeting and proceeded to do so. The next day Bernet heard about it and as Father Rodman reports, "Kept the phone hot between his office and mine until I thought I had better go upstairs and see him. He said to me, 'Don't have any more meetings of that committee. You know that the best committees are made up of three men, two deceased.' The conclusion was obvious. Let ME run the whole works. I smiled internally at this, as it showed me how really interested he is."[50]

Father Rodman was high in his praise of Bernet and said, "We have to do all in our power to cooperate with Bernet. I was told just recently that there is not another man in town who can put this thing over as he can. Even with him it is one of the most difficult tasks that can be imagined. You have no idea of what I am up against and no one can tell except the one who meets the man and knows the obstacles that must be overcome."[51]

The year 1929 ended with a resounding appeal from Bishop Schrembs in a Pastoral Letter to be read at all Masses in all churches on Sunday, 15

December 1929.[52] It announced the public campaign for the week of 30 January 1930, reviewed the services of the Jesuits to the city and cited his own responsibility under Canon Law for education in the diocese. He emphasized this responsibility by saying,

> The Canon Law itself makes no distinction as to the auspices under which such schools are conducted. *It does fix, however, definitely and clearly our joint obligation—bishops, Clergy and Faithful—*effectively *to see that such schools of higher learning shall be provided and maintained.*
>
> With all my authority as Bishop I urge upon you my devoted clergy and generous laity, the fullest and most whole hearted cooperation with this plan.[53]

MEMORIAL CHAPEL

The strong verbal support from Bishop Schrembs was backed up by his turning over to the Jesuits on 30 October 1929 a gift of a Memorial Chapel for which $203,000 had been pledged by the priests of the diocese. The chapel with a seating capacity of one thousand was to be the first building to be constructed on the new campus. Originally intended for Parmadale orphanage as a memorial of Pope Pius XI's Golden Jubilee, Bishop Schrembs's Ruby Jubilee, and the signing of the Lateran Treaty, the chapel was thought to fill a greater need on the Carroll campus.[54] The priests of the diocese met on 30 October at the Hotel Cleveland to present the chapel to the bishop as their gift through their spokesman, Monsignor Joseph F. Smith. After the bishop accepted the gift he then, as Father Rodman reported, "turned right around and gave it to the Jesuits—through me."[55] The move on the part of the bishop was a most welcome solution to a competitive fund drive; Father Rodman saw it as "clearing the track."[56] Reporting to Father O'Callaghan, Father Rodman observed:

> It took about four weeks to bring this about. But from the applause the priests gave, you could see that they were in favor of it. The bishop turned over the pledges of $203,000 to me. You know something of what has been in back of this so I need not repeat it. But we are all very happy at this outcome and Mr. Bernet feels very pleased. As I said before, it at least is clearing the track.[57]

Father O'Callaghan was quick to respond to the bishop's generosity, thanking him for the "extraordinary proof" he had given of his "kindness and . . . fatherly interest in the growth of the college."[58] In another letter about a month later Father O'Callaghan again expressed appreciation for the evidence of the bishop's satisfaction with the Jesuits by showing "cooperation in such an effective way."[59]

Father O'Callaghan also wrote to Father Rodman saying he had thanked the bishop as Father Rodman had suggested, and then asked, what was Bernet's reaction? "Your friend, BERNET, must be elated over the progress of the campaign, and no doubt is now using language more becoming to a follower of the college."[60] Father Rodman replied that it would be a good idea for Father O'Callaghan to send a congratulatory letter to Bernet on the campaign success thus far. Then Father Rodman added, "The night of the day we had the banquet at which the bishop presented the Chapel to me, I 'phoned Mr. Bernet and told him about it! 'That is fine,' he said, 'I think I will go upstairs and have a drink on it.' So you see how he felt about the good news. He is a good old boy just the same."[61] Father Rodman's own response to the gift was "I offer Bishop Schrembs the services of the Carroll Jesuits in the work of education for the good of the diocese and the salvation of souls."[62]

When Father Rodman had spoken of the length of time he had been working for such a gift and that its offer and acceptance had now "cleared the track," he was referring to his efforts to keep competing drives from endangering the success of the John Carroll campaign. Bishop Schrembs in 1929 had requested that Monsignor Smith take up with the priests of the diocese the building of a memorial chapel at Parmadale, a Catholic orphanage.[63] The course of the subscription drive did not go smoothly; at least one priest challenged both Monsignor Smith's authority to conduct a drive for the chapel and questioned the necessity of the chapel at Parmadale.[64] One of the issues involved was whether Monsignor Smith, the Diocesan Consultors and the Deans had "become the active voice of the Priests and parishes of the Diocese of Cleveland."[65] Tensions were sufficiently high for Monsignor Smith to appeal for support to the Apostolic Delegate in the bishop's absence.[66] The Delegate in reply told Monsignor Smith that he was "safe in following the directions you have received from the Right Reverend Bishop."[67]

By September 1929 the possible conflict of the chapel drive with the Carroll drive was worrying Father Rodman, who felt himself trapped in a difficult situation. Even Bishop Schrembs was becoming concerned. The bishop invited Father Rodman to dinner at the bishop's residence and in the course of conversation said, "I suppose the priests are telling you I am trying to block your drive," referring to the Parmadale Chapel Fund.[68] Father Rodman's reply was that he was getting a "great many reactions" as he went around. At that point Father Rodman had planned to ask the bishop for a donation of $100,000 but told Father O'Callaghan that "of course [I] will be lucky if I get $10,000."[69] As Father Rodman further explained:

I went to dinner with Bishop Schrembs the other night fully prepared to tell him something rather strenuous in regard to this campaign but Mr. Bernet advised against it when I proposed it to him. I might add he is very much worked up now, as he sees what a job he has on his hands and he is getting some other prominent men worked up too. The more they get worked up, the better I will feel.[70]

The presentation of the priests' pledges to Father Rodman ended the potential conflict of the two drives. This was only the beginning of the first phase in the Chapel story; the problem of collecting the rest of the pledges remained. Failure to collect the balance due, which was about half the total, was to halt permanently construction of the Chapel after the foundation had been built.

CAMPAIGN PUBLICITY PROBLEMS

Publicity for the campaign of 1929 was from the beginning far superior to that in the campaign of 1923. It was well handled, timely, and generously supported by the local newspapers. The numerous pieces of campaign literature held the general theme that John Carroll had given Cleveland much in forty years but Cleveland had given John Carroll very little in return. One campaign pamphlet capitalized on Father Odenbach's reputation, describing him as "Cleveland's 'man-with-the answer' " who "sits alone in his observatory . . . among the dials and the pendulums and the switch plugs" answering frequent telephone calls.[71] For years Father Odenbach had the only telephone other than the main one at St. Ignatius College; it was a necessity because the calls for him were so numerous. There were calls such as one from a *Cleveland Leader* reporter aboard the fire-tug *John H. Farley.* One of the crew had discovered some kind of an animal whose identification was being disputed. The reporter who described it said it would not eat meat or grain but had bristles and swimming webs on its hind feet. "Give it a banana and call me in twenty minutes," said Father Odenbach, who went to his bookshelf "muttering: 'Page 96, right hand column, bottom.' "[72] When the call came back the reporter announced that the animal had snapped up the banana. Father Odenbach then identified the animal as a South American Cuypu. On many occasions he was called upon to answer questions about phenomena such as the "Cleveland Comet" which was caused by heat from a steel mill's huge Bessemer crucible, which formed an ice cloud five miles up; a clear atmosphere produced the reflection. He also assured people who thought ghosts had moved into their homes and were causing pictures to swing or windows to rattle that there was no need to worry. It was his ability to explain earthquake vibrations and distinguish them from local blasting projects that earned the title of "earthquake man."

Another Jesuit whose accomplishments were capitalized on during the campaign was Father Fox, whose oratorical ability soon became known to Clevelanders after the Lenten season of 1929 when he gave a series of sermons at the Cathedral.[73] Father Fox himself was on the publicity committee and composed a substantial part of the publicity material. His experience in Marquette University's building campaign was invaluable.

Some publicity problems could have become serious but did not. One of these was the appearance in the *Cleveland Plain Dealer* for Sunday, 19 May 1929, of the announcement of plans for the new buildings including, so the article said, a $700,000 gymnasium.[74] One of the Jesuits had clipped the article and mailed it to Father O'Callaghan, who immediately wrote Father Rodman that the proposed cost was "way out of proportion"[75] and hoped that a copy of the article would not reach Father General's hands. Father Rodman replied that the $700,000 gymnasium was the reporter's fantasy, not his, and wondered why, when the other Sunday papers the same day carried the correct story, "the man who informed you had to pick the wrong paper and send that, although the other was there too."[76]

Far more serious was the last paragraph of the same *Plain Dealer* article, which spoke of the institution as not being "confined to those of the Catholic faith . . . because John Carroll though manned by the Jesuits, provides education with no religious bias."[77] Father O'Callaghan's informer had made a charge of "non-sectarianism" and the Provincial was worried that this charge might get to Rome. Neither Father Rodman nor his four consultors could see how anyone could confuse nonsectarianism with no religious prejudice or bias. "Of course," Father Rodman wrote to Father O'Callaghan "if a man wants to read his own subjective interpretation into an article or a sentence, he can color it any way he wants to."[78] In order to forestall any further misunderstanding, "I took up the matter of 'religious bias' and have instructed the men in charge to leave that side out altogether after this, so expect no more worry from that quarter."[79]

Father O'Callaghan's concerns about the nonsectarian label were not without foundation. Ever since the early 1920s when efforts to meet the requirements of accrediting agencies had forced changes in the traditional Jesuit pattern, there had been charges that the colleges were becoming less Catholic. In 1927 following complaints of some American clergy to Rome, Father General Ledochowski sent a detailed questionnaire to superiors and officials of American Jesuit colleges seeking information on "the situation from a religious standpoint."[80] The report on the questionaire was followed by a letter from Father General Ledochowski, dated 7 June 1928 in which he warmly thanked superiors and officials for their replies and apologized for having to stress "weaknesses and deficiencies."[81] In the letter the General objected to the presence of non-Catholics in the colleges, particularly on the faculty even in professional schools, and also to the presence of non-Catholic deans in the colleges.[82] He also criticized the quality of religious instruction but he was "pleased that terms, 'non-sectarian' or 'undenominational' have been eliminated from official documents," but not pleased that there was "much too little religious news in journals published by our universities."[83] As the General saw it, "The atheistic situation has gotten out of hand and reform must be begun."[84]

With that letter in mind, Father O'Callaghan in the fall of 1929 again warned Father Rodman to be careful about publicity for the campaign

You will recall that in more than one letter to you, I mentioned the need of the greatest caution in the publicity in connection with the coming drive for the college. One of my reasons for putting you on your guard was the fact that some of ours are given to writing to Rome,—a privilege they have, and besides newspapers, especially Catholic ones regularly reach the curia, in which news items relating to our colleges are read with interest.

Now to the point. I have sent no clippings or papers to Rome, but, that some have reached Rome is quite evident from a letter that arrived today. . . . you are quoted as having said that John Carroll was a "civic institution." The letter goes on to say: "There is a sense of course in which the expression is perfectly harmless,—in fact even commendable, but the objection is that if we beg money under the plea of being a civic institution, which we are not, we are not only getting money under false pretenses but we are laying ourselves open to difficulties in the line of claims that may be made upon us as a civic institution." Back of all of his objections (Fr. General's) is the fear that this may be compromising the fact that ours are strictly Catholic institutions, and you know how solicitous he is on this point. I ought to tell you that his anxiety on this point is not unfounded. He is in intimate relations with the Vatican. He has had experiences along this line in two countries already, and is particularly anxious to save us from any disagreeable regulations or restrictions. Then there was another slip in a printed public statement, to the effect that John Carroll was not a rival of—I think Western Reserve, but on the contrary, could, would or might,—I don't remember the exact words now,—act as a *feeder* to Western Reserve! I am afraid that we would have a hard time explaining that statement to the Holy See. The negative part of it is all right, but it is the positive part of it that went too far. Ours cannot realize how careful they ought to be in such statements now. One slip might bring a fulmination that would hit us very hard. . . .

As far as I can make out from the letter of my informant, the news items referred to above, did not reach Fr. General, but I am told that he would "go clear up in the air if they got to his ears—or eyes."[85]

It seems as though Father Rodman was getting it from all sides on publicity issues. Just as the public campaign was about to get underway in January 1930 he received a letter quoting a line from a signboard on Carnegie Avenue advertising the college as "open to boys of all faith." The writer informed Father Rodman, quoting Pope Pius XI, who said, "We, therefore, confirm our previous declarations and sacred canons forbidding Catholic children to attend non-Catholic, neutral or mixed schools, by the latter being meant those schools equally open to Catholics or non-Catholics alike." The writer went on to say, "Every dollar obtained by the John Carroll Building Committee on the strength of the first quotation is obtained UNDER FALSE PRETENSES."[86]

In no instance in the campaign of 1923 or 1929 were there complaints about the publicity from Bishop Schrembs. When Donald Dougherty wrote to the bishop after the campaign ended inquiring whether the publicity had been satisfactory for the "award of contract and groundbreaking ceremony,"[87] he received an answer that the bishop was pleased.[88] Yet in all of the publicity, many of the implications of the statements worrying Father O'Callaghan and Father General could be found.

SUCCESS AT LAST

By the end of 1929 the preliminary campaign came to a close; preparations were now begun for the public campaign to be carried on in the last half of January 1930. On 15 January a mass meeting of all campaign workers was held at the Music Hall to hear a list of speakers urge the workers to do their utmost for the success of the campaign. Charles Adams presided at the meeting, whose principal speaker was Ray Lyman Wilbur, secretary of the interior. The affair was carried over a local radio station whose audience heard Wilbur say, "This institution could do its work very well 43 years ago when it was founded. But now it finds itself hampered, cramped for room, unable to meet the demands made upon it. . . . You should build here an institution with the reputation of Georgetown, Loyola or St. Louis."[89] Other speakers were Bishop Schrembs, Father Rodman, and Alexander C. Brown, civic and business leader and former president of the Cleveland Chamber of Commerce.

Within a week, pledges in the amount of $280,260 were collected. At a dinner meeting on 24 January it was announced that pledges of $50,000 each had been received from Samuel L. Mather and John J. Bernet; pledges of $25,000 each from W. G. Wilson and C. L. Bradley were also announced.[90] A major gift from the Grasselli family, Thomas, Josephine, Ida, and Aloise (Mrs. William T. Cashman), was to provide for a library with a bell tower, which would bear the Grasselli name. Father Rodman in accepting the gift wanted it understood that at present the library would be put in a large section of the main building; he also suggested that an illuminated clock striking the hour and half hour would be more useful to the community than the chimes.[91] The tower was to be a memorial to the Grassellis' mother and the library a memorial to their father. The gift of $110,000 was, with the exception of the bishop's Chapel gift, the largest single gift of the campaign.[92] One of the larger gifts was the John Carroll Guild's pledge of $30,000. The Guild had been founded in 1925 as an organization of the mothers of Jesuits. Results of the campaign showed that at the close of the Drive, $2,514,625 had been pledged; the final total reached $2,541,322.[93]

In reviewing the results of the campaign, Father Rodman said, "Words cannot express my feeling of gratitude on the outcome of this wonderful display of good will and generosity by the people of the city and diocese of Cleveland."[94] He was particularly grateful for the "generous and eloquent appeals" of W. G. Rose, Newton D. Baker, W. E. Wickenden, president of Case, and Dudley Blossom, director of welfare in the city.[95] In a handwritten note to Bishop Schrembs, Father Rodman expressed his appreciation "for the magnificient support you gave us in the recent campaign. May the dear Lord bless you and leave you with the diocese for years to encourage and strengthen us in the work for God."[96] The *Carroll News* expressed the appreciation of the students and the university to the city of Cleveland for answering so generously the call for support. To the student newspaper, a civic duty had been performed by the people of the city and the future students now owed a great debt to the city which had made it possible for them "to fulfill their obligation to the Community."[97]

Bishop Schrembs made a special effort to thank all who participated in making the drive such a success. Among his letters were ones to Donald Dougherty, "the Master Mind that planned and directed it all,"[98] to Herman Neff, to Thomas Coughlin, and to Charles Adams, to whom he said, "you gave unselfishly of your time and your personality; you gave what is more—your heart, and that at a time when the shadow of suffering was hovering over your home."[99] Bishop Schrembs praised the Grasselli gift as "an 'Ideal Monument' perpetuating the noble character of your good father and mother, as well as the filial devotion of their children;"[100] to the Van Sweringens Bishop Schrembs also wrote words of praise for the "courage and zest" their "noble gift" gave to those in charge of the campaign.[101] The bishop expressed his gratefulness to Samuel Mather and the "exceeding kindness and generosity and your untiring cooperation in connection with the John Carroll Drive."[102] To Alexander C. Brown the bishop said he was particularly impressed with Brown's "masterly presentation of the claims of John Carroll University upon the community and your sympathetic pleas for the generous cooperation of all classes of citizens." What many had called a "foolish dream is now realized and its success stands as a glorious monument to the vision, generosity and untiring energy of those who conceived it and carried it to successful completion."[103] Bishop Schrembs also thanked Father Rodman for the "little token in appreciation of what you did for us during the strenuous days of the drive," which Father Rodman had sent him.[104] The bishop wrote to Father Rodman, "I assure you I needed no such token, but since you were pleased to send it I will treasure it always."[105]

Singled out for special thanks and praise was of course John J. Bernet. As the bishop was quoted in the *Carroll News*, "when all is said and done, it was the wonderful leadership of Mr. John J. Bernet, successful president and builder of railroads, that was able to unite all elements for the triumph of the cause."[106] A scene at the meeting on 30 January that was held to review the final reports of the campaign showed the "mettle of the 'square-jawed' president of the Chesapeake and Ohio."[107] According to the story, Herman Neff, the campaign chairman, had approached Bernet and said they were $75,000 short of the goal:

> So everybody looked sheepishly at the tablecloth. "It isn't enough," he continued. Now everyone knew it was the truth and everyone looked even more intently at the tablecloth as though seeking the thousands there.
>
> "Well," said Gloomy Herman, "here is $50,000 more from John McNichols of Detroit." [Father John McNichols, S.J., president of the University of Detroit]
>
> A wild cheer broke from the lips of the assembly. Things were becoming rosy and—it was still possible.
>
> "Mr. Bernet has something to say," Mr. Neff announced.
>
> When John J. Bernet arose to speak, pandemonium broke loose. The men jumped up and cheered and cheered and cheered out of the depths of their hearts and the fulness of their throats. There before them stood their general. He had performed a great deal of work and had donated personally a great deal of money. He had produced and brought from others a great deal of money. So they began to sing that human song of praise: "For he's a jolly good fellow." This they followed up with "who's all right?"
>
> Amid all this acclamation and uproar Mr. Bernet was whacking and pounding away with a gavel until the dishes began a merry dance on the speaker's table. At last he saw the futility of his attempt and waited until the cheers were over.
>
> When silence reigned again, he declared he had forgotten what he was going to say. So he started to tell of a friend of his who had told Bernet two months ago that he would give $5,000 to the fund. Later, this gentleman from Chicago boosted it to $10,000.
>
> "Last night he called me on the phone," Bernet went on to say, "and asked how we were coming along. I told him we were going to be a little short. Then my friend said, 'John I'm going to boost it. I'm going to give $35,000 more. If it puts

you over you can announce my name. If it doesn't I don't want my name used.' His name is Patrick H. Joyce of Chicago and he's president of the Standard Steel Car Co."

The miracle was accomplished and among those who made it possible John J. Bernet led all the rest.[108]

Bernet's own version of that meeting can be found in his letter of appreciation to Monsignor McFadden, who had thanked Bernet for all that he had done in the drive. "While I never have been able to talk on my feet," said Bernet, "of all the times for me not to try was last Thursday night, when I got up and thanked the workers of the army that put John Carroll across, because my brain was on a dead center and would not function."[109] Another version of Bernet's remarks that evening cannot be documented but has the support of those who say it was Father Rodman's own version. This story says that when Bernet did get the floor he said, "I am a genius on my ass, but an ass on my feet."[110] This is not an impossible version; the letter to Monsignor McFadden may have been a translation.

A letter written by Leo A. Lux, a member of the "rank and file," to the Speakers' Table on behalf of the four hundred who were present addressed each of those who were at the table with some appropriate comment. Of Bernet the letter says, "You stand for the spirit of the drive. How much more you have to stand for—or sit for—we know well. You have been thanked and re-thanked. The milk of human kindness was poured on you in a never ending stream and your opinion of the kind of cows it came from is the same as ours."[111] Among the other speakers addressed by Lux was Charles Adams: "The plaudits of the multitude are ever and rightfully yours. But to us of the common herd the brightest gem in your crown of glory is merited by you—the only man who ever limited the Right Reverend Bishop to a fifteen minute speech."[112]

There was no doubt in anyone's mind that the campaign was an outstanding success. Neither was there any doubt that the aggressiveness, dedication, and determination of Father Rodman and John J. Bernet as well as the experience and organizational skills of Donald Doughterty were the driving forces. The success is all the more significant since Dougherty said that the campaign was "by far the most difficult campaign of my entire experience—and required the longest period of planning and buildup ever given by me to an institutional fund raising account."[113] Perhaps this underscores the lack of recognition which the Jesuits had in the city in spite of their work of the previous forty-four years. The impact of the campaign on the public can be seen in the remarks of Dudley Blossom, who testified to his "better understanding of John Carroll University and a greater love for the school. I always thought it was a purely Catholic school. Now I find its doors are open to boys of all faiths. Every big city with a cosmopolitan population ought to have such a University."[114]

Dougherty submitted his final report on the campaign to Father Rodman on 22 February 1930.[115] The report reviewed the history of the campaign from January 1929 when Dougherty had been contacted by Father Rodman. According to Dougherty the Jesuits were then "still suffering a mental depression from the crushing defeat in its 1923 campaign for funds," but "faced such a severe physical crisis" that they were determined to make another appeal in the spring of 1929.[116] It was then that Dougherty had said that longer preparation was needed to insure success. The first idea was to erect a "single structure, all duty plant for $1,250,000; the inadequacy of such a structure before many years and the necessity of a third appeal caused the abandonment of this idea." The conferences with architect Graham gave rise to the plan that was finally agreed upon and the goal was set at $2,500,000 by Dougherty himself; this plan was acceptable to Father Rodman and his consultors. According to Dougherty there were three goals in addition to the principal one: offset the memory of the 1923 failure, make John Carroll understood for the first time, and collect $1,000,000 from non-Catholic sources.

On each of the phases of the campaign Dougherty gave an evaluation of the effort. The forecast for the alumni-student campaign was that it could not be counted on for more than $200,000; its proceeds amounted to $262,265.51; the per capita average of alumni pledges was $232.33 and of the students, $69.23, comparing "very favorably with other collegiate campaigns." Dougherty felt that the percentage of alumni giving was too small, only 32 percent, and it pointed to the "need for a much better conducted Alumni Association."

It was hoped that the Preliminary Campaign would bring in at least 50 percent of the goal. This campaign dragged until John J. Bernet accepted the general chairmanship in June 1929 and secured Herman Neff to head the preliminary gifts campaign. Under Neff's direction, $1,400,000 was secured; there were only "one or two Cleveland capital account preliminary campaigns with so large a total." Dougherty pointed out that "The remarkable feature of this showing is that it was accomplished despite the most unexpected and disturbing influence of the stock market crash of November 1929." Dougherty also had praise for the part Bernet played in this campaign.

While Mr. Neff mapped out the plays and called the signals in the Preliminary Campaign, it was Mr. Bernet who carried the ball for large and consistent gains. The General Chairman made Catholics of means give more liberally than ever

Faculty, St. Ignatius College, 1920. *Seated:* R. Meschenmoser, S.J.; F. Haggeney, S.J.; J. Kessel, S.J.; C. Bilgery, S.J.; E. Bracken, S.J.; T. Smith (rector); J. Neustich, S.J.; F. Vallazza, S.J.; S. Blackmore, S.J.; J. Doyle, S.J. *Second row:* _____; Hartmann, S.J.; V. Winter, S.J.; _____; F. Odenbach, S.J.; L. V. Carron, S.J.; A. Hackert, S.J.; H. Brockman, S.J.; _____; Bro. Gastl. *Third row:* L. Cunningham, S.J.; W. Roemer, S.J.; F. Ryan, S.J.; Bro. Holland, S.J.; F. Betten, S.J.; F. Mc-Kernan, S.J.; Bro. Weber, S.J.; _____. *Top row:* _____; J. Malley, S.J.; E. O'Leary, S.J.; A. Wilwerding, S.J.; E. Bork, S.J.; _____; _____; J. Kleist, S.J.; Bro. Mueller, S.J.; _____.

Faculty, University Heights, 1936. *Front row:* R. Gallagher, S.J.; W. J. Murphy, S.J.; C. Uranker; B. Jablonski; H. Graham; L. V. Carron, S.J.; C. LeMay. *Second row:* G. Pickel, S.J.; R. Hopkins; F. Graff; E. Reilley; F. O'Connell; F. Burke; J. March; F. Cosgrove Mulcahy, secretary to the dean; T. Ewing, S.J.; W. O'Donnell. *Third row:* A. Bungart; R. C. Miller; D. Gavin; F. Weiss; J. Joliat, S.J.; F. Suhadolnik; L. Puhl, S.J.; E. Mittinger; J. Schmitt, S.J.; J. Quinlan, S.J.; L. Otting, S.J. *Missing:* 11 Jesuits, 8 Laymen before (first setting a good example himself); made opening and significant successful approaches to the non-Catholic of large wealth; broke down some corporation obstacles and brought thousands of dollars from out of town into the Carroll total.[117]

The gifts from non-Catholics in this phase amounted to $800,000 or roughly one dollar for every two dollars of Catholic money.

The Parish campaign aimed at raising $500,000. The many demands on Pastors for funds and difficulties in agreeing on the proper approach were complicating factors. The amount pledged was $450,893.78 including the $203,000 of the bishop's Chapel Fund.

The General Campaign was directed for the most part at non-Catholic prospects; the outcome of this endeavor exceeded all estimates; it amounted to $477,245. The total cost of all campaign expenses was $87,915. Dougherty pointed out that $246,600 of the total pledged "can hardly be regarded as money raised by the campaign. This amount covers one pledge of $100,000 and another of $96,000 representing property and money of the Society of Jesus and reported as pledges by Father Rodman. The other $50,000 of this amount is a pledge signed by President J. P. Nichols [*sic*], of Detroit University." The adjusted cost of the campaign expenses would be close to .0295 percent. In commenting on this aspect of the campaign, Dougherty said, "Viewing the total expenditures in relation to the money raised, I believe the total cost of the campaign will be one of the most pleasant things the Society of Jesus will remember."[118]

The Corporate College of John Carroll University
1929–1933

The early 1930s were not only a time of transition to the East Side but also a period of close association with other Catholic institutions of higher education in the Cleveland diocese. They were also a time when the question of standards in Catholic educational institutions was being raised by the Committee on Accreditation of the National Catholic Educational Association. The Jesuit Educational Association was in its formative years; the midwest Jesuit colleges and universities were under special pressures from the North Central Association of Colleges and Secondary Schools to conform to North Central Standards. The issue among Catholic colleges, and in particular the Jesuit ones, was whether to conform to external standards or to adopt their own agencies to enforce what were referred to as "Catholic" standards.

The period also witnessed the development of teacher training institutions. In Catholic circles, the need for the training of Sisters to teach in parochial schools had been met in some dioceses by the established Jesuit colleges. The admission of women to Jesuit colleges thus became an issue. The circumstances were such that questions of who should train the teachers and who should set the standards of accreditation also arose.

DIOCESAN HIGHER EDUCATION 1922–1928

By 1922 the development of the parochial school system in the Cleveland diocese had reached a point where the need for Sisters to staff it had exceeded the ability of diocesan institutions to train them. Since 1920, John Carroll had listed education courses for teacher training in secondary education in its *Catalogue*, but even if these courses had been offered it still would not have solved the need for teachers on the elementary level. Father John R. Hagan, more commonly known as Dr. Hagan, who became Diocesan Superintendent of Schools in 1922, sought to remedy the deficiency by developing a diocesan-controlled institution for teacher training.

Meanwhile, in April 1922, both the Sisters of Notre Dame and the Ursuline Sisters sought permission from Bishop Schrembs to open colleges.[1] The bishop took the occasion to express his own concern over the training of teachers and said that he had thought about a diocesan college staffed by members of several religious communities, but the religious communities were not enthusiastic about the idea and the bishop had come to agree with them. Because the nuns were willing to build and maintain their own institutions, he readily gave permission. In fact any religious community of the diocese that could give sufficient guarantee of ability to conduct a college would be given permission to do so.[2] The question as to who would train elementary teachers was left open at this time.

In 1928 the State Department of Education in Ohio conducted an inspection of both Notre Dame and Ursuline colleges. Among the recommendations of the State Department of Education was the suggestion that training for elementary education be consolidated elsewhere.[3] One of the reasons for the suggested consolidation was the scarcity of both students and teachers in either of the institutions run by the Sisters. The need for general supervision of student teaching was also stressed as a reason for consolidating elementary training.

In his report on diocesan education for the year 1927–1928, Hagan called attention to the need of a diocesan viewpoint in the college field.[4]

> There is urgent need of creating amongst both priests and people the feeling that the colleges are the concern of all—not merely of the present students and their parents and not merely of the religious orders conducting these schools. It is this isolation of interest which perhaps accounts more than any other item for the relatively feeble condition of our colleges. No college can thrive unless its roots be firmly planted in the interest of the community from which it draws both students and maintenance.
>
> On the other hand, whole hearted support will never be accorded the colleges unless those contributing such support are invited to participate in the direction and the general policies of the institutions. This implies that there should be on the Boards of Trustees some members other than those belonging to the religious orders which conduct the college. This policy has been employed with remarkable results by several of the more flourishing Catholic colleges and universities of the country.[5]

Hagan was ahead of his time when he suggested outside participation in Boards of Trustees, although it is unlikely that he envisioned the kind of change that came in the late 1960s. As far as the local colleges were concerned he saw both Ursuline and Notre Dame expanding while he considered "The housing facilities of John Carroll . . . are such as to cause concern amongst all those interested in the cause of Catholic higher education."[6]

Bishop Schrembs upgraded the status of St. Mary Seminary to that of a major seminary in 1929, and gradually eliminated from it the preparatory work of a minor seminary. He also moved the seminary from its old quarters on Lakeside Avenue to its present location on Ansel Road. John Carroll University still continued to supply a major share of the applicants.

With the training of priests provided for, the problem of training the Sisters for their teaching certification was the most significant educational problem remaining for the diocese. At that time such training was provided in the nine different religious communities of women in the diocese under diocesan supervision. There was a movement within the Catholic Educational Association to establish a diocesan teachers' college in each diocese where teacher training could be uniformly given and effectively supervised. The four dioceses in Ohio—Cleveland, Cincinnati, Columbus, and Toledo—were in the forefront of this movement and Hagan came to be its principal spokesman. Hagan in 1932 defined the diocesan teachers' college as:

> an independent, professional school of collegiate rank, which is under the direct control of the bishop, which functions in organic unity with the parish school system, which is attended by members of the religious teaching communities and by secular candidates for positions in Catholic schools, which has a four-year curriculum leading to a professional degree, which prepares chiefly, if not exclusively for the elementary school field.[7]

Hagan felt that the differentiation between training for teaching in the elementary and secondary schools was even more pronounced in Catholic education than it was in the public system because he considered teacher training as a sole prerogative of the diocesan administration. The diocesan teacher training college bore the same relationship to the bishop that the Seminary did; in the former instance, the bishop regulated the training of teachers for the parish schools, in the latter, he governed the training of priests for the parish churches.[8]

The establishment of Sisters' College in Cleveland in 1928 met with some opposition from the religious communities of women. In an undated memorandum to Bishop Schrembs, Dr. Hagan complained that the communities were not living up to their agreement to send nuns to the newly formed Sisters' College.[9] Hagan suggested to the bishop that he should withdraw from parish schools all those nuns who should have been attending Sisters' College but were not. "The above matter is serious enough," the Superintendent claimed, "to threaten the continuance of Sisters' College."[10]

Sisters' College was in part the result of Hagan's philosophy and in part the result of pressure from the State Department of Education. In a memorandum on the educational system in the diocese in 1926, Hagan noted that high school teacher training was already being handled by Ursuline and Notre Dame; John Carroll had no department of education although courses in education for secondary teachers had been listed in the *Catalogue* since 1920. The attendance at Sisters' College for those receiving elementary teacher training was only forty-four; a minimum of seventy-five was needed to make the institution acceptable to the state. By 1928 Hagan had brought about the combination of the existing nine separate schools in the new Sisters' College with quarters in the old Cathedral School, which had been used for high school girls.[11]

At the time Hagan was preparing to combine the instructional efforts in diocesan elementary education, he received a letter from the associate supervisor of teacher training of the State Department of Education, L. L. Louthian, asking him to get the advice of the bishop "relative to the entire situation," suggesting the consolidation of Catholic teacher training into a single institution in Cleveland.[12] Louthian also advised that since high school teacher training was already being given in the liberal arts colleges, it should be left there and not questioned since it seemed "essential to the welfare of an institution."[13] He cautioned against small enrollments in educational programs and against a two-year normal school. Louthian also felt that the diocesan superintendent of schools "should have *general* supervision over the elementary teacher training institution and also over any high school teacher training department."[14] A four-year college was suggested as the ultimate goal.

It is clear that Louthian and Hagan were in complete agreement, as expressed in a subsequent letter of Louthian's:

> we believe wholeheartedly in the advisability of consolidating the various elementary teacher training departments in the Catholic Schools in Cleveland. This project will have far-reaching consequences and will enable you to organize under diocesan auspices an institution with a two year and also a three year curriculum which should soon be compared with the best of its type in this country.[15]

Until the opening of the Catholic University in Washington, D.C. in 1889, the Catholic Church as an organization had made little provision for higher education and the training of teachers in the United States. What higher education there was had been sponsored principally by religious orders of men and women. Between 1890 and 1920 increasing numbers of Catholic young men and women sought preparation in the professional fields of medicine, law, and education. The only institutions available to them were non-Catholic; this was especially true in the case of women, for whom there were limited opportunities. In Cleveland John Carroll University was too involved in using its energy and limited resources in effecting a move to the East Side to participate in the addition of professional schools such as occurred at the Jesuit colleges in St. Louis, Milwaukee, and Chicago. Bishops in Buffalo, Boston, New Orleans, Mobile, Los Angeles, Milwaukee, and Chicago brought pressure on the Jesuits to open their doors to women.[16] The appointment of Father Fox, who had experienced the expansion at Marquette, which was already coeducational, might have indicated a similar course for John Carroll, but Hagan's plans for the role of a diocesan teachers' college enjoined squarely the question of control.

Another possible solution to the teacher training problem was the corporate college concept as illustrated by St. Louis University in 1924. In order to provide the nuns with an opportunity to obtain advanced degrees, St. Louis offered courses in several convents much as John Carroll had been doing. Programs for nuns were eventually provided on campus leading to the development of a School of Education and a Graduate School in 1925. In 1924 an affiliation of Webster College, Fontbonne, and Maryville with St. Louis brought the Corporate Colleges of St. Louis University into being.[17] Financial independence and considerable educational autonomy were retained by the affiliated colleges, but all faculties and students of the affiliated Catholic colleges were treated as if they were faculty and students of St. Louis University. Through the efforts of Father Alphonse Schwitalla, the arrangement was given the blessing of the North Central Association of Colleges and Secondary Schools. Although Archbishop Glennon of St. Louis approved the plan, the diocesan seminary was not part of the project. This affiliation of colleges was reported in the *Carroll News* in 1926.[18]

Of necessity such an affiliation involved the question of coeducation and the teaching of women by Jesuits. The drift of the corporate colleges of St. Louis University into nonexistence occurred for many reasons but coeducation was probably one of them. A letter from Father General Ledochowski to American Superiors in 1928 raised any number of questions about how Catholic the Jesuit colleges in the American Assistancy were; the letter also condemned coeducational practices of many of the colleges and universities.[19] In forceful terms Father Ledochowski made known where he stood on the matter of coeducation.

> The problem of admitting women into our schools . . . must be solved by established standards of the Church and the time-honored traditions of the Society. The whole idea of co-education is disapproved by the Church, . . . we cannot

under any circumstances adopt it as a principle. . . . Our high schools and colleges must continue to close their doors against female students, no matter what pressures may be brought upon them.

As regards our universities, almost all of them report that owing to unavoidable circumstances they admit women to certain courses taught by externs. I wish it to be clearly understood that as soon as this special urgent necessity no longer exists, the permission hitherto granted by Father General or presumed by Provincials or local Superiors, must be considered revoked. In the meantime the attendance of women must be discouraged rather than invited, nor must they be admitted to any department where they are not already at the present time. The terms "coeducational," and "coed," etc., being misnomers in our institutions, must be carefully avoided, and must never again appear in catalogues, prospectuses, advertisements, etc., nor in the journals and magazines published by our students.

Should any colleges of women apply for affiliation to our universities for the purpose of profiting by our curriculum and our degrees, all such applications must first be referred to Father General, who alone can give permission for affiliation of this kind.[20]

At least some Jesuits in the United States were convinced that Father General did not understand the situation and was confusing the European concept of colleges, which was attended by pre-adolescents, with the American concept of college. A Commission on Co-education eventually requested by Father General and appointed by the American Provincials released a report in 1939; among other recommendations, the report said that undergraduate colleges that were already co-educational should remain so, but no new requests for undergraduate co-education were to be made. Women were to be admitted to professional and graduate schools; separate classes for men were to be set up where possible.[21] After 1942 further work by the commission ceased.[22] Meanwhile, through registration in Evening Colleges women found their way into classes in liberal arts colleges where, officially, co-education was not permitted.

Proposed Merger With Western Reserve

Father General Ledochowski's letter of 1928 was to have an impact of another sort on a potential affiliation of John Carroll and Western Reserve. The letter undoubtedly influenced the Chicago Provincial, Father O'Callaghan, in his negative response to an offer from Western Reserve University in the spring of 1929 to work out a kind of affiliation with John Carroll University similar to that of the University of Toronto and St. Michael's College. Had this offer been acceptable, and Father Rodman seemed willing to discuss it, the future development of John Carroll would most likely have been considerably different.

In May 1929 while plans for the building fund campaign were being considered and before there was any thought of affiliating the Catholic colleges, President Vinson of Western Reserve telephoned Father Rodman and invited him to lunch along with Newton D. Baker. Informing Father O'Callaghan of the invitation, Father Rodman said, "You know what that means. I'll take Father Fox along and let you know what comes of it. I do not know what proposition they have but they must be thinking of us anyway and they have all the money, the Catholics have not got it."[23]

There appears to be no record of exactly what the offer was but Father Rodman thought enough of it to inform his consultors and seek their advice. As the consultors' minutes show, "Rev. Fr. Rector explained the offer of Dr. Vinson of Western Reserve and Newton D. Baker about the affiliation with Western Reserve University. Certain offers of property and money were made in case of affiliation. The opinion arrived at was to wait and see the outcome of the campaign in the fall."[24]

Father Rodman also discussed the offer with Monsignor Joseph F. Smith, who apparently was very much in favor of accepting it and wrote a letter supporting the affiliation; Father Rodman sent the letter immediately to the Provincial. In reply, Father O'Callaghan quoted from Monsignor Smith's letter a part which said the "people of the town wonder, 'why should we be asked to duplicate in the matter of non-sectarian studies and furnish the money to the Jesuits for departments of medicine, law, and others of a University nature when we have them etc.' "[25]

Father O'Callaghan reminded Father Rodman,

> You and I will know that it is in these very departments that harm is being done at the present time by the professors who have no religious principles, and who frequently go out of their way—as we know is being done in certain schools in this vicinity—to scoff at all religious and who don't hesitate to say that there is no objective standard of right and wrong.
>
> The other day I mentioned the plan casually in the presence of two of ours—men of good judgement, and they showed unmistakably that they did not favor it.
>
> At any rate you see that we shall have to go cautiously in this matter, and make no promises that would compromise us in any way.[26]

Father O'Callaghan was worried even more about what Father General would say, particularly since his permission would be required for such an affiliation.

> You will recall that it was only last year that he sent out that rather strong letter about making our schools truly Catholic, and that the occasion of that letter was the severe criticism passed on many of our American schools for what was said to [be] lack of the real Catholic spirit.

If we hitched up with Western Reserve in any way, we would it seems to me, bring a storm of adverse criticism on ourselves from the laity and the clergy—and especially the bishops of the country if at any time some of the learned professors of Western Reserve were to come out with views on religious or kindred subjects out of harmony with Catholic doctrine.[27]

The Provincial was skeptical about some other points made by Monsignor Smith:

I suspect that in looking for an affiliation with them, the authorities of W.U. are not trying to do us a good turn, but are simply trying to keep everything in the educational line in their own hands.

To say that the scheme has worked out satisfactorily in Canada is to my mind not a very convincing argument since conditions there are entirely different from those that hold in our country.[28]

The Provincial's concern about Father General's attitude was understandable. The General had taken particular exception to non-Catholic professors and especially to those in the office of dean. He even suggested developing a fund to train Catholics for university faculties.[29] Father Ledochowski was also "pleased to note that terms 'non-sectarian' or 'undenominational' have been eliminated from official documents."[30]

Father Rodman must have left the matter open with Vinson and Baker, for in March 1930 he received a letter from Baker recalling their conversation of nine months before on affiliation. Perhaps Baker felt that now that the campaign had succeeded the offer might still be welcome. In the letter Baker enclosed a clipping of an article from *Current History* of January 1928, giving the history and an assessment of the St. Michael's College and University of Toronto relationship.[31] Father Rodman's attention was called to the favorable comments of Father E. J. McCorkell, superior of St. Michael's College. Baker was suggesting a rather quick response to the offer since, as he said, "This subject may not become active with us again, but I confess I have a strong feeling that it would be helpful all around if we could coordinate the educational activities of Cleveland so as to overcome some of the religious separatism here, at least in educational matters."[32]

Father Rodman's reply was obviously influenced by the fact that John Carroll was by this time engaged in trying to make work the affiliation of the Catholic colleges which had begun in December 1929. He agreed with Baker that the "educational activities in Cleveland should be coordinated," but the undertaking to coordinate the Catholic colleges would prevent him from devoting any time to the Vinson-Baker proposal. He agreed with Baker "that there is religious separatism here in Cleveland. I have noticed it more than in some of the other cities in which I have been stationed."[33] On that note the matter ended.

The new 1928 standards for teacher-training schools in Ohio forced some changes on the newly formed Sisters' College. The need for degrees for the teachers meant that Sisters' College would have to expand to a four-year college or affiliate with some existing senior college. In a letter to Hagan, Louthian approved the idea of a single teacher-training system for the diocese including the training of high school teachers. This idea had apparently been suggested by Hagan; Louthian said that he favored the suggestion that "you be responsible for and control all Catholic high school teacher training in the geographic diocese of Cleveland."[34]

The idea of creating a single responsibility in each diocese of Catholic education was proposed to Father John Murphy, Superintendent of Schools in Columbus, Ohio, in the spring of 1928. It was after this that Louthian visited the four dioceses in Ohio explaining and inaugurating the plan. When Louthian was in Cleveland, he informed Hagan that "inasmuch as there would be some difficulties raised from time to time, all letters and communications sent to Columbus relating to teaching training would be sent in copy to the Superintendent of Schools of Cleveland, and that all sending or making any communication on this head would be so informed."[35]

The problem of degrees still stood in the way of completing Hagan's control. Louthian suggested a concession by which the women's colleges in Cleveland would cooperate in establishing a senior college which would be under Hagan's direction and thus provide a single teacher-training institution.[36] In the fall of 1928 Hagan attempted to secure approval by Catholic University of the Sisters' College curriculum. Approval of the curriculum was granted, but affiliation for purposes of granting degrees was not possible at that time.[37]

Meanwhile the illness and hospitalization of Father Fox from the time of his arrival as dean at John Carroll in August of 1928, had prevented him from responding to Hagan's attempts to contact him. In February 1929 Father Fox did contact Hagan, saying that Louthian had asked Father Fox to talk over the secondary high school certification with Hagan, which Father Fox "gladly agreed to do."[38] The business of the building campaign was keeping Father Fox "unusually busy," but he was "sure a working program can be arranged to the advantage of us all."[39]

According to Hagan, the reason for Father Fox's letter was the dean's visit to Columbus on 23 February 1929, when he tried to seek reentry of

John Carroll into high school teacher training with Notre Dame and Ursu-line colleges operating under the John Carroll charter. Hagan also claimed that Father Fox told Louthian that Sisters' College was not competent to direct this work and was told in turn that Hagan was already negotiating with other colleges for degree-granting purposes and was already officially recognized as director of Catholic teacher training in the diocese of Cleveland.[40]

Hagan replied to Fox,

> The matter of amalgamating the Teacher Training activities of the Cleveland Diocese has been up for some time. The whole subject is totally changed from what it was two years ago. Just what will be the outcome I don't know, although I have pretty definite instructions from Columbus. I will be glad to see you at any time to discuss this and other kindred matters.[41]

This communication was followed shortly by another requesting Father Fox to consider what courses the three-year graduates of Sisters' College would need to complete their degrees at John Carroll.[42] Hagan informed Father Fox that Catholic University and the University of Notre Dame also had been contacted but he thought that resident students of Sisters' College would probably attend one of the three local institutions for the fourth year, if that could be arranged. There was some urgency in the matter. "I must know by Easter whether or not, a satisfactory continuance of Sisters' College programs can be arranged in Cleveland. In case of failure in working out such arrangements I would be forced to provide such a fourth year in our own institution."[43] Hagan claimed that this letter was never answered.[44]

In April 1929 Hagan received word from Catholic University that they "would accept the work done at the Sisters' College of Cleveland to the extent that it fits in with our requirements (prescribed and group) for the A.B. degree."[45] Some loss of credit was usual in such cases and was to be expected, but the Board at Catholic University expressed concern over what they saw as a failure of Sisters' College to offer courses in Latin and Greek when the college claimed to stress liberal arts. As the Board said, "this omission seems strange to say the least."[46]

With Father Fox busy in his role as a member of the publicity committee for the coming campaign for John Carroll and Hagan organizing his office as superintendent of diocesan schools, there were no further developments until the fall of 1929. Meanwhile Hagan was considering continuing his graduate studies in education. There had been talk of foreign study, but Hagan thought that was "beyond his powers at present."[47] He complained of overwork and "nervous strain" which led him to prefer Catholic University, especially since he had already completed one year there.[48] By October he was back at Catholic University. He wanted no publicity on the move because he said, "So far as publicity is concerned, no one will bother where I am after three days."[49]

With Hagan in Washington and Father Fox still otherwise occupied, the educational situation in the diocese might have remained quiet for some time were it not for the initiative of Bishop Schrembs on a different but related matter.

CORPORATE COLLEGE PLAN ADOPTED

The specific impetus for the Corporate Colleges of John Carroll University came neither from an attempt to provide teacher training for the nuns nor from any generally felt need for coordination of higher education institutions in the diocese. It came rather from Bishop Schrembs's long-standing desire to have the seminarians obtain college degrees as they finished their seminary training.

When, in autumn 1929, the bishop brought the matter up to Father Rodman he was referred to Father Fox who was familiar with the problem. On 3 October Father Fox spent the morning with the bishop discussing possible ways of providing the degrees; an affiliation of the seminary with John Carroll University seemed to be one way. According to Father Fox, the bishop, "threw up both hands and fairly shouted, 'Wonderful!' "[50] The bishop said, "I have tried for seven years to get degrees for my seminarians from John Carroll University but without success. I said to myself, I will try once more and if I fail, I fail."[51] Father Fox had wider vision than the bishop, and so he proceeded to lay out a plan of affiliation that included not only the Seminary and Sisters' College but the women's colleges and schools of nursing as well. The meeting ended with the bishop requesting Father Fox to write up the proposal and submit it to him so he could discuss it with the institutions involved. According to Father Fox, the bishop was "enthusiastically happy" about the possible solution.[52]

That very afternoon Father Fox drew up a proposal to create an incorporation in a *non legal* sense of the seminary, Sisters' College, Notre Dame College, Ursuline College, Charity Hospital School of Nursing, St. John's Hospital School of Nursing, and St. Alexis Hospital School of Nursing under the title of "Corporate Colleges of John Carroll University." Father Fox in his letter to the bishop agreed that "in a very real sense the Catholic Educational System extends from the kindergarten into the realm of higher education, including our universities and seminaries. At the same time, the growing complexities of modern education increasingly urge a union and co-ordination of all our available Catholic educational resources."[53] Fa-

Top left, Albert C. Fox, S.J., Dean, 1928−34; *right,* Hugh Graham, Education, 1930−51; *Bottom left,* John R. Hagan, Auxiliary Bishop of Cleveland, 1946; *right,* Charles H. Metzger, S.J., History, 1930−34

ther Fox noted particularly that "in the case of the Sisters' College it will enable us to assume a single responsibility before the State Department for the teacher training.[54]

The bishop was delighted. He wrote to Father Fox,

> The plan you outline in your letter appeals to me in every way. At the earliest moment I will take it up with my consultors and also with the heads of the various schools involved and come to a final decision.
>
> I hope to go over the plan with you at my earliest opportunity.[55]

Precisely what transpired between the presentation of the plan to Bishop Schrembs in October and the meeting in December, at which the plan was approved, is not entirely clear. It is evident that Father Robert Navin, who replaced Hagan as dean of Sisters' College during Hagan's absence, was concerned about the question of degrees for the Sisters but not informed on Father Fox's proposal. Responding to an inquiry from Louthian in November, Navin said that the files contained correspondence between Fox and Hagan on completing the fourth year at John Carroll but no action had been taken. Navin also observed that John Carroll had no certification program for teachers and there was, he thought, no indication that the university expected to start one.[56] Navin, apparently unaware of Father Fox's proposal, thought that he could "take immediate steps towards uniting" Notre Dame, Ursuline, and Sisters' College as a single institution, "but in case we do this we do not wish to relinquish our present charter nor even modify it, unless the latter becomes absolutely necessary."[57]

It is difficult to believe that one month after Father Fox's proposal had been presented to the bishop, the dean of Sisters' College was unaware of it. Yet, Navin makes no mention to Louthian of the proposal, even as something of which he would not approve. It may be that Bishop Schrembs did not move immediately as he said he would to discuss the proposal with the heads of the colleges involved. It is quite probable that Hagan was the only one with whom the bishop conferred. In a letter dated 11 December 1929, three days before formal approval of the Corporate College Plan, and from its contents clearly written by Hagan, reference is made to the attempt of six years earlier to get degrees for the seminarians through John Carroll.[58] When that effort failed, the author said, an approach was made to Dean Winfred Leutner at Western Reserve, who agreed to take twelve priests for master's degrees. Bishop Schrembs first approved and then "reneged," saying it would be a reflection on John Carroll. The author of the letter speaks of a proposed affiliation which was advanced some time before whereby Notre Dame, Ursuline, the Seminary and John Carroll would have equal representation and right in an "assembly of equals." According to this arrangement John Carroll would be "merely one like the rest" unlike the Corporate College Plan. According to the author, the proposal was referred to St. Louis and no more was heard from it. The writer says of this proposal, "You will note this is different from the present." The earlier proposal provided for a common charter under the direction of a board which was subject to the supervision of the bishop. There appears to be no other reference to this proposal in the respective archives of the diocese of Cleveland or in the archives of John Carroll or the Missouri Province.

The letter also reviews the developments in 1928 leading to Louthian's request of Hagan to bring Notre Dame and Ursuline College together and place them under Sisters' College to form a single teacher-training department. The writer thought it was a "mistake" to have teacher-training programs at the women's colleges since their graduates could not get positions in the public school system. As far as John Carroll was concerned, he said they were allowed to resign the charter for teacher training acquired in 1924. Also mentioned is the attempt of the Jesuits in Toledo to institute teacher training at St. John College there but they were forbidden to do so by Bishop Samuel A. Stritch.

On the question of diocesan normal schools the same letter refers to the debate of Father Schwitalla of St. Louis University and Father George Johnson of Catholic University over "the wrongness" of such schools and the "rightness of religious orders of men taking over all such." The writer of the letter claimed that ever since the establishment of Sisters' College, the Jesuits have been "frantic" and said further that he had been informed by a teacher at John Carroll that "all sorts of confabs" have been held to discuss it. He concluded that "the only thing the Jesuits want is Srs. College." As kind of an afterthought the writer added, "Mons. Smith's motives in the matter you can guess readily enough." Because of Smith's defense of the Jesuit position in the Loyola high school controversy, he had always been suspect in any affair involving the Jesuits. When St. Louis University awarded him an honorary degree in 1922 "in recognition of years of interest and helpfulness in the work of the Society in Cleveland and elsewhere," he became even more suspect.

The author of the letter then proceeded to downgrade the quality of John Carroll as an educational institution.

John Carroll is only an arts college—a poor one at that. The North Central demands 8 Ph.D.'s for a college. The Jesuits have not got a single one over there. Fox's degree is the honorary one. They cannot confer an MA that will be recognized anywhere. If Carroll were to be examined by an impartial committee of the North Central they would be thrown out even on the basis of an arts college. Look at their list of teachers.

There would thus be no point in affiliation with John Carroll because, "Educationally throughout the city they have no standing. Such promises as 'getting better men' is [*sic*] so much wind. None of the corporate colleges have anything to say as to the policy or condition of John Carroll. They can do as they please and stay in the North Central" through "wrongly filed reports" and "political maneuvering." The entire Corporate College proposal is referred to as "effrontery and bluff," and the suggestion is made that a general committee of equals be formed.[59]

What is difficult to understand is the bitterness of Hagan at this early stage and the unsubstantiated charges against Father Fox and John Carroll. Even many Jesuits had differed with Father Fox, but none questioned his national academic reputation. What is an even greater difficulty is to explain why none of these views surfaced and at least delayed if not prevented the signing of the agreement on 14 December 1929, an agreement which at least one party, Sisters' College, feared would place the bishop in the position of taking orders from the Jesuits. It would take time before Hagan would be able to convince the bishop that the plan was not workable and an affront to his authority. In the beginning no one seemed willing to oppose openly a plan that provided degrees for the seminarians and pleased the bishop.

According to Father Fox, the meeting on 14 December 1929, which approved the plan, was held in Bishop Schrembs's office and the agreement "was read paragraph by paragraph, discussed, voted upon, accepted and signed by all present including the bishop himself."[60] The meeting lasted three "solid hours." The signatories were Mother Mary Evarista for Notre Dame College, Monsignor James J. McDonough for the Seminary of Our Lady of the Lake, Sister Mary Amanda for St. Alexis Hospital, Sister Mary Patricia for Charity Hospital, Sister Agnes Therese for St. John Hospital, Dr. Robert B. Navin for Sisters' College, Mother Mary Eulalia for Ursuline College, Father Albert C. Fox for John Carroll, and finally Bishop Schrembs.

Publicity on the formation of the Corporate College plan appeared not only in local papers but also in those of cities throughout the country, producing both news articles and magazine editorials such as the one in *America*, a copy of which Father Fox sent to the bishop, whose response was, "it is now up to us to make the reality correspond to the idealism of the plan."[61]

At the luncheon meeting for the John Carroll building fund at which the bishop donated the Memorial Chapel, Father Fox discussed a chance for even better publicity for the Corporate Colleges. Father Fox thought that there was need for some visible manifestation of what the agreement really meant. He therefore suggested to the bishop the idea of a combined commencement of all the institutions involved to be held in the Public Auditorium, which had a seating capacity of ten thousand. According to Father Fox, "again the bishop threw up his hands and exclaimed, 'Wonderful.' "[62] Accordingly, plans were made for such a commencement on 11 June 1930.[63] A packed auditorium of ten thousand people witnessed the ceremony. Many photographs of the capacity crowd appeared in the newspapers and congratulatory letters from many bishops were sent to Bishop Schrembs. The visible sign however magnificent did not prevent what Father Fox called "the little rift within the lute" which appeared shortly thereafter.[64]

TERMS OF THE AGREEMENT

The incorporation of the schools and colleges into the Corporate Colleges was neither legal nor financial; it depended upon the "good will of the signatories," who retained "such autonomy as is consistent with the letter and spirit of this Incorporation." The financial interest of each institution remained outside the governance and supervision of corporate agreement.[65]

One particular item of the agreement seems to have caused much of the difficulty that came about in later years. A provision under the heading "Unity of Aims" said that the "Incorporation, founded and depending upon the good will of the signatories, shall not function as mandatory or compulsory in any matter *other than educational policies and standards*" [emphasis added]. In nearly every subsequent dispute, particularly with Sisters' College, there was a tendency to act as if that qualification did not exist. Claims of autonomy in educational standards and policies could hardly be justified if the statement were read as written.

The Corporate Colleges were to be governed by John Carroll University through a body to be known as "The Administrative Board of the Corporate Colleges and John Carroll University." The Board was to be composed of the bishop or his representative and two representatives from each institution, one of which should be an administrator. The Board elected its own officers and had advisory and recommendatory powers. A regent, Father Fox, was the link between the university and the board.

The university pledged to make all of its resources available to the corporate colleges and in turn the corporate colleges pledged to accept the direction of the Administrative Board. There were provisions for amendment and termination. In the case of termination a six-month's written notice was required. The whole bitter controversy probably could have been avoided if Sisters' College had simply exercised this prerogative. On the other hand, an early exercise of this option probably would not have met with the bishop's approval.

UNEASY BEGINNINGS

In April 1930 Father Fox, as regent of the Corporate Colleges, made a move to settle the question of John Carroll University's role in teacher training. He announced that he had hired Dr. Hugh Graham, who had been supervisor of teacher training at St. Louis University, to become director of the new department of education and supervisor of teacher training at John Carroll. Father Fox informed Louthian of the appointment saying that he hired Graham "with the understanding that Doctor Graham is to be *liaison* officer of John Carroll University under my direction. I take it for granted that you expect the applications from Notre Dame College and Ursuline College to be sent to you through my office."[66]

When Louthian responded to Father Fox, he kept his agreement with Hagan to send him any correspondence to and from the State Department of Education that involved teacher training in the Cleveland diocese. Consequently, Hagan received not only a copy of Father Fox's letter but also Louthian's reply, which did not indicate that a copy was being sent to Hagan; the letter said that in the future Louthian would no longer be dealing with Hagan or Navin, but the new arrangement would not be implemented until September. Louthian hoped that whoever was in charge of elementary education be "trained in elementary education and sympathetic to our purpose in that field."[67] Meanwhile, elementary education would be accredited to Sisters' College at least for the next year. Louthian had some doubt about what was meant by Graham reporting to Father Fox since he felt a liaison officer should have some freedom of action.

Father Fox's reply was somewhat imperious in tone particularly in reference to accrediting elementary education to Sisters' College.

> You know as well as I do . . . that no *senior* college is ever asked or expected to accept direction in matters educational from a *junior* college and yet this is precisely what you are insisting upon and have insisted upon endeavoring to subject Notre Dame College and Ursuline College to Sisters' College. I pointed this out to you in our very first interview in Columbus and I thought you got the point then.[68]

Father Fox saw no difficulty in Louthian working with Hagan or Navin but reminded him that he had asked for a single individual to deal with, hence, Graham's appointment as liaison officer. This letter was sent by Louthian to Navin with the notation to send it on to Hagan.

Within a week Hagan sent all copies of the correspondence he had received to Bishop Schrembs together with a letter of his own. The enclosures, Hagan said, were "too important" not to be brought to the bishop's attention.[69] As an explanation for how he had come by the letters of Fox and Louthian, Hagan pointed out that as a result of dealing

258/ John Carroll University

ethically with public officials at all times there has been a spirit of confidence between the School Board and the various city and state agencies. Among other things, the State Department has been scrupulous to transmit to me any matter with which they dealt which touched upon the interests of our schools. Sending me the present communication is merely in line with this code of ethics.[70]

Having explained his possession of Fox's letter, Hagan then said he was sure that Father Fox's action was without the bishop's knowledge and that having the dean of Sisters' College report to a "Carroll subordinate, who in turn would act under the direction of the Dean of Carroll" would prevent the Sisters' College dean from taking orders from the bishop.[71] Hagan did not show any great knowledge of the Corporate College Agreement when he said, "From what little I know of the late merger, each college was to retain full autonomy." This is the first instance of many to follow where the phrase about limiting autonomy to "other than educational policies and standards" was ignored as well as the statement that the institutions enjoyed the "fullest measure of freedom consistent with the common purposes of the colleges." Hagan chose to put a sinister label on the whole matter by telling Bishop Schrembs that, "As long as I was present in Cleveland I did not concern myself overmuch with his [Fox's] activities, but in my absence from the City things may be carried through, so disguised as to mislead those not intimately informed."[72]

Using a curious bit of logic, Hagan also saw a real danger in the Sisters' certificates coming through John Carroll rather than Sisters' College because "what these certificates mean is permission to teach in Diocesan Schools. Only the bishop may give this and only he, or his representative may hand them out . . . the bishop's right in this matter is [to be] upheld."[73] It would seem that Hagan was confusing certification that one had complied with the State requirements to teach with an appointment to teach in Catholic Diocesan Schools.

None of this unpleasantness affected the bishop's enjoyment of the first combined commencement in June, which turned out to be an overwhelming success. Even Father Fox's report of a challenge to his role as regent at a faculty meeting at Sisters' College failed to disturb the bishop's good feeling. A proposal made by Navin at the faculty meeting was met with a question about what Father Fox's response might be to the proposal. Navin's reply was, "Father Fox has nothing to say about this place."[74] The bishop listened to Father Fox and then dictated a letter to the heads of each of the Corporate Colleges, thanking them for their participation in the June commencement, "praising the Corporate College movement in unmistakeable language" and pointing out that "We must expect that at times there may be flaws and misunderstandings but with patience and the spirit of charity these little things will be ironed out . . . we will learn gradually that united efforts are infinitely superior to broken units."[75] The bishop seemed thus far unaffected by Hagan's fears and warnings.

Meanwhile, Father Fox sought to explain to Navin the appointment of Graham, saying he could not understand why there should be any concern. He saw no need for conflict among the deans and noted that John Carroll had dropped teacher training under his predecessors because of what were then considered the "extraordinary demands of the State Department, but it will be resumed this fall under Dr. Graham."[76]

A suggestion of the Missouri Provincial that a younger man replace Father Fox as dean of the college at John Carroll and thus give him full time as regent of the Corporate Colleges appealed to Father Rodman, but it was not implemented.[77] At the second quarterly meeting of the Corporate College Board in October 1930 it was agreed that work completed by Sisters at Sisters' College would be accepted at any college of the corporation towards a bachelor's degree that would be granted by John Carroll.[78] On 8 October 1930, the Solemn Mass of the Holy Spirit was celebrated in the Cathedral by Bishop Schrembs. This was the first time that students and faculty from all Catholic higher education institutions attended as one body, filling the Cathedral to the doors. Both Bishop Schrembs and Father Fox addressed the group.

On December, Father Fox wrote to the State Department of Education seeking to get permission to grant degrees retroactively to those priests who had attended John Carroll and the Seminary but who had completed their studies prior to 1929.[79] The Department replied that as long as the present conditions for a degree were met in all cases, there would be no problem.

STORM CLOUDS

Father Fox was aware from the beginning that there was "a ceaseless antagonism toward the movement. . . . it became evident that the Diocesan Superintendent of Schools was openly opposed to the Corporate College plan."[80] One of the many reports that Father Fox seemed to get from time to time claimed that when Hagan first heard of the plan he "blanched white with rage."[81] Father Fox also claimed that Hagan "openly flouted the bishop's directions given to him in Father Fox's presence to submit catalogues and other similar publications issued by Sisters' College for Father Fox's revision and approbation."[82]

The first half of 1931 saw no external evidence of an impending collapse of the Corporate College structure. In March, Bishop Schrembs thanked Father Fox for his good wishes on the occasion of the bishop's twentieth anniversary of his consecration and added, "We have done a splendid work here in Cleveland and I shall always gratefully remember your hearty and generous co-operation without which it could not have been accomplished."[83] The second combined commencement in June was an even greater success than the first. The selection by Father Rodman of Dr. George Johnson of Catholic University, who held views similar to those of Hagan, as commencement speaker served to increase the bishop's enthusiasm. Meanwhile Father Fox, who was already a member of the Committee on Revision of Standards of the North Central Association, was elected president of the Ohio College Association.

The first official break that marked the beginning of the end of the Corporate Colleges came in the fall of 1931. Pressure from the State Department of Education for a four-year degree program at Sisters' College along with what Hagan called "The failure of John Carroll to act, first as a separate college, then as head of the Corporate Colleges was imperiling the existence of Sisters' College."[84] It was also felt that John Carroll discouraged Sisters from attending classes at Sisters' College after they had completed two years there, thus making the third year at Sisters' College "meaningless." The action of the Corporate College Administrative Board's second quarterly meeting in October of the previous year encouraging such use of the senior colleges was now considered to threaten the future of Sisters' College. Instead of taking advantage of the provision that allowed any unit to terminate its association with the Corporate Colleges, the bishop called a meeting of religious superiors on 16 September 1931 to reorganize Sisters' College as a four-year college with power to grant degrees. The cooperation of the Superiors was asked in requiring all Sisters to continue and complete studies at Sisters' College.[85] Not only were the Sisters required to attend Sisters' College, they were "forbidden to attend the courses of any other institution. No exceptions may here be made."[86] According to Hagan, Bishop Schrembs felt that as president of Sisters' College, he had a "right to organize Sisters' College without asking permission from Father Fox."[87] Both the bishop and Hagan were now acting as if the Corporate College agreement was nonexistent. The question of the bishop's authority had been raised.

Hagan charged that Father Fox now began to show "real interest" in writing a "vehement letter of protest" to Father Rodman which was to be forwarded to Bishop Schrembs.[88] Father Fox's letter is not as vehement as Hagan claims. It rather factually reports that Fox had received letters from the Sisters who said they could no longer attend John Carroll. Father Fox contended that what was decided at the Superiors' meeting was certainly a matter of educational policy and as such should have come before the Administrative Board of the Corporate Colleges. The letter does say that "little by little," Father Fox came to learn that "it was not Dr. Navin but Dr.

Hagan who was fostering the movement [reorganization of Sisters' College]."[89]

Perhaps one of the best examples that the Corporate College agreement was not understood can be found in Navin's letter to Bishop Schrembs in October 1931, when, in explaining the reorganization of Sisters' College in relation to John Carroll, he said the action was not contrary to the original agreement because "complete autonomy" of institutions is "guaranteed."[90] Navin contended that what the Sisters' College did affected no other college because Sisters' College was the only one permitted to train elementary teachers. If Sisters were now withdrawing from other colleges it was because they should not have been there in the first place.

Bishop Schrembs still thought no real problem existed for the Corporate Colleges. In a letter to Father Fox in October 1931, he said, "I feel we have every reason to be proud of the work thus far accomplished and there seems to be a great future for us. Let us work in perfect harmony and mutual good will."[91] One can only conclude that the Corporate College agreement was never really understood. Perhaps Hagan's absence from the meeting at which the agreement was made was crucial.

THE STORM BREAKS

In the spring of 1932, Hagan and Monsignor McDonough, rector of the seminary, made a trip to Columbus to seek an opinion of the state attorney general on the validity of degrees granted by John Carroll through the Corporate College arrangement. This visit was inspired in part at least by the inability to reconcile the Corporate College arrangement with Canon Law so far as the seminary was concerned, an issue that seems to have bothered no one when the agreement was discussed and signed in 1929. When the pair returned with what they claimed was an adverse oral opinion of the attorney general they were challenged by Father Fox. Fathers Fox and Rodman then made their own investigation of the problem and got a written opinion from the same attorney general, John Bricker, to the effect that the degrees were valid. Bricker suggested that to remove the slightest doubt, each of the Corporate Colleges should insert in their charters the words "corporate college of John Carroll University."[92] The dispute over the validity of degrees continued until the spring of 1933 when the demise of the Corporate Colleges made the question academic. Neither the bishop nor his attorney agreed with the attorney general's written opinion and maintained that the degrees were not valid.[93]

Simultaneously with the attack on the validity of the degrees, the bishop appointed a committee to study ways of improving the constitution of the Corporate Colleges. A new constitution was presented at a meeting designed to set up "The Collegiate Conference of the Diocese of Cleveland." According to this arrangement, probably inspired by Hagan, all members were equal; there was no central institution. All degrees were to be conferred by the bishop himself! According to Hagan, Father Fox said, "John Carroll would enter into a merger only as the controlling element or would not enter at all . . . since the Jesuits were a recognized permanent body of scholars and could not enter into an educational pact with any other groups on the basis of mutual equality."[94] It was at this time that Fox first became aware of Hagan's earlier plan to merge Notre Dame and Ursuline Colleges with Sisters' College.[95] He wondered why the bishop, who must have known of the plan, never mentioned it when the Corporate College proposal was first made.

Events now began to move more rapidly as the June Commencement of 1933 approached. In the spring there was a State Department of Education visit by Dr. W. W. Boyd to inspect Sisters' College. Hagan charged that the visit was instigated by Fox and Graham. They were also charged with getting the State Department of Education to withhold sending teaching certificates to Sisters' College that year.[96] Boyd's visit resulted in accreditation being withheld from Sisters' College.[97]

The publication in 1932 of Hagan's doctoral dissertation, *The Diocesan Norman School*, provided another opportunity for intensifying the local conflict. One of the points made in the dissertation was that the "supreme control of the Diocesan Teachers College must be in the hands of the bishop."[98] The teachers' college, he contended, bore the same relationship to the bishop as did the seminary. Hagan criticized the existing relationship of diocesan teachers' colleges to outside standardizing agencies, saying that this relationship

> has caused many of our leaders to look askance upon all standardizing bodies, whether these be State Department of Education or voluntary and unofficial organizations. In any case, such standards are thrust upon us from without and, in so far, imply compulsion. A feeling of resentment is only natural. The Church is essentially a law *giver*, not a law receiver.
>
> In the matter of education this is supremely true.[99]

In Hagan's view, the liberal arts college was no place for teacher-training programs. "The singleness of purpose is lacking, the equipment is lacking, the properly trained instructors are lacking."[100]

An editorial in the *Catholic School Journal* on the issues raised in Hagan's dissertation appeared in June 1933. The editorial, written by Dr. Edward Fitzpatrick, editor of the journal and professor of education at Marquette University, was critical of the diocesan normal school concept and questioned whether it was the only approach to teacher training for parochial schools.[101] The editorial asked a series of questions which the editor said must be answered before launching a program of establishing diocesan normal schools throughout the country. Father Fox was accused by Hagan and Bishop Schrembs of writing the editorial, or of at least causing it to be written. Fitzpatrick testified by an affidavit that "Father Albert C. Fox, had nothing whatever to do with the editorial or other matters in the *Journal* in any way whatever, direct or indirect, nor has he ever had anything to do in any way whatever with anything that ever went into the *Journal*." [102] Even the publisher of the *Journal*, Frank Bruce, wrote to Hagan stating that he could also testify that Fox had nothing to do with the editorial, which, Bruce said, was "merely a preliminary raising of questions to discuss and determine upon diocesan normal schools of the future."[103] In Hagan's mind there were no questions to be raised; everything was settled by the bishop's authority.

Arrangements were made, with the bishop's consent, for the June commencement in 1933 to allow the six nursing schools to hold separate graduations; John Carroll, Ursuline, and Notre Dame held a joint ceremony, and the Sisters' College held a separate graduation ceremony in the Cathedral on 14 June. The bishop's address at the Sisters' College graduation was a philippic against anyone who would interfere in any way with Sisters' College. Although the bishop mentioned no one by name, it was clear to everyone that he meant Father Fox and John Carroll. Hagan had finally convinced the bishop that episcopal authority was at stake.

Let me lay down one first principle, that is not mine but a principle of canon law, a principle of the Council of Baltimore, which is the law of the Church for this country, a principle taught centuries ago by our Divine Lord, and that is that the bishop is the supreme authority in questions of education in his diocese. The Bishop is supreme. . . . No man, no institution, whether inside the Church or outside the Church, may stand between him and his subjects. . . . And I say to any man or to any institution that attempts to interfere with that authority: "Hands off," and I want that distinctly understood.[104]

Bishop Schrembs made it clear that he was also speaking for the other Ohio bishops, Karl Alter of Toledo, James Hartley in Columbus and Archbishop John McNicholas in Cincinnati. After having explained the origin and purpose of Sisters' College, he repeated his warning about interference with Sisters' College, saying,

Now I have no quarrel with any private institution but I want to tell every private institution of education in the Diocese of Cleveland, I do not care what its name and I do not care what its members are, but I say to them "Hands off" on the question of Catholic education in the Diocese of Cleveland. That is my business; that is my function, and I will not stand or brook any interference nor will the other bishops of Ohio.[105]

THE BISHOPS AGAINST FATHER FOX

Why did Bishop Schrembs choose to lash out at Father Fox and the Jesuits at this time? The answer lies in part at least in the pressure being brought to bear on him by the other Ohio bishops. A few weeks before the June 1933 graduation at Sisters' College, Archbishop John McNicholas of Cincinnati wrote to Bishop Schrembs expressing concern that the diocesan teacher-training institutions were in a "very precarious condition." In very forceful language Archbishop McNicholas asked Bishop Schrembs,

should we not unite to eliminate Mr. Boyd, who if not a bigot, is not in sympathy with Catholic institutions, who is using an organization within the Church against us bishops and is trying to divide our forces? From many sources I get the same impression of Mr. Boyd. I greatly fear that delay is dangerous in this manner.[106]

The Archbishop then suggested a meeting in Cincinnati of all of the diocesan superintendents the following Friday, warning,

The situation seems so grave to me that I am very much disturbed about it. I cannot write as freely as I wish, but I am sure that you will understand that a strong opposition is being exercised within our own ranks against us bishops. If we wish to control our schools, and to see that our Sister-teachers are properly prepared for their work, we must act together immediately and positively.[107]

There was no question that the unnamed enemy within the ranks was Father Fox and the Jesuits.

Archbishop McNicholas met with Bishop Schrembs in Cincinnati on 2 June 1933. Also present were Hagan, Father Francis J. Macelwane of Toledo representing Bishop Alter, Father John Murphy of Columbus representing Bishop Hartley, Father Carl Ryan of Cincinnati, Father Floyd L. Begin, and Father James O'Brien of Cleveland. The purpose of the meeting was to present a unified front against obstacles to Catholic education in Ohio. It was "unanimously agreed" that Boyd was one of the obstacles and that "steps should be taken for his removal."[108] The activities of Father Fox, who was described as the "unofficial representative" of Catholic Education before the state department, "playing into the hands of Mr. Boyd to the detriment of Teacher Training Institutions for the advantage of Liberal

Arts Schools" were considered the enemy within. "It was agreed that Father Fox in addition to presenting an acute local problem, was disturbing the equanimity of Catholic Education all over this State and was a menace to Catholic Education in the State of Ohio."[109]

The course of action to be followed by the bishops was to seek Father Fox's removal from the state by writing to his Provincial and, "if necessary" to the General.[110] If a letter to the General were to be necessary it should include mention "of a marked tendency on the part of the Jesuit Order toward the education of women, particularly of religious women, which is not in accordance with the constitution and spirit of the Order as followed by St. Ignatius."[111] It was also agreed that the four superintendents as a group would represent the bishops in educational matters and provide any necessary publicity. After some further discussion it was agreed that Bishop Schrembs would talk to Father Rodman and demand Father Fox's removal. Only if Father Rodman refused to act would Bishop Schrembs then write to the Provincial.[112]

After the meeting Bishop Schrembs received a letter from Dr. B. O. Skinner, director of the state department of education explaining that the "action taken [withholding accreditation of Sisters' College] would result in a much better college than we could possibly build for you by approving what was not actually meeting our Standards, I think you will get the conception of our real desire to be of assistance to you. . . . Dr. Boyd could not honestly recommend the school for approval. If we were to wink at delinquencies, it would bring this Department into criticism for not fully sustaining the standards we are requiring of other institutions."[113]

The whole question of standards was something neither Bishop Schrembs nor Hagan, or for that matter, the other bishops cared to understand or appreciate when it worked against them. Father Fox's efforts to improve the standards of John Carroll, in fact of all Jesuit colleges, were seen as an attempt to undermine Catholic education. There was little appreciation for and perhaps even a lack of knowledge of the efforts of the previous two decades to bring Catholic institutions of higher learning up to recognized standards. To equate the enforcement of standards with bigotry was hardly a rational approach.

Bishop Schrembs' reply to Skinner shows that it was easier to charge Skinner and Boyd with bias than it was to correct deficiencies.

I feel that your action has been dictated by vindictiveness, and bigotry. Dr. Boyd's findings were not based upon an objective standard. The last thing I would ask of you is "to wink at delinquencies . . ." but I do insist that you deal with us fairly and squarely and do not make of us a target of vendictiveness [*sic*].[114]

It was agreed later that another committee would examine Sisters' College.[115]

On 3 July Bishop Schrembs performed "a very painful duty" and told Father Rodman that the four bishops of Ohio wanted Father Fox transferred out of the state.[116] When asked on what grounds the request was being made, the bishop replied that it was the bishop's duty to look after the education of primary teachers and that "Father Fox is a hindrance to me and he is objecting to my plan. I made my position clear in my address given at the graduation exercises of Sisters' College, 14 June at the Cathedral."[117]

Father Rodman sought to disabuse the bishop of any idea that Father Fox had anything to do with Boyd's inspection. The effort failed and the bishop said of Boyd's report, "Well—it speaks his [Father Fox] sentiments anyway."[118] Further efforts on Rodman's part to point out that it was not true that Fox influenced either Boyd or Fitzpatrick's editorial were to no avail. The bishop contended that the "outrageous report" of Boyd "would never have been given if it hadn't been because of the influence exercised by Father Fox."[119] Bishop Schrembs told Rodman of the four bishops' demand for Father Fox's removal and that they would take it to Father General, if necessary.[120] Father Rodman agreed to bring the matter to the Provincial's attention.

Prior to another conversation between Bishop Schrembs and Father Rodman on 22 July, Father Fox testified in an affidavit of 17 July that he had not played any part in the Fitzpatrick editorial or Boyd's inspection and that he had not acted "by any word, action or influence of hindering, opposing or objecting to the education of his primary school teachers by the bishop of Cleveland in the manner he thinks best."[121]

In preparation for his second meeting with the bishop, Father Rodman contacted Monsignor Smith, who would by this time probably know all about the matter. Monsignor Smith, who had been away with the bishop for about ten days, was fully informed. Rodman concluded that the priests of the diocese had also picked up the story from the staff in the bishop's office. According to Father Rodman,

Msgr. Smith admitted that Dr. Hagan had "all" to do with it and that he played up to the bishop's authority and got hold of all the weaknesses of Father Fox to use against him. Msgr. Smith urged that I go to the bishop and assure him of how much we thought of his authority and then tell him that we all understood what a magnanimous man he was; finally to show him that, if the matter got into writing, it would have to follow Canon Law."[122]

At the meeting with the bishop, Father Rodman acted as Monsignor Smith had suggested but the bishop was not impressed. Father Rodman said that he would have to have the charges, with proof in writing and signed by the four bishops and, if this were done, the case would be out of his hands. Bishop Schrembs said he had no charges except the demand of the bishops which he thought it was in their right to make. Father Rodman thought that Bishop Schrembs was reflecting Archbishop McNicholas's tough stand rather than his own views and was "hedging." Rodman said the word "demand" was rather "harsh" and suggested that the word "request" be used. There was agreement between Father Rodman and the bishop that if an open fight ensued no one would be the better for it.[123]

To Father Rodman it was evident that the whole affair was based on

a false prejudice, a pre-conceived notion that Father Fox is detrimental to the authority of the bishops and their system of educating primary teachers. He is condemned without a hearing, without specific charges, merely on false assumption. . . . They, the bishops, seem to think that once he is out of the State that they can do as they want with the Department at Columbus. What a false presumption that is! The more we delve into this, the more the injustice of it all appears and that a good fight to clear the atmosphere would be the best thing for all concerned.[124]

In August two more meetings between Bishop Schrembs and Father Rodman occurred. The bishop was adamant and said that the "demand" of the bishops was "categorical" and, "if necessary, they will go to the Pope."[125] Father Rodman had had enough. "Disgusted with the reiteration of the man, I said very little and listened *per longum et latum* about his arrangements for a trip to San Francisco."[126]

The next day Father Rodman visited the bishop at St. John Hospital to say what he thought he should have said on the previous visit, "that there were no charges, there was no proof and the whole thing was contrary to justice," and to add that it was simply a case of *"persona non grata."* The bishop's response was, "I have no charges, or specific accusations or definite complaint against him. It is just his mental attitude against the teacher-training schools of the Diocese. I wish you would hurry up and get something definite."[127]

Bishop Schrembs later reported to Archbishop McNicholas that he had met the Jesuit Provincial in Chicago recently and had a letter from him through Father Rodman:

The Provincial insisted that to remove Father Fox without a hearing and the opportunity to defend himself would ruin his good name. He claimed that the entire question had become *"publici juris"* especially by reason of the occasion of the reopening of Sisters' College. I called his attention to the fact that Father Fox's name was not even mentioned. He replied that it was quite well understood that Father Fox was the principal man at whom my remarks were aimed. I told him that if this were true, it proves beyond a shadow of a doubt that he was guilty, in the matter of undue interference.[128]

The next move of the bishops was to request Hagan to draw up written evidence of the "wrongdoings" of Father Fox. This Hagan did under the title, "Conflict between the Sisters' College and JCU," a copy of which was sent to each of the four bishops.[129] The so-called "written evidence" is a collection of letters and correspondence together with Hagan's comments. None of the affidavits of Father Fox and Boyd and Fitzpatrick are included or even mentioned. There is a repetition of the accusations already made with no specific evidence to support them. A summary at the end claims that the Provincials of St. Louis and Chicago are opposed to teachers' colleges conducted under Diocesan control, that "Father Fox never has been disowned by his Order for what he has done." Hagan continued, "Father Fox has inaugurated in Ohio relations with the State Department of Education which never existed previously, which have given officials of the State Department a hold over Catholic Education which they never had before, and which has brought the Catholic name into disrepute." In Hagan's report it is never a question of standards; it is always a question of authority.

Perhaps the most significant part of this document is the statement that,

The issue has been simple enough; Whoever controls the education of the teaching Sisters controls the parochial schools.

This is not an isolated affair. It is a test case as to whether the bishop of the Diocese and the Secular priests have any rights in Catholic Education.[130]

The bishops were delighted with the document and left the follow-up in the case to Bishop Schrembs.[131] Archbishop McNicholas, backing off a bit from his previous position, suggested that perhaps Bishop Schrembs should see Father Fox personally and get him to resign or request a transfer out of the state. "It is giving him entirely too much importance to bring the matter before the Superior General in Rome. If he is 'persona non grata' to the bishops—there is nothing else for him but to leave."[132]

Bishop Schrembs was more than displeased with the stand the Provincial, Father Charles Cloud, had taken: prefer charges and we will consider them. Writing to Father Cloud, Bishop Schrembs argued, "To prefer charges and submit them to you would mean that you are to be the Judge of the Bishops of Ohio, which, to say the least, is a strange assumption."[133]

Another meeting between Bishop Schrembs and Father Rodman took place on 3 December at St. John Hospital, where the bishop was spending a few days. Father Rodman asked the Bishop to come to the Jesuit Community for dinner and added that, "Father Fox need not be there."[134] The bishop replied, "I can look Father Fox in the eye, I have nothing against him personally." The conversation followed much the same pattern as the previous ones with the bishop admitting that, while he had "a stack of papers that high" on Father Fox, there was "nothing definite—all inuendos—but all point to Father Fox."[135] Bishop Schrembs would not tell Rodman which bishop had asked for Fox to resign and said he would have planned to go to Rome personally on the case if his health had permitted.

When the Provincial informed Bishop Schrembs that he had again talked with his consultors and all were still of the mind that charges must be preferred before they would act in any way,[136] the bishop replied that this meant taking the matter to Rome.[137] Again Father Cloud wrote to Bishop Schrembs reminding him that such action as the bishops were demanding "presupposes grave wrongdoing and thus the matter necessarily takes on the character of punishment." The Provincial again cited the address at Sisters' College graduation exercises as a public attack on Father Fox, which demanded that charges be made and that Father Fox be given a chance to defend himself.[138] An impasse had been reached, but there is no available evidence of subsequent action on the part of the four bishops.

AFTERMATH

Whatever may have happened to the Corporate College plan as a result of the unwillingness of the bishop to continue it as originally planned, the visible sign of the Corporate Colleges, the combined commencement, posed a real problem. It was true that in 1933 there had been no joint commencement but the prospect now was that not even the modified 1933 pattern would be acceptable in the future. As early as January 1934, Mother Evarista of Notra Dame College asked the bishop what was to happen.[139] Bishop Schrembs scheduled a private conference with representatives of Notre Dame and Ursuline Colleges and told them that as in the previous year there would be joint exerciese for them and John Carroll in 1934, but that each college would confer its own degrees. "We will have to continue," the bishop said, "in order to show up our Catholic groups to the State authorities. We must do it especially this year because the State authorities are so strongly opposed to the Catholic schools and their needs."[140] The bishop told the Sisters that their schools were in danger of losing their charters if the Corporate College structure continued and, in spite of written evidence to the contrary (the attorney general's opinion on the validity of degrees), he said, "Why the men down in the State Department of Education laugh at us conferring degrees as we have done in the past. . . . We are being made fools of! . . . I'll not be made a fool of any longer!"[141]

Bishop Schrembs approached Father Rodman in April about holding a joint commencement. Father Rodman brought up the attorney general's opinion on the validity of the degrees and asked if, in view of that favorable opinion, John Carroll would confer the degrees. The most the bishop would concede was a conference of lawyers to settle the matter. Meanwhile, he wanted a joint commencement with each college conferring its own degrees. Father Rodman said he would think it over and discuss it with his consultors.[142]

Another meeting was held on 5 May between Bishop Schrembs and Father Rodman with Father Wilfred Robb, treasurer at John Carroll, also present. This meeting was in answer to a telephone call from the bishop wanting to know Father Rodman's answer to the question of a joint commencement. Father Rodman began by asking the bishop if Father Fox's presence on the stage at commencement would be an embarrassment. The bishop said he would not be embarrassed. Then Father Rodman called the bishop's attention to the "blast" that he had delivered at the Sisters' College graduation exercises the year before against one of the institutions of the diocese and a member of its faculty. Would there be a repetition? "Oh no! By no means," said the bishop. Father Rodman said he would let the bishop know within a week what he would do. Bishop Schrembs replied, "The Sisters are crazy to know. Don't keep them waiting."[143] The commencement was held as the bishop requested.

Even before commencement, the bishop's attack on Father Fox appeared to quiet down. In August Father Fox made his retreat and on 29 August he suffered a heart attack which resulted in his death on 8 September. A tremendous amount of space in all newspapers was devoted to his accomplishments in service to education both locally and nationwide. An editorial in the *Plain Dealer* summed up his local achievements by saying, "When the larger John Carroll finally comes into its heritage it will be monument in part to the service of Dean Fox."[144]

Father Rodman received numerous letters and telegrams, all of them attesting to the great esteem with which Father Fox was held in educational circles. President Wickenden of Case spoke of his "great respect and warm affection" for Father Fox; Dan Freeman Bradley, Pastor of Pilgrim Church in Cleveland, described Father Fox as "a man to love, courteous, gracious, a scholar without pedantry—a man to create in youth the desire to achieve worthily." To Jared Moore, professor of philosophy at Western Reserve University, he was a "delightful gentleman." C. R. Thomas, president of Fenn College, spoke of Father's Fox's death as "so great a loss."

Newton D. Baker noted that "The fine educational work of Dr. Fox had won for him the respect of educators everywhere. . . . in his spirit may we not rather pray that all his devoted and loving labor may be a foundation for the college in a great and useful future."

W. W. Boyd referred to the "esteem in which Dean Fox was held in the educational circles of this state." The State Director of Education praised Father Fox's "struggles to raise the standards" and his "modest simplicity and personal greatness." George F. Zook expressed regret over the loss of a man who "possessed a fine Catholic spirit and lived a "life of devoted service."[145]

Father Fox's funeral was held on 10 September in St. Mary's Church across the street from where John Carroll University was then located. Before a capacity congregation, one third of which was clergy, Bishop Schrembs, who delivered the funeral sermon said, "John Carroll has suffered an immeasurable loss. Let us pray that God will raise up others of his stamp. He was a 'teacher' in the best sense of the word."[146] Father Fox was buried in the Jesuit Cemetery at St. Stanislaus, Parma. What was left of the Corporate Colleges was interred with him.

Father Rodman paid tribute to Father Fox in a memorial address sponsored by the Ohio Poetry Society, of which Father Fox was the first president. In this address, given over a local radio station, Father Rodman said there were those who felt that Father Fox, "broken in health," would do little in Cleveland after his epic achievements at Marquette University. "Despite the epic quality of his mind," said Father Rodman, "I know that Father Fox carried within him the lyric heart." Father Rodman continued:

> At times when we would converse of the day when our John Carroll University would be established in its new home in University Heights, I could see the epic quality of his mind flame to life again, and he would begin envisioning once more the possibilities of serving the public along the broad lines of culture with which he was so well acquainted. But with each new rebuff to our hopes, he would sink back and smile resignedly: "I guess it will not be for me."[147]

Shortly after Father Fox's death, a nationally known Jesuit writer, Father Paul Blakely, S.J., made the following comment:

> I did not always agree with Father Fox on questions of policy, but I always recognized his outstanding ability. He did a work not only for the Society but for the Church that no other man of his generation, I think, could have done, for he was listened to and heeded by leaders of the opposition who turned a deaf ear to the rest of us. Clouds came in his later years, unmerited suspicion, opposition, and even calumny from those who should have supported him. How utterly mad this is, and yet it seems to be the story of every man who sets out to do great things

for God and his fellows. . . . Is there something perverse in human nature that rises in revolt against a nobility which it cannot itself reach? I should not like to think that, in spite of the evidence.[148]

The writer of the obituary of Father Fox in the *Province News Letter* appropriately commented:

It is pleasant to record that the last days of his life were probably the happiest and most serene. . . . Most of the unwarranted suspicions and misunderstandings that had fallen to his lot because of his militant championship of his principles and ideals were dispelled. There came to him a feeling of physical and mental well-being that had not been his for many a year. He was looking forward to a period of increased activity.[149]

Precisely whether and how there came to be a resolution of the issues dividing Father Fox and diocesan officials is not revealed in the written record. Sometime between March of 1934 and the June commencement of that year, a truce appeared to have been declared. Certainly, Bishop Schrembs's words at Father Fox's funeral would indicate that differences had been reconciled. Perhaps Father Rodman's closing words in his radio address are a fitting conclusion to Father Fox's career:

John Carroll University salutes him as a moving spirit who pointed the way to higher and nobler aims. His memory with her will never die. He will be enshrined henceforth among the worthiest of her cherished heros—a priest, a poet, a scholar, and a gentleman *sans peur et sans reproche.* [150]

After the demise of the Corporate College experiment, Cleveland's Catholic colleges went their separate ways. A joint commencement of John Carroll, Notre Dame, and Ursuline continued for a while but that too was finally abandoned. Hagan was made a Domestic Prelate in 1934 with the title of Monsignor and consecrated Bishop to serve as an auxiliary to Bishop Edward Hoban in May 1946. On the first of September of that year, Bishop Hagan received an honorary degree from John Carroll University, and died on the twenty-eighth of the same month.

Preaching at Bishop Hagan's funeral, Archbishop McNicholas described him as "an ideal little priest wholly dedicated to his calling, enthusiastic, argumentative, crusading for the cause he espoused, industrious in an extraordinary manner in preparing himself for his tasks and faithful in performing the duties assigned to him!"[151]

"To Practice Patience and Wait"
1930–1935

Between the completion of the building fund campaign in January 1930 and the actual beginning of classes on the East Side in October 1935, faculty, students and benefactors spent a little over four years of waiting for the fulfillment of their dream. The long wait was forced upon them by the failure to collect enough of the money pledged to complete the project; the deepening economic depression of the 1930s was largely responsible for this failure of donors to fulfill their pledges.

Problems of approving a final set of plans for the new buildings, beginning construction, and later protecting the unfinished structures during a period of a little over four years were only a part of the story. Concerns equally important which required attention during the period of waiting were the general financial condition of the university, the determination of the site for the new Gesu parish, an attempt to coordinate all the Cleveland Catholic institutions of higher learning under the aegis of John Carroll, an amendment of the charter to permit broader educational scope, continuing difficulties with the North Central over athletics, and numerous efforts to secure a loan and collect pledges. It was the sheer determination and drive so characteristic of Father Rodman that resulted in eventual success in opening classes on the new campus in October 1935.

BUILDING PLANS

When, in March 1930, Edward T. P. Graham, the original architect, released his rights to the plans for the new buildings, Philip L. Small was hired as the new architect. The original plans, based on what buildings there should be rather than what could be afforded, were scaled down to include only essentials. The main building was to include classrooms, a library, offices and a cafeteria; provision was also to be made in it for a gymnasium which could also be used as an auditorium. Two science wings attached to the main building, a faculty building (residence for Jesuits), a dormitory, and a power plant completed the essential group. This was the basic plan for which funds had been solicited. A separate gymnasium was to be added if sufficient money was collected over and above the amount necessary for the essential buildings.

During the spring and summer, when plans were drawn up for submission to Rome for approval, two problems arose. One was the location of the library and the other the demand for a separate gymnasium. The addition of two more buildings demanded by some was not considered possible by fund-raising campaign chairman John J. Bernet under the circumstances. The Grassellis had contributed to the library with the understanding that the library would go in the main building. Bernet was hopeful that the Grasselli interest could be maintained until sometime later when there could be an appeal for a separate building to house the library. "Their enthusiasm in the undertaking, however," said Bernet, "must be stimulated in the meantime, which we will undertake to do."[1]

While the library issue was settled rather easily, such was not the case with the gymnasium. Insistence by Father Rodman and the Jesuits on the separate gymnasium caused some strong rebuttals from Bernet. One of the reasons for the sharpness of the controversy was faculty willingness to build a gymnasium instead of a dormitory. Still hoping to achieve football fame, the Jesuits suggested a change in plans that already had been agreed upon. Bernet's reply to the suggestion was to point out that there was an implicit agreement with benefactors that the basic group of buildings which had been outlined was to be built. He placed particular emphasis on the fact that the basic plan envisioned an enrollment of about 1,200 undergraduates, some of whom would live in dormitories. Since the appeal for funds was geographically unrestricted so also would be the areas from which students might come. There was a particular appeal to out-of-town donors. Since a "very substantial part of the total pledges was from people who were non residents of Greater Cleveland," not to build a dormitory would be breaking faith with them.[2]

In a rather lengthy reply to the proposed changes, Bernet said,

> The plan you propose now contemplates an auditorium to seat 1500 people, which is more than your final enrollment is expected to be, and which is estimated to cost (including cafeteria, etc.) $270,000. I assume that the auditorium may be used more than once during the year.
>
> It is proposed to provide a faculty building that will use up more than 10% of the total funds received.
>
> It is proposed to change the plan to have two separate science wings. For that I have no criticism to offer.
>
> We were uncertain when we talked about raising the funds as to whether we would receive enough to build a gymnasium but it was generally thought that that would be a later consideration. It is now planned to have a gymnasium, and it is

also planned to abandon any dormitory buildings. Some of the excuses that I have heard were that it would be difficult to police, and place an unfair burden on the faculty. This is the first time I have heard a Jesuit teacher complain about the burden that is placed upon him. Of course, I have not associated with them very much, and that may be the reason. If you were contemplating an old priests retreat, which will incidentally look after boys from greater Cleveland who will be forced to go home every night, and a few that may enroll from out of town, but will be forced to seek their own lodgings, without any supervision or policing, I think you are working up an ideal plan but, so far as I am concerned, I do not see how I can consistently go along with the changed plan because I feel that if I gave my approval to such a plan, I would have taken money from people whom I had solicited, under false pretenses, because it was specifically stated, and with full authority, that there would be some dormitory housing provided.[3]

Needless to say, Bernet had strong feelings about building the dormitory. The Jesuits' arguments that the need for a good gymnasium superceded that for a dormitory and that it would be easier to build a dormitory later than it would a gymnasium, did not prevail.[4] The dormitory was built as part of the original group and appropriately named Bernet Hall. Bernet's interest in the dormitory was not personal; he was concerned with future fund-raising. "In going to the people of Cleveland for further contributions in the future, those undertaking the appeal I believe would be embarrassed by a failure to carry out one of the important features of the plan as represented in the last campaign."[5] Once there was final agreement in the plans they were submitted to Rome and later approved as having "exceptional merit."[6]

Before a gathering of some three hundred people, including the faculty and students, ground was broken for the new John Carroll on 7 April 1931, near Hadleigh Road and Carroll Boulevard. Bishop Schrembs, surrounded by Fathers Rodman and Fox, Monsignor Smith, Bernet, Neff, and Small, and C. A. Lohmiller and G. E. Conkey representing the general contractors, drove a silver shovel into the ground and turned over the first shovel of dirt; a second shovelful of earth was turned by Bernet and a third by Monsignor Smith.[7] Bishop Schrembs in his talk paid tribute to the work of John J. Bernet and Charles L. Bradley in bringing about the movement for expansion of the university. "We have gathered here for a simple ceremony," said the bishop, "the turning of the first soil for the John Carroll University. It is impressive in its consequences as well as in its simplicity. It tells of great things to grow. We can visualize now the great buildings that will grow, which will proclaim the Jesuit order as the order of the educator."[8]

In an elaborate ceremony on 5 July 1931, the cornerstones of both the main building and the bishop's chapel were laid. Bishop Schrembs again

Herman R. Neff, Chairman of 1929 Preliminary Gifts Campaign

John J. Bernet, General Chairman of 1929 Building Campaign

Benedict J. Rodman, President, John Carroll University, 1928–37

Ground Breaking of University Heights, 1931. *Front row:* Msgr. J. F. Smith, Fr. Fox, J. Harwood, Bp. Schrembs, H. Graham, Fr. Rodman, J. Bernet, H. Neff officiated, assisted by many of the priests of the diocese. U.S. Sen. Robert Bulkley was the principal speaker.

CONSTRUCTION SUSPENDED

Toward the end of 1931, it was becoming increasingly difficult to collect enough pledge money to support continued construction. There seemed little hope of immediate improvement in the general economic condition of the country and the city, and little promise of any future rapid recovery. Construction was finally suspended as of 19 January 1932. By that time the six buildings were in a semi-complete stage. The order suspending further work anticipated a delay of some length of time and so certain work was authorized to put the building in a state which would allow as little deterioration and weathering as possible. All roofing, composition roofing, connecting flashing, downspouts, and sewer connections necessary to make the buildings weather-tight was to be completed. Interior metal door jambs were to be painted, and glazing completed. All material that was on the premises such as radiators, motors and other equipment was to be placed in the halls, and a statement showing the state of completion was to be drawn up. Watchmen were to be hired and proper protection against vandalism was to be taken.[9]

It was considered advisable to complete the exterior work on the Grasselli Tower. The *Carroll News* commented that, unlike the occasion of groundbreaking and cornerstone-laying ceremonies only six people were present and as the "stately Gothic structure floating in a sea of mud" was completed when the last stone was in place.[10] The newspaper called the occasion important because although it did not mark the completion of the building, it did signify that "dreams of Carroll are becoming reality."[11] The reporter was more perceptive than he realized. Grasselli Tower has indeed become the visible symbol of John Carroll University. Although not of great height, it does stand out particularly at night under a lighting arrangement that enhances its splendor. Its nighttime appearance has been so attractive that the photograph of its lighted beauty has become a University trademark. The Tower bells, too, have their history. The larger of the two bells rang the hour and the smaller one the Angelus until 1937, when a local ordinance limited the ringing of the hours. The restoration of the ringing of the Angelus was discussed in the 1950s but no action was taken. The two bells were cast in the McShane Foundry, Baltimore, Maryland and were donated by Thomas A. Grasselli and his three sisters.

The halting of construction did not deter Father Odenbach from moving into the Tower in April 1932, where he remained until he was recalled by his Superiors to the West Side shortly before his death in March 1933. He had been given permission to move to the Heights with his instruments and it was assumed that he would stay there unless the buildings would be finished; the consultors were optimistic.[12] Accompanied only by his dog, Hector, and a canary, he set up "camp" in the Tower, which now became his workshop. He did his own cooking and slept in an Arctic sleeping bag. His return to the West Side early in 1933 was prompted by concern for his health. He was hospitalized for surgery in February and seemed on the road to recovery when he died in March. He never lost his sense of humor even after his operation; "I am being made over like an old Ford," he said to reporters, "I'll be out of here in two or three days."[13]

Well known, admired, and respected, Father Odenbach was eulogized by Dean Winfred G. Leutner of Western Reserve University: "In the many years I have known Fr. Odenbach, he was one of the most interesting and picturesque figures in scholarly circles. He was keenly alive to scientific development and was a genuinely human person."[14] President William E. Wickenden of Case said, "The scientific life of Cleveland and the nation has lost greatly by his death."[15] Dr. Dayton C. Miller, also of Case, considered him "eminent in his study of earthquakes."[16] Bishop Schrembs described him as a "scholarly yet humble priest" and a "great scientist."[17]

FINANCIAL PLIGHT

The failure to collect pledges was not the only financial problem confronting the university. The demand of the Chicago Province for payment of the old Buffalo Mission debt required the borrowing of $100,000 in 1932 from a bank to pay off the debt. The consultors would have preferred to mortgage both the West Side and East Side property, borrowing $500,000 to pay off the debt and finish the buildings.[18]

To alleviate the financial situation of the university, Father Daniel O'Connell, Prefect of Studies of the Chicago Province, suggested that Father Rodman "reduce the number of lay Professors" as an economy measure.[19] Out of a total faculty of twenty-four, ten were laymen. A compromise was later effected whereby salaries were reduced ten percent.[20] The death of one layman brought the total number of laymen for the following year to nine out of a total of twenty-four faculty. The summer school which had operated at a loss in 1931 had to be cancelled for 1932 because of the new diocesan regulation prohibiting nuns from attending John Carroll. In explaining the cancellation to the Bishop, Father Rodman said,

> Your Excellency can well understand that with John Carroll itself facing financial difficulties for the payment of the necessities of life, we dare not burden ourselves with obligations for payment of which we have no funds available. I

have discussed the matter thoroughly and repeatedly with Father Fox and the rest of my Consultors and they are unanimously agreed that, as much as they regret it, we shall have to omit summer school courses this year.[21]

Efforts to secure a loan to complete the new buildings were frequent and unsuccessful. Toward the end of 1932, an attempt was made to secure a loan through the Reconstruction Finance Office of the Federal Government. The mayor of Cleveland, Harry L. Davis, lent his assistance but to no avail. The Huron Road Hospital, the second oldest in Cleveland, also applied for a similar loan at the same time. Both requests were refused on the technical ground that the pledges in both cases were not negotiable paper. An editorial in the *Cleveland News* critized the RFC for denying the requests and urged Cleveland industry and business to come to the rescue of both institutions.[22]

Early in February 1933, there seemed to be hope that a loan could be made. A Newark, New Jersey financier by the name of Hollender had come to Cleveland to talk to diocesan officials about a loan to the diocese and was willing to discuss a loan of several hundred thousand dollars to John Carroll. Hollender, a furrier and fur manufacturer, even invited Father Rodman to come to his home in Montreal for a visit. Talks continued for a while but nothing came of them.[23]

At an Alumni meeting in January 1933, Herman Neff reported reasonably good results, considering the depth of the economic depression, from a quiet drive to collect on pledges.[24] Neff also reported receiving suggestions from all over the country on how to bring about the completion of the university buildings but, "of all the hundreds who have come to my office with suggestions, never has a Catholic man come to me."[25]

There is an unsigned and undated memorandum among Father Rodman's papers listing urgent reasons why the Jesuits should complete the new college buildings.[26] Eighteen reasons are listed; among them the inability of the Jesuits to meet their obligations if they remained on the West Side seemed to be the principal one. The feeling was that parents would send sons only to an East Side school and the enrollment necessary to operate could only be achieved on the East Side; over six hundred students, high school and college, were crowded into the West Side quarters with no room for expansion. Weighing the cost of maintaining and protecting the incompleted buildings against interest payments on a loan large enough to complete them, the Jesuits thought the loan was worth the risk. There was confidence also that the pledges would eventually be redeemed. A constant effort to collect them had already produced $185,000. As the author of the Memorandum put it, the "Jesuits were working under a cloud with no inspiration" on the West Side and "there is no appeal." The high school, too, was suffering. The only answer seemed to lie in making a loan and completing the buildings as quickly as possible.

In August 1933 at the peak of the Corporate College controversy Bishop Schrembs lent his support to the idea of a loan by writing to Father General Ledochowski, reviewing the history of the property from its purchase in 1923, describing the current situation, and saying, "you will pardon me I am sure if I presume to write to you on a subject which, while it belongs to your jurisdiction, means much for the interest of the Church here in Cleveland."[27] Bishop Schrembs said he had planned to go to Rome and, in the course of other business, "hoped to lay this matter before you personally." The bishop finished his letter by saying, "I plead with Your Paternity with all the earnestness of my heart to give favorable consideration to my humble petition."[28] A good part of the bishop's letter repeated many of the reasons already listed in the Memorandum including the suggestion that a $500,000 loan would provide the necessary funds.

Father Ledochowski responded to the bishop rather quickly and sympathetically. After thanking Bishop Schrembs for his "personal practical interest in the work of the Jesuit Fathers," Father General said it would not surprise the bishop to learn that "the Fathers themselves are almost in despair about their inability to complete construction," and that many appeals for cooperation had been received in Rome.[29] The General explained, "It is certainly not owing to any indifference or lack of appreciation on my part," that nothing had been done thus far, "I simply did not see how I could relieve the situation under present conditions, having no money to give or to lend."[30] Moreover, "The Chicago Province having other houses threatened with bankruptcy, could offer no assistance."[31] The only "prudent course to follow" was "to practice patience and to wait."[32]

Father Ledochowski's letter shows serious doubt as to whether John Carroll could handle a $500,000 loan. He was willing to verify his judgment one way or the other by making it his "immediate duty to communicate with Father Provincial and other Superiors, and to ask them to study the matter thoroughly, to get the advice of experts, and to report to me."[33] His one caution was that the "Sacred Congregation has been much more severe lately in granting indults to borrow money. It requires in every case serious guarantees showing how loans can be paid."[34]

A report on the financial condition of the university in 1933 surprised the John Carroll consultors when it showed that they were "running behind $20,000 a year as things are now."[35] What was even more surprising to them was that even with a loan to complete the new buildings, they probably could not stop that loss. The important factor was the expected enrollment forecast of 700 students on the East Side, and 700 students in the high school on the West Side if the new building could be finished and occupied.

A later estimate put the numbers at 500 in the high school and 900 to a thousand in the college.[36] At the November meeting of the consultors, Father Rodman suggested that a plan be drawn up to allay any doubts that the Provincial might have that the enrollment projections had a valid basis.[37]

An inspection of the unfinished buildings early in 1934 was made with a view to seeing whether only part of the buildings could be completed, thus reducing the amount of the necessary loan. It was finally decided that this plan would cause trouble with the contractors and suppliers.[38] A report by the treasurer, Father Wilfred Robb, that there was $33,500 of tuition in arrears led to a program to collect that sum, which represented approximately 25 percent of the tuition due in both regular semesters.

In spite of the conditions on the West Side there was an increasing number of out-of-town students, not all of whom were athletes but all of whom had to seek their own lodging. Father Robb proposed to provide housing on the West Side without waiting for completion of the buildings on the East Side. There was a large house at the corner of Carroll and West 28th streets, former headquarters of the Knights of St. John, which could be had for a reasonable rent. A couple hired to cook and look after the house would provide resident supervision. Father Robb felt that such a move was required because of "the assurance we feel must be given parents of out-of-town students that the University will exercise some supervision over the boys that will in a measure satisfy the parents as to the welfare of their boys."[39]

In the course of the discussion on the advisability of renting the house it was decided that such a plan would provide a good beginning for the new dormitory on the East Side even though the house could accommodate only twenty students. In order that athletes should not be the only ones allowed to live there, it was also decided that the number of athletes should not exceed one half of the total.[40]

THE MEMORIAL CHAPEL

When the bishop donated to the Jesuits the Memorial Chapel originally intended to be built at Parmadale, it was understood that it would be built from the funds resulting from the pledges made by the priests of the diocese. Income and construction costs for the chapel consequently were managed as a separate fund. The plans for the chapel were subject to the approval of the bishop and the budgeted cost was $204,063.[41] The pledges were due according to a schedule that required a certain percentage of the pledges to be paid as the construction advanced from laying the foundation to the complete structure. If the schedule were followed, 40 percent of the pledged amount was due by the middle of July 1931; the next three installments of

20 percent each would be due within a year from that date.[42] For many reasons the three installments were not forthcoming and it became impossible to collect on the pledges once construction on all the buildings was halted. Efforts to get the bishop to assume any responsibility for collecting the pledges resulted in the bishop informing Father Rodman in October 1931 that it was not his responsibility to collect the pledges for the Chapel.[43]

The correspondence between John J. Bernet and Bishop Schrembs over the collection of pledges for the Chapel is a lively one. The bishop had made a personal pledge of $10,000 to the campaign fund. Bernet wrote to the bishop on 5 December 1931 to point out that the building schedule had thus far been maintained but that further progress was dependent upon payment of pledges. The bishop's pledge was now in arrears, and therefore it was important that the bishop as "one of the more generous contributors . . . make every effort to liquidate payment on his pledge."[44] In a reply, Bishop Schrembs said that his personal pledge should go to the Chapel fund and said that he had stated this "quite clearly" at the time he made the pledge.[45] The bishop then called Bernet's attention to what he considered to be an "unfortunate misunderstanding with regard to the Memorial Chapel;" that is, when the bishop turned over the pledges for the Chapel he assumed "full financial responsibility for the total of these pledges."[46] The bishop contended that,

> They might as well hold me financially responsible for all the pledges made to John Carroll University because I authorized the drive and inaugurated it and repeatedly insisted that I meant the drive to be a success.
>
> John Carroll University has a General Committee in charge of the collection of pledges. Well, the pledges for the Memorial Chapel are exactly on the same basis as the general pledges for the John Carroll University and I can see no valid reason why your General Committee should not collect these pledges the same as they are collecting other pledges.
>
> Both Monsignor Smith and Monsignor McFadden, who were active in soliciting the priests' pledges, are most willing to cooperate with your Committee in seeing that these pledges are honored, but, of course, the general depression has hit these pledges just as it has hit many of your other pledges. I feel satisfied, however, that the priests who made the pledges, both for themselves and their parishes, are going to honor them.[47]

There are two versions of the bishop's letter to Bernet, one marked "not sent" and another sent at a later date. Up to the point already discussed they are the same in content; they differ in language but not in tone in reference to matters concerning the chapel. The bishop resented having contractors sent to him for his signature on contracts. In the letter not sent he called this practice "foolish and impertinent," and in the letter sent later he referred to the practice saying he was "rather provoked."[48] In the letter not sent, the bishop said, "I resent this action. I resent likewise the fact that while the rest of the buildings are being put up, all the work on the Memorial Chapel has stopped. Such action is not of a nature to conciliate the good will of the priests of the diocese."[49] In the revised version the bishop merely "noted" that the Chapel was not progressing as were the other structures. The reason, to which the bishop did not allude, was that the Chapel could progress only to the extent the priests' pledges were paid.

One other matter appeared in both letters in the same language. The bishop referred to the "constant rumors passing among priests that the University Memorial Chapel is going to be made the Parish Church of the new Gesu Parish. This, too, has created bitter criticism on the part of priests who say they never subscribed for a Jesuit Parish Church but for a Memorial Chapel, which I in turn dedicated to the University."[50]

In his reply, Bernet stated "very frankly I do not have the same recollection your letter indicates you have," and then proceeded to take up each point in turn. Bernet was willing to concede that the priests' committee and the General Committee could cooperate but, "something more than that is needed. Our committee cannot undertake to collect those pledges, and if you will again refer to your pledge of 22 January I believe you will agree that it never was intended that they should collect the pledges from the priests."[51]

With regard to approval of contracts for the Chapel, Bernet called the bishop's attention to some previous correspondence concerning those contracts, in which the bishop did approve a contract and reserved the "right to pass on every item of religious furniture which goes into the Memorial Chapel before its final approval."[52] The halting of construction on the Chapel was attributed to the fact that money from the priests' pledges was not coming in and the committee "certainly could not take any money from the general building fund to pay for the Chapel."[53]

As to the rumors about the Memorial Chapel becoming the Gesu Parish Church, Bernet said he knew nothing, but he had met Monsignor Smith recently in White Sulphur Springs, West Virginia, and had discussed the matter. Bernet certainly did not advocate such a use of the chapel and felt that the Parish Church should be built on the location originally intended for it.

Bishop Schrembs's recollections obviously did not agree with those of Bernet and so the correspondence continued. Ignoring the implication of Bernet's remark that "something more" was needed than the cooperation between the Priests' Committee and the General Committee, the bishop said that, "If the Priests' Committee is shirking its responsibility or is slow in carrying out its pledge of cooperation with your committee, I think your committee should get busy with them and urge upon them the need of a strong effort to collect the priests' pledges especially in view of the fact that all other buildings are nearing completion."[54] With regard to contract approval the bishop said, "The fact that I reserve the right to pass on the various items of religious furniture that were to go into the Memorial Chapel before its final approval cannot by any stretch of the imagination be meant to indicate that I personally assume financial responsibility therefore." The bishop felt the fact that "all ecclesiastical buildings and their furnishings are subject by law to my approval," entitled him to "that much of a courtesy."[55]

Subsequent correspondence between the two men failed to achieve any measure of agreement. In the course of this exchange the bishop learned that all construction had been halted. He expressed optimism that "things are bound to improve, and that as we come back to normal conditions, the priests' pledges will be honored."[56]

PARISH MATTERS

In September 1929 Bishop Schrembs had expressed a desire to sell the "triangle" property located near Warrensville Center Road originally intended for the East Side Jesuit Parish. Writing to Father O'Callaghan, Father Rodman explained that he could understand the bishop's thinking since the property located a short distance from the university had been valued at $450,000 and its sale would help in liquidating the large parish debt already acquired.[57] Monsignor McFadden, secretary to Bishop Schrembs, called attention to the complaint of many people of the parish that the church had not been built on the "triangle" site as was originally planned.[58] If it had not been for the activities of the first pastor, Father Rudden, some parishoners claimed, the church would have been built and by now the parish would be in good financial condition as were others founded about the same time. Instead there had been nothing but court suits and disputes about politics and zoning.

If the "triangle" were to be sold and the church located permanently on John Carroll property, the sale price of the necessary university land to the diocese had been set at $50,000. Monsignor McFadden felt that this would put an impossible burden on the parish and suggested that John Carroll donate outright the property to the parish:

> I, therefore, do not hesitate to recommend to you [Father Rodman] and your Consultors with the real interest of John Carroll University, my Alma Mater, at heart to give the piece of property absolutely without cost to the parish.
> It will be a real master stroke for the John Carroll University to put an end to

the disquieting situation that has prevailed for these past four years. . . . The generous thing is to give it absolutely. Then these people will become an asset in the coming campaign [1929–1930] instead of being a drag. . . .

I am sure you will realize that it is only the desire to help John Carroll University that makes me so audacious as to propose this free gift to the Gesu Parish.[59]

Father Rodman did take the matter up with his consultors, who agreed to follow Monsignor McFadden's suggestion, and a deed was drawn up giving a piece of the University property to the diocese for the church.[60] There were problems about the university's legal ability to make such a gift. Joseph A. Schlitz, acting as the University's attorney, pointed out that many would take the position that a corporation organized for education cannot dispose of property without a court order.[61] Such an order would involve time and expense and probably be necessary if in the future the diocese wished to dispose of the property.[62] The parish was to stand all expenses if such an order was needed. The diocesan attorney, M. P. Mooney, raised the same question.[63] The university was not in any hurry to proceed with the transfer but there was pressure on the parish since a note was soon coming due.

Father Rodman did ask the Provincial to draw up the necessary request to Rome for permission to give the property to the diocese. In August 1930 Father Rodman received a letter from the new Provincial, Father Charles Cloud, notifying him that he had received the "Faculty from Rome of alienating the piece of property on which the Gesu Church stands in favor of the diocese of Cleveland."[64]

A year elapsed before any further action was taken. Neither Father Rodman nor the bishop was entirely satisfied with the proposed arrangement and many more serious matters intervened, particularly diocesan education problems arising from the controversy over teacher-training for parochial schools and the validity of degrees granted under the Corporate College arrangement. In October 1931 Bishop Schrembs informed Father Rodman that he wished the Gesu Church moved to the original triangle site.[65] Writing to Father Rodman, the bishop said,

it was a mistake to have abandoned the original property which was given for the establishment of a parish and to have attempted the building of a parish proper on the University grounds.

In the first place, I do not think that a parish church belongs on the University grounds and, in the second place, I feel that the property now on your hands with no apparent chance of a sale is an incumbrance rather than an asset.

Fortunately, you have not gone so far as to not remedy the blunder and it is my conviction that you ought to go back to the original agreement. Use the original property for the purpose for which it was given and leave the University grounds for the University. . . .

Unless you can present to me some cogent reason why this should not be done, I hereby direct you to make this change effective at once.[66]

Father Rodman's "cogent reason" for not doing as the bishop ordered is to be found in plans for purchase of the property across from the university on Miramar Boulvevard. This property had been intended for Cleveland Heights Board of Education purposes and had been so designated by the Van Sweringen Company but it was later discovered that the five-acre site was not large enough for the Board's purposes. Father Joseph Milet, who had become pastor of Gesu Church in 1931, had been involved in the negotiations that would have brought about the acquisition of this property in exchange for the "triangle" or in some other way. A resume of the discussions was sent to Father Rodman, who thanked Father Milet for his efforts and said he would do whatever he could to bring acquisition about.[67] Although permission was received from the bishop to proceed with the arrangements to acquire the Board of Education property, the action was not completed until Father Rodman became pastor of Gesu Church in 1937.[68] By that time crowded conditions in Gesu School made some action necessary. The site was purchased, thus settling the permanent location of the parish.

FACULTY CONCERNS

During the wait for construction to be resumed Father Fox took measures to organize the faculty for more effective work. In 1931 he began a publication called the "Faculty Reflector" whose purpose was to provide a record of action taken at faculty meetings. Most of the contents dealt with procedural matters such as the requirement of syllabi, students' and professors' absences, and the like. It was made clear that the Dean's Office would handle policy.[69] An item occurring frequently in the pages of the "Reflector" was the need for departmental cooperation particularly in the enforcement of good English usage. There was also a good deal of discussion on the requirements demanded by the North Central. Included in the agenda was the discussion of letter versus numerical grades and the proper handling of graduate work.

At one meeting the faculty discussed a long list of the complaints reported by Father Lionel Carron, Assistant Dean.[70] Among these subjects were the poor scholarship of many students who lacked adequate high school preparation, a noticeable lack of refinement and culture among some students, untidiness in dress, students whose outside work interfered with their studies, inadequate library facilities, and the basis for granting scholarships. The "most animated" discussion centered around the over-emphasis on athletics; this was the closest the meetings came to dealing with policy issues.

AMENDMENTS TO THE CHARTER

On 1 November 1932 the Trustees met to consider and approve the adoption of two amendments to the Articles of Incorporation. The first amendment was for the purpose of dropping the "The" from the title, "The John Carroll University." The second amendment dealt with the "purpose clause" of the original charter. The revised clause read,

> The purpose or purposes for which said corporation is formed is to establish, maintain, and conduct a University in which may be taught, cultivated, or promoted all branches of learning and which may comprise and embrace, separate or combined departments for literature, theology, law, medicine, nursing, dentistry, pharmacy, pedagogy, commerce, journalism, music technology, agriculture, the various branches of science both abstract and applied, the various branches of the fine arts.[71]

The list continues and includes almost every conceivable form of subject matter as well as action "to organize, or cause to be organized, under the laws of Ohio, or of any state, territory, or country, or the District of Columbia, a corporation or corporations for the purpose of accomplishing any or all of the objects for which this corporation is organized."[72] There was hardly anything the corporation could not legally do in the field of education. The revision was occasioned by the challenge to the Corporate College structure of institutions of Catholic higher education in the diocese of Cleveland under which arrangement the validity of the degrees granted by John Carroll University to the Corporate Colleges had been questioned.[73]

In 1935 the John Marshall Law School of Cleveland proposed that it affiliate with John Carroll. The consultors were favorable since it would "insure the permanence of our University Charter."[74] Concern over the move to the Heights prevented more thorough consideration of the matter. A School of Journalism was proposed about the same time by Eugene Mittinger, director of the University news bureau.[75] The proposal was sent back to Mittinger for more details.

NORTH CENTRAL CRITICISM

One reason no action was taken on these proposals for adding professional schools was the visit of the North Central in 1934, and the immediate necessity of dealing with its report. This report "commended the manner in which all the academic records of this college are kept," found that the college was adhering to the admission standards, praised the faculty for having twenty out of twenty-six meet the standards—a "very good showing"—and recognized that the ratio of students to faculty (20 to 1) was good even though some few classes had as many as sixty students.[76]

What did not please the review team was favoritism toward athletes in granting scholarships, the cramped library and laboratory conditions, and the discovery that three students had been graduated with fewer than the 128 required semester hours. The charge that "requirements for graduation are not enforced wtih sufficient diligence" was easy to refute since the review team had overlooked the transfer credits of the three students in question. The cramped library and laboratory conditions were excusable in view of the impending move to the new quarters in University Heights. The scholarship and the charge of irregularities in the athletic situation was not so easily dismissed. As the report said, "All the emphasis has been placed on athletics with no attention to date upon a physical education program, except the intention to set up something in the near future."[77] The report criticized the eligibility determination procedure and observed that a good proportion of the players were very weak scholastically; too many of the basketball players were on probation. There was also a question about how probation had been removed in some instances. In one case, cited in the report, the student had been given an examination in Liturgics without any lectures in the course and only one assignment; in another instance the probation was cancelled without comment. The review team was "of the opinion that favoritism has been granted the athletes."[78]

When it came to assessing the financial condition of the university, the examiners found that "The actual financial condition of this institution is quite difficult to determine under the present circumstances," since the accounts of both high school and college were not separated but kept as a single account of the Jesuit Community. "However, the entire organization seems to be living within its income," concluded the review team.[79]

In summary, the North Central Report stated that the development of a physical education program and the welfare of the student body should take precedence over the "specialized attention to the members of the athletic squads"; also, the institution should give more attention to its bookkeeping and accounting system and arrange for an external audit.[80] The most pressing problem, the report pointed out, was to collect sufficient funds to complete the move to the new buildings and to reduce the University's indebtedness. The recommendation of the report was that John Carroll remain on the accredited list but be subject to reexamination in no less than two years.[81]

PATIENCE REWARDED

In May 1934 the Hunkin-Conkey Company, general contractors for the new buildings, informed Herman Neff that it was one year since it had received any cash. Noting that meanwhile there had been some payment on pledges, the company wondered when it would receive some of that money. "We have ridden along with you in the best of spirit and as long as money is being received, please do your part."[82]

Meanwhile in October 1934 Province Consultors had been considering the financial problems facing John Carroll. Their plan was to make the effort to collect about $250,000 in pledges and then borrow $250,000. That recommendation was not acceptable to the consultors, who contended that such a plan might have been acceptable in the spring of 1934, but not now.[83] Moreover, they said, the plan "had all the earmarks of a move to prevent the borrowing of any money to complete the buildings. We are patiently waiting now for Father General's decision."[84]

By January 1935 Father General Ledochowski had made his decision. He appointed Father Edward C. Phillips, Provincial of the Maryland Province, to visit John Carroll. Writing to Father Rodman, Father Phillips said he was coming "Chiefly with a view to assisting, by such light as I could throw on the situation towards the best solution of the financial problem upon which the future of the university vitally depends."[85]

Father Phillips had already received Father Rodman's memorandum of 13 November 1934, entitled, "Why the Jesuits Should Get to the New Place Even by a Loan," as well as the Provincial Consultors' report, the financial statements for John Carroll for 1931 to 1934, and the statement of the Building Fund as of January 1932.[86] He had also a financial statement indicating what was expected to be the situation if a loan were approved. After visiting John Carroll, Father Phillips also contacted Bishop Schrembs, whom he informed that Father Ledochowski was favorably disposed towards granting permission for the loan.[87]

On 4 February 1935 in a letter to Father Rodman, Father Phillips reported that, "Today I sent my report to Rev. Father General and I hope it will speed the day when John Carroll will 'move into its own' and start an era of new progress and greater service to Catholic youth of Northern Ohio."[88] Father Phillips recommended a loan of no more than $300,000 to complete the buildings sufficiently to allow their use for the college; the high school was to remain on the West Side for the present. The rest of the money needed should come from collections on pledges with the hope that a sum equal to the loan would be collected from the unpaid pledges. It was also Father Phillips's recommendation that it was neither "necessary nor advisable to change the rector at the present time."[89] Normally there would have been a change of rectors in 1934, since Father Rodman would have completed six years in office. A further recommendation was that it was

> very desirable that the supervision of the finances and the determination of the order in which contracts are to be filled, should not be left to the sole judgment of Father Rector, but should be placed under the direction of a special committee including besides the ordinary Consultors of the House, two or three other experienced Fathers.[90]

Father Phillips also suggested an order in which the buildings should be completed. The priority list was headed by the administration building and the two science wings with the student dormitory next on the list. The Jesuit Faculty Building could be placed near the end of the list because "for a time the teaching staff can live on the West Side and commute by auto."[91] Last on the list was the bishop's Memorial Chapel which could wait until funds were available for it.

Meanwhile, Father Rodman attended a meeting at the Hotel Cleveland with Bernet, Neff, Dougherty, Monsignor Smith, and Alumni president Harry Hanna to stir up interest in collection of unpaid pledges. Personal solicitation was the keynote of their plan. In March Father Rodman informed Father Phillips that he had received a favorable response to the request for a loan from Father Ledochowski through the Provincial.[92] Father Rodman planned to hold up any public announcement of the news that construction would be resumed until the quiet drive was a little further along. Over 1,200 persons had already been contacted representing a potential $300,000, at least half of which he expected to receive in 1935.[93]

At some point in these developments Father Rodman decided to inform Bernet that the construction would definitely be resumed and classes would open on the East Side in the fall of 1935. Father Rodman called in Eugene Mittinger and asked him to go to Bernet's office and inform him of this intention. According to Mittinger, Father Rodman warned him that after he had made this announcement to Bernet he would be treated to a most rapid flow of colorful language, including many words he probably had never heard before. Mittinger was instructed to sit quietly and listen until Bernet was finished. Mittinger was then to repeat, "Father Rodman says we will be out there in the fall." Father Rodman knew Bernet so well that everything happened as he had predicted. Bernet, it seems, did not see how any such timetable could be met and considered Father Rodman's prediction something of an idiot's dream.[94]

The committee recommended by Father Phillips was set up. It was composed of Fathers Pickel, Joliat, and Otting meeting with the consultors to arrange plans for starting construction and the further collection of pledges. An initial loan was to be $100,000 and available not later than 15 May at which time public announcement was to be made of the resumption of construction.[95] Publicity was planned to accompany the renewal of activity; a "John Carroll Day" in the parishes, radio talks, and other appeals to the general public were part of the publicity program.

Meanwhile the Congregation of Religious had inquired of Archbishop Amleto Cigonani, Apostolic Delegate in Washington, about the advisability of John Carroll contracting a debt. The Apostolic Delegate in turn asked Bishop Schrembs for his opinion.[96] Bishop Schrembs willingly endorsed the action, stating that the reasons for his approval had already been given to Father Ledochowski. As the bishop put it, "We are now at the close of the school year, and unless something is done without any further delay so as to insure the opening of the new university for the fall session, John Carroll might as well close its doors."[97]

At a weekly meeting of the building committee in May 1935 Herman Neff made the public announcement that the resumption of construction was to begin on May 27.[98] Neff gave four reasons for the resumption of work, the principal one of which was that many subscribers would not honor their pledges until work was resumed. Other reasons were the impracticality of continuing college-level work on the West Side, the economic loss resulting from the unfinished buildings, and the need of the city of Cleveland "to see success in a community that lately has been lacking in courage."[99]

Although nearly $200,000 in pledges had been collected by May, the results of further effort were not quite sufficient to get the minimum of $250,000 that had been hoped for. As a result a loan was needed to make up the amount required to finish the buildings. In September another loan was arranged and put into a separate account.[100] The registration date for the fall classes was pushed back to 30 September to give the workmen a little more time to complete their tasks.

Two events in July of 1935 were of special significance to John Carroll followers. One of them, the death of John J. Bernet, was a great loss to the university. There is no question that but for his leadership the move to the East Side would not have occurred. Father Cloud, Chicago Provincial, wrote to Father Rodman, "You have lost a wonderful friend, and we share that loss too."[101] It is most regrettable that Bernet did not live to see the completion of the work to which he committed so much of his time, energy, and money.

The other event was a "John Carroll Day" on Sunday 21 July on which the public was invited to inspect the progress in the new buildings. The event was announced at all the Masses in the parishes of the diocese on that Sunday at the request of Father Rodman and with the cooperation of Bishop Schrembs, who also gave a radio talk on the "Open House" with special emphasis on Bernet's role in the project.

After the event, which was well attended, Herman Neff wrote to Bishop Schrembs thanking him for his cooperation, saying, "Personally I was greatly pleased to have you emphasize Mr. Bernet's great leadership in the project which has always been so full of problems. He was anxious to get part if not all of the buildings ready for the Jesuits' use in September. It was one of the last things he and I talked about."[102]

Classes formally opened in the new buildings on 7 October under rather chaotic conditions as both teachers and workmen competed for time in the classrooms. The dormitory was not ready until after Thanksgiving. The twenty-five dormitory students were housed meanwhile in private homes and since the cafeteria was not immediately ready, ate their meals at the Cedar Center Restaurant through arrangements made by Eugene Mittinger. The restaurant, according to the students, served a "powerful good meal."[103] The library was not ready until after the Christmas holiday, and many of the classrooms were still being finished as an attempt was made to continue classes in them. Classes were frequently moved on almost a daily basis to allow carpenters with hammers to complete their work on blackboards and lockers without disturbing teachers and students. Classes often passed each other in the halls on the way to quieter rooms.

The mayor of University Heights extended a warm welcome to the new residents expressing on behalf of the community his "deep appreciation for the fine cultural influence the University will bring to their community of homes."[104] Conditions were primitive in those early days; plank walks in many places were tests of ability to walk without getting splattered with mud. But the move to the East Side had at last been accomplished and the inconveniences did not seem too great.

One of the first things that had to be done was to arrange for transportation from the Fairmount car line, which ended some distance away from the college. The consultors gave approval for the purchase of the bus to replace the old "Black Maria" and charged it to the Building Fund as "necessary equipment"[105] The bus, whose colors "fairly shriek John Carroll," was driven by the newly arrived Brother Kopf and Brother Hay. The cost of the ride was twenty-five cents a week. It operated on a fifteen-minute schedule during class hours.[106]

The move to the Heights saw a new treasurer, Father James Quinlan, who cooperated with Fritz W. Graff and James March, faculty members in the new department of Business Administration, in setting up a new accounting system. A general audit of all books was to be made by Graff.[107] Also approved by the consultors at that time was an extended rest for Father Rodman, whose physician had strongly recommended it.[108]

John Carroll University, 1936. Original buildings and chapel foundation

Cut stone surrounding Bishop's Chapel foundation, 1936

Above, Student Lounge, 1936. Now Communications Department; *Left,* Cafeteria, 1938. Now faculty office area; *Bottom,* Zippered cats, 19500 Anatomy Laboratory

A New Rector-President

Once the University had completed the move to the East Side the question of replacing Father Rodman as rector, and therefore as president, again rose. In July 1936 Father Rodman wrote to Father Samuel Wilson, president of Loyola University in Chicago, asking his assistance in an effort to prevent any immediate change:

> Nothing in the world can be gained at this time by a change. Of course I will gain personally but the school will loose [*sic*]. This is said in all humility as you know . . . I started the entire refinancing program and cannot finish it before thirty days. . . .
>
> I have three good prospects I am nursing for new money . . . but, of course, I cannot tell when they will come through. The help of our committe [*sic*] in handling sub contractors and difficult labor conditions . . . will not be forthcoming to a new man. . . . It is hard for me to personally bring these matters out, but maybe you can and thus forestall the entire affair.[109]

Father Rodman also wrote to Father Zacheus Maher, American Assistant in Rome, in January 1937 about a choice of a successor when it appeared certain that he would be replaced. Referring to the "latest 'terna,' the third in eleven months," Father Rodman argued that it would be

> far better to wait until the summer and leave me to try to finish the faculty building and to push the quiet campaign we are having at present. I am only giving you my candid opinion. I will be happy to abide by whatever decision Father General makes but there is one thing sure. If I am wiped out completely, and all prestige is taken away by not giving me some official position or title, I will not have the entre to moneyed men that I would have with such prestige. Personally, prestige and title mean nothing, as you know, but for the good of the school and certainly for obtaining entre which means contact you cannot otherwise have. The prestige that comes from the title of President means a lot. If they insist on putting a new President in it will be all right if they let me for a time have some kind of title that will carry prestige with it.[110]

Father Rodman had written in much the same vein to Father General. He made the same points that he had made to Father Maher but devoted more attention to the *terna* suggesting that the choices were excellent and that one man in particular could give the college the "scholastic prestige" that it needed because of "our constant rubbing with Western Reserve, Case School of Applied Sciences, and Baldwin-Wallace."[111] Any new man, however, "would be at a disadvantage in getting money for too long" even if he had "scholastic prestige."[112]

On 28 February 1937 the change of rectors was made; Father William Magee, president of Marquette since 1928, succeeded Father Rodman as rector and president. Father Rodman became pastor of Gesu Church, which allowed him some of the "prestige" he claimed was necessary to continue fund-raising. It is interesting to note that a newspaper article announcing the change dealt almost entirely with the new president's views on football prospects for John Carroll. The article referred to the fact that, "A number of years ago John Carroll played the toughest teams it could schedule. But Blue Streak elevens of recent seasons have been thumped by their Big Four rivals, Western Reserve, Case and Baldwin-Wallace, and also by Buckeye and Ohio Conference teams."[113] It was clear from Father Magee's remarks that John Carroll would do well to remain in its own class. " 'We expect to win games,' Father Magee said, 'but do not expect a coach to do any better than the nature of his material permits.' "[114]

Father Magee's term as president of John Carroll was a brief one. On 3 October 1937 Father Magee became Provincial of the Chicago Province. An acting rector and president was appointed at John Carroll until a more permanent choice could be made. With a certain sense of justice, Father George J. Pickel, now seventy years old, was selected as acting rector and president, assuming a post he had left twenty-seven years before. As a prime mover in the establishment of an East Side college it was perhaps fitting that he have the post even if only temporarily. Again, a reporter totally unaware of Father Pickel's role in the history of the institution was concerned only with whether John Carroll would still have a football team.

Meanwhile, although busy in his new post as pastor of Gesu, Father Rodman had some unfinished business with Bishop Schrembs. Remembering the unhappy Loyola High School situation, Father Rodman wrote to Bishop Schrembs saying, "Away back in 1930 and 1931, you gave me over and over again oral approval for the establishment of a new Jesuit Community. . . . For the sake of permanent records I am asking your Excellency to give this approval in writing on diocesan stationery and to date the letter of your approval as of July 1931."[115]

The bishop complied, but not entirely as requested. His letter was dated 20 August 1942, but he did say,

> I am very happy to convey to you the renewal of my approval for the establishment of John Carroll University in University Heights with the new Jesuit Community House there.
> The new University is an honor to the Diocese of Cleveland and to your Community, and I am sure your Fathers will always continue to be worthy of the good will and high esteem of the bishop of Cleveland.[116]

The request of Father Rodman was made just a few months before the Most Reverend Edward F. Hoban was made Coadjutor Bishop of Cleveland. Father Rodman did not want any slip-ups this time.

A Second Beginning
1935–1946

As part of the move to the East Side there seems to have been an implicit understanding that the West Side roots would be ignored; John Carroll was somehow a "new University" without previous existence. The understanding manifested itself in countless ways. Perhaps most interesting is that the large framed pictures of the first ten presidents, after hanging briefly in a corridor in Rodman Hall, disappeared. They were found much later in the process of preparing this history in a closet in the library. A plaque in the lobby of the new administration building reads, "John J. Bernet and Benedict J. Rodman, Founders of the John Carroll University Campus." The name St. Ignatius College seems not to be part of the tradition. Maybe it was Monsignor Joseph F. Smith's advice that all connection be broken with the West Side in order to change the German image that influenced the approach.

GOLDEN JUBILEE, 1936

In early June 1936 John Carroll University celebrated its Golden Jubilee with the theme a "Half Century of Service to Cleveland." In his invitation to Bishop Schrembs asking him to participate in the program, Father Rodman pointed out that in the fifty years over four hundred clergy had attended the institution for their preparatory studies, earning for the university the title "Alma Mater" of priests.[1]

On Sunday 7 June the baccalaureate Mass was celebrated on the altar that was first used in the chapel in old St. Ignatius College.[2] That afternoon there was an open house civic celebration with a series of talks given by Father Rodman, Father Ralph Gallagher, acting dean of the college, Father William L. Newton, professor of scripture at the diocesan seminary, Harry Hanna, representing the Alumni, and John A. Smith, president of the Cleveland chapter of the National Federation of Catholic Alumni. Solemn Benediction closed the afternoon affair, which was attended by some

2,500 visitors. Bishop Schrembs was celebrant at the Benediction with Father Pickel as deacon and Father Furay as subdeacon.

The Alumni Banquet on Monday evening was attended by four bishops—three of them former students, McFadden, LeBlond, and O'Reilly. Six former John Carroll presidents, Schulte, Pickel, Furay, Sommerhauser, Smith, and Boylan, were also present. Local institutions were well represented by Monsignors Hagan and Navin from Sisters' College, President Leutner from Western Reserve, President Wickenden from Case Institute of Technology, and Monsignor McDonough from the Seminary. The president of the University of Dayton, Walter Tredtin, S.M., the president of the University of Detroit, Aloysius Poetker, and the president of St. John College, Toledo, Gerald Fitzgibbons, were also present. Judge Joy Seth Hurd of the class of 1903 was the principal speaker. National, state, and local governments were well represented by Sen. Robert J. Bulkley, Congressmen Martin L. Sweeney, Robert Crosser, and Chester C. Bolton; Gov. Martin L. Davey and Mayor Harold H. Burton completed the group. A special honored guest was Father Francis Haggeney, who had spent many years at the college as a professor of philosophy and confidant of students. He must have been agreeably heartened by the public recognition that had been so hard to come by in his day.

It had been hoped that Monsignor Peter Guilday, author of the biography of John Carroll, could be secured as the commencement speaker, but he was unable to come. The Jesuit consultors then agreed that Bishop Schrembs should be asked;[3] the bishop readily accepted. The Golden Jubilee commencement was the first event to be held on the terrace of Rodman Hall, then known as the Faculty Building. It was a joint commencement with Notre Dame and Ursuline Colleges; seventy undergraduate degrees were awarded by John Carroll, forty-one by Ursuline, and thirty-five by Notre Dame, along with four master's degrees by John Carroll. The second and third honorary degrees ever awarded by John Carroll went to Bishop Schrembs and Herman Neff.[4] Because Bishop Schrembs was also celebrating the Silver Jubilee of his consecration as a bishop, Father General Ledochowski took the occasion to send congratulations to him and express his "gratitude once more for the benevolence" which Bishop Schrembs had always shown toward Father General and the members of the Society.[5] Bishop Schrembs replied with thanks and noted that John Carroll University had "progressed marvelously."[6] The bishop even suggested that he might go to Rome to thank Father Ledochowski personally.

As might be expected, there were not many living former students of St. Ignatius College from the first class in 1886, but Louis Litzler was among the first students registered in 1886 and available to help celebrate the Golden Jubilee.

UNFINISHED CONSTRUCTION

At the time of the move to University Heights in 1935 neither the Jesuit Residence, usually referred to as the Faculty Building, nor the bishop's chapel was completed sufficiently for use; the Faculty Building had at least its roof and exterior finished, but the bishop's chapel had not yet risen above its foundation. Work on the Faculty Building could not start until the general contractor had been paid off; work on the chapel awaited the payment of outstanding pledges.

The secretary of the Cleveland Federation of Labor, Thomas A. Lenahan, spearheaded a drive among the various labor unions in the city to raise funds to assist in the completion of the Jesuit residence.[7] One of Father William Magee's principal objectives when he became president in 1937 was the completion of the residence. He realized that, while many things needed to be done, there was an urgency to eliminate the problem of Jesuits commuting from the West Side each day. Jesuits who taught evening classes were assigned rooms in Bernet Hall, but the increasing number of dormitory students ruled this practice out as a long-term solution. Some Jesuits were adventurous enough to develop makeshift living quarters in their offices. Those in the sciences were particularly lucky in this respect. Father Terrence Ahearn in biology, Father Joliat in seismology, and Father Pickel in chemistry attempted to live in their offices. Father Ahearn was quoted as saying, "If anyone entered my room at night, I'm afraid they'd receive quite a fright; I hang my coat, necktie and towel on the laboratory skeleton."[8] Father Pickel, who designed the chemistry wing, probably wished he had had even more foresight now that he slept in his office.

In July 1938 work began on the interior of the Faculty Building and by September the Jesuits who had been in Bernet Hall moved in; the first Mass in the domestic chapel was celebrated on 8 December of the same year. Not until two years later did the workmen begin to finish plastering the first floor. Pressure from Father Maher, the American Assistant in Rome, to finish the dining room was resisted by Father Edmund C. Horne when he became rector, because of lack of funds and no immediate chance of getting them.[9] The Faculty Building, which in the mid 1940s began to be called Rodman Hall, was not completely a Jesuit residence until the exodus of the Navy V-12 boarders and some civilian students in 1945.

The bishop's chapel was to remain unfinished. There was no formal decision not to finish it, but the agreement had been that it would be built only as pledges for it were paid. Father Thomas J. Donnelly, rector from 1942 to 1946, made an effort to collect on outstanding pledges from the diocesan priests in October of 1942. By December he said he had no results from his letters; "at least they did no harm."[10] Even if these pledges had been collected it is doubtful they would have made much difference in the fate of the chapel. The structural steel which was lying around the foundation since 1931 was sold for scrap in July 1941; at the same time the area around the chapel was filled in with dirt from the excavation for the Fairmount theater building at Fairmount Circle.[11] Cut stone for the superstructure which had long since lost its markings disappeared into the ground or was carried off. The interior wood furnishing eventually found its way into the faculty building.

Not all of the attention of the rector was devoted to the East Side campus buildings. Until 1939 the rector had the responsibility of the Jesuits on both sides of the town. Before he left John Carroll to become pastor of the Gesu parish in 1937, Father Rodman had to deal with the problem of renting the barracks and other buildings along Lorain Avenue on the West Side. These buildings were standing idle and were producing no income. After first authorizing the rental of the buildings, Father Rodman changed his mind, fearing that rental to outsiders would adversely affect the high school property.[12]

When he became pastor of Gesu, Father Rodman purchased land across the street from the John Carroll property and by 1940 had built a combined church-school structure. This meant that the original church and school buildings on the John Carroll property could be torn down or put to other uses. Before the end of 1940 it was decided to tear down the church and school buildings, leaving the rectory still standing for Joseph Muller and his family to use.[13] Muller did most of the interior carpentry work on the campus, especially in the dining room and recreation room of Rodman Hall.

In spite of the attempts to protect the college buildings from the elements while they were lying unfinished from 1931 to 1935, some damage did occur. Roofing particularly on the auditorium needed repair and replacement.[14] The floor in the auditorium went through a period of buckling because proper procedures in laying it seemed to have been ignored. Not until a new tile floor was laid in 1943 was the problem at least partially solved.[15]

CAMPUS LANDSCAPING

The Jesuits in University Heights were faced with a problem that did not overly concern the early German Fathers on the West Side. The original college property was relatively small in size and fronted on three public streets; landscaping on any great scale was neither urgent nor practical. It was sufficient to erect the necessary buildings and to try to provide as much room as possible for student activities in the restricted gravel yard campus area. In University Heights it was expected that the sixty acres would need proper landscaping. The current visitor to the campus is often struck by its beauty and attractiveness; it took a long time and great effort to create the present picture.

Elaborate plans for landscaping had to be set aside in 1935; whatever funds were available went into putting the buildings in shape for classroom use. Two conspicuous mounds of top soil, one at the rear of the auditorium and one between Miramar Boulevard and the biology wing, remained to be spread. The front area between the administration building and Fairmount Circle, covered with thick underbrush and several smaller mounds of earth, together with ungraded land to the rear of the administration building represented the work to be done in 1935. It fell to Father William Haggerty, Minister of the Jesuit Community, to attempt to bring some order out of the early chaos.

The top soil mound to the rear of the administration building was spread before the first classes opened in October, but the mound near the biology wing remained until December 1941, when as the Minister's Diary put it, it was removed "at long last."[16] The expanse in front of the administration building was sufficiently cleared for a temporary nursery for trees that were donated by Cyrus Eaton, a local industrialist with an international reputation.[17] The front area remained untouched until the mid 1940s. Certain members of the faculty often enjoyed hunting pheasant and quail in this area. These hunters usually took aim from the fourth floor of the tower; when they worked at ground level trying to flush pheasant out of the bushes they appeared to city officials as poachers. It was also possible to find pheasant toward the rear of the property.[18]

Shrubs and other nursery stock continued to be acquired through the 1940s. In 1939 some of the smaller nursery stock was planted in rows along one side of Rodman Hall for later use. A rose garden, known as Father Pickel's rose garden, was planted in the terrace area of Rodman Hall and the Kmieck Garden area was also completed. In 1940 the work of grading was begun; help from the county engineer in grading the area along Belvoir Boulevard was gratefully received. University Heights officials also cooperated in leveling and clearing the area. This land between the power house and Belvoir Boulevard had originally been intended for an athletic field. Work on this part of the property had been delayed because there was one lot in the center of the area which the university did not yet own. The university was finally able to solve the legal problems involved in the acquisition of this lot, known as lot number fifty-one on the survey map, in 1943.[19] However, not until the presidency of Father Frederick E. Welfle (1946–1956), was there real progress in making the campus take on some of its present attractiveness.

PRESIDENTIAL SHUFFLE

The period from 1937 to 1946 saw five presidents take turns at directing the fortunes of John Carroll; four of these presidents served in 1937—Fathers Rodman, Magee, Pickel and Horne. The loss of Father Rodman was a serious blow. His dynamic personality was praised by the student newspaper, which considered Father Rodman the "finest man Carroll will ever know. In the nine years that he has been with us and our institution he has so 'extended his personality' over us that anything but progress was impossible."[20] In a later edition of the paper praise for Father Rodman continued to fill the columns. "When he walks into a student convocation he is greeted by a thunderous roar of sincere applause. Carroll men realize that before them stands the truest friend any college student has ever known."[21] He was credited with "surprising knowledge of the student body;" he was "more than a president, more than an educator;" he was "one of the greatest men Cleveland has ever known."[22]

Father William Magee, Rodman's immediate successor, did not remain long enough to become very well acquainted. Within a few months of his arrival he became Provincial of the Chicago Province and was succeeded by an acting president, Father Pickel, who was also Superior of the Community but not rector.[23] On 6 December 1937 Father Edmund C. Horne became the fourth president of the year. The civic reception given to Father Horne was the first such affair since the one given Father Rodman ten years before; it was in a way also testimony to the impact Father Rodman had had on the Cleveland community.

Father Horne's regime, though it lasted only four years, was influential. His academic training was in sociology in which he was considered an expert in labor problems. He had been in Japan in 1937 as a delegate to the World Federation Educational Association meeting. It was remembered after the Japanese attack on Pearl Harbor that Father Horne, in addressing a meeting of the John Carroll Senior Guild one month before the attack, had said, "War between the United States and Japan is inevitable. Most likely the first action will take place in Hawaii."[24]

Father Horne was frequently called upon for consultation in labor affairs. The Cleveland community appreciated his willingness to give considerable time to community problems. When illness forced Father Horne to retire from the presidency, the *Cleveland Press* editorialized that under Father Horne unfinished buildings were completed, scholastic progress was undeniable, enrollment increased, and the evening session was expanded.[25] It was also generally agreed that under Father Horne's regime the influence of John Carroll on the community had increased. In 1940 Father Horne was president of the Ohio College Association.

Top left, Edward F. Hoban, Bishop of Cleveland, 1945–56; *right,* Thomas J. Donnelly, S.J., President, John Carroll University, 1942–46; *Bottom left,* William M. Magee, President, John Carroll University, 1937; *right,* Edmund C. Horne, President, John Carroll University, 1937–42

Father Thomas J. Donnelly (1942–1946), who succeeded Father Horne, had the impact of World War II to face. He was by temperament and training more on the conservative side. Much of the credit for the survival of the institution during this period must go to the dean of the college, Father Edward C. McCue who, given a relatively free hand by Father Donnelly, served not only as an extremely capable academic leader but also as a fund-raiser.

PROFESSIONAL SCHOOLS

Ever since the charter of the university was revised in 1932, Father Fox had dreamed of establishing a school of business administration. When the name Cleveland University was acquired in 1923, there was a requirement that at least one professional school be established within nine years. A number of circumstances including a desire to fulfill the requirement combined to bring about the creation of a department of business administration in 1934. In June of that year two members of the business administration staff of Cleveland College resigned over differences of opinion with Dr. Caswell Ellis, president of the college, concerning policies in their department. These two professors, Fritz W. Graff and James H. March, met with Father Rodman and in August agreed to form a department of business administration at John Carroll. A recent study had revealed that Cleveland was the only city among the seventeen largest that did not have a university school of business.[26]

The new department was intended to train men and women who aspired to positions of responsibility in the business world. Classes for men in the day and men and women in the evening began in September 1934. The first year was spent in planning the curriculum; additional staff were soon acquired to cover a variety of fields. Within three years six seniors, fourteen juniors, forty-six sophomores, and seventy-six freshmen were preparing for the business degrees. In 1945 Provincial approval was received for the creation of a separate school of business to be known as the School of Business, Economics, and Government.[27] It was expected that the school would "give John Carroll another mark of distinction, as no other college in the vicinity has such a school."[28]

In 1940, some years after the Mittinger proposal to establish a school of journalism had been turned down by the consultants, a student petition revived the idea of establishing such a school. But all that was achieved was an agreement to send representatives of the Cleveland newspapers to lecture at Carroll.[29] In 1942 requests were made by newspapermen of Fathers Donnelly and McCue to allow them to offer a course in journalism. The requests were turned down because "under the circumstances we are doing all we can to train students in the field of journalism."[30]

The addition of professional schools was never pursued with serious intent after the collapse of the 1923 campaign in which professional schools were included as part of the overall plan for the East Side location. Although there is no direct evidence to indicate that this inaction was deliberate, it may have been that Father Rodman was listening to the advice of Father Samuel Wilson, President of Loyola University in Chicago. Father Rodman and Father Wilson were frequent correspondents and a letter of Father Wilson to Father Daniel O'Connell, Chicago Province prefect of studies, cautioned against the rush to add professional schools; he saw more important direction in the expansion of graduate work for Jesuit colleges and universities. Writing to Father O'Connell in early 1936, Father Wilson said,

> I may tell you now that the ignorance prevailing about graduate work among our own people is, as far as I can see, rather abysmal. Perhaps only in the case of very few is there any realization that the whole trend of education is now pointed toward graduate work, and that unless we bestir ourselves I am afraid we shall be put back several years in the progress we should secure mainly because of other divisions of the University instruction in which our officials are more interested.[31]

Financially and academically, John Carroll University was in no position to establish either professional schools or a graduate school. Graduate work was offered in the early 1930s but the Chicago Province had laid down conditions for the establishment of a graduate school that John Carroll could not yet meet. Adequate finances and staff for five strong departments were not yet available.

FINANCIAL MATTERS

Moving to University Heights under financial restraints made it even more urgent to attend to the North Central's insistence in 1934 on proper accounting procedures and better financial management. The consultors in March of 1935 sought to make use of the talents of Graff in examining the financial condition of the university with a view toward providing a budgeting procedure for all departments.[32] A report showing a $10,000 deficit for the 1934–1935 year made necessary some means of cutting expenses or increasing income.[33]

When Father Phillips visited John Carroll prior to the approval of the loan necessary to complete the move from the West Side, he had left a set of recommendations for future financial management. The consultors appointed the suggested special committee to carry out these instructions. One of the first moves intended to save money was the elimination of the position of Building Fund Director Donald Dougherty. It was agreed that he would be retained for one month after the move to University Heights and then, with the assistance of Father Ralph Gallagher, Father Rodman was to act as director of the fund.[34]

In April 1936 it was thought that money could be saved by refinancing the total debt of $530,000.[35] By September of that year the matter became more urgent when the general contractor was trying to force the institution to borrow more money or be subject to a lien on the buildings.[36] Meanwhile, there was belt-tightening on the Jesuit Community expenses, which had been rising; a more strict enforcement of guidelines for tuition reductions was also needed.[37]

The seriousness of the financial situation resulted in the creation of the office of comptroller. The consultors debated the advantages and disadvantages of having a layman fill this position, since it was such an important post.[38] A suggestion that a layman be appointed but assited by a committee was considered. Some consultors wanted to give full authority to the committee; others said this arrangement would not work. Final agreement was reached by allowing a layman to hold the position but to be assisted by a committee in making his recommendations to the president.[39] In practice the office of comptroller was held by Father William Haggerty, who was Minister of the Jesuit Community; Graff held the title of assistant comptroller with John Seliskar as auditor. In 1938 Charles J. Cooney replaced Seliskar as auditor. In 1940 Father Clement Singer replaced Father Haggerty as Minister and comptroller. There was as yet no desire to put control of university finances in the hands of a layman however competent he might be.

The practical working out of this arrangement was not satisfactory and illustrated the increasing difficulty of combining the financial management of the university with that of the Jesuit Community. By 1942 the new treasurer of the community and the university, Father Laurence J. Eckman, was complaining that "members of the administration transact most of the school business with Mr. Cooney, the lay auditor," rather than with him.[40] As a consequence Father Eckman "did not get any opportunity to learn the university business setup."[44]

Father Gilbert Krupitzer, who became treasurer in 1943, reviewed the financial condition of the university and emphasized the continuing need to curtail expenses.[42] He cited the loss of $2,000 by the student newspaper in 1943–1944, band purchases made without supervision, and repairs to heating equipment and the auditorium roof as the types of things that represented a drain on resources.

The problem of refinancing continued to complicate the fiscal situation. Deferred payment of bills, sometimes as much as six months, was not helping the credit rating of the institution. A mechanics lien of $53,000 was an additional burden on the credit standing. Efforts to collect pledges had come to a complete halt by 1939 since it became general knowledge that all money collected would go to the contractor for past bills.[43] This situation undoubtedly was the source of many of Father Horne's worries and helped complicate the illness that forced him to resign in 1942. Bishop Schrembs often sought to suggest possible fund sources to Father Horne. On one occasion Father Horne replied to the bishop about a newspaper clipping he had received from him.

> It is difficult for me to express verbally my gratitude for your many acts of kindness towards John Carroll University since my advent as rector. Not only the generosity of your gift yesterday, but your continued tolerance of my mistakes, your fatherly counsel and encouragement have made me very much your debtor. I have never had a conference with you which has not given me new strength. May God reward the charity of your true shepherd's heart.
> The valued suggestion accompanying your gift will be quite helpful.[44]

The separation of the high school and college in 1939 into two distinct Jesuit communities created the problem of the relative share of each in the total debt. After a long and sometimes bitter exchange of views, the Provincial and the rectors of the two communities finally agreed in 1945 that the high school should assume $100,000 of the total debt.[45] Arrangements were also made for the division of the Province tax and the disposition of the Vermilion property to the high school. It was agreed by the John Carroll consultors that money received from the high school in the settlement of the debt should be used to replenish the John Carroll scholarship fund, which had suffered losses through the withdrawal of funds to cover various emergencies.[46]

Father Donnelly, recalling a Provincial directive, again brought to his consultors the matter of budgeting the operating expenses. Neither Father Donnelly nor the majority of his consultors could see "how in the light of our uncertain income for the immediate future, that this [budgeting] was practicable."[47] In spite of the presumed futility of it, Father Krupitzer was asked to work something out.

In early June 1946, Father Donnelly received a letter from Bishop Edward F. Hoban, Bishop Schrembs's successor, in which was enclosed a check for $50,000 to cover the university deficit of the previous year.[48] On 19 July Father Donnelly met with Bishop Hoban and proposed giving an honorary degree to Bishop John R. Hagan, who had recently been appointed as an Auxilary Bishop; Bishop Hoban agreed but did not want the donation of $50,000 publicized.[49] On the 31st of July, Father Donnelly notified Bishop Hoban of the change in rectors; Father Frederick E. Welfle replaced Father Donnelly as rector and president. Other discussions between Bishop Hoban and Father Donnelly prior to the change of rectors resulted in the decision to give an honorary degree to Bishop Hoban as well as Bishop Hagan. Father Donnelly then informed Bishop Hagan that he was being given an honorary degree; Bishop Hagan "expressed his great pleasure at being thus honored."[50]

An important factor in the financial picture was the lack of sufficient endowment. The "endowment of men" which covered the services of the Jesuit Fathers when coupled with an almost complete dependence on tuition income made the size of the enrollment a very critical matter. The last year on the West Side saw the enrollment reach 509 in the September semester of the college of arts and sciences, 126 in a Saturday session, 177 in the Evening Session, and 126 in the preceding Summer School. The year 1934–1935 was only the second year in which the enrollment in the college of arts and sciences reached the 500 mark while the institution was on the West Side; in the 1932–1933 academic year, the enrollment reached 517 in the September semester.

In 1939–1940 the number of students in the September semester of the college of arts and sciences was 658, but from there on the number dwindled until the Navy V-12 program was inaugurated in 1943. From 1943 to 1945, the number of civilians ranged from 110 to 79 while the Navy contingent went from 403, its peak enrollment in November 1943, to 153 in 1945. The Evening and Summer sessions were eliminated during the V-12 program. The first postwar surge came in March 1946, when the enrollment reached 594; in the fall of 1946 the number of students was 1,346.

From the first year in the new quarters the need for some form of organized recruiting of students was recognized. In the spring of 1936, representatives were sent to the various Catholic high schools. Because a "lay man and not a Jesuit" represented the university at the different schools there was criticism by some of the clergy of the diocese.[51] In the fall of 1936, Father Haggerty suggested that Father John Weber be brought to Cleveland to organize and prepare for recruiting work.[52] Father Weber did come later and became quite famous as a recruiter as well as the man who lured freshman with the promise of a swimming pool that was not to materialize until 1975.

FACULTY

Although in 1936 there were twenty-two laymen on a faculty of forty-one, the term "faculty" almost invariably meant Jesuit faculty. Even in 1946 this was still true when the laymen numbered thirty-seven out of a total faculty of fifty-eight. There had been no real change in the status of the lay faculty since the time in 1934 when Father Rodman made it clear that all of them were expendable if financial necessity required it.[53] In 1936 there were a total of five doctoral degrees on the faculty of forty-one, two among the Jesuits and three among the laymen. In 1946 there were sixteen doctoral degrees on the total faculty of fifty-eight, six among the Jesuits and ten among the laymen.

In 1939 shortly after Father McCue had become dean, he made an attempt at "a more definite understanding (or contract) between the university and lay teachers in the matter of rank and tenure."[54] Nothing came of it since the laymen saw no advantage in signing what amounted to a unilateral contract. Salary matters were decided by the consultors without any regular schedule or framework; increases were occasional rather than regular, and the basis for making them was not always clear.

The matter of fringe benefits was not considered, although in 1941 Father Horne proposed a hospitalization plan for the Jesuits which was open to laymen if they wished to join.[55] Father Horne saw advantages of such a plan for the Jesuits because it was likely that the free hospitalization they had been receiving from the three Catholic hospitals in the city would soon end. The plan was approved by the consultors but the laymen did not participate.

The policy of whether laymen who taught at John Carroll could run for political office was a confusing one. During the short presidency of Father Magee a laymen, Walter G. O'Donnell, became a mayoral candidate in Cleveland. He received a telegram from Father Magee telling him that he would have to choose between teaching political science and practicing politics.[56] Later in the year, Ray C. Miller, the registrar, also sought political office. Father Magee's ruling was reversed by the consultors on the recommendation of Father Bracken because of Miller's "excellent work."[57] There was no clearly defined policy on the relation of teaching to other activities outside the university.

Among the Jesuits of the first years on the Heights there were at least two who stood out as carrying heavier than usual assignments. One was Father William J. Murphy, who was appointed faculty moderator of athletics in 1936; by 1941, his eleventh year at John Carroll, he was also moderator of the band, prefect of Bernet Hall, moderator of the Carroll Union and dean of men. In spite of all of his duties, he still found time for playing the violin. Father Joseph Teply, who joined the physics department in 1936, gradually acquired all sorts of functions, most of them related to the heavy work involved in sprucing up the campus. He also ran the printing shop and was most generous in supplying tickets to students and others who were unable to get them for the various affairs supervised by Father Murphy. Father

Top left, Joseph M. Teply, S.J., 1936–48; *right,* Charles Cooney, Auditor, 1936–56; *Middle,* Eugene R. Mittinger, Professor of Mathematics, 1928–66; *Bottom left,* Richard T. Deters, S.J., Evening Division, 1949–62; *right,* Joseph S. Joliat, S.J., Seismology, 1933–47

Teply was so gracious in complying with requests for printing almost anything, usually replying, "surely, surely" that he was known as "Surely
Teply." Father Murphy often had difficulty reconciling his books when all
of the free tickets that Father Teply printed showed up at the door; receipts
and tickets seldom matched.

The period was marked by the death of Father Charles M. Ryan in 1941,
the debate coach who led John Carroll debate teams to a string of victories
over such major universities as the University of California, Purdue, Ohio
State, New York University, University of Vermont, Detroit, Marquette,
Northwestern, and a team from Oxford-Cambridge. Another death, that
of Monsignor Joseph F. Smith in 1943, marked the departure of a "friend
of Jesuits and Benefactor of Carroll."[58]

NAVY V-12 PROGRAM

The outbreak of war in Europe in 1939 caused Father Horne to prepare for
its impact on future enrollment by seeking an ROTC unit for John Carroll.
A formal application for such a unit was made with the approval of the
consultors; an anti-aircraft unit was preferred since it was "best accommo-
dated to present facilities" and would "have greater appeal to students."[59]
Word came in September 1940 that for the moment no new ROTC units
were being established.[60]

After Pearl Harbor, the university sought to anticipate enrollment decline by streamlining the course work into a three-year program. The
summer session was extended to two sessions in twelve weeks instead of the
customary one session in six. Almost simultaneously came an inquiry from
the Navy about the possibility of the university's facilities being adequate to
house, feed, and instruct Navy men.[61] Father Horne was authorized by his
consultors to tell the Navy that John Carroll would cooperate in any way
possible,[62] but the Navy did not respond immediately.

Meanwhile, the Army made overtures to use John Carroll facilities as an
Army hospital. The consultors were unwilling to turn the facilities over to
hospital use since too many changes would have to be made and it would
distort the educational purpose of the institution. Meanwhile, the Navy
was willing to consider John Carroll for a V-12 college training program.
Negotiations for a Navy contract continued throughout 1942; Father
McCue handled most of the negotiations working with the approval of the
consultors but without a committee specially appointed for that purpose.[63]
Father McCue was convinced that by July 1943, there would be few regular
students left and a "Navy contract for students would come in mighty
handy."[64] The Jesuits were willing to turn Bernet Hall over to the Navy and
worked out an agreement with the nearby Jewish Orphanage, Bellefaire,

for the use of two of its buildings for about two hundred students. The Jesuits were even willing at this time to consider leaving Rodman Hall, if necessary.[65] It was discovered later that only one building at Bellefaire could be spared for Navy use, raising the question of whether the university could provide sufficient space for the Navy program.[66]

By the middle of March 1943, it seemed almost certain that a Navy contract would be awarded John Carroll even though the issue of the availability of Rodman Hall had not yet been settled. The Jesuit residence was not completely finished; there was plastering and terrazzo work yet to be done. Toward the end of May word from the Navy made it clear that partial use of Rodman Hall was unacceptable, but neither the Provincial nor the consultors approved of turning over the entire building.[67] Shortly thereafter the Navy gave approval for partial use of Rodman Hall.[68] The portion of the building that was newly finished and unoccupied by the Jesuits was approved for Navy use.[69] One benefit of the Navy's arrival was the finishing of the Jesuit refectory in Rodman Hall. The Jesuits had up until then used the university cafeteria, which was less than a satisfactory arrangement; overcrowding with the arrival of Navy personnel made finishing the Rodman Hall dining room a necessity.[70]

The Navy occupied Rodman Hall until November 1944, when the Provincial gave permission for civilian boarding students to occupy the rooms vacated by Navy students. The purpose was to form a nucleus of boarding students for Bernet Hall after the war and to provide some revenue. Thought was given to seeking temporary housing for such students but that was considered too uncertain, expensive, and full of problems.[71] There was a suggestion that an addition be built on Bernet Hall but there was no money available for such construction. Since it was agreed that dormitory facilities after the war would not be sufficient if local applicants were accepted as boarding students, only out-of-town students were to be accepted for boarding.[72] This policy changed when funds for additional dormitories were available.

On 1 July 1943, 389 Navy students arrived to begin a program that changed the school calendar by establishing a three-semester year with beginning dates on 1 July, 1 November, and 1 March. Summer school and evening classes were discontinued although Saturday classes continued to be held. There were 110 civilians in that first session, bringing the total enrollment within about 60 students of what it had been in 1942–1943. For the remainder of the program the number of civilians ranged between 75 and 100.

The work of Father McCue and Father Clement Singer, as Minister, had been invaluable in securing the program, which provided a life-line for the university during the war period.[73] After one year it was clear that the program had served the nation as well as helped John Carroll.

The program produced some changes in university traditions. The *Carroll News* observed that "The ban on smoking in the halls brings back old nostalgia of when one had to have a co-pilot to navigate through the lower halls."[74] Another tradition that disappeared was that of free days on Holy Days of Obligation; the new schedule made no provision for them.

Except for some differences over accounting procedures, relations between the university and the Navy were amicable. Father Donnelly was at times worried that "perhaps he had gone along too confidently on the soundness of our financial condition based on our income from the Navy. He tried to leave the impression on outsiders that "we were not on 'easy street' "[75] in spite of assistance from the Navy program.

From 1 July 1943 to 1 November 1945, there were 787 Navy men who went through the V-12 program. Upon leaving Carroll 265 went on to V-6 or regular duty, 202 to midshipmen's school, and 133 to the Air Corps or V-5 program. Six went on to the Naval Academy and others into varying departments of the Navy service; 148 were on board and unassigned at the end of the program. Many returned at the end of their service to finish degrees.[76] A Veterans Readjustment Council set up by Father Donnelly in late 1944 with Father Lionel V. Carron in charge developed later into a more general counseling center.

PREWAR STUDENT LIFE

The change in location of the university in 1935 seemed to have little effect upon an increase of school spirit. In later years the term "student apathy" was used to describe the condition that remained a perennial complaint. The *Carroll News* of 15 January 1936 carried a front-page editorial entitled "Here's a Real Joke for you—John Carroll's school spirit." The editorial noted that a pledge drive by the Carroll Union produced no results, there was low attendance at the basketball games—an average of twenty-five students per game—and only fourteen students attended a smoker given by Heights businessmen to aid the university. The list of complaints continued; only fifteen students attended the recent meeting of the American Catholic Philosophical Society in Cleveland, five students showed up for tryouts for the play, and but ten students showed up for the Glee Club concert in the auditorium.

Five years later a letter to the editor of the student newspaper pointed out another direction in which lack of spirit seemed evident. The writer claimed that "the student body at Carroll was about twenty years behind the times and extremely inactive with regard to great movements in the social field, Catholic Action, etc."[77] The writer blamed the attitude on the disillusionment of the youth of that day with the country's leadership, which sought to enter a war on behalf of England. "How can we fight in behalf of Britain with what we know of British history," the writer asked.[78]

Whatever validity there may have been in the charges of lack of spirit and activity, life was by no means dull in the early days on the Heights. Apart from the standard complaints about cafeteria food, students managed to continue some West Side traditions. Father Pickel had achieved a reputation for precision and attention to detail in chemistry. His oft-repeated reference to "John Bonehead, the perpetual member of the chemistry class" served as a constant warning to students. One of the brighter students managed to qualify for the title in the very first year on the Heights. The student seemed unaware of the difference in melting points of the sample he was testing and the glass on which he put it. He wound up with a lump of glass when he put it in a thousand-degree oven; he was awarded the title of "prize John Bonehead of the year."[79]

More enterprising were the freshmen biology students who were running frog races every quarter hour, and the students in the anatomy laboratory who were inventing zippered cats. William McGannon '41 apparently got tired of the process of cutting, sewing, and unsewing the cats; so he equipped his cat with a zipper. The zippered cats were first displayed at an open house in the spring of 1939. It was such a popular idea that all students in anatomy were required to equip their cats with zippers; various zipper colors were used to match the cat.[80]

Students in physics decided they needed a coat-of-arms. They designed one with a scroll in Greek at the top of the shield saying, "Physics is an Exact Science." There was a lamp between the first and second quadrant with a question mark on either side of it. One explanation of the lamp was that Father Lawrence J. Monville's courses in heat and light made the students burn the midnight oil. Other symbols represented characteristics of other professors' courses.

Other students not so scientifically inclined tended to gather in the student lounge on the basement floor in a room which is currently the home of the department of communications and the television studio. In the early days it was inhabited by what were called "pinochle majors" whose enthusiasm for betting once forced Father Bracken to close the place to card playing.[81] Many students, particularly those from Cathedral Latin and Holy Name high schools, tended to congregate on the second-floor passage way between the administration building and the biology wing. The antics of those who frequented the area caused it to be called "Screwball Hall." Most of those who congregated there were freshmen and sophomores who engaged in "bull sessions," football, and even hockey in the narrow confines of the area. The place was described as the "zaniest, screwiest place at John Carroll University . . . where a unique comradeship and friendship is fostered by its inviting atmosphere."[82]

The need for a satisfactory student lounge continued throughout the period. The class of 1942 started a "lounge fund" which was eventually successful.[83] Not until 1943 did the room visualized in 1941 begin to take shape; a successful raffle by the John Carroll Junior Guild provided the funds to furnish the room. The old room with its dense clouds of smoke and sleeping students who should have been in class, gave way to brighter and more comfortable surroundings that received heavy use during the period of the Navy V-12 program.[84] In March 1945 the room, "consistently littered with paper, orange skins, 'coke' bottles, and the like," was closed. Eugene Oberst, the athletic director, finally prevailed upon authorities to reopen it. For about five or six months order was maintained and then it returned to the downhill route.[85] There really was no greater provision for student recreation on the East Side than there had been on the West Side, but the situation was now more difficult with resident students on campus. The Snack Shop in the basement of the Administration building, however popular, was hardly adequate.

The annual play and intercollegiate debating were still traditional activities. *Yellow Jack*, the first play produced on the East Side, presented a problem that brought forth a solution from Father Murphy worthy of King Solomon. There was one female part in the play, a nurse. The plan to have students from Notre Dame and Ursuline colleges try out for the part succeeded in getting two women, one from Notre Dame and one from Ursuline, to apply. Father Murphy at first suggested writing another part into the play; no one was willing to try. The next solution was to add another nurse just for decorative purposes. Finally, Father Murphy decided that the play would remain as written but that the two women would alternate performances in playing the part of the nurse.[86] This decision came at the same time that Eugene Mittinger, moderator of the student newspaper was told to "adhere strictly" to the "repeated instruction concerning the appearance of women in advertisements of the school paper."[87]

The highlight of the intercollegiate debating activities in 1937 was the defeat of a team from Oxford and Cambridge Universities by the brothers Thomas L. and James M. Osborne. They defended the negative of the question, "The absolute veto power of the Supreme Court is an anachronism." The debate sponsored by the Cleveland Knights of Columbus took place before an overflow crowd of 3,200 people at the Carter Hotel ballroom.[88] An invitation to debate New York University on the radio on an undetermined subject in 1940 was turned down, ostensibly for lack of sufficient information. The consultors said, "This was to prevent any possible involvement with other Jesuit schools in the East or in some subjects better left untouched."[89]

The role of student counselor during this period was filled by Father Clifford LeMay, who tried to provide a relaxed atmosphere in his office where the student could discuss his relationship to God and the things that affected that relationship.[90] In addition to scheduling appointments with the students, Father LeMay also was moderator of the Sodality. In this latter capacity, he found great difficulty in setting times for Sodality meetings because of the full schedule of classes. Father Bracken offered him the noon hour on Tuesdays and Thursdays which Father LeMay refused as totally unsatisfactory.[91]

Father James J. McQuade came to John Carroll in 1939 as professor of religion and also took charge of the Sodality. He wrote frequently in the *Carroll News* in a column called "Sodality Notations." His purpose was "to keep Carroll conscious of its distinctive nature as a 'Catholic school' by bringing to the attention of Carroll men and friends of Carroll the distinctively Catholic features of Carroll life."[92] The articles continued for some time, demonstrating Father McQuade's intense interest in the Catholic Action movement. Sometimes the articles were commentaries on various phases of campus life; other times they might contain prayers, meditations, or adaptations of Gospel parables to student life. Father McQuade sought to make the Sodality an integral part of the Carroll experience. The dedication of the university to the Sacred Heart of Jesus in March 1940 by Father Francis X. McMenamy was hailed by Father McQuade as an example of "aggressive Catholicism" gaining headway at John Carroll.[93] The statue of the Sacred Heart in the lobby of the main entrance was the symbol of unity.

During the war years, Father LeMay became chaplain for the Navy V-12 program and took over Father McQuade's column in the *Carroll News*. The presence of the Navy required reorganization of the Sodality in January 1944 into two groups, Navy and civilian, because of conflicting schedules. After the war, in 1948, the overflow membership in the Sodality again required a second Sodality. Father Joseph O. Schell became moderator of the second group, which was composed of freshmen.[94]

Father LeMay, in addition to his many on-campus duties, had charge of the Catholic Collegiate Council, which arranged symposia for the students of the Catholic colleges in Cleveland on a variety of current topics on ethics and morality. One of these symposia held in February 1936 produced a sharp rebuke from Bishop Schrembs. Even though Father Daniel Lord, national Sodality leader, had not been invited, Bishop Schrembs, to whom Father Lord was *personna non grata*, had heard that he was invited. Father Rodman explained to the bishop that Father LeMay was unaware of the

Top left, Clifford J. LeMay, S.J., 1933–63; *right,* Lionel V. Carron, S.J., 1917, 1930–41; *Middle,* John A. Weber, S.J., 1948–61; *Bottom left,* William J. Murphy, S.J., 1930–59; *right,* Charles A. Castellano, S.J., 1934–36, 1947–76

bishop's feelings toward Father Lord and in any event Father Lord had not been invited.[95]

Although the bishop approved the subjects to be discussed at the symposia—euthanasia, birth control, mixed marriages, sterilization, divorce, and premarital chastity—he did not like the reports he frequently got after a symposium had taken place. On one occasion the bishop was disturbed that one of the priests at the symposium "did not handle it [sex] with great prudence."[96] A year later, prior to the next symposium, the bishop was still contending that the sex questions were discussed "too frankly for the mixed group of young people" and warned that future discussions must be kept "well in hand."[97]

Bishop Schrembs was also not happy with the proposed combined social affairs of the local Catholic colleges. The bishop's secretary wrote to Father Horne in 1938, that he was advising him "under the bishop's direction, that he considered a combined social affair involving the four colleges of Greater Cleveland as unwise. Hoping that you will be able to avoid the issue with diplomacy. . . ."[98]

The bishop's desire for a joint commencement of all the high schools and colleges of the diocese at the Cleveland Stadium in 1939 on the occasion of his Golden Jubilee, provided another opportunity for misunderstanding between the bishop and the Jesuits. There was an original agreement that, for John Carroll, everything would be as it would have been had the commencement been held at John Carroll. St. Ignatius High School, fearing a mixup on the diplomas, used blank diplomas, saving distribution of the real ones for later. Bishop Schrembs upon learning of this charged that it was a personal insult to him.[99] When the bishop next learned that what he thought were commencement exercises for St. Ignatius High were to be held at John Carroll on the Sunday preceding the Stadium affair, he threatened to bring the matter to Father General and demand ecclesiastical penalties.[100] The Sunday exercises were not intended to be commencement exercises. "What makes the entire pill difficult to swallow," noted the consultors, "was the fact that a local parish high school had their real graduation diplomas granted" ten days before the Stadium event. "A priest from Sisters' College delivered the commencement address and nary a word of lack of cooperation, personal insult and opposition."[101]

The period was also noted for more pleasant things. In response to a request of alumni and students, Father Joseph A. Kiefer undertook the writing of "Sons of Carroll," which was first presented at the forty-seventh annual Glee Club concert on 2 May 1937. In 1940 the song was presented by Fred Waring and his orchestra on national radio. There was an abortive effort of the class of 1939 to donate a statue of John Carroll to the university. Even with Bishop Schrembs's support the contributions proved insufficient. The proceeds were eventually used to provide a side altar for the Sodality chapel.[102] The first student Annual, *Carillon*, was produced by the class of 1938, the culmination of over a year's effort to get permission for such a book. The new rector, Father Horne, gave his approval shortly after his arrival. A chapter of Alpha Sigma Nu, a Jesuit honor fraternity, was established in May 1939. It took a long time to get the chapter established because of the ban on all fraternities at John Carroll.[103] A weekly radio program under the exacting supervision of Father William F. Ryan gave the students plenty of opportunity to participate in plays, discussions, and a variety of types of radio programming.

An experiment was tried in 1939 to let students address students at a general convocation on such things as rowdy behavior, student dress, smoking, and "moving things about" such as desks, etc.[104] The program turned into a general criticism of the college, faculty included. An outgrowth of this was permission for the first "Stunt Night" on 21 April 1939. An editorial in the *Carroll News* after the affair hoped that it would become an annual event but also wished that the "rowdy element" could be eliminated in future performances. It seems "a few wise guys" threw water on the Juniors in the middle of their act in which precision was required. Slippery footing could have injured the participants.[105] Some improvement in behavior was noticed in the next performances; there was no particular comment except on the poor quality of scripts. Another first for the period was the revival of the old custom of a freshman-sophomore "Ball Rush" in May 1939. For the first time in memory, the freshmen won.[106] Meanwhile the students managed to avoid any serious difficulties with the local citizens or police. The only source of community irritation seemed to be with the red light Father Teply had put on top of Grasselli Tower. The police said they confused it with the red light on top of city hall. Father Teply changed the light to green. The bells in the Grasselli Tower soon became a community issue. The Angelus Bell was disconnected in 1937, because of complaints. The larger bell, which rang the hours around the clock, was put on a limited daytime schedule because of local city noise ordinances.

The Student Union came in for considerable criticism from the students for not being very effective as a promoter of student interests. A writer in the *Carroll News* in 1938 declared that the Student Union was "An august body that never knew, does not know, and never will know its function."[107] The arrival of the Navy in 1943 made it even more difficult for the Student Union to function in its effort to coordinate activities, which were limited to the Speech Club, Glee Club, *Carroll News*, Sodality, Band, and Athletic Association. After the Navy left, the revived Union saw as its most urgent business the "problem of Freshman initiation, the freshmen protesting the brutality of it all, while the upper-classmen demanded that the Union 'put teeth' into the hazing."[108] In November 1944 the permission for limited initiation of freshmen was looked upon as providing "only a shadow of the old times. The ice cold shower and the combination shoe polish and tomato sauce massage which highlighted the last dorm initiation—that of '42—must be postponed until the upper classman are again a substantial majority."[109]

Father McCue's warning of a little more than two years earlier apparently had been forgotten. Addressing a student convocation shortly after Pearl Harbor, the dean had declared, "Joe College with his racoon coat is dead and gone forever."[110] The student newspaper commented, "Joe I. (stands for fun while it lasted) College died 7 December 1941. Requiesat in Pace."[111]

INTERCOLLEGIATE SPORTS

The two years of Tom Yarr's tenure as head coach of football, 1934 and 1935, were far from successful. After the miserable 1935 football season it was decided to release Yarr and his assistant, Mike Koken. Shortly thereafter, a North Central investigation in February 1936 raised a number of questions about the athletic situation and in particular about scholarships, much as it had in 1934.[112] Favoritism in giving scholarships to athletes was the specific charge. Father Robb, treasurer, answered the complaint by pointing out that scholarships had decreased in value and covered only a third to a half of tuition. Those who could not supply the difference were required to work to make it up.[113] It seems that six athletes were unable to pay the difference and were not required to work. The final recommendation of the North Central was that the university be retained on the accredited list and reinspected within a year or two with emphasis on the development of a physical education program and the outcome of the effort to retire indebtedness.[114]

The next inspection had been looked forward to with a considerable amount of concern and uneasiness. Father Rodman was fearful that the North Central visitor would jeopardize John Carroll's standing by repeating what was considered to be an unfair investigation of the Xavier University athletic situation two years earlier. So concerned was Father Rodman that he wrote to his friend, Father Samuel Wilson, President of Loyola University in Chicago, asking him to intervene and help to secure a different examiner. Father Wilson, who was a major influence in the developing Jesuit Educational Association and had assumed Father Fox's role in dealing with the North Central, first thought he would try to get the appointment of J. R. Sage of Iowa State College of Agriculture and Mechanical

Arts as examiner changed.[115] After some reflection on the matter, Father Wilson thought it would be better not to ask the North Central for a change, but he did "believe that some outsider, Father Allan P. Farrell, should be present at John Carroll when the inspection takes place."[116] Rather than incur the North Central's displeasure by a request for another examiner, Father Wilson advised Father Rodman to be content with Sage and await the report of the announced examiner.[117] Father Rodman would have preferred Father Wilson and Father O'Connell to be present. According to Father Wilson, the Provincial's fear was not the academic record of John Carroll, which was "quite all right," nor with the football situation following the dismal record of the past seasons, but with the "general temper of the faculty," which was not "sufficiently in repose to make a good impression at the time of the inspection."[118]

Father Wilson reassured Father Rodman that there should be nothing to fear from Sage's visit but cautioned that "one must always wear a velvet glove when dealing with the North Central authorities but the hand wearing the glove must never be flabby or nervous."[119] Father Wilson did feel that the cause of trouble might be the recently fired coaching staff "whose talk might have gotten back to the North Central as evidence that the athletic situation at John Carroll is not technically correct."[120]

Meanwhile, Father Wilson thought it wise to visit Sage in Iowa as a representative of the Jesuit Educational Association in order to clear up in advance any potential misunderstandings. Before Father Wilson set out on his visit, he received a letter from Father Rodman assuring him that the coaching staff (Tom Yarr and his staff) had been fired because of their "lack of success" and there were no athletic irregularities to be afraid of, nor should Father Wilson "worry about our hands being flabby or nervous."[121]

The visit to Sage was productive. Father Wilson learned that the reexamination of Xavier in 1934 was the result of some careless remarks made by the Xavier representatives at the North Central annual meeting of that year. Sage had been immediately dispatched to check things out, but could get no answers from the authorities at Xavier, which made him suspicious. When he questioned students, he was accused of unprofessionalism. Sage pointed out to Father Wilson that a visit to the University of Detroit that same year produced no such difficulties.

Father Wilson concluded that Sage was a "meticulous and honest man" who would cause no difficulties at John Carroll if he met with cooperation.[122] The examination did go off well. Father Robb's letter, written from a bed in St. Vincent's Charity Hospital, seems to have answered any questions on athletic scholarships.

The selection of another Notre Dame man, Tom Conley, as head coach in 1936 occasioned a review of the athletic situation by the *Carroll News*. A poll of members of the varsity teams showed no agreement on the cause of the difficulties: a new coach means little, "the faculty is always with us;" the need is money; centralization of direction under Conley may help; we need an intramural system to support the varsity; if a Notre Dame coach is the answer, why did Yarr fail?[123] Conley did have considerable success, but it took some time for him to build a winning team. After the formation of the Big Four in 1933, there had not been many victories for the Blue Streaks. The year 1935 was probably the worst ever experienced, the football team winning but one of nine games. From there on the path was upward with the first Big Four title in 1939 climaxing the most successful season thus far in university history.[124]

Athletic contests between local college teams often prompted escapades of one sort or another. In 1939 after Carroll had defeated Case 19–0, about a dozen Case supporters arrived on the Carroll campus in the early morning hours with a flag on which C-A-S-E was printed and attempted to hoist it on the flagpole. Alert Carroll dormitory students came out to thwart the Case followers' ambitions. They seized the flag, dispersed the invaders and proudly hung the flag in the room of one of the rescuers where it could be viewed on request.[125] A similar incident occurred in 1941 when a banner stolen by Case followers after an 8–6 defeat of Carroll in 1934 was unfurled after Case had scored two touchdowns. Some Carroll freshmen dashed across the field and after a brief battle recovered the banner.[126]

Whatever the football fortunes of the first years on the Heights, the cost of fielding the teams was considerable. In 1942 Father Eckman wanted a definite policy on subsidies for athletes. It was his recommendation that athletes should pay fees and buy their own books and that all "driftwood" should be removed at the end of the first semester.[127] Subsidies for athletes from 1935 to 1941 amounted to $51,127.50, with a total deficit for the athletic operation of $35,344.50. Financial help from various sources, including alumni, kept the deficit down. The number of athletes subsidized in 1935–1936 was thirty-five; the number rose to eighty-two in 1938–1939 and dropped to sixty-two in 1941. The total amount of tuition allowance rose from $7,000 in 1935–1936 to $17,250 in 1940–1941.[128] Father Eckman proposed cutting the number of athletes that would be given tuition allowances to forty-eight in 1942–1943.

With the advent of the V-12 program all such problems vanished with the announcement on 12 June 1943 that intercollegiate athletics would be suspended for the duration. "It seemed clear to the University," reported the *Carroll News*, "that these (Navy regulations) called for a concentration on academic excellence which left little or no opportunity for 'athletics as usual.' "[129]

Among sports other than football, hockey was by far the most successful. By 1940 the team under coach Herb Bee, with such stars as Eddie Arsenault, Fred Rancourt, Don Meyers, Clem Rannigan, Ted Lempges, and George Otto, had won its third straight championship title in the Ohio-Penn league. In the 1939 season, the team was undefeated and untied in fifteen games and had run up a string of forty-one consecutive victories. Until the cessation of the sport in 1941, Carroll's hockey teams "were the terror of this part of the country."[130]

A new sport, wrestling, was introduced during the Navy V-12 program. All the Navy trainees engaged in elimination tournaments staged in the rear of the gym (auditorium) while basketball was being played on the floor and boxing matches were going on up on the stage.

A good example of how people often tend to think that history begins with their own existence can be seen in the remark of a *Carroll News* writer in 1940 about the possibility of having a baseball team. An alumnus had offered to back a baseball team and the writer exclaimed, "If this dream of a baseball team materializes, it will be the first baseball team in the history of John Carroll."[131] One would have to deny that John Carroll University was ever known as St. Ignatius College for that statement to be true.

The Navy V-12 program was introduced just as efforts were being made to develop an athletic field. When John Carroll first moved to the Heights, Bellefaire Orphanage was most generous in allowing Carroll the use of its football and tennis facilities together with shower rooms and dispensary. Later a field was developed on the quadrangle near Rodman Hall. This field was often too muddy for practice and so the players tended to drift in the direction of the grass on the lawn in front of Rodman Hall. When Father Donnelly became rector in 1942, one of his first problems was to admonish coach Conley about players who strayed onto the Rodman Hall grass. Father Donnelly had thought this matter was settled before his arrival.[132]

Efforts were then made to renovate the rather unsightly strip of land on university property adjacent to Belvoir Boulevard. In 1935 this strip was filled with sand and dirt from the Belvoir paving project along with all sorts of debris. On 1 August 1943, the strip was levelled and graded to provide for a football field, track and drill field. With the advent of the V-12 program and the abandonment of intercollegiate athletics, these plans were dropped. In 1945, however, Gene Oberst and a corps of assistants prepared an area for a skating rink which became known as Oberst Park.

In 1944 Oberst, who had been retained as athletic director after Conley left in 1942, asked for the return of organized football. He pointed out that the Navy would assume no responsibility or expense but did favor the physical training and competition the sport provided.[133] Father Donnelly was unwilling to make a decision until one year later, in December 1945, when the consultors agreed to resume football on a "purely amateur scale."[134] The consultors were firm in their opposition to subsidizing athletes and revived the athletic board to supervise athletics.[135] Intercollegiate sports and a broad intramural program were resumed in the fall of 1946. It was further agreed any profits from athletics should not be put into scholarships for athletes.[136] In spite of its earlier success hockey was not to be among the revived intercollegiate sports, which included basketball as well as football.

DEVELOPMENT OF ADMINISTRATIVE ORGANIZATION

One of the most significant features of the years 1936 to 1946 was the sowing of the seeds of a new university administrative structure that would slowly depart from the traditional pattern of control by the rector and consultors. The Provincial requested in 1936 that the rector, deans, heads of departments, and two appointees of the university board of trustees (personnel almost identical with that of the consultors) draw up an outline of duties and responsibilities of the several offices in the university.[137] Although a committee was formed there were few immediate positive results.

One stimulus to action on the Provincial's request came from a faculty study club developed during the Navy V-12 program. While the club, under the leadership of Father Frederick Welfle, chairman of the department of history, devoted a large percentage of its time to international problems and presented panel discussions on them for students and faculty, it was not long before the club began to look into university structure and organization.

The visit of Father Leo Sullivan, Provincial, in 1945, pointed out the necessity of a definite code of regulations. The Provincial suggested something similar to the statutes adopted by the University of Detroit to govern its administration. Father Donnelly's response was that such a code had been in existence at John Carroll for many years and was recently supplemented by a document outlining rank and tenure of faculty "adequate to our needs. The Fathers consultors concurred in this."[138] The Provincial was then informed that John Carroll already had a code that was adequate and would be brought up to date in the summer of 1945.[139] What Father Donnelly had in mind is hard to say, but he and the Provincial were not talking about the same thing.

During that summer the faculty study club, unconvinced that existing regulations, whatever they might be, were adequate, continued to discuss at length a set of statutes for the university. In February 1946 there was a meeting of the faculty, both Jesuit and lay, to discuss the new administrative organization plans. These plans included rank and tenure, a salary scale, and a retirement plan.[140] The statutes drawn up by the faculty study group were approved, but were not promulgated and not generally known.[141] It remained for Father Welfle when he became president to follow through on the study club's recommendations.

The entire discussion of statutes proceeded without any apparent knowledge of the recommendations of the Jesuit Educational Association in February 1935 of a form of statutes for Jesuit colleges and universities, copies of which had been sent to all rectors.[142] While these recommendations were more urgent for the complex universities, the principles in them were in keeping with the idea of bringing all Jesuit institutions into the mainstream of American higher education.

The recommendations provided for a separation of the functions of rector and president. The rector, assisted by his consultors, was to confine his activities to those of the superior of a religious community. He was not to act in university affairs. The president was to be appointed by Father General on the recommendation of the legal board of trustees, which was to be separate from the consultors of the community. The president was to be assisted by an academic senate of the faculty. An executive committee of a faculty senate was to function when the senate was not in session. Other recommendations covered the entire structure of a university. The formation of these statutes had been greatly influenced by Father Thurber Smith, dean of the graduate school of St. Louis University. There were differences of opinion about the function of the academic senate but the recommendations were adopted by some of the Jesuit institutions.[143]

Because of his leadership role in the development of statutes for John Carroll, Father Welfle was chosen to succeed Father Donnelly as rector-president in July 1946. The ten years of Father Welfle's tenure were spent in trying to construct a university organization within the bounds of the traditional Jesuit system but nevertheless having some modifications to bring it into greater conformity with other colleges and universities. His successor, Father Hugh Dunn, spent his eleven years building on the foundation Father Welfle had laid, but moved more rapidly, and probably too rapidly in the direction of a university with a minimum of the traditional ties to the Jesuit Community.

Postwar Plans

Beginning in the summer of 1944, the consultors carried on serious discussions concerning the future of the university. Agreement was reached that "we could not hope to compete with Fenn College and Western Reserve University, but that we would be able to provide something interesting and profitable for the returning war veterans."[144] It was then that the decision was made to feature business administration and to organize the school of business, economics, and government. Father McCue felt that there was also a future in adult education and the Provincial suggested an effort to develop a labor school.[145] There was also talk of seeking a Navy ROTC unit for the postwar period as a "*temporary* means of obtaining our operating expenses."[146] A labor school was begun in March 1945; the Evening School had been resumed earlier.

When Father Donnelly asked his consultors in 1945 if it was true that, in spite of its years of existence in the city of Cleveland, the university was not well known in the area, he was assured that this was so. It was agreed that an office of publicity director should be created to help remedy the situation. Father William Murphy was suggested for the post although some thought a journalist hired on a part-time basis would be more effective. Father Murphy's manifold duties were reason enough not to consider him further for the post.[147] Not until much later was such a position established.

A discussion initiated by Father Donnelly with his consultors toward the end of 1944 sought to address the question of what specifically John Carroll should do to meet the expected return of veterans. There was the impression that any increase in students over prewar numbers would have to depend upon recruiting out-of-town students. One solution was to add a wing to Bernet Hall. The Bernets felt that the building costs were too high to add a wing, but they were willing to give $10,000 to refurbish Bernet Hall for civilian students.[148]

High on the priority list of things to do was the attention to be given to long-deferred repairs. Leaking walls in the administration building and repair of the front drive, which had crumbled under heavy bus traffic, demanded attention. Most of this work, including the pressing need for a new physics building, still had to be deferred.

The first decade on the Heights closed with major changes in Jesuit personnel. Father Welfle had become president of the university. Father Benedict Rodman was transferred from Gesu parish to Detroit after differences with Bishop Hoban over diocesan building program. For Father Rodman this was the first time since 1928 that he would not be associated with the Cleveland Jesuits.[149] Two other Jesuit faculty members were also transferred. Father Dennis Burns had been at John Carroll since 1931 as head of philosophy and religion. He had left John Carroll at one time to go to Xavier University as rector-president. In 1944, he was leaving to be retreat master at Manresa in Detroit. The *Carroll News* considered his reassignment "probably the greatest blow to Carroll's scholastic and academic framework."[150] Father Remi Belleperche had come to Carroll in 1940. Known as "a great classicist a 'greater despiser of sophomores,'" he instilled his spirit into all his classes and probably was responsible for the scores of budding philosophers now roaming the campus of JCU."[151]

A final note to the first ten years on the Heights is the wishful thinking expressed by the *Carroll News* in 1945 regarding coeducation. Quoting from the student newspaper of Creighton University, "Girls, Girls. During the war years, the gym was 'out of bounds' for girls, but the boys' monopoly has been broken with this announcement; Every Monday at 7 P.M. the gym will be open to girls only for swimming, badminton, volley ball, and other sports;" the *Carroll News* comment was, "Well we can dream, can't we!"[152] Judging from the later bitter quarrel over coeducation at John Carroll, there was a marked change in attitude between 1945 and 1960.

"The Decisive Years"
1946–1960

The appointment of Father Frederick E. Welfle to be rector-president of John Carroll University in 1946 was a fortunate one. He was to provide leadership in the next ten years in making the critical decisions necessary to help John Carroll University meet the challenges to higher education in the postwar years. His presidency was to be the longest since that of Father Rodman, thus providing a desirable continuity that would prepare the way for the next president, Father Hugh E. Dunn, who would follow through and expand upon the foundation that Father Welfle laid. In this sense the regimes of Fathers Welfle and Dunn from 1946 to 1967 constitute a period in which John Carroll University developed into a modern institution of higher education. In personality and style of administration the two men were as vastly different as were the circumstances under which they worked, but their goals were much the same.

Father Welfle stood firmly in the tradition of Jesuit rectors, but he was willing to explore possible new relationships between the role of rector and that of president. He also sought to provide a positive role for the layman. Before he was three years in office Father Welfle perceived the great difficulty in reconciling the role of rector with that of the president in the light of modern university demands on time and energy. He explained to his consultors that the demands on his time "from within the University alone," were so great that he could not find the time for necessary contacts with the public.[1] Father Welfle proposed the appointment of a Superior for the Jesuit Community and an executive assistant to handle the many internal details of the president's office.[2] It is ironic that the executive assistant, Father William J. Millor, was appointed just before Father Welfle's death in 1956 and the Superior, Father Douglas Pearl, arrived in time to give Father Welfle the last rites as he rode with him to the hospital after his fatal heart attack.[3]

The progress of John Carroll University as envisioned by Fathers Rodman and Fox had been interrupted by World War II and the stand-pat policies of Father Welfle's immediate predecessors, Fathers Horne and

Donnelly. What had given John Carroll some hope of breaking out of the mold of the traditional small Jesuit college after the war was the energetic and forward-looking endeavors of Father Edward C. McCue who, as dean of the college since 1939, tried to upgrade the academic life of the institution. Father Welfle, as one who had done his doctoral work in other than Jesuit universities, was sympathetic to the views of Father McCue. Father Welfle saw rather clearly the difficulty in reconciling the expanding role of the president with that of his duties as rector of a religious community. Although there is no clear evidence to support the view that he was consciously suggesting the recommended solution of the Jesuit Educational Association to this problem, he seems to have worked along the lines of the recommendations. Years would pass, however, before the recommendations were given more specific form and were more generally adopted in Jesuit colleges and universities. Meanwhile, Father Welfle proceeded to lay the groundwork for bringing the university up to date.

By temperament Father Welfle was well suited to an office he said he had wandered into through his leadership in the faculty study club that had proposed the university statutes. He was popular with faculty even though some criticized what they considered to be his ineptitude. He had the ability to laugh at himself. He could, as even his critics admitted, put his foot in his mouth, take it out immediately, and laugh with his critics. His humor was one of the things that took the sharp edges off the notes he often wrote to those whom he thought were out of line. In fact an entire chapter could be written on those notes, but few have been preserved. Father Welfle was also a "learner" with an open mind to sound propositions and arguments. He knew that the position of president would require information and experience he had not yet come by; he therefore attended courses and seminars where he filled in the gaps in his knowledge and experience.

In accomplishing his objectives he relied heavily on Father McCue and Fritz Graff. In a very real sense these three formed the group that had the most to say about final decisions. Even the students were quick to recognize the concerted action of the trio. A Student Stunt Night skit on one occasion had the three doing a soft shoe dance with straw hat and cane to the tune of "Freddie, Fritz, and Eddie." Rarely did the three act independently of each other.

In 1946 Father Welfle became president of a university that had a total enrollment of 1,998; of this number, 1,343 were registered in the day school, the rest in the Graduate and Evening Divisions. There was a faculty of sixty full-time teachers of whom twenty-three were Jesuits. In addition there were thirty-one lecturers. In a message to the students in 1946, Father Welfle pointed to the increase of faculty over the war years, the reactivating of the departments of Speech and Sociology, a new major in electronics and an autonomous School of Business, Economics and Government as evidence that the university was on the move.[4]

In a message to the Lay Advisory Board of Trustees dated 14 November 1956, Father Millor as executive dean commented on Father Welfle's presidency,

> As President for ten difficult years—during the stage of intense "growing pains," he distinguished his administration by manifesting excellent foresight. Through his efforts and leadership, John Carroll is now beginning to take its place among the leading Universities of this area.[5]

To be fully understood, Father Welfle's accomplishments must be seen against a background which included a view that John Carroll should remain a typical small Jesuit college of former times.[6]

FUND-RAISING

In order to insure the projected educational growth, Father Welfle sought to build better accountability into the university financial structure. As a first move he provided for separate accounting of the Jesuit Community's expenses and those of the university. The Provincial had also requested that this be done in order to get a clear picture of Jesuit expenses, which he wished the university to pay.[7] Father Welfle also set up a budget and staff council which would oversee all university financial matters. Its members were Father Welfle, Father McCue, Charles Cooney, Father Weber, and Dean Graff. It didn't take long for conflict to develop over issues of rank, tenure, salary, and control of promotion. Although the Faculty Study Group had been very clear about separating academic and financial matters, it was some time before agreement was reached that the nonacademic members of the budget and staff committee were not competent to pass upon individual salary and rank; the setting of salary brackets was left to the budget and staff committee.[8]

After attending a seminar on university fund-raising in the summer of 1947, Father Welfle discussed with his consultors the various possible means of adopting some sort of long-range plan under the direction of a capable and experienced person. Outlining the needs of the university was the next step. It was decided to aim for a school of some 1,200 to 1,500 with no expansion of curricula but rather an intensification of what was already in place—liberal arts, a school of business, and pre-medical, pre-dental, and pre-engineering programs.[9] A new dormitory and an addition to the service building were listed as immediate building needs. The consultors also "urged that a lay advisory board of the right prominent laymen be appointed."[10]

In spite of the determination not to expand, an offer of the Northern Ohio Druggists Association to establish a school of pharmacy on campus was considered briefly in 1949. The closing of the Western Reserve School of Pharmacy in June of that year provided the opportunity. The consultors wanted to seek the advice of some other Jesuit universities which had such a school before approaching Father General for permission to accept the proposal. The result was the decision not to establish such a school.[11]

Father Welfle engaged the American City Bureau to conduct a survey at a cost of $3,000 to determine the best procedure for fund-raising for John Carroll.[12] An advisory board of lay trustees was also selected.[13] When the report on fund-raising was made in April 1949, the lay trustees approved hiring the American City Bureau to conduct the program. A new dormitory was to be the first priority of the campaign.

Within a short time objections arose among the Jesuits to a new dormitory. Some felt there was greater need for classroom space, thinking that a new dormitory eventually would be a "white elephant."[14] Further discussion convinced the consultors that existing classroom space was not fully utilized and that Bernet Hall could not always be kept at its overcrowded condition. Moreover, the use of rooms in Rodman Hall by students was becoming a nuisance to the Jesuit Community.[15] The consultors now supported the drive for the new dormitory.

The new plans for fund-raising produced many questions. Since large sums of money would be involved, should the consultors attend Budget Council meetings, since the consultors had a "higher deliberative authority"? It was finally agreed to keep the two groups separate "since it gives the rector an easier out if a proposal has to be vetoed or reversed."[16] An allied issue was control of the investment. In this instance the consultors voted to retain the right to withhold approval of sales and transactions of securities.[17] When the lay advisory board of trustees wished to supervise the funds that were collected in the campaign, the consultors approved a special fund for this project.[18]

Two other financial matters were handled without much controversy. The university owed the Jesuit Community a considerable sum of money by reason of several loans made to the university some years earlier. It was decided to convert this amount into a fund whose interest would be used exclusively for scholarships.[19] At the same time, Father Welfle contacted Bishop Hoban, who gave his approval for the campaign.[20]

In May 1949 the Advisory Board of Lay Trustees was formally launched. Joining them as *ex-officio* members were the Provincial, the president of the university along with the vice-president, the treasurer, and the alumni president. The purpose of the Board was to advise the president on physical and financial affairs, development of the university and such related matters as the president proposed. The *Carroll News* observed that the new development program represented planned progress within the framework of Father Welfle's goal to become not "larger" but "better."[21]

Father Welfle soon appointed an assistant to the president, J. Patrick Rooney, who was to advise the president on development plans. Father Welfle also began a series of dinners for prominent Clevelanders in order to explain the "Carroll Story." In April 1952 in order to correlate better the services of John Carroll with the needs of the city of Cleveland, Herbert H. Kennedy, a former General Motors executive, was made vice-president for development. The Advisory Board of Lay Trustees then laid out a list of priorities. A field house was near the top of the list because of the need for recreation facilities for the increasing number of dormitory students who would be on campus. A separate library building was an even greater need. Also listed were a heating plant adequate to handle future buildings, a physics building, and a business school building. Expansion of ROTC facilities was also included. Although there were no immediate plans for any of these buildings, collections of funds continued under the very successful leadership of Kennedy.

Meanwhile, Charles Cooney, the auditor, was concerned that all the promotional activity was an unnecessary drain on the budget. He recommended that publicity and promotion be curtailed and that something be done about the $20,000 deficit in intercollegiate football.[22] There seemed to be no immediate solution to the football deficit, but the consultants agreed that although the expenditures for publicity and fund-raising were high, it was better to continue them than to risk their curtailment.[23]

CAMPUS DEVELOPMENT

When Father Welfle took office there was a long backlog of postponed maintenance from the war period; landscaping, waterproofing, painting, and general repairs were now demanding the attention which Father Welfle proceeded to give them. The large prairie-like tract at the front of the campus needed to be graded and landscaped according to the original plan. Formerly, buses used the drive in front of the administrative building. The damage to this drive caused by the bus traffic forced the buses to stop in the area near Kerwick Road between the chemistry wing and Bernet Hall. The University Heights Council then proposed a new route along Washington Boulevard to a street east of Belvoir.[24] A long controversy ensued but the new proposal went into effect and cleared the former bus stop area for university use. Even though there were no immediate building plans for the front area, a decision concerning the design and materials of any future building to be erected specified that original architectural material and style should be followed. Temporary structures such as quonset huts, very popular in postwar days on other campuses, were ruled out.[25] It was felt that money would be better spent in permanent construction and remodeling.

Through the efforts of Father Raymond Mooney the Community Facilities of the Federal Works Agency offered a building in 1947 that could serve as a temporary gymnasium. The building, placed on the unused chapel foundation, provided a gymnasium and relieved the pressure on the auditorium-gymnasium in the administration building.[26] The structure was completed by spring 1947. It was a frame building painted a color intended to correspond with the brick in the other buildings. In addition to serving as a gymnasium it also provided offices for the School of Business. The building soon became known as the "Pink Barn" as well as by a number of other names reflecting the less than exact match between the paint and the brick. The building served as a gymnasium until a new one, planned under Father Welfle's building program, was completed and dedicated on 3 November 1957.

Two other buildings in the idea stage were not fully planned until Father Dunn's presidency: the library and the student activities center. Other plans for renovation and changes in location of some offices were also incomplete at Father Welfle's death. One of these plans was the idea of converting the old cafeteria into a chapel when a new student activities center containing a new cafeteria was completed. Another project was the construction of a physics building.

Pacelli Hall, completed and dedicated in May 1952, was built through the efforts of Father McCue and Dr. James Peirolo, modern language professor, who gained American-Italian support of the fund drive. Another dormitory, Dolan Hall, was scheduled and completed in 1955. Herbert Kennedy, Charles McCahill, and Thomas Dolan were among those who successfully carried out the drive for funds. With the completion of these dormitories, rooms used by the students in Rodman Hall were turned back to the Jesuits. The Muller residence became vacant in 1954 on the death of Muller. As a partial solution to the need for office space, the Department of Education together with the Employment and Counseling Service moved into the little "White House," the former Gesu parish rectory.

Between 1956 and 1960, efforts at new building projects centered around a new library, a science center and a student activities center; Father Welfle's death in 1956 prevented him from seeing these projects to completion. The library was completed in 1961, and the student activities center in 1959. The old cafeteria was then converted to office space rather than a chapel. A science center in place of just a physics building was planned as a possible seventy-fifth anniversary project.[27] Its completion in 1968 allowed the original chemistry and biology wings to be converted to other uses. The School of Business eventually moved into the chemistry wing; some administrative offices and the department of modern languages moved into the biology wing.

FACULTY ROLE IN GOVERNANCE

The new statutes provided for an academic council, which was a compromise between merely an advisory council chosen by the president and a council that would be a policy-making body representing the faculty.[28] The result was a body appointed by the president to advise him on matters brought to it by either the president or the faculty. In many ways the new body resembled a group of consultors on academic matters paralleling the Jesuit Community consultors, similar to the arrangement recommended earlier by the Jesuit Educational Association. The council was to devote itself to the working out of the details of the new statutes as its first order of business. Its original membership consisted of Fathers Welfle, McCue, Lawrence Monville (physics), Leonard Otting (philosophy), as well as Dean Graff, Eugene Mittinger (registrar), John Seliskar (business), and Doctors George Grauel (English), and Hugh Graham (education). There was agreement at its second meeting in December 1946 that all discussion be kept in confidence and that information be released only through the president.[29] The first item of business turned out to be the hiring of a new football coach, Herb Eisele, with most of the arrangements being conducted outside of the council.[30] The second meeting of the Academic Council listed its priorities as confidentiality, public relations, student discipline, duties of department heads, and criteria for teaching standards.[31]

A good example of how the first Academic Council operated can be seen in the handling of the matter of a public relations policy. A report which served as the basis for discussion suggested a structure in which there was to be a director of public relations assisted by an executive committee. Since it was agreed that only the Academic Council could pass final judgment, such a committee would not work. No mention of the discussions or the report appeared in "Faculty Notes."[32] Later, it was agreed that the "Faculty Notes," which was published by the President's Office, should be the medium for publicizing the minutes of the Academic Council after Father Welfle had expurgated some material.[33]

Work on a faculty and administrative handbook occupied most of the early meetings of the Academic Council, culminating in the publication of the first faculty handbook in 1953. Other problems discussed included the relation of the School of Business to the college of Arts and Sciences, the clear definition of the type of graduate desired as a product of the university, interdepartmental relationships, the role of Christianity in course work, a policy for student activities, and a way of dividing up the tasks involved in running a university.

Just before the publication of the *Faculty Handbook* in 1953, Father Welfle said he had been getting some criticism that the Academic Council was failing in its purpose.[34] Much of the criticism stemmed from the fact that the Council was a compromise between what Father Welfle thought was possible and the faculty's desires. The faculty was still thinking of the council as originally intended, a semilegislative body. Although the Council by 1951 had begun to take votes on issues, complete authority remained in the hands of the president.[35] One of the principal complaints from the faculty was that the body had become a body of executives with too many *ex-officio*, members; it did not represent the teaching staff.[36] On another score, secrecy in the deliberations of the council had the unfortunate effect of diminishing the confidence of the teaching staff in the Council. One solution which recognized the preponderance of Jesuits in administration, was to have two bodies, a council of deans and *ex-officio* administrators, and a lay faculty council elected by the lay faculty. One member of the Academic Council, Father Deters, dean of the Evening College, cautioned that the Jesuits might prefer a single Academic Council which included them.[37] There was still a question of whether the laymen were an integral part of the faculty. As a result of further discussion, confidentiality was modified so that henceforth only when it was specifically agreed upon would a matter be confidential.[38] Another change allowed the lay faculty to elect representatives to the council. The issue of equalization of membership of administrators and faculty and of Jesuit and lay faculty remained. A solution providing some balance was finally approved with safeguards for the president's veto power to be taken care of in the rewriting of the Statutes.[39]

In spite of efforts to meet the objections of faculty critics of the Academic Council the situation had not improved by 1955. Even Father Welfle felt that the most effective work of the Council was accomplished in the beginning when it produced the *Faculty Handbook of 1953*. Too much confusion had developed between the role of deans and that of the Academic Council. Father Welfle had often failed to report back to the Council during the later years when he, Father McCue, and Dean Graff effectively controlled the administration. A suggestion that Father Welfle remove himself from the Academic Council did not meet with his approval.[40] He felt that he gained a great deal from being present at the meetings. The original purpose of the Academic Council, to make relations between faculty and administration more harmonious, was not being accomplished.

Top left, Frederick E. Welfle, President, John Carroll University, 1946–56; *right,* Edward C. McCue, S.J., Dean, 1938–61; *Bottom left,* Edward Eggl, History, 1945–56; *right,* Fritz W. Graff, Dean, 1934–56

There seemed to be no solution to the problem caused by the admitted right of Father Welfle as rector-president to make whatever arrangements he wished with the deans.[41]

When Father Dunn became president in 1956 he inherited this unsolved problem of conflicting function. Within a year he presented the Academic Council with his solution, explaining that he saw the first task of the Council to be the updating of the *Faculty Handbook.* For the time being, he said, the updating should concern itself more with ideas than with wording.[42] Father Dunn wanted the budget procedure changed so that the department head and not the dean would be responsible for control of his own budget and would receive reports on it. The role of the president was to be reexamined and the "splintering" effect of the Academic Council was to be corrected. In Father Dunn's mind the key person, operationally speaking, was the department head, who should be represented on the Council. Thus the Academic Council was reorganized in 1958 to include all eighteen department heads, as well as the assistant dean, the dean of men, and the librarian; the president was to be responsible for the agenda. In this way planning with the cooperation of others could be accomplished. The president's secretary was to be secretary of the Council and a clear distinction was to be made between when a matter was in the idea stage and when a report was ready for action. Father Dunn also wanted a clear distinction between standing committees and *ad hoc* committees. Committees whose purpose was served in other ways were to be dissolved; committees with overlapping functions were to be reconstituted.[43]

ROTC PROGRAM

The consultants agreed in May 1949 "that it would be a good thing to have an ROTC transportation unit here."[44] The news of the approval of the application and the announced starting date in the fall of 1950 were received by the students "with mixed emotions."[45] Everyone, including the consultants, was surprised by the speedy action of the Army, which "anticipated by one year our expectations of the beginning of a unit."[46] Simultaneously, the consultants hoped that one of the four armories planned for the Cleveland area could be secured for the property on the east side of Belvoir Boulevard.[47] The possibility of acquiring the armory existed because the site originally selected by the city of Cleveland was not available for lease. The armory would be available for ROTC activities and there were sufficient guarantees in the contract to protect the rights of the university during the lease. The city site, however, eventually did become available and so nothing developed for that use of the Belvoir property. An ROTC building on the campus was dedicated on 26 October 1950.

ENROLLMENT AND CURRICULAR ISSUES

Father Julian Maline, Province Prefect of Studies, after his annual visit to John Carroll in November 1951, reported that the activities of the Academic Council, the Budget Council, and the general concern and activities of the administration showed that the university was "very much alive to its problems."[48] One of Father Maline's concerns was the "disturbing remarks about the quality of students," but he hestitated to recommend a general education program as had been begun at St. Louis University.[49]

At a meeting of the Academic Council 13 December 1950, Father James A. McQuade introduced into the minutes some notes from Father General Ledochowski on the type of student to be admitted to Jesuit colleges and universities. Father General's remarks placed emphasis on the maintenance of discipline and cited an example of enrollment actually increasing after some extensive dismissals of problem students.[50] At that same Academic Council meeting three standards of admission criteria were recognized: moral, social and intellectual; only the third was to be considered for possible modification.

Some of the concern for student quality undoubtedly came from possible enrollment decline as a result of the Korean War. By 1951 there was talk of a one-third decline in enrollment. Father Welfle reported that St. Louis University planned to reduce faculty, but that he would prefer that John Carroll try to keep its faculty as it did in World War II. He therefore proposed an "aggressive hunt for new students."[51] The Academic Council endorsed such efforts as well as plans for an accelerated program which would help expand the summer school. Under an accelerated program, freshmen were to be accepted in June. For this reason the two-term summer session was retained as a means of accelerating a student's course of study. The problem of student quality, however, remained. Continued pressures of military mobilization called for further action to stabilize enrollment as a matter of survival.

Father Deters suggested that there might be some merit in considering the suggestions of Father Robert Henle, dean of the college of arts and sciences at St. Louis University. Father Henle's suggestion was basically a policy of open admissions with the first college terminus at the end of the sophomore year, if the student made it that far. Acceptance of students after three years of high school was also recommended on the ground that the fourth year was not that profitable for the student academically.[52] Another suggestion was to eliminate Saturday classes so that John Carroll would not be identified with a six-day week.[53] The total university enrollment did drop by about 150 students in the years 1950 to 1952 but it rose 170 in the fall of 1953 to a total of 2,433. Steady growth continued through succeeding years to a total of 3,896 in 1960.

A problem of the 1950s, not unrelated to enrollment, was that of a curriculum overloaded with required courses which made it impossible to finish some programs in four years; only the AB and BS in SS (Social Science) degrees could be finished in the required 128 hours. Certain programs in business and science required as many as 153 hours. Father Maline in his report of 1951 felt that the *Catalogue* should state that only the AB and BS in SS could be finished in 128 hours.[54] Father McCue opposed the inclusion in the *Catalogue* of any such statement and Father Welfle decided to leave the matter to the deans.[55] Even changes in the curriculum in 1959 did not reduce completely the excessive hours in some programs. Among other changes that year was the shift to the four-point system and the dropping of the double minor. Father John A. Weber thought additional scholarships would be an aid to recruiting and suggested that these scholarships be offered to boys in public high schools. The consultors decided that boys from public high schools could apply for the scholarships already offered.[56]

If too many degree requirements were a matter of concern so also was the heavy teaching load of some members of the faculty. Perhaps because of the enrollment uncertainties there was a reluctance to spell out the teaching load in any specific terms except to say that it was fifteen hours plus counseling. The question of research was minimized in favor of student contact. Another factor inhibiting research was the teaching load in excess of fifteen hours allowed during the postwar years. These excessive teaching loads, sometimes eighteen or more hours, were the only available means of augmenting a faculty member's meager salary.

"THE DECISIVE YEARS"

Discussions on future enrollment led Father Welfle to take steps in 1955 to authorize a study of the possibilities and the choices that the university might make as to its future size. All of the suggestions of the previous years needed some coordinated approach that would carry out Father Maline's admonition to distinguish *ad hoc*, or emergency solutions, from long-range planning. In 1955 the Jesuit Educational Association representing the American Assistancy had submitted a statement on Jesuit education in the United States to Father General. The statement read,

> We should be ready to accept as many students as "furnish solid grounds for the hope that they will go through with their studies to the end with real success"—and for whom we can provide the teaching and physical facilities necessary to give the kind of education we wish to give.
>
> We will be ready to expand present physical facilities and teaching staffs to the extent of compatibility with our financial resources, actual or readily available.[57]

There had been no overall development plan for Jesuit colleges in the United States, nor did the colleges and universities fall into one homogeneous group. There were basic liberal arts colleges, a group of what were called complex colleges in which John Carroll was classified, and the multiuniversities such as Georgetown, Fordham, St. Louis, Marquette, Creighton, University of Detroit, and Loyola of Chicago, all of which had numerous professional schools. It was up to John Carroll to make its plans in the light of its own history. There were no intentions of moving into the class of multiuniversities; the orientation towards liberal arts was clear and traditional. In order to explore the possibilities for improvement of John Carroll as a liberal arts college, Father Welfle in 1953 invited President Gordon Chalmers of Kenyon College in Ohio to talk to the faculty about the role of a liberal arts college. The argument for bringing to Carroll such a distinguished educator was that at John Carroll "a great deal has been done for the poor student but not much to explore the relationship between the teacher and the better student"; some successful experiments at Kenyon could serve as models.[58] Some thought that the speaker would only succeed in highlighting the differences between Kenyon and Carroll. Listeners would suffer from frustration in reviewing "what Kenyon had accomplished in its atmosphere of wealth and leisure. It was pointed out that Carroll was a poor man's school not a rich man's school."[59]

It was within this context that Father Welfle appointed a steering committee in April 1955 to develop an enrollment self-study. In October Father Welfle sent a letter to each faculty member outlining the purpose of the study. The letter said in part,

> The most pressing need at John Carroll University is an analysis and appraisal of the current problems and challenges in the operation of a college, which will serve as a basis for formulating general overall policies to meet the demands of the "Rising Tide" of college age students.[60]

The final report, entitled "The Decisive Years," came out in June 1956. Although it touched on many problems it was basically an enrollment self-study which reached the conclusion that enrollment could be doubled, but that it was too early to formulate an enrollment policy. The most difficult task would be to provide financing and facilities for any increases in enrollment. Inadequate endowment and a 90 percent dependence on tuition income were serious financial handicaps. There was some thought of becoming more selective in admissions with a more than adequate pool of available students. The educational program, however, was considered "inadequate" and the curriculum too rigid to attract students.[61] The study had really only scratched the surface, but it was an initial step in planning.

It would be the task of Father Welfle's successor to determine how to follow it up.

Sessions for students, usually part-time, who could attend only in the evening had been inaugurated in the 1930s; an Evening Division was established in 1933 offering undergraduate as well as a few graduate courses. Between 1933 and 1942 the number of students attending ranged from 170 to 250. In 1943 evening sessions were suspended, resuming again in 1945 with 104 undergraduate students in addition to 100 in a special adult program and 105 in a Labor School. In 1946 the number of students jumped to 575 and remained at that level until 1953 when it rose to 766 and from there reached its peak year in 1959, with 1,650 students.

Much of the growth of the Evening Division from 1949 to 1959 must be attributed to Father Richard T. Deters, its director. When the division was made a college in 1959, Father Deters became dean. His energy, vision, resourcefulness, commitment, and dedication to the student earned the Evening College an enviable reputation. Working from scratch, scrounging for office space, battling other administrators when necessary, Deters demanded equal treatment for the student who could attend only at night. Father Deters started with a desk in the corner of the registrar's office. As the division grew into a full-fledged Evening College using the regular faculty augmented by a competent and loyal group of part-time faculty, Deters became not only dean, but janitor and general handyman as well. He was expected to run an Evening College without any claim to the services provided students during the day. He began his own newspaper, *The Sundowner*, for Evening College students; it was a far more elaborate paper than its predecessor in 1941, which was only a mimeographed sheet called the "Blackout." He and his staff developed a reputation for sound counseling that many felt exceeded that of the day school in quality.

It is true that Father Deters incurred considerable criticism for some of the "courses" which he added from time to time. Most notorious was the "course" in flycasting. The array of flycasters along the sides of the quadrangle aiming at the flagpole in the center made it exceedingly dangerous to attempt to cross the campus or even proceed along the edges. Father Welfle was apparently constrained to bring the matter up to his consultants by whom it "was decided to be more conservative in this respect."[62] As Father Deters explained to the author, the publicity was more positive than negative and the fringe benefit of fishing tackle and other equipment supplied by various manufacturers was too good for a dean who was also a fisherman to pass up.

Shortly after he became director of the Evening Division in 1949, Father Deters experienced the difficulties of having responsibility for an operation over which he had no well defined authority as director and few guidelines to assist him. He finally requested a purpose statement for the Evening College from the Academic Council.[63] In reply he was told that the operating rule would be that the direct instructional cost should not exceed 50 percent of the total income; this rule was to apply to the Evening Division as a whole and not to its individual operations. The idea was to yield as much surplus as possible in order to help support the day school. This still left the director's authority in limbo. Not until the director was made a dean in 1959 was that problem at least partially solved.

One of the problems associated with the growth of the Evening College was the tendency of students registered in the college of arts and sciences to enroll in Evening classes with the deans permission as "guests." Sometimes the reason was a more convenient schedule; on other occasions, the student's teacher preference might be the reason. There was also a growing tendency to cycle certain advanced courses so that they might appear one year in day and the next year in the evening. Since the Evening College was coeducational, the possibility of Evening College students "guesting" in the college of arts and sciences was later to raise the issue of whether the day school should also become coeducational; successful promotional efforts to increase the number of women in the Evening College brought more women into the college of arts and sciences as "guests." In 1952 Father Deters was quoted as saying,

> Coeducational! That is perhaps the main idea which we have been driving at in our promotion for the past eighteen months. Every piece of mail which leaves this office has the word "Coeducational" printed in two different places on the envelope, and once on the letterhead. . . .
>
> This hammering away is beginning to pay off. Few now ask whether we accept women in our Evening Division, and about half of our counselees have been women.[64]

This policy intensified the coeducation issue, which was not resolved until 1968. Meanwhile, in 1958 Arlene Dorsey, a sophomore in the Evening College, was elected secretary of the Student Union; she was the first woman to hold such a position. Another sign of things to come was the hiring of the first full-time woman faculty member in 1956, Mary M. Neff in the Department of Mathematics.

MATTERS SPIRITUAL

One of the outstanding student events of the postwar years was the annual retreat given by Father Charles W. Clark, a former army chaplain, in December 1947. "Observers at the retreat," reported the *Carroll News*, "were at a loss to decide which was the more remarkable . . . the complete meditative silence of the 650 retreatants, or the waiting in line for eight and nine hours in order to have their confessions heard by Father Clark," who was kept in the confessional until 2 o'clock one morning and until 4:30 the next morning.[65] Father Clark was invited to return for another retreat even before that one was completed.

The attendance at the regular student Mass was another story. When twenty-five students were suspended in 1948 for nonattendance, the issue of compulsory attendance at Mass was raised. In view of the university's desire for corporate worship, voluntary attendance seemed impractical.[66] A compulsory plan developed by Father Joseph A. Kiefer was considered "impossible to be put into effect."[67] Scheduling difficulties had previously ruled out the traditional compulsory daily Mass in favor of attendance once a week. Increased enrollment had changed the requirement to once every two weeks.[68] Hope was expressed that a solution could be found by the beginning of classes in the fall of 1948.

BEYOND THE CLASSROOM

The literary efforts of the students were given an outlet in the *Carroll Quarterly* beginning in 1947. The *Carroll News* continued its publication, winning an All-American Rating given by the Association of Collegiate Presses in 1949. The yearbook, the *Carillon*, was not so fortunate. It merited the censure of Father General for its 1953 edition; it contained too many pictures of women in evening gowns.[69]

Radio was not overlooked as an outlet for student activity. An FM radio station was first proposed by Father Lawrence Monville in 1947, but it was not until 1966 that this proposal became more than an idea. In 1952 a closed-circuit radio hookup was set up to serve the campus and also to provide a laboratory workshop.

Meanwhile, "Freshman Hell Week" was revived in 1948 and stunt night proceeded as usual with Father Murphy being frequently caricatured. Social life on campus operated under rather severe restrictions and automobiles were prohibited to the dormitory students. In 1954 at a meeting of dormitory prefects, a social where beer was permitted to be served under supervision was approved.[70] Parental reaction was not in full support of such action when a local brewery wanted to use the letter announcing the permission for advertising purposes, and the United Press wanted to make a national story out of it.[71] The result was that no beer socials were permitted.

Vaughan Monroe and his band brightened up the campus on 15 January 1949 by broadcasting his weekly program from John Carroll before a packed auditorium. There was an encore performance on 21 May; only the University of Alabama had a similar encore performance. Monroe said he enjoyed broadcasting from John Carroll more than from any other university.[72] In terms of outdoor activities, the "Big Snow of 1950" provided not only exercise but also a fringe benefit for the dormitory students.[73] With everything closed down for several days after Thanksgiving, the boys "made a killing (money-wise) shoveling snow from driveways in the neighborhood."[74]

MYTH AND REALITY

One of the legendary members of the John Carroll community in the 1940s was the "Raven." A "faculty nemesis and terror" of Bernet Hall, the Raven, reappeared in the fall of 1946 after a short absence. His advent was announced by a huge banner draped on the side of the auditorium with large letters, "Beware the Raven is back."[75] Students inclined to play pranks of all sorts took refuge in the mythical Raven.

A more persistent legend can be found in Harry Gauzman. Harry has been in the picture at John Carroll since 1948. Nonexistence never slowed Harry down. Harry, the creation of student Al Bieshada, so the story goes, was born in the South Pacific in World War II. While Bieshada, who had been wounded in heavy fighting, was waiting for treatment in an aid station, a corpsman was having difficulty bandaging another wounded Marine. Bieshada sought to relieve the tenseness of the situation by calling the corpsman Mr. Gauzeman. Bieshada was stuck with the name and Mr. Gauzeman became an all-purpose "fall guy." Bieshada later dropped the "e," added the name Harry, and came to John Carroll in 1948. His work in the bookstore and on the *Carroll News* staff gave him ample opportunity to use Harry Gauzman as the man for students to see when difficulties arose. Harry even won an award for sports photography from the Ohio College Press Association. Harry was at his best at freshman registration, where freshman were told he was the one to give final approval to their programs. He occasionally registered for class himself; one year he registered for twenty-six semester hours. As the *Carroll News* put it, "Harry is Kilroy, Yehudi, and Sad Sack all rolled into one. As such he is a perennial Carroll legend."[76] Through the years Harry has been ghost writer for any number of imaginative students whose identity has not always been disclosed. Harry has been given some permanence in recent years when a new student lounge in the lower corridor of the administration building was named the "Harry Gauzman Lounge."

The flesh and blood reality of the Carroll student is to be found in Robert Beaudry, killed in an airplane crash in 1951. The traditional award, "Man of the Year," was named after him in 1951. On 28 October 1951 a shrine in honor of "Our Lady Mother of Grace" was dedicated, erected with the financial help of Robert Beaudry's family, friends, and the sweat of Father Weber and his co-workers. Over 400 attended the dedication, which was part of the Parents' Day Weekend in 1951. In his senior year Beaudry had been president of Alpha Sigma Nu and the Boosters Club. A writer in the *Carroll News* said, "Perhaps the story of Bob Beaudry will grow into legend; undoubtedly the memory of him will never fade. His memorial will remain a symbol of one man's love for his school and his faith."[77] Beaudry's name "represents that intangible quality, school spirit."[78] He was a worthy successor to Raymond Gibbons, '24, who exemplified all of the qualities of the award long before it was established.

STUDENT APATHY

One aspect of student life in the late 1950s was generally referred to as student apathy or lethargy. If one were to be specific about the nature of this apathy it could be defined as lack of interest in cultural and intellectual activities. Father Herman Hughes, director of the University Series, in his attempt to bring some outstanding artists and cultural productions to campus, claimed that the atmosphere on campus did not promote intellectual curiosity; there was too much conformity of dress, speech, and even slang.[79] He decried the lack of intellectual "bull sessions" and the carrying over of the dogmatic authority of the priest into the classroom and other areas. Removed from the culture of the city, the students, particularly those in the dormitories, tended to become a restricted and closed society.[80] Father Hughes later modified his criticism when five hundred students attended a John Gielgud performance.[81]

A year later, reflecting the then current criticism of Catholic education, Father Hughes regretted the lack of motivation at John Carroll. He attributed this in part to the lack of preeminent scholars on the faculty which in turn he saw as the result of the lack of professional schools.[82] Father Hughes also thought that Catholics were crippled in dialogue with themselves because of a ghetto mentality; they were not sufficiently open to the outside.[83]

THE PENDULUM OF ATHLETIC POLICY

The dreams of making a name in "big-time" intercollegiate football, born in Father Bracken's time, faded in the 1950s; not, however, before a few brief moments of glory such as the Great Lakes Bowl game with a victory over Canisius in 1948, and the victory over Syracuse in 1950. By 1954 the dream had faded completely with the formation of the Presidents' Athletic Conference. The attempt at "big-time" basketball with the assistance of Al Sutphin, Cleveland Sports promoter, was less than a glorious experience, although a certain amount of notoriety rather than fame was the result of this venture.

If there was ever a president opposed to subsidizing intercollegiate athletic teams, it was Father Welfle when he first took office. When an argument arose within the first month of his tenure over charging meals for the football team to the university during preseason practice, Father Welfle was forced to take a stand. The auditor's advice was that "as it is evident that we cannot have a football team without some form of subsidization, I recommend that football be abolished until such time as it can be resumed on a purely amateur basis."[84] Father Welfle was not willing to go as far as abolishing football, but he did announce a policy stating that the resumption of intercollegiate sports was to be on a purely amateur basis. Nevertheless, doubt still remained as to the status of athletics because of differences of opinion about what expenses could be legitimately charged to the university.[85] On 16 September 1946 Father Welfle issued what he called a clarification of policy. The first principle was that the regulations of the Ohio Conference and the North Central Association would be observed, so that there would be no outlay of money not considered legitimate by these two organizations.[86] By November 1946 the picture changed somewhat. The *Carroll News*, in referring to the report that a new coach, Herb Eisele, was to be hired said, "if the teams warrant bigger games they will get them."[87]

At the suggestion of Herb Eisele at the time he was hired, a meeting of some John Carroll football supporters was held to determine whether a group could be formed whose purpose would be to subsidize football players each year on a continuing basis so that the university would not have to subsidize them and lose money. In preparation for an address to this group, Father Welfle made a rough draft of the talk in which he revealed the department of his thinking about athletics. After dealing with football in earlier discussions with faculty, he said he came out "4 square for deemphasis." The past history of football at John Carroll convinced him that subsidization was too costly to meet the competition and produced only deficits rather than winning teams. The faculty attitude was also against subsidy. As president he inherited the present situation and felt he must "brave it." He was not against football but rather opposed to its abuses. Father Raymond Mooney, he implied, helped him to see things in a more favorable light. He rapidly became aware of an interest in football at John Carroll that he had not experienced anywhere else. He was "still stubborn" but finally found a solution. "My attitude began to change: it would be wonderful if JCU could have a WINNING TEAM." There would be a winner or there would be no team at all. The problem: where to get the players? Loss of $80,000 on football since 1917, plus tuition, ruled out any university support even if conference regulations did not. Then Herb Eisele entered the picture. This was the turning point; if successful in forming an organization that would supply and support players then Eisele would be assured the necessary resources for a winning team.[88] And so the Eisele era was launched.

Father Welfle still had some misgivings about the course he had taken as is evident from a letter sent to him by Father Mooney, a rabid football enthusiast. The letter read in part, "Since I did have some part in encouraging you to sign Mr. Eisele, I do want to reassure you, Father, that you have done nothing whatever to jeopardize the University with any accrediting association. The school is NOT subsidizing athletes."[89]

The *Carroll News* saw the signing of Eisele as the beginning of the new era to put Carroll on the map. The fame of the victorious hockey team of 1940 was to be duplicated in football and basketball. To symbolize the new era there was even an attempt to drop the name Blue Streaks.[90] "Let's be optimistic," said the student newspaper, "Let's put Carroll on the map where she belongs."[91] In the fall of 1947, after a successful start of the football season the *Carroll News* again claimed "That elusive 'New Era' of JCU athletics shows strong indication of becoming a reality."[92] Optimism was also expressed by writers in the local newspapers, particularly by sports writers who were Carroll graduates. "The old school is really going somewhere on the football field," wrote Ed McAuley of the *Cleveland News* when he was a guest writer in the student newspaper.[93]

Victory in the Great Lakes Bowl game, the addition of girl cheerleaders in 1948—which "sent another Carroll tradition rolling down the road to the land of worn out customs,"[94]—the fact that Herb Eisele was being sought by other colleges as their coach, the hiring of Jack Hearns as band director on a full-time basis, the hiring of Norb Rascher as basketball coach, and the appointment of Al Sutphin as chairman of the Athletic Board in 1949, all clearly pointed the way to potential glory. The victory over Syracuse before nearly 18,000 people at the Cleveland Stadium in 1950 seemed to mark the turning point on the road to fame.[95] The victory also had a stimulating effect on local collegiate football in general. A sportswriter in the *Cleveland News* thought it was now time to revive the Big Four so that the other colleges could keep pace with Carroll. The concern of a prominent athletic official was that, "if any more local schools drop Carroll it looks to me like Herb Eisele's squad is going to grab off the limelight by playing a major independent schedule."[96] There was, however, a note of caution based upon the previous experience of Western Reserve. The same *Cleveland News* sports article pointed out that "Reserve tried to go it alone and look where they are;" the article observed that Carroll got away with it against Syracuse but it might be difficult to keep it up.[97]

The year 1951 marked a change in the apparent upswing of the football fortunes of John Carroll. In January Father Welfle, speaking at the football banquet, said, "We shall not only keep our football, our basketball, our intramural and minor sports as we have them at present; we shall do our best to develop them as time and space permit."[98] In December Father Owen Englum, substituting for Father Welfle, who was making his annual Retreat, gave an address on football at John Carroll that indicated increasing pressure on Father Welfle to emphasize athletics. Father Englum conceded the interest of the average alumnus and a great majority of fans in high-caliber football and said he had no quarrel with the interest as long as it remained within the bounds of reason. "But when the alumni and fans become so fanatical and so powerful that they can demand 'Big Time' football with all its commercialism or get the scalp of whoever fails to provide it, then affairs are not within the bounds of reason."[99]

Father Englum then went on to say that the present system of scholarships was available for both athletes and non-athletes, with each holder of a board, room, and tuition scholarship being assigned work around the school after the season was over. "Under this system we cannot dream of so-called 'Big Time' football. . . . The fact is, unless our venerable alumni wish to mortgage their possessions; unless it is their desire to make the Athletic department supreme at the cost of the school's academic standards, all wishful thought that John Carroll should become 'Big Time' has reached the end of the rainbow."[100] Father Englum concluded his remarks by saying, "the real competition of the Cleveland backyard area, regardless of whether any of the teams are listed among the first 20 teams of the nation, or among the first 200," should be John Carroll's competition.[101] Father Englum's remarks clearly reflected a rough road ahead for alumni advocates of "Big-Time" football.

In spite of promised support, the drain on university funds for athletics was considerable in the years 1949 to 1952; the total estimated deficit for football alone for 1951–1952 was over $23,000.[102] A North Central Association's ruling in 1952 prohibited "the subsidization of athletes in any form by members of the Association"; Father Welfle wanted time to study the rule's implications for John Carroll.[103] In 1953 a warning letter from Father General concerned intercollegiate football and some of the practices associated with it. [104] Father Englum was assigned the task of examining the letter's implications for John Carroll.

Other local colleges, facing many of the same problems that John Carroll faced, were interested in reviving the Big Four. Some were interested in a broader base which would include nearby colleges. Under the circumstances

John Carroll was receptive to suggestions even though an alumni group was reported to be trying to schedule a game with the Army for 1951.[105] What resulted was the Presidents' Athletic Conference as an answer to common problems. Father Welfle presented the proposal to his consultors in March of 1954 and said it had been discussed with other presidents in the "utmost secrecy." The proposal presented "a down-to-earth amateur program of intercollegiate athletics: no scholarships, no guarantees—games restricted to members of the league and all members are to be close to Cleveland so as to involve no overnight stand."[106] The consultors agreed that the proposal should be given a fair trial.

Ironically, the "April Fool" issue of the *Carroll News* in 1954 carried an article on dropping football at Carroll. The 9 April issue confirmed that this was probably a true report. Many students when they learned the news of the formation of the PAC agreed with an editorial which said, "We are sorry to see Carroll abandon its big time football and basketball ambitions." The editorial conceded nevertheless that the new program was necessary for "practical reasons."[107] An appraisal of the PAC after five years of experience seemed to be summarized in the phrase, "it is good, but." The slumping football fortunes of the mid-1950s had been rescued by the PAC, but a totally acceptable football and basketball program had not been established.[108]

In a surprise move in 1959, a new football coach, John Ray, was hired and Eisele became director of the department of physical education. The 1959 season was the first undefeated season in the history of John Carroll football.

Basketball at John Carroll in the late 1940s and 1950s suffered most of the problems of football. The major feature was the attempt, with the assistance of sports promoter Al Sutphin, to play a big-time national schedule under the auspices of the Cleveland Arena. Sutphin sought to center the Arena schedule around a local college which would engage in playing the games he arranged. Questions as to who was in control of John Carroll basketball and whether the university even had the right to hire its own coaches surfaced during the experiment. The release of Norb Rascher and the hiring of Elmer Ripley, former coach at Georgetown, began the controversy.

Cleveland newspapers charged that the Arena ran college basketball. The *Cleveland News* reported that the opinion expressed by several leading coaches and athletes was that "College basketball is dribbling its way right off the campus into the hands of professional promoters and arena owners."[109] One unidentified midwestern coach was quoted as saying, "You have a hell of a situation in Cleveland when a coach has to please the Arena owner to keep his job. The colleges don't even own the ball they play

Top left, Father Welfle and mascot; *right,* Owen J. Englum, S.J., Treasurer, 1950–57; *Middle,* Eugene Oberst, Athletics, 1936–71; *Bottom left,* Herbert Eisele, Athletics, 1947–70; *right,* Jack Hearns, 1931–72

with."[110] Sutphin denied this, claiming that a flat sum was given to the college which enabled it to hire a higher-priced coach.[111]

Fred George, who had had winning teams in both basketball and football at St. Ignatius High School, replaced Ripley in 1951 when the latter quit because of the mismatch between the quality of the players and the demands of the schedule. In 1950 John Carroll had played eight of the leading thirty-six teams at the NIT Tournament that year. George was of the opinion that Carroll should pull out of the Arena setup because it was impossible to pursue a sound basketball program under the conditions the Arena required.[112] Father Welfle expressed his concurrence in a letter to Fred George shortly after a meeting on the subject of Arena basketball: "I, for one, am in favor of letting you take the ball and run with it."[113] By 1953 John Carroll had won three city titles and was finding it much easier to schedule games. In 1954 the PAC included basketball.

ROLE OF THE LAYMAN 1946–1960

The June 1946 issue of the *Jesuit Educational Quarterly* carried an article by Father Albert H. Poetker, former president of the University of Detroit, on laymen in Jesuit schools. The problem had arisen, he said, because of the increased enrollment of many of the Jesuit colleges. In the sense that the subject of laymen was not treated in the *Ratio* it was an entirely new problem. In 1900 the lay teacher was virtually nonexistent except in a few preparatory and commercial classes. If only the available Jesuits were used to teach the Jesuit college and university enrollment of 1946, the ratio of students to teachers would be 500 to 1; obviously large numbers of laymen were needed. Laymen were also necessary because of the growth of the professional schools in Jesuit institutions. In the liberal arts college "laymen continued to be looked upon as temporary lay assistants without clear status or academic rank and certainly without tenure; they were barely regarded as a member of a learned profession. . . . When special needs arose rectors thought first of Jesuits, . . . That situation still remains."[114]

Father Poetker contended that apart from the obvious need for laymen, they should be thought of as an integral part of any Jesuit educational institution, including liberal arts colleges and high schools, for several reasons. Among these were the need for "breadth of faculty outlook," the more general appeal laymen provided by carrying the name of the institution into areas only partly reached by Jesuits, and the role of laymen as an essential part of the Church's apostolic work.[115] It was therefore time to set up policies that included the laymen.

John Carroll was no exception to the situation described by Father Poetker. The early years of Father Welfle's presidency brought out the difficulty of trying to reconcile the role of a university financial administration which included laymen with that of the role of the consultors in running the school. Jesuits took exception to Dean Fritz Graff in particular. The specific difficulty lay in an unwieldy arrangement of four business officers of differing status, "conflicting personalities and indeterminate authority setting policy."[116] The four were Fathers Gilbert Krupitzer and William Schmidt, and Graff and Charles Cooney. As an attempted solution, it was agreed to make Father John Weber superintendent of buildings and grounds and Father Krupitzer would take over Father Weber's classes. Graff was to retain the name of associate treasurer, "but in a purely advisory capacity without jurisdiction."[117] A year prior to that action Dean Graff, in response to long-standing criticism by some Jesuits who found him arbitrary and difficult to deal with, offered his resignation from the Committee of Business Officers and as associate treasurer. After discussing the matter with a layman, Edward Eggl, Father Welfle did not accept the resignation.[118] Friction over the role and influence of Dean Graff lessened, but it was not eliminated; financial relations between the Jesuit Community and the university continued to present problems.[119]

There were difficulties not only on the administrative level, but also within the faculty itself where there was a perception by the liberal arts faculty of preferential treatment of School of Business faculty in the matter of salary.[120] An enrollment decline in the School of Business in 1951 added fuel to the fire. The decline was attributed to the rule that students in the Business School were not allowed to take extra hours; if ROTC were added to their programs there was no way they could graduate in four years. Father Englum also echoed complaints about the "high handed and uncompromising attitude" of Dean Graff.[121]

It was against this background that the twelve-month salary plan was proposed as a means of improving salaries generally. The plan extended payment of the then current monthly salary from nine months to twelve in return for required teaching in the summer session with every third summer off. Success of the plan depended on increased summer enrollment. Father Welfle got very little encouragement from his consultors to adopt the plan. Other Jesuit presidents whom he contacted were equally skeptical.[122] All of them considered the risk of building up the summer sessions to a point where they could support the plan too great.

Father Welfle, realizing that something had to be done about salaries, tried many ways to find enough money to underwrite the plan, which he felt had considerable merit. He finally asked Bishop Edward Hoban's assistance in February 1952 and reported the bishop's favorable reaction to his consultors.[123] Within a month Bishop Hoban agreed to underwrite the plan to the extent of $25,000 for each of three successive years; no publicity was to be given to the bishop's gift.[124] At the same time Father McCue proposed new salary scales which were discussed by Father Welfle with the laymen. The twelve-month plan was approved and made public in May 1952; it went into effect on 1 July of that year.

The replacement of Father Lionel Carron by a layman, Dr. Walter S. Nosal, as head of the vocational services in 1951 was seen by some Jesuits as an instance of favoring laymen over Jesuits. Father Maline did not agree with this perception, but he did think that the matter was not handled very well and that the duties of the administrator and director of the services were not too well defined.[125] Father Welfle inadvertently contributed to the controversy when, in addressing an audience of parents, he apologized that he was not able to provide Jesuit teachers for all of the students. Present on the stage at the meeting was the layman who had replaced Father Carron.

A special report to the Academic Council in 1954 pointed to the need for defining a clear area in which the faculty, both Jesuit and lay, could participate in the formation of policy.[126] One Jesuit suggested that there was danger in consulting the faculty, "because you might have such a concentration of opinion that even greater frustration would result if the majority opinion were not followed"; the same Jesuit thought that faculty meetings were for indoctrination and instruction of faculty and not for deliberation.[127] There was no agreement on how to resolve the matter of faculty participation in a monarchical structure, nor how to provide an appropriate role for the layman.

At a faculty meeting in 1956 Father Welfle detailed the terms of a Ford Grant that provided an investment fund for faculty salaries and spoke also of the increase in tuition. He did not speak directly to the question of how the grant would affect faculty salaries and was completely surprised when a delegation of the lay faculty called upon him to express their concern at this omission. As Father Welfle said, "Perhaps I have heard only the bitter comment. But about this there seems to be no doubt; the meeting was followed by expression of dismay."[128]

In a moment of frustration Father Welfle asked, "just what does an administrator have to do to secure the confidence of his faculty? The reported dismay damns my record with faint praise. Let's take a look at the record."[129] Father Welfle then proceeded to review his efforts to raise salaries and integrate the lay faculty into the life of the university, and he reviewed plans to enlarge upon that participation. Father Welfle might have added to the list of his accomplishments the only fringe benefit then available to the faculty, a social hour following the Sunday faculty meetings. In order to insure attendance at these meetings Father Welfle had promised they would be followed by an opportunity to let off steam in a convivial atmosphere. Taking over what was then the student lounge the faculty mingled in a festive mood that often provided better discussion than that of the faculty meeting itself.

Welfle saw the issue as much larger than salaries and the place of the layman in the scheme of things because, "these are only symptoms of an underlying cause, and that something lies at the very heart of Catholic school organization. Government in a Catholic school is a monarchy. It is not democratic. There is no sprinkling of authority among various groups. Other bodies are essential to the functioning of a school, but they can never be more than advisory to the president. This stark fact I cannot change."[130] He was willing to consider some kind of an organization that would represent the lay faculty, not as a grievance committee, but in an academic, professional, and social way. Father Welfle said he had presented his ideas to Dr. George Grauel and Edward Eggl, who had come to him as lay faculty delegates.

The instrument finally proposed was called the Lay Faculty Association. By the end of May 1956 the necessary revisions had been made in the constitution of the association; the consultors and the Provincial approved the final draft.[131] Two remaining issues were ultimately ironed out. Part-time faculty were to participate in social affairs and the Association was to report to the president until an executive dean was named. Father Welfle did not live to see the implementation of the Association.[132]

The role of the laymen in Jesuit institutions came into focus in preparation for the 1961 annual meeting of the Jesuit Educational Association, a meeting concerned with problems related to the resources of Jesuit institutions in relation to its goals. Departments had been asked to contribute to these discussions by answering a number of questions, one of which dealt with the Province supply of Jesuit manpower and its effect on planning for faculty in the Jesuit educational institutions. Discussion on this question at a meeting of the Department of English at John Carroll brought out some strong views held by at least one Jesuit in the university. Father Herman Hughes, a member of the department, thought that only Jesuits could give a Jesuit education and that the more Jesuits there were on the faculty the more Jesuit an institution was. Laymen had no place as administrators although necessity caused them to be tolerated on the faculty.[133] The remarks did not lift the laymen's spirits; the consultors were not amused and "deplored" the "imprudent remarks."[134]

BLUEPRINT FOR THE FUTURE

Not all planning for the future concerned itself with the internal affairs of the university; there was also the consideration of John Carroll's role in the diocese and the community. A meeting of diocesan and university officials explored the possibility of degrees and teacher certification for priests who would be teaching in the new Borromeo Seminary. After the meeting, Father John Whealon, rector of Borromeo, wrote to the Auxiliary Bishop, John Krol, that the results of the conference were very encouraging. "The Jesuits promise to do all they can to see that any priests sent to them will be granted degrees in a minimum of time and that the new Seminary will thereby be accredited as speedily as possible."[135] After Bishop Hoban was notified of the plan he wrote to Father Welfle expressing his appreciation for the Jesuits' contribution which was "only one in the long list of contributions by the Jesuit Order to the priesthood of our Diocese."[136]

As a follow-up on the work done in the enrollment study of 1955, Father Welfle spent the early summer of 1956 planning a thorough study of the entire university in order to develop a plan for the future. He engaged the services of a consultant, Thomas Gonsor, and set up an interim committee on development with Father William J. Millor as chairman. The Lay Advisory Board was to be kept in close touch with all developments. The basic questions of the study were, what is being done now? why is it being done? and what impact does it have on the students and on the community? The committee was to determine enrollment goals together with the programs and facilities needed to support them. Father Welfle announced these plans to the faculty in a letter of 9 August 1956 which said in part, "A clear look at the stern realities of the present forces the conclusion that John Carroll must put its house in order and lay careful plans for the long range future."[137]

The sudden death of Father Welfle on 17 August momentarily interrupted the planning process; but solid groundwork had already been laid. The House Diary noted that August 17 was "a dark day for John Carroll." Two days after the funeral the entry was: "community still dazed by the suddenness of Fr. Welfle's death."[138]

When the students returned in the fall, they, too, were shocked. One headline in the student newspaper read "End of an Era"; Father Welfle's death did indeed mark the end of "the initial chapter in John Carroll's modern age." The article in the *Carroll News* pointed out that the university under Father Welfle had risen "from infancy to adolescence."[139] Father Welfle's talents and service were also recognized outside of the university community; in 1955 he had been awarded the University Heights Citizen of the Year Award and he had served as president of the Ohio College Association.

During the time between the death of Father Welfle and the appointment of a new rector-president in December, Father William J. Millor, who had been appointed executive dean, was named acting president. He continued the plans started by Father Welfle and announced to the faculty at the first meeting in the fall, in his own inimitable style, "It is my onerous duty to ride herd on you fellows when it becomes necessary." A steering committee for planning was appointed and a procedure to work through department heads for the necessary reports was established. In December Father Millor announced that the Graduate Division would become the Graduate School with Father Henry F. Birkenhauer as its dean. As chairman of the Steering Committee he also announced that classrooms, the library, office facilities, and new quarters for the School of Business were the principal priorities.[140] The participation of the Lay Advisory Board of Trustees in the discussions of the Steering Committee raised a question in the mind of some Jesuits, "would the Lay Board of Trustees supplant the legal trustees?"[141] Another question raised was whether there were plans for the day school to go coeducational. At the time the answer to both questions was in the negative.

In mid-December 1956 John Carroll had a new president, Father Hugh E. Dunn, who came from the University of Detroit where he had taught sociology. In a statement to the *Carroll News*, Father Dunn praised his predecessor for leaving "a rich heritage of accomplishments and a solid foundation on which to expand our services."[142]

Father Dunn met with the Steering Committee in February 1957 to explain his approach to planning. His training as a sociologist and his experience in counseling caused him to favor the group approach which he saw as more than a process of pooling knowledge. His first goal was to determine the educational blueprint before talking about buildings. He expected the groups to impose a certain amount of self-discipline upon themselves that would result in a desire to learn from others. He wanted an awareness of the role of nonlogical factors in a person's or a group's outlook and hoped that the majority would listen and learn from the minority. It was crucial to Father Dunn's approach that everyone have the attitudes he described. Deans and other administrators had to exemplify this attitude: "we can't just tell the faculty. Ask them what they think about this point. Let them open up and 'sound off.' "[143] In a comment on Father Dunn's remarks, Father McCue wondered whether what the new president wanted was unity in total university outlook rather than uniformity or "goose stepping." Father Dunn said that Father McCue had understood correctly, unity rather than conformity or uniformity. "If there are blocked attitudes, let's face them. The real issues are a lot of latent questions in the backs of peoples minds and they are loaded with emotional thinking."[144] Father Dunn listed five stages in the group process: doubt, conversion, enthusiasm, confusion, and finally, "let's do something."[145] Father Dunn thought that the Steering Committee was still in the doubt stage. Perhaps exemplifying the type of nonlogical thinking of which Father Dunn spoke, a sheet was circulating among the faculty with the title of "The Indecisive Years." The message on the sheet was easily paraphrased: why don't we simply teach and do research as we have been hired to do and forget all the planning and self-study nonsense?[146]

At his first meeting of the Academic Council in February 1958 Father Dunn explained that his attention to many matters had prevented him from meeting earlier with the Council. The purpose of his attendance now was "to initiate steps to gear the operation for the long haul."[147] He gave his evaluation of John Carroll's internal operation as he saw it. Organizationally, he found it very difficult to break into John Carroll. The *Faculty Handbook* was inadequate as a guide because the operation seemed to rest more on "effective and efficient agreements between individuals which were never set down in writing." The previous ten years were a "bootstrap operation of heroic proportions;" no one thought much of manuals, but just pitched in and did what had to be done. If the operation succeeded it was because of the workload of a few dedicated men. Father Dunn might have added that this procedure was characteristic of the university from its beginning in 1886. Father Welfle saw the problem and took measures to solve it, and Father Dunn was going to build on that foundation.[148] John Carroll, Father Dunn thought, was unique in that it possessed all the advantages of an urban environment without any of the disadvantages.

In December 1958 Father Dunn held an administrative workshop for faculty. His goal was decentralization of the operation with the department head as the key person, operationally speaking. In 1959 the report of the Blueprint Committee was made public. The purpose of the report, which had been announced in 1956, was "to formulate a sound, comprehensive and long range policy for the development of the University in all its physical, financial and educational aspects." The report was a composite of departmental reports and other studies with emphasis on educational considerations as a first priority.[149] Although the report had many flaws and omissions it served as a springboard for the kind of planning Father Dunn had in mind. It would be replaced later by the Decade of Progress Plan of 1963 and further academic planning in 1966–1968.

Traditions: New Ones for Old
1960–1970

Colleges and universities in the 1960s could not escape the influences of the Civil Rights movement and the Viet-Nam war. For Catholic institutions the impact of Vatican II raised questions about the role of a Catholic college or university in the modern world. It was Father Dunn's lot to tackle the new problems in an atmosphere far different from that which prevailed during Father Welfle's presidency. Moreover, the two men had quite different outlooks on problem solving. Father Welfle, a historian, tended to look for long-range solutions that took into consideration past traditions; Father Dunn, a sociologist, was more concerned with the present in the context of new approaches. He might be bound by tradition to some extent, but he was not afraid to break with it. Moreover, he did not have great patience with those who did not share his vision. Father Welfle moved more slowly; Father Dunn probably attempted too much too soon. The founding German Fathers of John Carroll might have still recognized many familiar things about the college in 1960; by 1970 they would have been hard put to recognize the college they had established, and most probably they would not have approved the changes.

Curiously, an editorial in the *Carroll News* in 1961 complained of the lack of tradition at John Carroll, citing only the sophomore's "Burial Tradition" at the beginning of the school year, and it regretted the wiping out of the "beanie" tradition and the seniors losing the Stunt Night award.[1] This very limited view of tradition was repeated a year later when a student in a letter to the editor said he could find only three traditions at John Carroll—standing while the school song was sung, not walking on the school seal at the main entrance of the administration building, and Homecoming-Migration days.[2] An attempt to add a fourth to the list was made in the fall of 1962 by staging a "new annual tradition," a freshman-sophomore tug of war.[3]

In the early sixties the students had not yet fully understood that John Carroll's traditions were more firmly implanted in the academic than in the social area. For example, the requirement of Latin for the bachelor of arts degree, the eighteen hours of systematic philosophy taken in proper sequence, and an extensive core curriculum requirement. The Blueprint Report had suggested that many of these traditions be reviewed. Many were willing to dispute the claims philosophy and theology made for their former places in the curriculum, to reject the use of certain sociology courses for theology credit, to question the exemptions of the non-Catholic student from the theology requirement, and to decry a deemphasis on liberal arts in favor of vocational or pre-professional programs. The Blueprint Report warned that, "The University is hardly in a position where it can ignore these interests and [vocational] demands of the student entirely and force the student into a purely liberal type of education. At best it can attempt to reduce the vocational aspect to a minimum."[4]

THE LATIN REQUIREMENT

There had been no fundamental change in undergraduate requirements at John Carroll and other midwestern Catholic Colleges since the 1920s. The difficulty, however, in retaining the Latin requirement for the bachelor's degree was recognized by Father Samuel K. Wilson in his response to a committee recommendation in 1935 to the National Catholic Education Association that the Latin requirement be retained. Father Wilson pointed out that the Catholic women's colleges were opposed to the Latin requirement and he thought that, "for a generation at least in this region [Midwest] classical studies are going to be minimized . . . I do not think that we can continue in this region at least to insist on Latin as a pre-requisite for the A.B. unless we wish to desolate our colleges several times." Father Wilson's solution was to offer the A.B. for any course of four years of college work and "to offer at the same time an honors course which would be rigidly one of classical and vernacular letters topped off with a stiff course in philosophy."[5]

For some time at John Carroll University there had been a clamor to eliminate the Latin requirement, but not until the late 1950s was the matter given serious consideration. This change would not be accomplished without protest. A passage in the Blueprint Report of 1958 refers to the problem in language that is typical of Father Millor, then executive dean and a classicist himself:

> Remembering that it is not always kindness to silence the waiting moppet with a lollipop, the Blueprint Committee recommends careful deliberation of the consequences of a too precipitous elimination of the Latin requirement from the Bachelor of Arts curriculum. Popular favor is a capricious thing. The University should concern itself with graduating students who have received the best education John Carroll can give them. It is a common complaint that the University has been in the past too accommodating in easing the specific degree require-

ments to permit marginal students to graduate. Such a practice is academically imprudent, and, in the case at hand, if the study of Latin is determined to be an integral phase of a liberal arts training, it must be retained in the curriculum.[6]

The Jesuit Educational Association had been discussing the requirement of Latin in the Bachelor of Arts curriculum for some time and had finally set up norms for a non-Latin A.B. In 1959 when the University Catalogue Committee recommended a non-Latin A.B., Father Dunn referred the matter to the Academic Council. Within two years, as part of a number of curricular changes, a non-Latin A.B. was approved along with an "A.B. Classics." Other curricular changes were the offering of a speech major including communication arts, revision of the basic pre-engineering program to qualify students fully for entrance into engineering schools, approval of the divisional major, and revision of the mathematics sequences. The curricular revision was not accomplished without strong differences of opinion over the changes and the intent of the revision. Meetings of the Academic Council in January and February 1961 were lively sessions.[7]

PHILOSOPHY: THE INTEGRATING FACTOR

Jesuits had always made clear that the objective of their educational enterprise was the spiritual and moral training of the student. The classical course was looked upon as the ideal instrument for achieving that objective. With the demise of the classical course and introduction of electives after the 1920s, philosophy came to be looked upon as the integrating force in the curriculum. It was thought that philosophy would offset the fragmentation and secularization resulting from the introduction of electives and a wide variety of new subject matter. Philosophy came to be considered the most important subject in the curriculum. To explain the distinctiveness of John Carroll University to the public during his presidency, Father Welfle never ceased to point out the special role of philosophy as a distinctive mark of a Jesuit education.

The required eighteen hours of philosophy were the capstone of the curriculum. The structured program had applications in all subject matter areas, putting them in their proper perspective. The concern for the "whole" person was thus expressed together with requirements for spiritual and moral training. The conviction was still strong in the 1950s that this integration could stand up under any challenge; the line between Jesuit and secular higher education was clearly drawn.

The philosophy courses were taught exclusively by Jesuits who used the thesis method; those who held different views were referred to as "adversaries" and given little, if any, attention.

The philosophy taught in these courses was based on neoscholasticism and closely identified with the Catholic faith. One result of this identification was that often students transferring to a secular university found their philosophy credits unacceptable or classified as religion.[8]

THE ROLE OF RELIGION

The role of religion as a course of study was not so well defined. Even with the curricular changes of the 1920s Catholic educators debated the role of theology as an academic subject. Religion was a more accurate term to describe the content and purpose of most courses. Other terms were, "Evidences of Religion" and "Christian Doctrine." However the content was described, it was seen as relating to instruction in proper Catholic religious belief and conduct. Such courses were given less credit than other courses, usually two credits or even one. The religion courses certainly did not serve as an integrating factor in the curriculum. Students tended to look upon them as an "extra" and put less effort into the courses which presumably any ordained priest could teach. Many of the teachers of religion courses were part-time.

John Carroll was the last of the colleges in the Chicago Province to change the name of the department offering such courses from religion to theology. Not until the fall of 1956 was the change made in the hope that well trained, younger and active staffing would be forthcoming. Except on a proposed graduate level the change in name did not signify a change in the content and direction of the department.

WINDS OF CHANGE

Developments in the field of philosophy by the 1950s and the impact of Vatican II on theology raised serious questions about whether the synthesis so long established would be able to survive the attacks upon its structure. The average Catholic was hardly prepared for the confusion and frustration that followed. Departmental faculties were divided, and unfortunately there was a tendency to personalize issues. An overcrowded curriculum resulting from the increasing requirements of professional schools put the eighteen hours of philosophy and eight hours of religion in further jeopardy. Some hedging had taken place in 1936 when two sociology courses, one each in the junior and senior years, were allowed to suffice for the religion courses in those years as a result of a directive to colleges of the Chicago Province. The courses were not to be pure sociology but rather applications of religious principles to modern problems; one course dealt with the family, the other with the Papal social encyclicals. Later, seniors were permitted to substitute an appropriate course in their major field for the philosophy course in ethics in that year. Meanwhile there was continued discussion over the relationship of the ethics course to the moral guidance course in religion.

In spite of the substitution of a course in the student's major for special ethics, criticism of the eighteen-hour requirement continued. In 1962 a motion in the Student Union to reduce the requirement to twelve hours and have more electives passed unanimously. Father Schell, chairman of the department of philosophy, spoke to the Student Union about the requirement in the other Jesuit colleges; fifteen of them required more philosophy than John Carroll, only five required less.[9] Father Schell was quoted as saying, "Philosophy is a characteristic of a Jesuit education. If part of it were to be removed, distinguishing a Jesuit education from the rest would be difficult. In my personal opinion you don't have a ghost of a chance."[10] An increase in electives, he thought, would be possible.

The theology requirement suffered from a number of criticisms. The two credit hours given for theology courses was thought demeaning, but the most important issue was the controversy over the content of the courses. Father John Gerken, the new chairman of the department of theology fresh from studies under Father Karl Rahner, had sharp differences of opinion with the dean of the college of liberal arts, Father Joseph Downey, over the content and sequence of the courses. While the dean maintained he had "consistently taken the progressive view," he did not "see why college theology *must* become an adventure in avant-garde concepts."[11] The main issues were over the newer historical approach to the study of Scripture and the role of theology as an academic discipline.

A Los Angeles Workshop on Philosophy and Theology and their place in the curriculum, sponsored by the Jesuit Educational Association in 1962, supported the new directions in both of these subject areas. Father Dunn made certain that a copy of the final report of this Workshop was given to each member of the Academic Council in December 1962. The Workshop was conducted on the general principle that "The Jesuit University is set within the Church, of whose mission it is a part." This mission included the total human being implying moral, religious, and spiritual formation. "To this formation all the activities and all of the personnel of the college must contribute, according to their natures and functions within the institution."[12] This assumption meant that "The academic disciplines of philosophy and theology, which are the core of Christian Wisdom, must foster intellectual formation of the student and, in harmony with this goal and with the academic nature of these disciplines, contribute to the moral, religious and spiritual growth of the student into personal Christian maturity."[13]

The application of the Workshop's recommendation to theology meant its task was "not to construct a faith; supernatural faith is necessarily presupposed in any theologizing, properly so called. Theology rather aims at a presentation and understanding of this faith-accepted communication made by God, our Salvation."[14] The new approach viewed theology as an academic discipline belonging to the library, seminar, and classroom and not to be confused with the office of the chaplain.

In philosophy, the Workshop recommended a "variety of methods and approaches to achieving basic insights and commitments proper to the *Philosophia Perennis*."[15] It also endorsed a variety of curricular patterns and suggested that "administrators should prudently encourage the presence on our campuses of lectures and discussions involving non-scholastic philosophers."[16] Teachers were to be selected who were basically committed to "a realistic metaphysics as possible and necessary for the adequate constitution of a philosophy of created being" as well as a commitment to the "dualistic constitution and social nature of man, spirituality of the human soul, freedom of the will, moral responsibility based on a realistic metaphysics," and finally commitment to a belief in the existence of "a personal and transcendant God known by reason."[17]

An Alumni Questionnaire sent out in December 1963 gave an interesting picture of how graduates saw their philosophy courses at John Carroll when they were given in the rigid pattern of the eighteen hours. On the positive side, most felt that their philosophy was an integral part of their education; the courses were difficult and it was hard to get good grades; those surveyed did not want the number of courses reduced. On the negative side the graduates regretted that there was no acquaintance with contemporary philosophy and some teachers were criticized for not taking a personal interest in each student.[18] An examination of the departments of philosophy and of theology in 1964 showed that the philosophy department was enjoying "excellent organization" and "high morale" in studying suggested options in the philosophy program. A graduate program and opportunities for appointment of distinguished professors or visiting lecturers were thought desirable.[19]

The department of theology was divided on the issues raised by the Los Angeles Workshop, but an attempt had been made to draw up a four-year program in theology. A survey of other Jesuit colleges had revealed that no other Jesuit school required less theology than John Carroll. The chairman, Father Gerken, felt that the faculty of the department needed considerable improvement.[20]

In curricular revisions during 1965, the philosophy requirement was reduced to fifteen hours including two courses in the history of philosophy, one each in metaphysics, philosophy of human nature, and principles of moral philosophy. In theology, three three-hour courses were now required, one course in the New Testament, one in Grace, and a third from Christian Origins, and Patterns in Comparative Religions.[21]

NORTH CENTRAL REVIEW 1964

The North Central visitation in May of 1964 provided an opportunity for assessing the results of recent changes and a projection of future needs. An oral report to Father Dunn at the end of the visitation commended the clear statement of purpose, excellent planning and self analysis, salary improvement, maintenance of a reasonable service load, good condition of the physical plant, sound graduate program, and large number of graduates going on to professional schools as particularly strong points. Several areas for continued improvement were singled out. Among them was the need for stimulating faculty research, the encouragement of experiments in teaching techniques, a greater academic challenge to the students, the development of a sense of independence and responsibility among students, as well as the separation of the office of dean of student affairs from the college of arts and sciences in order to develop its independence. Of special note was the need for a reduction in the core curriculum requirements and the provision for graduation in four years in the science and business curricula.[22]

The written report commended the efforts at administrative reorganization but suggested that some role for the voice of the layman be provided. "The impression could easily be obtained that the participation of the lay faculty in plans and policies is considerably overshadowed by that of the clerical faculty. . . . the potentialities of the situation for difficulty are obvious."[23]

Curricular reform was already in progress when the North Central report was made; in the fall of 1964 ground rules for reform were established: "based on the assumption that this university intends to remain in all of its degree programs basically a liberal arts college and will not become a technical institute, that it intends to meet contemporary needs but at the same time retain its distinctive character as a Jesuit university."[24]

Within a year the curriculum had been revised and approved; the changes went into effect in the fall of 1966. The minor was dropped in the A.B. and B.S. programs, the major required a minimum of twenty-four upper-division hours, the language requirement was dropped for the School of Business, a course in fine arts was added, Advanced Placement credit was permitted, and voluntary ROTC was left for further discussion. In October 1968 further changes were worked out by a committee of the Academic Senate; these changes, which now included a requirement in the social sciences, went into effect in the fall of 1969. The core still required at least sixty-three hours. The philosophy requirement was now fifteen hours including two courses in the history of philosophy. The theology requirement remained at nine hours.

Attention now shifted more to how the courses were being taught than what was taught. An editorial in the *Carroll News* expressed the view that too many classes were "cut and dry" and implied that some course presentation methods used elsewhere should be tried.[25] The faculty response that a student gets out of a course what he puts into it brought a student response that something cannot be gotten out of nothing.[26] Teacher evaluation now became a major issue.

Administrative Reorganization

In keeping with his plan of decentralizing the administration of the university, Father Dunn had reorganized the Academic Council in 1958 so that it included all departmental chairmen, the librarian, and the registrar. The Council's function was to assist in policy matters and interpret approved policy for departmental members. In 1962 the Council produced an evaluation report on the university with conclusions and recommendations, many of which were implemented in later curricular revisions.

Two areas remained as continuing problems. One was the improvement of the quality of students and the other the need for centralized data information to provide a base for studies of such areas as student admissions and achievement. Preparation for the North Central Visitation in 1964 was an added incentive to put the house in order. In order to coordinate these efforts better, the Academic Planning Committee, composed of administrative officers, became the Executive Committee in November 1962. It was more than a change of name. The committee of administrative officers was expanded to include development and public relations officers; its purpose was to review, advise, and develop material for all facets of the university for planning purposes. Since its members were the principal officials of each division of the university, it could deal effectively with any matter that affected more than one division. The Academic Council retained its status as an advisory body in academic matters; it was directly responsible to the president. All of the activities of the university were proper agenda for the Executive Committee and reports of sub-committees were coordinated by a steering committee. After discussions in the Executive Committee, reports went to the president for approval. The principal results of the Executive Committee's work were embodied in a ten-year plan, "The Decade of Progress, 1963–1973." This plan was to be continuously updated under the supervision of the director of institutional planning. It was the Executive Committee rather than any other body that now gave direction to university development.

The Executive Committee was a matter of concern to the Jesuit consultors since it threatened to replace them in university administration. Father Dunn spoke to his consultors about this relationship and the purposes of each body in an effort to allay their fears.[27] The Executive Committee, nevertheless, with a preponderance of lay members and with its agenda prepared by Dr. George E. Grauel, director of institutional planning, continued to be the subject of much Jesuit criticism. Not only to some Jesuits, but also to many laymen, the Executive Committee seemed to be the center of the decision-making process with little or no input from the faculty. A review of the work of the Executive Committee, which fills several volumes of reports on projects, would demonstrate that no phase of university life escaped its review. Whether it be the decision to appoint a coordinator of research, to require departmental self-evaluations, to provide an annual statistics report, to set salary brackets to achieve a "B" rating on AAUP scales, to establish an Honors Program, to approve departmental programs, to establish relations with other colleges, to analyze budget reports, or to determine staff policies, these and more were topics of Executive Committee Reports. Failure of a member of the Executive Committee to do his homework for the weekly meetings was a serious matter as was absence from the meetings. Many a member felt the stinging and often silent rebukes of Father Dunn, who acted as chairman. Grauel's close association with the Executive Committee caused him to bear personally a large measure of the criticism that was directed against the committee and Father Dunn.

The change of the twelve-month salary contract to a nine-month contract is an interesting example of how some matters could be handled not so much through the Executive Committee as through Director of Institutional Planning Grauel and Father Dunn. Difficulties affecting a change from twelve to nine months were ironed out through this channel. Approval was finally given in March 1963 for the nine-month contract at the then current twelve months pay and the elimination of the summer school obligation.[28] This set to rest the growing complaints about the exhausting requirement of teaching both summer school and regular sessions in two successive years.

Although the accomplishments of the academic Council were many in the years prior to 1964, there was a growing concern that the Council was in need of some changes. As a result, a committee composed of eight members of the teaching faculty, including two Jesuits, was appointed to inquire into the purpose of the Council to determine if that purpose was being accomplished and to make recommendations for change, if necessary.[29] The study required more time than seemed suitable to effect immediate remedies. Consequently, a compromise was reached in the creation of an "Interim Academic Senate." In September 1966 the Academic Council held its last meeting and the "Interim Academic Senate" took its place. The new body, designed to serve as a means of faculty participation in decision making while more effective means were being explored, was composed of the president, ex-officio, the academic vice-president, who was to act as chairman, the chairman of each department, and the deans of the college of arts and sciences, evening college, graduate school, school of business, and student affairs. There was also a significant change in the manner of selecting chairmen of departments; they were to be recommended by department consensus to the deans who would in turn make recommendations to the academic vice-president. The term of the departmental chairman was now limited to four years; successive terms were possible. Members of the new Senate were to represent the views of their departments, both majority and minority as well as their own. The president was to accept the recommendations of the Senate or give adequate reasons for his refusal to do so. The basic function of the Senate was to make recommendations in academic matters to the president and the Board of Trustees on behalf of the faculty.[30] The issue of student representation on the Senate was not settled until 1968 when two students were admitted. In 1969 the number was raised to five.

This Senate was busy in the years following its creation with procedural and curricular matters, but perhaps one of its more important achievements was the setting up of a student counseling system. Against objections originally made to the cost and effectiveness of such a system, some members of the Senate persisted in so presenting the case for the counseling arrangement that it was eventually approved.

In 1966 the Executive Committee like the Academic Council underwent a change; it became the University Council with a smaller membership. It now included the president, the vice-presidents, director of institutional planning, and two elected faculty members. On paper its function was the same as that of the former Executive Committee, but it operated with much less effectiveness and more as a review committee than a working committee. It did not originate projects and met only when the president wished to consult it. The faculty members of the University Council were often frustrated because it did not meet regularly or because when it did meet they felt inadequately briefed on the matters discussed.

THE FACULTY SERVICE COMMITTEE

In 1961 faculty morale had reached a low point. The exodus of a number of teachers whom students considered "top notch educators" was cited as proof that the university did not have the ability to retain an excellent faculty.[31] An editorial in the *Carroll News* placed some of the blame for these departures on the students themselves. "The immature attitude of many students is no small factor," the editorial claimed, "in the decision of many of these professors to quit John Carroll. To a great extent the students are not willing to support excellence."[32] It would be an oversimplification of the reasons for these departures to accept the student comments as full explanations.

In electing a new president in 1961, the Lay Faculty Association sought to raise basic questions about the role of the Association, which had been approved for three-years in 1956 and was now beginning the third year of a three-year renewal of that approval in 1958. Meetings between the new president, Dr. Robert Yackshaw, and Father Dunn provided opportunities for the discussion of the role of the Association in addressing faculty problems. In a letter to Father Dunn in June 1961, Yackshaw explained that he had discussed the role of the Lay Faculty Association with twenty-three members of the faculty including three Jesuits and that he was now ready for another meeting.[33] Areas of concern were the advisory area for the lay faculty, lay faculty thinking about Grauel's role in institutional planning, the future of the college, lay faculty-Jesuit relations, faculty morale, and *Faculty Handbook* problems. Yackshaw said, "In fact if we can't find a proper advisory area for the Lay Faculty Council, I want to be told that as soon as possible; or if you prefer departmental chairmen to run the [academic] council, I want to be told that as soon as possible."[34]

After the meeting with Father Dunn, Yackshaw wrote,

> I believe I got the impression you wanted to convey to me. You wanted to make it quite clear that you would cooperate in every way with the Lay Faculty Council, and that you sincerely hoped that we would be able to accomplish something that would be for the good of the University and for the good of the men. *But* you wanted to be sure that I understood that you wanted no wild-eyed 'malarky' and that I would convey to the men that you were disappointed and discouraged with certain unjustified attitudes.[35]

In 1961 a report to the members of the Lay Faculty Association, Yackshaw presented an agenda for the fall meeting of the entire Association and also a review of his talks with faculty and Jesuits about the future of the Association.[36] Yackshaw saw the future role of the Lay Faculty Association as that of a "responsible critic." In an informal interview with Father Dunn, Yackshaw reported that he had read to him the criticisms made by faculty members, including two Jesuits. The "aloofness" of the Jesuits from the lay faculty was attributed to the "*old* Jesuit attitude that the laymen are naturally inferior," and that in his infrequent appearances before the faculty Dunn was "not saying anything they wished to hear," reported Dr. Yackshaw.[37] Other criticisms were listed, including what some considered the waste of time involved in all the committee meetings when the faculty wasn't sure that such effort was considered important. In fact, the faculty was not sure what Father Dunn was aiming at and his "aloofness" was frequently taken as contempt when it was not interpreted as indicating Jesuit superiority to laymen. "This aloofness would break down if all were seen as *equally* involved in improving their respective departments. But barriers will remain as long as preferential treatment is given."[38] This latter reference was undoubtedly related to Father Hughes's remarks on the superiority of Jesuits in the English department meeting the previous February. At the same time Father Dunn was accused by many of the Jesuits of showing preference toward laymen.

Yackshaw suggested that one way to give the Lay Faculty Association more prestige was to put the members of the Lay Faculty Council on the Academic Council. Discussion of this and other suggestions went "round and round" with no resolution.[39] Yackshaw reported he "backed away" from Father Dunn's request to pin-point the breakdown in communications, questioning whether it was at the dean's or departmental level.[40]

The first general meeting of the Lay Faculty Asssociation since 1958 was held 6 October 1961. The minutes of the meeting refer to many "spirited moments" and the "usual amount of misunderstanding"; the meeting at times "degenerated into an attack on the Association president."[41] It is ironic that the minutes also record that one good thing was accomplished, the passage of a resolution of gratitude to Father Dunn, who had made notable improvements in organization of the University.[42]

Prior to this meeting, Dunn had called to his office four laymen to whom he expressed his concern about the unfounded criticism that was circulating. Father Dunn was particularly annoyed with the idea of the Association claiming to be a "responsible critic" standing off and playing no part in the decision-making process. He made it clear that he wanted this misunderstanding corrected and his views explained at the October meeting. He also wanted it made clear that, as faculty, he wanted no distinction between laymen and Jesuits; for this reason he considered that the very name Lay Faculty Association contributed to the maintenance of a false division in the faculty. It was clear to those at this meeting with Father Dunn that he was visibly disturbed by the recent exchanges with the Lay Faculty Association.[43]

Following the October meeting of the Lay Faculty Association a questionnaire was circulated among members of the Association to get views on academic issues. One concern expressed in some of the answers was that graduate assistants were replacing some full-time faculty who had left, a concern due in part to the antipathy of some faculty members towards graduate assistants.

Father Dunn dissolved the Lay Faculty Association in May 1962. In its place he created a Faculty Service Committee. In a letter to Yackshaw,

Dunn reviewed the past year's activities of the Lay Faculty Association, observing that the university was now more structured than in 1956 when the Association was first formed; the Association now had no clear-cut function; the Association was "divisive of the faculty and this in the pejorative sense."[44] Father Dunn rejected its suggested role of "responsible critic" because that implied denying the faculty a role in policy making, which would represent retrogression. Other roles for the Association were barred because of the nature of its constitution. The suggestion that the Lay Faculty Association should report directly to the president to provide him with "uncensored thinking" was a "blanket indictment of all department heads" and "contrary to the facts of experience in meetings of the Academic Council."[45] Other suggested functions of the Association would result in duplicate organizational structures. Thus no function seemed to be left for the Lay Faculty Association. Father Dunn felt that the trend in recent years of greater faculty participation should be continued. He was, therefore, constituting a new group designed to give even greater faculty participation; the specific type of organization was to develop from further discussions and experience.[46] This action formally dissolved the Lay Faculty Association and made it clear that the term "faculty" now officially included layman as well as Jesuits.

The new organization, the Faculty Service Committee, an interim title, held its first meeting in May 1962. Its basic objective was "To function as an advisory vehicle for effective interchange of ideas, questions, problems, and/or general information between the University faculty and the president through the exercise of responsibilities" in certain areas.[47] Included in these responsibilities was the duty to make sure that proposals made by faculty members were directed to the proper channels, to give information on policy, to promote faculty understanding, to inquire about the progress of proposals, to obtain faculty views on problems that arose, to arrange social events for the faculty, to meet at least monthly and submit minutes of each meeting to the president. Present at the first meeting were Father Charles Castellano, chairman, Father Joseph Henninger, Doctors Jean Cummings and John Gersting, and Robert Valyo; all were appointed by the president. At the request of the consultors, minutes of the Faculty Service Committee's meetings were to be submitted to the Jesuit Board "to keep the policy making body familiar with the needs and working of the lay [*sic*] faculty."[48]

THE MATURING STUDENT

The John Carroll campus in the 1960s shared many of the student issues which were making national headlines, but the student response was less

Francis A. Jones, Vice-President for Business, 1963–72

Herbert H. Kennedy, Assistant to the President, 1952–69

Robert F. Black, Chairman, Advisory Board of Lay Trustees, 1964–67

Joseph O. Schell, S.J., President, John Carroll University, 1967–70

Hugh E. Dunn, President, John Carroll University, 1956–67

extreme even though it might not have seemed so to those on campus. The 1960s began on the upbeat. In an effort to avoid the kind of freshman initiation of previous years, a new program called "Hello Week" was introduced in the fall of 1961. An editorial in the *Carroll News* praised the manner in which the week was conducted.[49] In fact, the week, which ended with a push-ball contest, was termed a great success by nearly everyone. The often unfortunate presence of the Kangaroo Court of earlier years was not in evidence during the week. The absence of "beanies" was regretted, but the "duffer" was considered a worthy substitute. Even the dean of the college of arts and sciences, Father Joseph T. Downey, praised the new style of orientation week. Father Dunn was quoted as saying, "Personally, I cannot think of a better possible start for our 75th anniversary."[50]

At a meeting of the Carroll Union in October 1960 which Father Dunn attended, the president was questioned about the planned demise of "Hell Week." Members seemed more than miffed that they had not been informed about the changes that were to be made. Father Dunn replied that the former " 'Hell Week' was always a bad start for the school year. Some of the activities of the week have been a little short of sadism."[51] Father Dunn also pointed out that the decision to abolish the Kangaroo Court was made more than a year earlier; apparently, he observed, some people took it for granted that the decision would be rescinded. The success of the new style orientation in 1961 quieted some of the more vocal critics.

A half-hour before the 1960 Student Union meeting, Father Dunn was presented with a new constitution for the Union; he refused to comment on it at the meeting because of the short notice. He cautioned the Student Union on the use of the term "administration" as a vague "catch all" term.[52] He then went on to urge the Union to engage in more positive thinking.

> The Code of the Carroll man is a project of the Union not realized yet. If you want a door that leads to better understanding between the administration and the students, this is it. We have not yet solved the problem of the place of student government, but may I suggest that your executive committee has not aimed high enough? Set a positive goal, a goal that can be accomplished only through the Union.
>
> We have an unsolved problem in communications. Human limitations apply to the officers of the administration as much as to the Union. We have to live with realities. We can improve, you can improve, we shall try, you will try. The interpretation of other people's motives is very dangerous.[53]

In response to a student criticism expressed as, "We propose, they dispose," Father Dunn answered, "I would like to reiterate and re-emphasize my interest in having vigorous student government at Carroll. We have fewer problems than most universities."[54] The Union approved, in the spring of 1961, a "Code of the Carroll Man" which set appropriate standards for student behavior.

Alpha Sigma Nu sponsored the first annual President's Convocation in September 1962 as a means of providing better communication between the president and the students. Father Dunn spoke of the responsibility for using one's talents with motivation to do more than stay out of the dean's clutches.[55] The following year Father Dunn touched a similar theme, speaking of the "tyranny of the average." He also emphasized the training of the whole man expressed in terms of real understanding, shared loyalties, responsibilities, and beliefs.[56]

Father Dunn often dwelt on a theme that was recurrent since the enrollment study of 1955: if the pool of students were as large as predicted, why should not John Carroll be selective and raise standards? This theme ran counter to the traditional one that John Carroll had an obligation to open its doors to Catholic students and raise them to the limit of their abilities whatever they might be. There was no real resolution of the issue but an attempt was made to accommodate both views as the records of the Academic Council and other bodies indicate.

The "Evaluation Report of John Carroll" prepared by the Academic Council in 1962 undertook to analyze the graduates from 1950 to 1961.[57] Of 3,328 graduates in those years 330 had received honors; 198 graduated cum laude, 120 magna cum laude, 12 summa cumma laude. In the School of Business 5 percent of its graduates had received honors while in the combined college of arts and sciences and Evening College almost 12 percent received honors. There were no previous studies on admissions so the Academic Council set out to develop studies that would provide enough data to chart a course toward upgrading admission standards. The consultors were also concerned with higher standards for admission, even though there was evidence that the attempt at higher standards was having a financial impact. "Income has slacked somewhat because of the University's effort to upgrade the caliber of her students," recorded the consultor's minutes.[58] There may have been another explanation for the slightly lower admission rate. The Academic Council was of the opinion the "a lack of reputation for 'name' programs, departments, or even students deters or, at least does not help attract the better students."[59]

Among a series of Academic Council reports in the 1961–1962 year was one dealing with the Mass and Sacramental life on campus. The report stated that

the university does not consider the attainment of a degree the ultimate goal of the student's college experience; a more desired end is the formation of moral and ethical principles which will enable the student to meet the challenges of his chosen way of life. The university provides explicit regulations which each student is responsible for knowing and observing.[60]

After listing the existing opportunities for participation in religious exercise, the report recommended more vigorous efforts to promote student responsibility, more closed retreats, and greater student initiative in accepting self-rule. The issues raised involved questions about the level of Christian maturity of the students. A student questionnaire revealed that while students were aware of regulations concerning Mass, retreats, and reception of the Sacraments, they were aware to a much lesser degree of the role of good example.[61] An analysis of the responses in the questionnaire by several Jesuits revealed that there was a significant segment of the student body whose answers raised the question, "Are some of Ours [Jesuits] uncouth and gauche in courtesy???"[62] About two-thirds of the students were considered practicing Catholics; objections to compulsory attendance at Mass and retreats came up frequently. The general conclusion was that something was wrong at John Carroll; the weakness seemed to be that personal conduct was not what it should be.[63]

The vulgarities and excesses of Stunt Night in 1961 are a case in point. As a result of that performance, one student was dismissed. In the future, any class skit which the judges deemed too vulgar would exclude that class from the following year's competition. For 1962 Executive Dean Millor had limited Stunt Night to the lampooning of students and organizations; this order had come shortly before the scheduled performance and caused a motion to be made in the student Union to cancel Stunt Night altogether. A bitter fight ensued over passage of the motion. When Father Millor contended that students in the past had demonstrated their lack of maturity to handle Stunt Night properly, students felt that they were being persecuted by an "all-powerful administration."[64] Others were willing to admit that "through abuses the program has completely lost contact with decency and objectivity. There is no room at John Carroll for individuals who place petty satisfaction above the good of the University."[65] The Student Union voted not to cancel Stunt Night and decided that it would lampoon current events.[66]

The Stunt Night performance in 1965 was considered a "concrete landmark in student responsibility, for the Student Union has definitely proved its ability to censor class scripts without the assistance of the Administration".[67] The writer in the student newspaper praised the peformance which was "without recourse to gaudy slapstick or biting bitterness" in professionally satirizing conformity "with a message that can only prompt all members of the Carroll community to reevaluate their roles in the system."[68]

A studet-sponsored panel in April 1964 examining the Catholic position on birth control tended to generate more heat than light. Clerical and medical representatives formed a panel of which the students were to ask questions. Differences of opinion reflected emotional rather than rational behavior. Student opposition to an unquestioning acceptance of the Church's position was strong.

A month after the panel was held, the North Central report of the 1964 visitation was released. Its comments on student life on campus stated,

> The visitor to the John Carroll campus cannot help but get the feeling that student life is still governed by patterns more appropriate to an earlier age in higher education. It is probably time that adequate recognition be given to the greater maturity of contemporary students. . . . They should be enouraged to take a responsible part in more spheres of their own extra-class life. . . .
> To a surprising extent the exercise of their initiative is limited, and they do not have available a wide scope of opportunities to learn the risks and costs of their own ventures.
> The students generally appear to be loyal to their school and academically conscientious. But they do not give the impression of being overextended in their learning capacities. Perhaps a greater challenge and a higher reach would be in order for a richer and more fruitful academic experience.[69]

A Student Personnel Workshop in July 1965, held under the sponsorship of the Jesuit Educational Association, reviewed the various student problems at Jesuit colleges and universities. The conference's report strengthened the belief of the Academic Council in the need for greater professional preparation for student personnel staff. A task force was set up to examine the local campus problems. In 1968 a vice-president for student affairs, Dr. James M. Lavin, was appointed. In making the announcement, President Joseph O. Schell said, "it is evident that students have become an increasingly assertive force on the American college campus. The importance of the ability of the University to channel this force toward constructive, not destructive change has never been more apparent."[70] The office of Student Affairs was now taken out of the Academic Division and set up as a separate and independent division.

A student bill of rights had a high priority on the Student Union agenda even though the initial positions in an early draft were considered too extreme by the faculty.[71] In 1970 another bill made its way into the Student Union, the third one since 1967. Action on it was again delayed.

On a more positive note many things were happening to improve campus life. In 1968 a rathskeller, managed by students, was approved and located in the basement of the original chapel foundation. A chapel was included in the Fritzsche Religious Center which, in 1970, occupied the refurbished former quarters of the School of Business on the upper floor of the "Pink Barn." Soundproofing between the two levels was no problem as long as only background music was played in the rathskeller. When the juke-box was installed, better soundproofing was required. An FM radio station with FCC licensing as an educational station was approved in 1966. In 1968 with the university matching the Student Union financial support, the station began operation. In 1967 a Student Community Action Program aimed at raising the students' awareness level of current social issues and the need for social service was begun. This program was part of a broader attempt to deal with issues outside the curriculum. The next step was to engage in social action, such as the lettuce boycott and peace movement. "Freedom University" was an extension of such action.

All the activity that seemed to be going on caused the *Carroll News* to comment in January 1969 that, "Within recent months a new spirit has been circulating around campus. It's a feeling that things are really changing."[72] The fact that only one-third of the students had participated in a recent teacher-course evaluation was cited as indicating that there was still much room for improvement: "The malady that affects the school isn't administration paternalism—it's student inertia. Here at Carroll the students don't have to fight the administration for their rights."[73]

In 1970 editorial comment in the *Carroll News* indicated that things were far from satisfactory and questioned whether the current spirit of the administration was totally acceptable. There was still need, the editorial claimed, to deal with the student as an individual, to improve the athletic program with at least one sport on a major intercollegiate status, to continue revision of the curriculum, and to put faculty and students on the Board of Trustees. "Some say the administration is inert," claimed the writer. "Perhaps their alleged inaction in the committee rooms is typified by their lack of any response in print."[74] The basic criticism seemed to be that the administration said "no" but never "why not."[75]

THE SPORTS SCENE IN THE 1960s

When the students were not pushing for voluntary ROTC, which was approved for the fall of 1969, or winning awards for the *Carroll News*, of which there were several in the 1960s, or attempting to get funds for the erection of a statue of John Carroll to commemorate the 75th anniversary in 1961, or trying to arrange socials with the women's colleges, or seeking open dormitories, much of their activity and interest turned to athletics, both intramural and intercollegiate.

Football and basketball had their ups and downs during the 1960s. After a losing football season in 1960, three successive winning seasons included two undefeated seasons, fifteen consecutive victories, and two PAC championships, all under coach John Ray. A break-even season in 1964 under a new coach, William Dando, followed. In 1965 Jerry Schweickert took over the coaching chores and finished 5–1–1. After a few mediochre seasons things improved in 1969 when a 7–1 overall record brought Carroll its fourth PAC championship since the conference was formed. The 1970 team finished with a 2–5–1 record.

Basketball fortunes improved somewhat in the 1960s. John Keshock in his nine seasons as basketball coach compiled a 75–67 record, making him the "winningest basketball coach in JCU history."[76] Keshock succeeded Eisele as chairman of the department of physical education upon the latter's retirement in 1970.

The wrestling team under coach Tony De Carlo did very well, taking four successive PAC titles between 1967 and 1970. There were enough successes in intercollegiate athletics during the period to whet student and alumni appetites for bigger and better teams. There were even momentary thoughts of abandoning the PAC. The complaint in 1969 was that the PAC was "a good league, but certain of the schools are allowing their intercollegiate athletics to deteriorate."[77] More sober reflection revealed that Carroll had not won a football title since 1963, had never taken a cross-country or soccer title, a track or tennis championship, and no basketball title since 1960. Carroll had not competed in baseball or swimming. The conclusion had to be that there was no basis for the feeling that Carroll was too good for the PAC.[78]

The brightest spot in the 1960s was Tim Wood, a Silver Medal Olympic winner. His career provided good publicity for Carroll. It is curious that with all the efforts to achieve a measure of glory in football and basketball it was on the rink and on the mat that a good measure of the long sought fame was achieved.

A new athletic field was made possible through the generosity of the John C. Wasmer family; Wasmer Field was ready for use in 1968. An athletic hall of fame was established in 1964 with Father Bracken, Gene Stringer, and Richard Walsh the first members to be installed.

For sports not on the official list as sponsored by the athletic department budget, the Athletic Club was a device for providing an outlet for those who wished to engage in such sports. The Rugby Club was often a center of controversy. One problem was the use of facilities for practice by a club which had a low priority in such instances. An attempt to form a baseball club was made in 1969, but the backers could secure neither funds nor a practice field. Some forty students were willing to revive the sport, which had been a major one in the period around World War I.

"COLLEGE FOR MEN" TRANSFORMED

Bishop Gilmour often referred to St. Ignatius College as the "college for men," and so it remained officially until 1968. Nuns attended Saturday classes from the mid-1920s on, and the Evening College and the Graduate Division in the 1930s also admitted women, but the college of arts and sciences was open only to men, at least in theory. Talk of coeducation at John Carroll, therefore, centered around the admission of women on an equal basis with men to the college of arts and sciences. As early as the 1940s coeducation had been an issue. An article in a local newspaper reported that "John Carroll University in University Heights, for 55 years a men's institution, is gradually becoming coeducational."[79] The changes, the writer observed, were being effected through the school's extension division in which women were registered. If a course could not be secured in the Evening Division, then room was found for female students in the day college.

There was not whole-hearted acceptance of this practice, called "guesting," nor for that matter, the idea of Jesuits teaching women in their own institutions. A request from Notre Dame College in 1943 for Father Donnelly to supply some Jesuits to teach there brought the response that there was "no objection on the part of the Society to that sort of work, it being about the only legitimate way we may engage in the teaching of women."[80] Referring to the teaching of women in the evening classes at John Carroll, Father Donnelly explained to the consultors that "the teaching of women is not in accord with the spirit of our Institute and contravened a general directive and order given him personally by Father Maher, the [American] assistant."[81] Father Donnelly was of the opinion that the Jesuits gained "neither financially nor in prestige by continuing the night school"; he also saw no "real contribution to the common good since the same courses could be obtained elsewhere."[82] As a result the night classes were discontinued in 1943, "at least for the present."[83] Father McCue thought that some exception should be made for those hospital nurses whom the university was to a degree bound to serve. Father Daniel Cronin, director of the extension courses, wanted to drop Saturday classes as well as evening classes since the former were more bother than the night classes. Evening classes were reopened in 1944.

At the time Father Donnelly raised the issue of the Jesuits teaching women in 1943, John Carroll University had already given eighty-two undergraduate degrees to women who had attended the Summer, Evening, and Saturday Sessions. There were fourteen lay women in the group, which was composed mostly of nuns. The first female graduates were three nuns in 1927, Sisters M. Ferrer Conroy, O.S.D., Mary Kieran Dowd, H.H.M., and Mary Thomasina Lynch, H.H.M. The first laywomen to graduate were Jennie Dignan and Agnes Loretta Meehan in 1936. In 1942 the first female to graduate in business administration was Antoinette Antoncic.

In 1946 Father McCue wished to consider the advantages of coeducation in the School of Business. He saw no violations of existing regulations since women were permitted to attend professional schools. Father McCue also thought that a working agreement with Notre Dame and Ursuline colleges could permit the girls to attend the first two years at those colleges and then enter the School of Business at John Carroll. Father Welfle, Father Donnelly's successor, promised to contact the Provincial but nothing developed.[84]

Except for an increasing number of evening students who seemed to find the courses they needed available only during the day, the official status of coeducation remained unchanged as the Blueprint Committee took up the subject in 1958. The Committee acknowledged the fact that what was needed was more a "question of liberalization than one of radical innovation"; the question really was, is such a liberalization desirable?[85] The Committee made two recommendations: extend the Evening College classes through the afternoon hours, and appoint a committee to examine the question of undergraduate coeducation in "extensive detail."[86]

Support for coeducation was found in a local study of higher education in the Cleveland area on the available facilities for growth in Cleveland by the Cleveland Commission on Higher Education. The opportunities available to women were not likely to meet the expected demand nor was there any planning to provide these opportunities according to the study. If John Carroll were to help fill the need it was considered that the appeal of John Carroll to women would be to those Catholic women who were choosing schools other than Notre Dame and Ursuline, the local women's colleges. Also, there was "fairly general opinion that coeducation would greatly enhance the cultural tone and student conduct at John Carroll."[87]

The influx of graduate assistants, mostly women, in the years after 1958 gave the impression that coeducation had arrived without any discussion of policy. This impression was reinforced when graduate assistants taught some undergraduate classes, and seemed to be confirmed especially by a front-page spread appearing in a local newspaper featuring a large picture of one of the assistants, who happened to have been "Miss Fiesta" of San Antonio.[88] The registration of a coed from Montana in the School of Business in 1962 sparked renewed campus concern about coeducation. The School of Business, which had been as the *Carroll News* put it coeducational "in theory," was "now coeducational" in fact.[89]

Neither the Academic Council nor the Executive Committee met the question of coeducation "head on" in spite of numerous opportunities to do so. When a study of space utilization in 1962 revealed that the afternoon periods from two o'clock on were rarely used, Father Dunn gave his approval for the extension of Evening College hours to two o'clock in the afternoon. The extension permitted the Evening College to offer a full undergraduate program from two in the afternoon to ten in the evening, thus theoretically eliminating guesting in the day school.[90] The policy on coeducation was, according to Father Dunn, not to

> envision unlimited expansion at Carroll. Our aim is to round out our facilities and get them in balance. If coeducation is introduced, it will be mainly to increase quality and not to add to enrollment numbers. Our eventual enrollment capacity will probably not exceed 6500 for all four units, including some 3500 full-time day students.[91]

What Father Dunn claimed was policy was not what many on campus, including his Jesuit colleagues, thought was being carried out. The public announcement of the new Evening College hours in the *Cleveland Press* on 13 November gave many the impression that the determination to make the day-school coeducational had already been made.[92] The headline "Bring on the Girls, is the New Carroll Slogan," did nothing to calm the fears of those who opposed coeducation, especially when the article stated that, "John Carroll has taken a long stride toward becoming a coeducational institution."[93] An article in the *Carroll News* considered the story as "one more link in the chain of stories unleased by the Public Relations Department in order to create what they think is a desirable 'girl' image for Carroll."[94] The fact that the newspaper article appeared before the announcement of the change of Evening College hours was made to faculty did not help; to the opponents of coeducation there was clear evidence of a conspiracy to bring it about.

The newspaper story carried neither the real reason for the extension of Evening College hours nor Grauel's statement as dean of the Evening College that not many full-time women would be added. The *Carroll News* also ignored the real reasons and was convinced that what motivated the "girl push" of recent years was the attempt of the Public Relations Department to change the "seminary on the hill" image.[95] The reporter observed that "this image has all but faded and is maintained by only a few of the 'old guard' who probably wouldn't approve of the 'girl' image either." The desired image, according to the writer, "should be one of an educated and cultured student body" and not that of

> a bunch of lonely college men seeking female companionship. . . . No twisted or exaggerated stories would be needed to present the intellectual and cultural side of Carroll to the press. It would only have to be a true picture of what is happening.
>
> In our midst we have many nationally and locally prominent faculty members, scores of talented students engaged in useful activities, the best small college football team in the country, and a University Series that yearly brings world famous performers to our stage.

These are the things that should be capitalized on to the fullest extent when obtaining publicity for the University.[96]

The blame for the undesired publicity was not placed entirely on Public Relations, but also on other administrators for not seeing to it that the Public Relations Department was fully informed of what the school policy was.

In May 1963 a subcommittee of the Academic Council recommended that "coeducation not be extended to the college of Arts and Sciences;" a minority report indicated that the recommendation was incomplete because it implied that coeducation was not to be extended "*at any time or for any reason.*"[97] Meanwhile, the argument continued with one Jesuit challenging the assumption that coeducation would improve the quality of the student body. He also noted that the majority report of the Academic Council numbered only nineteen lines while the minority report numbered fifty-eight lines.[98] Continued study of coeducation was urged by the Academic Council as the number of coeds in day classes increased under the "guesting privilege" in spite of limitations on its use.

The *North Central Report* in 1964 suggested that a separate women's college might be an answer to coeducation.[99] This suggestion was ignored while controversy on coeducation continued in the student newspaper with considerable space given to the subject.[100] A student poll in 1965 brought out all of the aspects of the controversy but indicated that most students saw the inconsistencies in the official policy and wished for a resolution of the issue. The editor of the *Carroll News* was so strongly opposed to coeducation that he suggested the following epitaph for the university: "John Carroll University, an institution of higher learning for men, 1886–1965."[101]

One aspect of "creeping coeducation," increasing use of the "guesting privilege," led to a change in deans of the Evening College in 1965. George Grauel was now to devote full-time to institutional planning; he was replaced as dean by Donald Gavin who had been chairman of the department of history since 1946. "Guesting" was presumably to be restricted, but it was not considered good policy to turn away well-qualified applicants because they were women. With Father Dunn's tacit approval, an increasing number of such applicants were accepted, resulting in even more women "guesting" in day classes. Although the local Catholic women's colleges disputed the fact, most of these applicants wanted to attend a Jesuit college and would go to state colleges rather than a Catholic women's college if they were not admitted to John Carroll.

A program in 1965 for approximately fifty women in a nurse's program at a local hospital, Cleveland Metropolitan General, registered the women in the Evening College but scheduled all of their courses in the day to avoid conflict with their hospital schedules. The only consolation for opponents of coeducation was that the nurses were there for only two semesters;[102] this view tended to overlook the fact that a new group replaced them every third semester.

In 1966 complaints continued about the increasing number of women students, although there was also an element of resignation. Even the *Carroll News* editor admitted that "they are here and will probably continue to grow in numbers during the ensuing years."[103] The Student Union in May 1966 passed a resolution that "John Carroll is a coeducational University."[104] The *Carroll Quarterly* in 1967, for the first time in its twenty-year history, had a woman, Susanna O'Neil, appointed to an editorial post. A women's Glee Club was formed in the same year. Also in 1967 the Evening College became University College because, as Father Dunn said, "The name 'Evening College' no longer adequately describes the nature of the school."[105] University College was to add programs for non-degree students and continuing education. The logical effect was the registration of women in the College of Arts and Sciences for degree programs.

Shortly after he became president, Father Schell reported to the Jesuit Board of Trustees that Bishop Issenman had indicated "he thought John Carroll University should be the Catholic college of Cleveland for both men and women."[106] In December 1967 Father Schell announced to the Jesuit Board of Trustees "that the University's proposal to become coeducational had been brought to the attention of the Provincial consultors; that the proposal was now being considered in Rome."[107] Father Schell had also informed the presidents of Notre Dame and Ursuline colleges of the change. By January 1968 the requested approvals from the Province and Rome had been received and Father Schell announced that in September 1968 the college of arts and sciences would be officially coeducational.[108] The Academic Senate approved the changes.[109] Mary Kirkhope became the first dean of women, and in the spring of 1968, Sandy Cervenak became the first female editor of the *Carroll News*. In the fall forty-eight women registered in the College of Arts and Sciences occupied the self-contained first floor of Murphy Hall.

INTERINSTITUTIONAL RELATIONS

During the year 1962–1963 the Academic Council explored the possibility of cooperation among the Catholic colleges of Cleveland, then turned its findings over to the Executive Committee for some form of implementation.[110] As a first step, Father Dunn announced a policy of free tuition for students of Borromeo and St. Mary seminaries, which he said reflected "our avowed purpose by assisting education in the Diocese of Cleveland."[111] All priests, nuns, and brothers in the diocese were to receive a one-third remission of tuition.

During the summer of 1963 agreement was reached by all of the officials of Catholic institutions of higher education in the diocese to work together on interinstitutional planning. The specific instrument through which this planning was to be accomplished was called the Liaison Committee. The committee was to establish "an atmosphere and attitude of reciprocal help out of which can grow collaborative measures tending to academic improvement, financial economy, operational efficiency, and public prestige."[112] The Liaison Committee served its purpose from 1963 to 1966 when a review of its work indicated the need for a more formal structure.[113] Grauel, John Carroll's representative on the committee, suggested the need for more basic planning. It was agreed that future meetings would be devoted to the submission and discussion of the separate plans of each college, but Grauel's death in February 1967 temporarily halted the work of the Liaison Committee. Before Father Dunn left office in the fall of 1967, he obtained the necessary funds and arranged for consultants with national experience and reputations in higher education to come and make recommendations in what was called a feasibility study. The Liaison Committee had laid the groundwork through agreements on complete transfer of credit, shared use of classes, interchange of faculty, joint social and extra-curricular activities, a common library card, and the sharing of lecturers.

The committee of consultants, consisting of Dr. Theodore Distler, Dr. Manning Pattillo, Sister Ann Ida Gannon B.V.M., and Monsignor William L. Baumgaertner, presented a report in December 1967 which concerned itself with the direction the institutions might take and envisioned a "structure for Catholic Higher education in Cleveland in which each college or seminary, while retaining its special character, will become part of a larger complex in which a board, legally incorporated and broadly representative of the participating institutions and community, will determine overall policy."[114] The first step was intended to be the establishment of strong boards of trustees in each institution. A committee of presidents of the institutions was formed and continued to meet to discuss common problems, but the goal the consultants had in mind was never attained.

As might have been expected, not all of the presidents were completely receptive to the recommendations of the feasibility committee. Institutional autonomy as it had been in the Corporate College days of the 1930s was a major stumbling block. The training of elementary teachers was also a thorny issue as it had been in the 1930s. Even the Liaison Committee which attempted to do something about allowing institutions other than St. John College (Sisters' College) to engage in the training of elementary teachers found the issue exactly where it was in the 1930s. As chairman of the Liaison Committee, Grauel attempted in 1965 to bring the subject of elementary education up for discussion. He received a sharp rebuke from Monsignor William M. Novicky, who was then director of high schools and academies, questioning the "propriety and rationale" of submitting the matter for discussion.[115] The letter pointed out that the matter had "already been decided by episcopal decision."[116] Fearing that the Liaison Committee's knowledge of that decision was inadequate, Monsignor Novicky proceeded to state the essentials for Grauel. The consultants on the Feasibility Study Committee, however, made recommendations that St. John College still considered threatening. The subject of training teachers for elementary education was no more discussable in the 1960s than it had been in the 1930s.

REORGANIZATION OF THE BOARD OF TRUSTEES

Catholic institutions of higher education, originally established by religious orders, found the continuation of the traditional rector-president administrative arrangement increasingly difficult to maintain in the face of modern developments in higher education. Catholic colleges and universities in the 1960s no longer had as their mission catering "to the 'poor but good,' " boy and were "no longer formally and immediately apostolic."[117] The descendants of immigrant Catholics were moving into the mainstream of society. The "first duty of the college," it was now claimed, "is to serve the community according to its needs and modern demands."[118] Recognition of the changed role of higher education and proposed solutions were major issues in the late 1960s, and caused bitter division within religious communities over the proposed changes.

A major difficulty in any solution was the reconciliation of the demands of canon law governing the institutions as an extension of the religious community and the civil law under which the institutions operated by reason of a state charter. As discussions progressed, a major contribution toward solution was made by Father John J. McGrath of Catholic University relative to the ownership of educational property and canon law governing disposal of that property.[119] Father McGrath's conclusion was that the property of the collegiate institution was not the property of the sponsoring religious community; neither was it ecclesiastical property but property held under a state charter for educational purposes. The combined rector-president office, many remaining European traditions, shortsighted financial policies, less than professional university administration, confusion between pastoral and academic areas, and insulation from the mainstream of contemporary American thought in higher education were additional issues to be resolved.[120]

Father Welfle had recognized many of these issues, particularly the difficult task of trying to be rector of a religious community and president of a university at the same time. Father Dunn also recognized the problem which during his presidency was complicated by the impact of the changes resulting from Vatican II. Where Father Welfle was reasonably patient in trying to work within the system and make changes slowly, Father Dunn chose the path of trying to keep abreast of the movements on other Jesuit campuses where the pace of change was faster. The necessity of Father Dunn's going out to the public even more often than did Father Welfle meant frequent absences from the community where, as rector, he was expected to be. Because there was a Superior to take care of the community matters, Father Dunn gave his priority to university affairs, but this arrangement did not work.

In addition, Father Dunn's personality and style of administration complicated any resolution of the issues. A man of vision, Father Dunn often sought to be alone with his thoughts. When he sought advice on hard decisions, he frequently relied on Father Millor. Although they differed sharply on many occasions, the two men were very close and in many ways complemented each other; their six-month motor tour of Ireland in 1968 after Father Dunn left office is a story in itself. More often than not during his tenure at Carroll, Father Dunn would call upon some layman to drive him to unspecified and frequently distant destinations while he sorted out his thoughts. At other times he would call a layman to his office late in the afternoon to serve as a sounding board for new ideas and changes which might be made. He hoped that his administrators would know what he had in mind and that they would fulfill their assignments without asking him what to do; he was disappointed when they did not act as he had hoped. Father Dunn appeared to many as an unsympathetic man difficult to approach.

In many respects the high point and low point of Father Dunn's regime at Carroll came within a year of each other. In October 1966 a civic dinner in his honor was given at the Hotel Sheraton-Cleveland, where he was toasted for his contribution to the Cleveland scene during his ten years as president of John Carroll University. John H. Sherwin, chairman of the committee sponsoring the event, said that it was the wish of many in the city that the contributions of Father Dunn to the community be publicly recognized. "There isn't anyone among us tonight," said Sherwin, "who is not aware of the impact John Carroll University has on the life of our city and thus on the lives of us all, whether we be management or labor, government officials, professional people or what have you."[121] Within a month of the civic dinner Dunn was given the "Citizen of the Year" award by the University Heights Council. Merle Marxe, council president, said, "Father Dunn has elevated the entire community with his initiative and his contribution to education."[122]

When Father Dunn introduced the subject of adding laymen to the governing board at John Carroll, he was doing so against a background of the increasing importance of the laymen in Catholic institutions of higher education. The decisions of the Jesuits in the late 1920s and 1930s to expand the size and scope of their colleges and universities meant that laymen would have to take the place of Jesuits when the latter were not available. In the following years the numbers of available Jesuits did not keep pace with the expanding enrollments. The second Vatican Council further enhanced the role of the layman in the Church, and the General Congregation of the Society of Jesus in 1965–1966 issued directives for the participation of laymen in Jesuit activities. In Father Dunn's thinking these developments were a natural evolution in recognizing the division of labor in the Church under the principle of collegiality.

It was, nevertheless, a case of moving too fast too soon under the circumstances. Father Dunn's reliance on the Executive Committee almost to the exclusion of the consultors in university affairs made dealing with his fellow Jesuits difficult. Some who were otherwise inclined to support him criticized what appeared to be a step more in the direction of a business corporation rather than an academic institution. Father Dunn's perceived preference for laymen in key positions was a further matter for criticism by some of his fellow Jesuits, who felt they were losing control. In the minds of some, Father Dunn was more concerned with informing the newspapers than his own community of any impending changes. As the *Carroll News* was later to comment, "Change on this campus is, admittedly, slow moving due primarily to the conservative nature of the administration, faculty, and student body."[123]

While the pace of changes involving the addition of laymen to the legal board of trustees was more rapid on some other Jesuit campuses, the pace was speeded up by the public announcement in early January 1967 that Webster College in St. Louis, under the sponsorship of the Sisters of Loretto, was in the process of being turned over to a lay board of trustees.[124] The announcement that its president, who was herself becoming laicized and did not think that a religious community should run a university, caused further confusion on those campuses already contemplating adding laymen to the legal board, but not turning the institution over to lay control. Almost at the same time the *Cleveland Press* ran an article by its religion editor, Jack Hume, in which he said there was a trend in religious orders to retreat from their colleges and universities and "turn over to laymen" the control of their institutions so that there would be no problems with applications for federal funds.[125] The article also stated that the Jesuit presidents had agreed in principle that laymen should share control and pointed out that John Carroll was included. Confusion grew when there appeared to be no clear distinction between what Webster College proposed and what the Jesuit presidents were seeking.

On 27 January 1967, within about ten days of the Webster College announcement, the *Carroll News* carried an article which said, "For the first time in the history of John Carroll, laymen—not necessarily Catholic—will become members of the Board of Trustees of the University." Father Dunn was quoted as saying that the exact number was not yet decided "for we are still working on the legal details."[126] The board referred to, the legal Board of Trustees, included the consultors.

At a faculty meeting on 30 January Father Dunn sought to clear up the confusions resulting from the publicity of recent months. The impression of laicization given by Webster College's action, he said, made it necessary, in order to avoid identity with the Webster model, for other colleges to announce plans for addition of laymen to the boards without turning control over to the laymen.[127]

In his visit to John Carroll in May 1967 Father General, Pedro Arrupe, commented on the changes taking place in religion, education, and society, citing John Carroll as a good example of the progress that was needed. He described the growth of the university as an

indication of a dynamic spirit of progress marked by a strong support with the secular as well as the religious elements of the Cleveland area.

This is as it should be. Our Jesuit colleges and universities relate themselves to the world they strive to serve. This is our guarantee of relevance in the changing and complex times.[128]

Father Arrupe went on to speak of the partnership with laymen as fruitful because:

at institutions such as John Carroll University this relationship began many years ago with lay faculty members. Later laymen were welcomed into positions of higher authority in the administration. Now a new charter is being studied which would include laymen in the governing board of the institution.

He continued his remarks by saying that "The Jesuits do not fear change." He was more concerned about lost opportunities. He also made it clear that with the winds of change blowing strongly, the Church was "looking to America, with its pluralism and its democracy, as a source of inspiration and example."[129]

Father General's support of change did not allay the Jesuits' criticism of Father Dunn, which had been continuing for some time. The criticism was broader than the question of laymen on the board of trustees producing division in the community and finally resulted in Dunn's removal as rector by the Provincial. In July 1967 Father Joseph O. Schell succeeded him as rector and became president on 1 September after being elected by the traditional Jesuit Board of Trustees.[130]

Members of the Lay Advisory Board of Trustees were quite shocked when they were told of the change, but, publicly, they said little. Robert Black, one of the members of the board and in charge of the Decade of Progress campaign, said, "The University was blessed with outstanding leadership during the tenure of Father Dunn. He has the respect and admiration, and the confidence of the entire Cleveland community."[131] Kenneth King, owner of Kenny King restaurants, also praised Father Dunn:

> If he has his way, he'll slip out of town without any fanfare.
> He's that kind of guy; this quiet, unassuming, talented powerhouse, . . . persuaded businessmen that education was "everybody's business." . . .
> I guess that really is the word to describe him, 'genuine.' In everything he does he is straightforward and that most avoided of all virtues, sincere. As a Jesuit he epitomized the kind of priest the order develops. He lives up to his vows with gracious strength that gives courage and hope to anyone who comes in contact with him.[132]

Father Dunn did slip away quietly, but he was known to have felt that with two more years he could have put university affairs in proper order.

The student newspaper reviewed Father Dunn's accomplishments during his presidency; listed were four major buildings with a fifth ready for occupancy, a policy of service and cooperation with the Greater Cleveland community through a series of programs and institutes, growth of the student body from 3,600 to 4,500, an increase in faculty from 141 to 225, and a 100 percent increase in faculty salaries. "His works can best be described by an overheard comment made by an unknown senior last year who claimed he had never seen Father Dunn: 'Father Dunn?' he said, 'I think it's a name of a committee composed of many administrators. It certainly can't be one man.' "[133]

There were many things that could have been listed by the writer of the editorial. Among the omissions was Father Dunn's partially successful effort to restructure the administration of the university. There had been a tendency to make nearly every decision an *ad hoc* one. He hoped to correct the situation by adopting a structure that would make it easier to determine responsibility, establish criteria for performance, provide a wider base of faculty input, and develop long-range planning.

Father Schell continued the process of determining what form the Jesuit

Board of Trustees should take in the future. At a November 1967 meeting of that Board, Father Schell divided the office of secretary so that the House Consultors and the legal Board, though practically identical, were now served by different secretaries. At least functionally there was a separation between the consultors and the Jesuit Board of Trustees.[134]

Next was a sort of integration of the legal Board and the Lay Advisory Board in January 1968.[136] The Lay Advisory Board selected five members to serve with the Jesuit Board in what was known temporarily as the "Joint Council of John Carroll University." Father Schell warned that, "if there should be any pressure from any quarter to move to a formalization and legalization of this Jesuit-lay board structure, it should be resisted."[136] Father Schell felt that John Carroll "should stay with this experimental structure for a long time."[137] In the meantime it was "intended that the Lay Advisory Board be retained and strengthened.[138] Although legal power was retained by the Jesuit Board of Trustees, the meetings of the Joint Council were open to thorough discussion of issues by all; all members were to express opinions by vote.[139] Ben Hauserman, chairman of the Lay Advisory Board, praised the "foreward step taken by the university in combining members of the Advisory Board with Jesuits in a functional board."[140]

At the first meeting of the Joint Council, attorney Joseph Mullaney suggested that incorporation of the Jesuit Community as a separate entity might be a desirable step regardless of whether there would be any change in the university's structure of governance.[141] Such action would provide a legal separation needed for the "transfer of monies, salaries, and other legal purposes."[142]

By September 1968 discussions had progressed to the point where Father Schell, in a meeting with the Jesuit community, asked for an expression of opinion on adding laymen to the Jesuit Board of Trustees.[143] One of three positions was possible: opposition in principle, undecided, and in favor in principle. Twenty-nine of the forty-one voting were in favor in principle. Two were opposed in principle, eight were undecided, and two abstained.[144] The understanding was that, if the vote was favorable, "an effort would be made to have a mutually satisfactory proposal ready within a year to submit for approval."[145]

Shortly after this action, a letter from Father Provincial Walter Farrell was read by Father Schell at a Jesuit Board of Trustees meeting, expressing "concern that the fears, real or otherwise, of the Community be allayed for a smooth conclusion to the discussions currently approved by the Community for the adjustment of the ownership and management settlements of John Carroll University."[146] The trustees agreed and approved separate meetings of the Jesuit Community and the Lay Advisory Board at which all pertinent material and plans would be discussed. There would then be a joint discussion by the two groups.[147] The plan was to give the Jesuit Community sufficient time for discussion of any proposals and to have an acceptable proposal ready by the end of the 1968–1969 academic year.

It was Father Schell's hope that the proposal would provide for a governing board composed of both Jesuits and lay persons. He "noted that officials of the Jesuit Order have pointed out separation of the Jesuit Community from the University corporation would be a prerequisite of the establishment of a new governing board."[148] Although there was no end of problems, the discussions continued with the capable assistance of Father Henry Birkenhauer. Father Schell favored a pattern of organization followed by Holy Cross College, the ideas of which he thought could be incorporated into two documents: one would be a set of norms for the Jesuit Community covering relationships with the university, the other would be an agreement between the Community and the University covering matters of common interest.[149] By the end of January 1969, plans for separate incorporation of the Jesuit Community were ready for presentation to the Community for consideration.

At a 21 April meeting of the "Joint Council," Father Schell announced that agreement had been reached on separate incorporation and that the proposal had been sent to the Provincial.[150] In August the Provincial's approval was received and by September word came that Father General had also approved.[151]

Meanwhile, discussions on the composition of the board of trustees had also proceeded "in line with the thinking of Father Dunn and present trends in private institutions of higher education."[152] The new board was to be one fourth Jesuit and three fourths lay. The members were to be chosen by the Board and submitted to the new Jesuit corporation for approval. The property of John Carroll University was to continue to remain in the hands of the members of the Jesuit corporation which was not necessarily identical with the Jesuit Community; only those Jesuits who signed the roster were members of the corporation. The new board was to choose the president of the university, who was required to be a Jesuit but no longer would be rector of the Jesuit Community. All that remained was to determine when public announcement should be made of the changes; that date was set for 27 October 1969, the date of the first meeting of the new board of trustees.

The difficulty of accomplishing the changes should not be underestimated. Tensions were great and perhaps Father Schell's own conviction that the change was inevitable and that qualified lay persons could no longer be induced to assist unless they were members of the legal board played an important part in convincing his fellow Jesuits that the change

New Governing Board: In 1969, the Jesuits at John Carroll University created a new Board of Trustees made up of twenty-one laymen and seven Jesuits. The Board combines the functions and most of the personnel of the former Jesuit Board of Trustees and the Advisory Board of Lay Trustees. It has legal control over the management of the University. Ben M. Hauserman, vice-president of E. F. Hauserman Company, was appointed chairman of the new Board. Vice-chairmen are: Dr. James C. Hodge, chairman of Warner & Swasey Company; Frank E. Joseph, partner, Jones, Day, Cockley and Reavis; and Rolland F. Smith, manager, Cleveland Fisher Body Plant, General Motors Corporation.

The first meeting of the University officers and new Board of Trustees included *(seated clockwise starting second from left):* Rev. Joseph O. Schell, S.J., president; Mr. Hauserman; Frank J. Schulte, Jr.; James S. Reid, Jr.; Francis X. Feighan; John R. Wall; F. William Dugan; Rev. Joseph P. Owens, S.J.; Rev. Ernest G. Spittler, S.J., secretary; Joseph H. Keller; Mr. Joseph; Rev. Laurence V. Britt, S.J.; Mr. Smith; Rev. Glenn F. Williams, S.J.; Campbell W. Elliott; Joseph C. Coakley; Morris A. Bradley; Dr. Hodge; Rev. William H. Nichols, S.J.; Thomas F. Dolan; and Hugh M. O'Neill. *Standing are:* William D. Fissinger, vice-president for development; Rev. Thomas P. Conry, S.J., academic vice-president; and Herbert H. Kennedy, retired vice-president and assistant to the president.

Not present when the picture was taken were: Rev. Henry F. Birkenhauer, S.J.; Rev. Eugene P. Simon, S.J., treasurer; Robert F. Black; Kenyon C. Bolton; Edward L. Carpenter; Allan W. Fritzsche; Edwin T. Jeffery; Van H. Leichliter.

392/ *John Carroll University*

should be made. The important role played by Father Birkenhauer was also a significant factor.

GATHERING LOOSE ENDS, 1967–1970

Because of the time consumed in the process of the creation of a new board of trustees, Father Schell found that he had insufficient time for other pressing issues. He had, of course, settled the question of coeducation but many other issues remained. The Academic Senate agenda for 1968 included further revision of the core curriculum, reduction of the teaching load, automatic sabbaticals, a pass-fail option, and a number of other matters. As Father Schell looked to the future he said, "We still need a real focus on the educational effort at John Carroll University—what makes it distinctive, how is it to be implemented."[153]

An important task that could not be neglected was the revision of the optimistic enrollment projections that had been made in 1965; they needed to be adjusted downward after the seeming peak in 1967. The revision was made in 1969. A new emphasis on counseling, particularly at the freshman and sophomore levels, was insisted upon by the faculty. As a result of the Feasibility Study the Association of Catholic Colleges and Seminaries was formed and its presidents continued to meet regularly.

As 1970 approached, rising costs, financial aid for students, and the effort to provide low-cost education became important concerns. After a leave of absence for health reasons, Father Schell resigned and Father Birkenhauer became president in 1970. The new president inherited a university that was markedly different from the one which any of his predecessors had inherited. The ten years between 1960 and 1970 had produced basic changes in almost every phase of the university's operation. The long-range effects of these changes had to be dealt with; emphasis on long-range planning was needed now more than ever.

In Search Of a New Balance
1970–1975

As John Carroll University entered the 1970s both internal and external pressures were forcing an assessment of what the university had become and precisely where it stood as a Catholic and a Jesuit institution which, by agreement with the Jesuit Community, it was expected to remain. The tradition-shattering changes of the 1960s by which more laymen had assumed key administrative roles, the content and role of philosophy and theology were changed, coeducation had been made official, and the offices of rector and president separated, had been too much for some and not enough for others. Some saw the departure of the institution from the traditional pattern of a Jesuit college as an irretrievable loss. One of the Jesuits interviewed in 1970 in the search for a replacement for Father Schell as president commented that some Jesuits still hoped to preserve John Carroll as a traditional small Jesuit college.[1] Others saw little progress being made in the areas of student rights and the faculty's role in governance. For them, more change was desirable. The expected decline in the future enrollment pool of available pool of available freshmen, rising costs, and inflation added external pressures to the search for solutions to problems. Other external factors could be found in the general questioning of the value of a college education, particularly a liberal arts program in a Catholic college.

Nationally, higher education was coming upon hard times; it was not likely that John Carroll could escape budget deficits without constant attention to keeping expenses within bounds. It would be difficult to manage budget restraints in a way that did not affect educational quality. A report from Francis A. Jones, vice-president for business, showing the relationship between the income and expense per credit hour from 1963 to 1971, made clear that the expense was rising disproportionately.[2] In 1966–1967, the peak year for credit hours enrolled, 117,107, the differential had been three dollars; in 1970–1971, it was nine dollars with the credit hours dropping to 105,537. In that period tuition had almost doubled. Since the differential had to be made up either by increasing tuition or finding other sources of revenue or both, the choice was not easy. During the 1970s, enrollment in terms of credit hours continued to decline at the rate of 2 to 3 percent a year until leveling off at 92,000 credit hours in the 1976–1977 year. Even with tuition increases, the John Carroll tuition was well below the median for Ohio private colleges, leading some to argue that the educational program was being sold too cheaply. By 1979 the John Carroll tuition was double what it was in 1970, but there was still a serious problem of keeping up with rising costs and inflation.

Vice-president for Business Frank Jones in his budget notes for 1970–1971 proposed a cutting back in basic costs to provide a balanced budget. He saw the problem as one of how to finance operations with over 77 percent of income derived from tuition in the face of a declining or static enrollment. A $300,000 cut in basic costs for 1970–1971 together with an increase in tuition would be necessary to balance the upcoming budget.

In summary, Jones was worried about the continued decline in reserves with the probability of the cash bind becoming worse. To stay in balance he felt that there would have to be an annual tuition increase and also a commitment to a level of at least $600,000 in unrestricted gifts. Enrollment, particularly in the Summer Session, would continue to decline. "The lack of coordinated planning and control becomes more evident with each passing year," observed Jones.

> Instead of planning what we want to do within the context of sound principles or policy we are forced to react with expedients to meet current pressures. We are not solving problems, we are papering them with greater expenditures. Probably the strongest evidence of our current weakness is the elimination of the financial principles with which we operated in the past.[3]

The optimistic enrollment projections and staffing tables provided in the 1963–1973 Decade of Progress Plan had been revised in 1969 to give what proved to be a much more accurate picture of the future enrollments. It remained, therefore, to implement a course of action to meet the financial needs required by the new projections. In order to supply pertinent statistical data about university operations since 1963 and to provide priorities and guidelines for the implementation of new policies, the University Council presented a report in April 1970 which became known as the University Council Report. This report, which contained a brief foreward on educational philosophy, was presented to the Academic Senate and approved by Father Schell before his resignation; it became a basic document of the 1970s. Its four parts, educational philosophy, priorities, operational guidelines, and statistical information, were somewhat revised and updated in 1976. Major changes did not come until 1977, when the educational philosophy section became the basis for an improved Mission

Statement, and in 1978–1979 when a faculty committee with university-wide representation revised the priorities and guidelines. Later, in 1980, all of the changes were embodied in a planning report of the new president, Father Henry Birkenhauer.

When Father Schell tendered his resignation in late spring 1970, the student newspaper expressed regret that students often failed to understand the achievements of his short tenure. During his regime, the Board of Trustees had been reorganized, students were represented in the Academic Senate, the second phase of the Decade of Progress Plan was continued, and, above all, close rapport with the students was established. Father Schell's presence at the Student Union meetings and his visits to the Rathskeller showed the "depth of his concern, his abiding love for the student."[4]

For the first time since its reorganization in 1969, the Board of Trustees was to choose a new president. After an extensive search, the committee appointed by the Board recommended Father Henry Birkenhauer, who was unanimously approved by the Board and became the nineteenth president of the university in 1970. Father Birkenhauer was no stranger to the John Carroll community. A nationally known seismologist, former dean of the Graduate School and assistant to Father Schell, he had been at John Carroll since 1947 as professor of mathematics and director of the seismological observatory. In 1958 Father Birkenhauer spent the year in Antarctica with a United States geophysical expedition. From 1962 to 1968 he spent time in theological studies and as director of Jesuits in Tertianship. He returned to the university in 1968 as assistant to the president.

There was also a change in the office of vice-president for academic affairs when Father Thomas P. Conry resigned to return to theological studies. For the first time a layman, Dr. Arthur J. Noetzel, was chosen to hold this office. Noetzel had been dean of the School of Business since 1956; he was replaced in that capacity by Francis J. McGurr, professor of accounting and chairman of the department since 1963.

Father Birkenhauer stated that one of his major goals would be "to maintain financial stability, and to increase the personal development of the student."[5] He also saw the university playing a role in the surrounding community because although John Carroll University was a "private institution, yet it is a public trust."[6]

In reviewing the budget for 1971–1972, Father Birkenhauer took into consideration the recommendations of Jones and the priorities and operational guidelines of the University Council Report. Stating that John Carroll "very definitely is not in crisis," Birkenhauer said, "We see difficulties ahead and we are trying to meet them now and alleviate them before they grow."[7] As a result, $310,000 was trimmed from the 1971–1972 budget.

Approximately $70,000 of this amount came from the academic category, most of it originally intended for capital expenditures. Faculty salaries over $20,000 were frozen for at least one year.

While all areas except the library were affected by the cuts, some of the most controversial cuts came in the area of cultural programs. The University Series, which had shown a net loss of some $26,000 coupled with poor student attendance, was to be eliminated, as was also the *Quarterly* and the *Carillon*. The University Events Committee, which supplied money for programs sponsored by the departments, was also cut. In February 1971 Father Birkenhauer approved a revised budget for the University Series saying that, "total cancellation of the Series would have serious adverse public relations effects."[8] The *Quarterly* was not so well treated, although it managed to survive. As for the *Carillon*, it was given a year of grace. An editorial in the student newspaper pointed out that the recent history of the yearbook showed lack of student support, attributed in part to the limited scope of the book, and a failure to meet deadlines and stay within budget.[9] The elimination of class and faculty pictures also had not helped to gain support.

The cutbacks made under the new fiscal policy were not popularly received but Father Birkenhauer insisted that the fiscal situation must be forecast and met accordingly. He considered that "brinksmanship technique is not only dangerous but senseless."[10] In the president's *Annual Report* for 1971–1972, Father Birkenhauer said, "In the midst of change John Carroll has kept a sense of direction. The human values of a liberal education and the religious orientation which is a fundamental heritage continue to be our goals. Personal interest in the individual student guides our choice of means (curriculum, activities, special programs)."[11]

With the Decade of Progress fund-raising activity about to end in 1973 and with Phase II of that program lagging, a new effort to complete the project was launched in 1972 with the title, "Fresh Start," under the chairmanship of Board member Rolland H. Smith. The president's *Annual Report* for 1973–1974 reviewed the accomplishments of the Decade of Progress Plan. Among the benefits were a 40 percent increase in physical resources, a 3.5 percent increase in endowment, and the raising of $13 million from corporations, foundations, alumni, and individuals. It was now time for a new plan, which would be called the "New Dimensions Campaign."[12] The goal was $10 million over five years which would assist the university in establishing "new horizons of educational service" including programs for business education, adult women, minorities, the aged, and other "people-building needs of the community."[13] Also included was the consolidation of past gains, recruiting of students, adaption of physical facilities to

Henry F. Birkenhauer, S.J., President,
John Carroll University, 1970–80

William J. Millor, S.J., 1949–77

Laurence V. Britt, S.J., Dean, 1966–77

new needs, and an increase of endowment. In the first seventeen months of the new program $2.73 million was committed in gifts and pledges.[14]

Although unsophisticated by later standards, The Decade of Progress Plan accomplished important fundamental objectives. It provided an information base on enrollment patterns, academic trends, budget projections, and fund-raising; it also identified and analyzed problems. To continue updating and improving this operation, a new computer was installed in 1973, and a grant from the Gund Foundation was secured to provide for technical assistance for three years.[15]

On the academic side of the planning process a review was made of the former Executive Committee's actions to determine what needed to be revised and what areas remained to be covered. Father Birkenhauer formed a Planning Committee, composed of the vice-presidents and deans, which prepared an agenda on the basis of priority. High on the list of priorities was the need for a clear definition of objectives, the development of a planning mechanism, and an improved data base. Just as this procedure was getting under way in 1973, the Cleveland Commission on Higher Education sponsored a management study for some Cleveland institutions of higher education. It was conducted by Dr. Earl J. McGrath, formerly of the United States Office of Education and then director of Temple University's Higher Education Center. The purpose was to provide the type of professional service and advice a large university could often get from its own staff. John Carroll was included in this study during the year 1973. For many reasons the study failed to live up to its expectations.

COMMUNITY AND STUDENT RIGHTS

When news of the Kent State shootings in May 1970 reached campus just before the final examination period, there were meetings, resolutions condemning violence, and dialogue among students, faculty, and administrators. On 5 May 1970 the faculty passed a resolution commending the John Carroll students for acting in "a rational, intelligent fashion without violence."[16] In spite of this, the administration deemed it prudent, partly because of the proximity to Kent and partly because there had been outsiders on campus attempting to stir up trouble, to end the academic year abruptly without final examinations. Prior to the meeting of administrators to discuss this issue, students, for undetermined reasons, began lining the corridor through which those attending the meeting would have to pass to get to the board room adjacent to the president's office. To avoid any confrontation the meeting was held elsewhere.

It was not, however, the Kent State issue, but rather a local issue that was the real source of student unrest. The academic changes approved by the

Academic Senate and the president in the spring of 1970, such as unlimited "cuts" for juniors and seniors, a pass-fail option, and revised final examination procedures, failed to touch one of the more urgent problems affecting dormitory students. Even an approved liberalized dress code and the faculty-inspired new counseling program were not sufficient measures. The important issue was the demand that dormitories remain open twenty-four hours. The issue had been brought to a head in the spring of 1970, but the students were dissatisfied with the compromises which had been made. An editorial in the *Carroll News* in October 1970 claimed that the regulations were now

> openly and flagrantly violated. Is this because there is no enforcement or is it because the Administration does not care to enforce its rules, but would rather just like to have them on the books? We wonder. . . . conditions, however, are now reaching a critical point. A number of students seek private housing . . . others refer to the dorms as a prison. Certainly, something is wrong.[17]

There were student gatherings voicing disapproval of the situation and opinion polls confirmed the discontent.

Students had apparently accepted the regulations approved in the spring of 1970 on the ground that it was better to accept something rather than get nothing. Dissatisfaction reached a climax on 27 October when some five hundred students met with Father Birkenhauer to discuss open dorms. The student polls had shown 98 percent of the students in favor of open dorms and 75 percent in favor of nonviolent action in support of open dorms.[18] Father Birkenhauer was quoted as telling the meeting that he was

> prepared to request action by the Board of Trustees on proposals which do not jeopardize the university's fundamental commitment to religious and moral values. Such proposals, for example, would be to change the hours of visitation or to allow individual dormitories to vote for a change of hours.[19]

A meeting on 1 November of Father Birkenhauer, several faculty members, and dorm prefects reached the conclusion that the real issue was not the open dorms but rather "an increased degree of self-determination, leading hopefully to an improved University community."[20] Father Birkenhauer then requested the committee to put its philosophy on paper. If the policy were approved, it could lead to a revised dorm visitation policy.

An expanded committee that included students produced a thirteen-page draft of a "New Philosophy" which had unanimous Student Union approval[21] and was to be discussed and voted on by the faculty and then presented to the Board of Trustees. The final draft was entitled, "John

Carroll University—A Proposal for the Future." The report contained three proposals on dormitory policy which virtually assured an open dorm situation; it was hailed by some as affirming the trend of recent years, by which "the Carroll student has been losing his traditional stigma of conservatism," and would "alter the basic assumptions of power here at Carroll."[22] It was argued that John Carroll already had a policy that provided for restrictions; what was needed was a positve approach supplied by the proposal. "Why must negativism and skepticism greet every attempt at responsible change the students introduced?" asked the *Carroll News*.[23]

On the other hand, some articles in the *Carroll News* defended the "silent minority" who were "discomforted and disturbed by the claim that John Carroll University is backward and not producing the people they think they are producing."[24] The "silent minority" objected to the attempt to force the administration to accept the view that "dormitory bedrooms are actually kitchens, dining rooms, family rooms, night clubs and even hotel suites." The problem, as these students explained, was that those who questioned the "loyalty of student extremists who claim to have the interest of all the student body at heart," are accused of unfairness when they see the open dorm as a "violation of their right of privacy or of a simple moral autonomy to speak out against something they quite frankly believe unnecessary or unethical for John Carroll."[25]

When the proposals on self-determination were presented at a faculty meeting in mid-November 1970, approval in principle was given to the idea of an experiment in greater student democracy but the specifics of the proposals were voted down.[26] Father Birkenhauer then sent the proposals back to the dormitory council and formed a committee of students and faculty under the chairmanship of Father Michael J. Lavelle of the School of Business. The committee was called "The Committee on Community," and its purpose was to discuss ways of solving the problem. One faculty member was of the opinion that irresponsibility on the part of some students put other students' sense of responsibility in some doubt. Another faculty member felt that a few agitators wanted revolution under the guise of philosophy in seeking acceptance of "demands . . . above and beyond human decency."[27]

During the controversy, numerous articles in the *Carroll News* expressed varied and often perceptive points of view. A letter to the editor from one of the coeds expressed disappointment that the 20 November issue "was so taken up with matters settled on other campuses—even Catholic ones—4 or 5 years ago;" she felt that racism, intelligent awareness of the political scene, and academic freedom were the real issues. "Why are people," she asked, "wasting so much time on a relatively minor, self-centered matter as whether and when boys and girls might be allowed to see each other in their rooms?"[28] One editorial pleaded for more respect for others, compensation for student leaders, and a lessening of the administration vs. students vs. faculty situation before an explosion occurred.[29] An editorial in February 1971 argued that students were unwilling to understand the reasons and objectives behind proposals unless they were "related as personally as possible," and urged the president to help build even more effective rapport with the students. The editorial pointed out that many students came to appreciate Father Schell only after he had left office; it was hoped the students would not make the same mistake with Father Birkenhauer.[30]

Between 15 December 1970 and 29 March 1971, when the committee under Father Lavelle released its final report, many hours were spent in trying to reconcile the different points of view. A preliminary report submitted to Father Birkenhauer on 24 February was later presented for discussion at a Rathskeller meeting which was poorly attended by the students.[31] Father Birkenhauer said he would accept the recommendations of the committee even though they involved a change of hours, provided they met "standards of honesty and responsibility on which we can all agree."[32] Father Birkenhauer went on,

> Basically, my change in attitude has come about from this dialogue. I still believe that there are risks. But there are risks in any choice, any personal decision. The way in which we live as honorable men and women despite these risks is the measure of our maturity. As educators, let us give our students a chance to grow responsibly and to prove their maturity to us.[33]

The final report of the Committee on Community was presented 29 March 1971, with Father Birkenhauer giving assent to its recommendation. In fulfilling its purpose of being specific in its recommendations the Committee called for inter-mingling of classes in each of the four dormitories, a large measure of self-government in each dormitory, limitation of hours by a small unit within each dormitory if so desired, a positive approach to solutions, and a review within a year. Implementation was to begin in the fall of 1971.[34]

The Committee on Community found the dormitory issue so time-consuming that it was unable to devote itself to the broader aspects of the idea of community. The Committee did point out that education at John Carroll was expected to consist of more than courses; principles of life style were involved. Among these were Christian justice and charity in giving everyone his due and concern for the good of others; mutual trust through community living and accountability for one's actions must be accepted. "These principles," said the Committee, "mold or should mold the lives of men and women of the John Carroll Community."[35]

In a comment on the leadership of the movement for open dormitories, the *Carroll News* observed that "rallies in the fall were led and directed not by the Union leaders but by outside interested parties. The students listened to these men."[36] Even after the student meeting with Father Birkenhauer when Union leadership sought to help him understand the situation, the students still followed the leadership of those outside the Union. The newspaper saw the action as marking the end of an era when a few Student Union members worked through committees in dealing with the president for student privileges. "Carroll seems to have moved to an era where student support for various issues is more open and demonstrative, to an era where leaders are in front of the group leading the students."[37] A month later the same theme was repeated in an obvious reference to Viet-Nam when the student newspaper observed that, "Although a conservative Jesuit college, John Carroll University students are becoming more aware of the pertinent events surrounding them. . . . The commitment is becoming larger every day as students throughout the country are expressing their views on events directly involving them."[38]

After four years, two editorials in the *Carroll News* in March 1975 reviewed the implementation of the Committee on Community's recommendations. One editorial by Father Lavelle wondered what had happened to the attempt to provide an opportunity to allow each dormitory to develop an atmosphere where students could mature. The answer he thought was that "when the open dorm issue was settled all the rest of the recommendations were ignored and downplayed. . . . As a member of this committee I am periodically reminded of our work and must assess it as, at best, visionary and, at worst, a failure"; noise, vandalism, and disregard for privacy and the rights of others were at the same level as four years previous.[39] Father Lavelle thought that the committee should be revived. The other editorial warned all dormitory students "that the fun is almost over. The big crackdown is coming."[40]

An issue competing for attention along with the open dormitory question was the adoption of a "Declaration of Student Rights and Responsibilities" which passed the Student Union Senate in December 1970. Within a year, Father Birkenhauer had changed the position description of the University Council in order to allow it to take up such matters as a student bill of rights.[41] The Coordinator of Religious Affairs was added to the University Council membership which was now to be a working group on long-range planning in addition to acting as a review board for policy changes. During a series of meetings running to December 1971, the University Council decided to go through the proposed student bill of rights, item by item. An incident in the fall of 1971 involving the suspension of two students passing out birth control literature in the lobby of the Student Activities Center served to point up the urgency for action on a student bill of rights.[42]

While the dormitory issue was apparently settled by the Report of the Committee on Community, wrangling over the "manned desk" to screen visitors continued, and the discussions over the student bill of rights reached an impasse on crucial issues; the students were demanding absolute rights.[43] The problem, according to Father Birkenhauer, was to find "a way to give the students more freedom without sacrificing JCU's Catholic character and the ultimate right of the University, to govern all her members."[44] An acceptable compromise was found and the "Bill of Rights" was approved by the University Council on 14 March 1972. Also established was an appeals board as the "final recourse in student cases."[45] Father Birkenhauer said, "For me this means we have faith in the future of John Carroll University, and have faith in each other."[46] Father Schell called the Bill of Rights, "a statement of what you already have."[47]

In some ways, the various settlements of issues such as open dormitories and student rights could be more accurately described as a truce. The basic moral issues involved in student independence and responsibility remained; "don't dictate: Christian behavior on campus," declared the *Carroll News*.[48]

CATHOLIC AND JESUIT?

The external symbols that had traditionally identified a college as Catholic and Jesuit were the requirements in religion and philosophy, the annual retreat, and attendance at Mass. Scholastic philosophy rather than religion provided the integrating curricular force. The conviction was still strong in the 1950s that external symbols identified the Catholic college.

After the Jesuits sponsored the Los Angeles Workshop of 1962, philosophy and theology requirements came to be viewed in a different light. Vatican II also changed some viewpoints. Maturing Catholic colleges and universities were seeking acceptance as universities in their own right. In the Decade of Progress Plan 1963–1973, Father Dunn tried to reflect the changed environment without diminishing the substance of the Catholic and Jesuit character of John Carroll. In an introductory message to the document Father Dunn said, "It seemed essential to me that before determining John Carroll's role in meeting these national needs, we clarify our educational mission. What kind of an institution is this? What are we trying to achieve?"[49] Father Dunn went on to say that John Carroll was "first of all a university . . . a distinctive kind of a university—a Jesuit institution" where there was concern for the total person and where there was "a standard of values erected upon a sound philosophy and an acceptance of revealed truth."[50] There was also a "dedication to excellence" but not an identification of "excellence in education with excellence in admissions. We have no intention of limiting our enrollment to that extremely talented group of young people who take the lion's share of prizes and scholarships, although we do hope to have our share of students of this type."[51] Although the large majority of the students were Catholic, Father Dunn was "proud of the fact that we also have a substantial number of non-Catholics in our faculty and student body." He saw this as

> evidence of the sincerity of our educational convictions and also of the trust that non-Catholics place in us. There is no conflict between this trust and our convictions, and we shall not fail either. The Jesuits are proud to be among the pioneers in the ecumenical spirit of the Catholic Church. The only test for admission was whether a student could profit from the educational experience at John Carroll, or to put it another way, whether he can justify the investment the university and the faculty will make in him.[52]

When curriculum changes were discussed in 1971–1972, the requirements in philosophy and theology were still so identified as symbols of the Catholic and Jesuit character of the university that for some any change in them implied a loss of the traditional identity of the institution. The new approach to theology as an academic subject gave additional weight to the argument for loss of identity. Alumni found the changes, particularly the deemphasis of scholastic philosophy, hard to accept, as if a familiar song had been changed to "Should auld Aquinas be forgot and never more be taught."

The Alumni publication, *Carroll*, reported that the new curriculum of 1969 "raised a few eyebrows among faculty conservatives" because philosophy at John Carroll University has "taken on a new look and an unaccustomed vigor, and the winds of change are still blowing." Father John E. Dister, "tall slender British educated" departmental chairman, explained that the Carroll student now had a variety of philosophical viewpoints available to him; "the one system approach of the past based heavily on St. Thomas Aquinas had given way to a broader perspective." Father Dister felt that the change was for the best because "philosophy deals with questions about man and about life which no one system can answer completely."[53]

The meaning of a Jesuit education was described by the *Carroll News* as "the central ambiguity surrounding us" during the revision of the core curriculum in 1972.[54] Without any real resolution of the "ambiguity," a major revision of the curriculum was approved in 1972, in spite of the fact that some of the proposals appeared to be at odds with university goals.[55] Father Laurence V. Britt, dean of the college of arts and sciences, thought that the proposed curriculum was an attempt to respond to the student "wants" rather than any sound educational principle. He also thought that student selection of courses from five divisions "guaranteed superficial exposure" to a whole series of introductory courses.[56] Father Britt's experience with student complaints about the curriculum had led him to believe the problem was not with the core but with the quality of the courses.

The revised core divided subjects into five divisions: humanities; social sciences; mathematics, physical, and life sciences; philosophy; religious studies. Courses were not specified, but the requirement in philosophy was three courses and in religious studies, two. There was also a requirement in English composition and speech communication as well as provision for independent study and waiver of requirements; "Balance and Flexibility" were the words Father Birkenhauer used to describe the new core curriculum.[57] In spite of fear of financial implications resulting from a change in student demands on certain departments and a shifting away from others, the new core was implemented in the fall of 1973.

CLEVELAND CATHOLIC COLLEGES

While the university was trying to solve its internal problems of student issues and its own identity in the midst of financial difficulties, it was also seeking to determine its relationship with the other Catholic colleges of Cleveland. There had been no pressure on the colleges to set up the governing council recommended by the Feasibility Study of 1967, but no one was willing to consider merger or federation. There was so much competition and fear of loss of autonomy, that the seeds of suspicion planted in the days of the Corporate Colleges of the early 1930s had borne fruit in the image of John Carroll as an obstacle to cooperation. In the case of the Liaison Committee in 1964 and again in the Feasibility Study of 1967 John Carroll "provided the initiative and a good share of the resources for the study of options in which John Carroll had little to gain. . . . For these efforts John Carroll has been generally considered as . . . trying to dominate or swallow up the other schools," wrote the director of institutional planning at John Carroll to Father Birkenhauer in February 1971.[58] The occasion of this correspondence was the effort of the Catholic colleges to hire a coordinator without any prior agreement on the direction the group was to take.

The Feasibility Study was accepted by the presidents without any real commitment to its goals. On 14 and 15 November 1969, the consultants returned to Cleveland to meet with the presidents, and were surprised to learn that the recommendation of an executive director had not been carried out. The consultants felt that perhaps they had acted on a false assumption that the colleges were ready and committed to move in the direction suggested by the study.[59] In the discussions at these meetings it was clear that there was disillusionment among many of the original supporters of the study. The study had raised false hopes; efforts at cooperation had increased rather than decreased costs and had produced competition in certain lecture series and conflicts in cultural events. The independent action of John Carroll in making coeducation official in the college of arts and sciences was looked upon by the other colleges as further evidence of the university's lack of sincerity in a cooperative effort. The monopoly on elementary education by St. John College and the gentlemen's agreement that surrounded it was something neither the consultants nor the colleges other than St. John could quite understand. Under the circumstances the consultants thought that hiring a coordinator might help.

The minutes of the meetings of the presidents with the consultants in November 1969 caused further confusion. One of the presidents, Monsignor Lawrence Cahill of St. John College, criticized the pessimistic tone of the minutes both in their original and revised form: "A stranger reading them could conclude that the issue of cooperation between these institutions is now a dead issue. I am not willing to accept that conclusion. However, when I look for specific amendments I could propose to the minutes, it is hard to find any words or paragraphs to alter."[60]

Monsignor Cahill then sent a position paper on cooperation to the presidents of the other colleges.[61] In it he expressed his concerns that the meetings had generated a feeling of pessimism and expressed his reactions to points in the minutes. Stressing that the weakness of one institution was the weakness of all, he made it clear that elementary education must remain exclusively at St. John College; to lose it would weaken or destroy it. "To suggest that one must flourish at the expense of another is shortsighted and grossly cynical," said the president.[62] He was particularly upset at the "constantly recurring dichotomy between communications and liaison on the one hand and merger or federation on the other"; such dichotomy was "totally unacceptable as a basis of our discussions. Such a dichotomy could only destroy the present progress in cooperation."[63] He concluded by saying:

> If there are any among us who reject the total concept of inter-institutional cooperation, that should be stated clearly and honestly. That institution should then withdraw and allow the other members to attempt to grow in their cooperative fashion. That institution should then express its decision publicly so that its students, faculty, trustees and donors might understand its position.[64]

One of the presidents sought and received a grant from the Cleveland Foundation to support a coordinator for one year. One of the requirements of this grant was that the Cleveland Catholic Colleges incorporate. On 14

August 1970, the Cleveland Catholic Colleges were incorporated as The Associated Colleges of Cleveland. They were described as "a consortium for the joint planning and implementation of cooperative programs acceptable to the member institutions."[65] The search for an executive secretary resulted in the selection of Dr. Hugh L. Thompson, who had been director of institutional planning at Baldwin-Wallace College. He began his duties 18 January 1971. There was now clearly no intention of implementing the recommendations of the Feasibility Study of 1967.

One of Thompson's first actions was to attempt to file an application for assistance to "developing institutions" under Title III of the Education Act of 1965. When John Carroll was asked to fill out an application, the director of institutional planning informed Thompson that John Carroll was not eligible under the rules of the Act to file such an application. Thompson's reply was that he now realized that, and also that John Carroll might be put in an awkward relationship with any one of the Associated Colleges receiving such a grant.[66] Later in the year an unsuccessful attempt was made to create some symbol of unity by a proposal to a foundation for the endowment of a chair of humanities.[67] After the McGrath Study in 1973 had produced no results, efforts were made to arrange joint projects among the Associated Colleges by the executive secretary of the Cleveland Commission on Higher Education, Dr. Jack Burns. A variety of projects proposed included the establishment of cultural programs, encouragement of John Carroll students to enroll in music courses at one of the women's colleges, and participation of the students of the women's colleges in the John Carroll instrumental ensemble. Problems and complications arose largely because, according to Father Britt, "the academic deans were rather completely bypassed by the grass roots approach that was apparently encouraged."[68]

There was little progress beyond what had been accomplished by the Liaison Committee, but the presidents of the Associated Colleges continued to meet. In 1975 Bishop James A. Hickey, recently appointed Bishop of Cleveland, began to join the presidents in their meetings. The reason for his action was the need for Catholic colleges to work together and give visible evidence of a Catholic presence in the field of higher education in the diocese. The bishop felt that each institution had a special character and he hoped there would be no competition, but rather mutual help.[69] In March 1976 Bishop Hickey discussed with the college presidents Cardinal Gabriel Garrone's letter of 21 June 1975 to local ordinaries concerning the departments of philosophy and theology in Catholic colleges. Cardinal Garrone was Prefect of the Roman Congregation for education. The Bishop had commented on this letter at an earlier meeting of the Associated College presidents in September 1975, saying that it tried to bring too many things under one umbrella. He saw no problem with the independence of American Catholic colleges and universities. The bishop responded to a question in the letter concerning his relationship to the colleges of the diocese by saying that in the Cleveland diocese this relationship was largely carried out through the Associated Colleges of Cleveland.[70]

One instance of close cooperation of two of the colleges was the joint certification program at John Carroll and Notre Dame College for teachers of the mentally retarded. There was nevertheless, a tendency for the two women's colleges to work more closely together than with John Carroll. Although the cooperative arrangements accomplished by the Liaison Committee remained intact, they were less prominent in the relationships of the Associated Colleges.

EDUCATIONAL OPPORTUNITIES EXPANDED

The Soviet Institute at John Carroll University celebrated its tenth anniversary in 1971. Under the direction of Dr. Michael S. Pap, assisted by Dr. George J. Prpic, the Institute had provided annual forums attended by prominent scholars in the field of Soviet Studies. It also had produced eighty master's degrees as well as certification of competence in Soviet studies to fifty students. Over 350 high school teachers had received similar training. Some sixty nationally recognized lecturers in the field had been guest lecturers on campus. Through the efforts of the Institute, John Carroll University became the founding member of the Intercollegiate Academic Council on Ethnic Studies, a consortium of thirteen educational institutions devoted to research on ethnic groups, with Pap as the Council's first chairman. In 1972 Pap was given leave to serve the city of Cleveland as director of the Department of Human Services and Economic Development.[71]

Increased activity of the faculty in research and publication marked the 1970s. A ten-year report on acousto-optics research by the department of physics detailed the advances in which the Carroll research team, led by Dr. Edward T. Carome, played a significant role. The first major public seminar in northern Ohio on environmental problems of Lake Erie was presented by Dr. Edwin Skoch of the department of biology with the assistance of Republic Steel Corporation. With the help of a grant from the Cleveland Foundation, John Carroll began to offer a concentration in aquatic biology to serve as a focal point for research on Lake Erie. A three-year grant from the Cleveland Foundation enabled the establishment of a Chair in Aquatic Biology. Operated by the department of biology and coordinated by Skoch, the Chair planned conferences and was a center of information. Research in the environmental area broadened and in 1974

Dr. Andrew White of the department of biology was engaged in a major research activity in the problems of Lake Erie. A Chair in Ecology under the direction of Dr. Joseph T. Bombelles, professor of economics, was established in 1974.

There were also many other areas that attracted research and interest. Dr. A. Jerome Clifford, S.J., professor of finance, received a Fullbright-Hays Fellowship to study central banking in Yugoslavia, and later went to Fiji for the same purpose. Twenty-nine faculty members received George E. Grauel Faculty Fellowships for study and research ranging over a variety of areas. One problem with these fellowships was that often there were more quality proposals than available awards. One of the most prestigious awards was the appointment of Dr. Clement A. Miller, professor of fine arts, to a Guggenheim Fellowship to the Vatican Library to annotate the correspondence of Renaissance musicians. Dr. Robert Getscher, associate professor of fine arts, went to Scotland to examine prints and letters of American artist James A. Whistler in preparation for a major art exhibition. In addition, John Carroll University was chosen as one of eleven universities to participate in the government's Project Vela Uniform because of the expertise of Dr. Edward J. Walter, director of the seismological observatory at the university. The John Carroll phase of the project was to detect differences in the recording of nuclear explosions and earthquakes and was completed successfully in 1963.

The Jesuit Community established a Jesuit Fellowship to further the Jesuit presence on campus. The award was to be renewable for Jesuits who qualified but who could not otherwise be hired because of departmental budget limitations. This enabled the university to bring Father Emmanuel Carreira, a Spanish Jesuit, to campus for a semester each year. Since his field of expertise was astro-physics, interest in astronomy was revived.

Faculty activity was only a part of the expansion of educational opportunities. A television studio and the radio station provided new teaching tools in the area of electronic media. An executive-in-residence became part of the program of the School of Business. A new management program was also established. A Co-op Program in 1978 combined classroom theory with on-the-job experience. Father James E. Duffy, director of the program, received a grant to support it. New courses such as the physics of art and the physics of music broadened student intellectual horizons. "Choices for Women" offered an opportunity for adult women to complete degrees or to take non-degree work. "Early Admissions" made it possible for talented high school students to take college work for full academic credit. A Black Scholarship Program was sponsored by the Jesuit Community and the university. An Honors Alternative Program provided an opportunity for talented students to design their own program.

In 1974 an elementary education major was introduced. Although the *Carroll News* carried an article in which it was claimed that this was the first program initiated by student effort,[72] it should be remembered that were it not for the episcopal decision going back to the 1930s that St. John College should have a monopoly on elementary education in the diocese, that program would have been introduced much earlier by administrative action. The Liaison Committee tried in 1966 to launch such a program and was severely reprimanded by a diocesan official for even bringing the subject up. The Associated Colleges were unable to change the situation until the closing of St. John College was decided upon by diocesan authorities.

When the North Central visitation in 1974 was completed the report was said by the head of the team that reviewed John Carroll to be the most favorable of the fifty-one schools visited.[73] The general report was that John Carroll was doing what it claimed to be doing, with no serious deficiencies.

Problems surrounding the University Series led to the discontinuance of the program and produced a cultural vacuum, limiting student opportunities in this area. The *Carroll News* complained that, "Recreation on this campus consisted of a raucous spring fertility rite in the form of Stunt Night and a few beer mixers in the same vein."[74] The replacement for the University Series, Cleveland-on-Stage, encouraged the hope of increased interest in the performing arts. It was an attempt to bring to the campus some of the community's outstanding cultural organizations in the performing arts. By 1978 this, too, was experiencing financial difficulties; it had nevertheless given the university a good public image with slightly better student participation than the University Series.

The University College of Continuing Education, which in a large measure provided a public service function for the university, underwent some changes. The need for a statement of philosophy and objectives as well as criteria for course offerings was a matter of concern to the Committee on University Planning in 1976.[75] The presumption at the time was that the college would continue to exist, but the clearly academic courses would be placed in their respective undergraduate units.

THE GRADUATE SCHOOL

The original concept of the Jesuit college as preparatory to the university did not provide for graduate work as it is generally understood today. Such degrees as were granted beyond the baccalaureate degree were limited to the master's level. These degrees were usually granted a year after the baccalaureate degree and the requirement was a paper on a topic, usually philosophical, approved by the rector-president. Two such master's degrees were granted by St. Ignatius College in 1895 and one in 1896. Efforts were made by the Jesuit Interprovince Committee after World War I to promote graduate studies in conformity with American standards and the accepted practice of the accrediting agencies. At the 1922 meeting of the Interprovince Committee it was agreed that, "In view of the fact that the standing of a University is largely measured by its graduate work, it seems advisable that our universities should strive to introduce such courses wherever possible."[76] Not until the 1930s did John Carroll feel that it had the necessary resources to begin graduate work in certain departments. Additions to the faculty at that time included several with doctoral degrees in various fields; Father Charles H. Metzger in history, Hugh Graham in education and teacher training, Father Elmer Trame in biology, and Father Ralph Gallagher in sociology provided opportunity for graduate study in their respective fields.

In December 1934 a meeting was held under the chairmanship of Father Edward Bracken, who had replaced Father Fox as dean of the college, to consider whether graduate offerings should be continued. Attending the meeting were Professors Fritz Graff, newly appointed head of the Department of Business Administration, Frank Burke (chemistry), Hugh Graham (education) and Bernard Jablonski (French), as well as Fathers Pickel (chemistry), Charles Ryan (English), Patrick Lomasney (history), and Ralph Gallagher (sociology). There was unanimous agreement to continue offering graduate work in selected departments: those approved were chemistry, English, biology, education, history, business administration, and languages. Two degrees were to be offered, the master of arts and the master of science; the program in each case was twenty-four credit hours plus a thesis for six hours credit. After credentials had been approved by the registrar, each student's direction was in the hands of the major advisor; the dean was to be involved only in case of difficulties. At least 60 percent of the work was to be in those courses given only for graduate students. Since enrollment was quite low, formal classes were often replaced by a kind of tutorial system.

A difference of opinion existed among Jesuit leaders in the American Assistancy over the desirability of encouraging the growth of graduate programs in any of their colleges that felt they had the necessary resources. Some would have preferred the concentration of graduate study in one or two schools. The program at John Carroll was included in an investigation of graduate programs in Jesuit colleges by Father James B. Macelwane, a St. Louis University seismologist. Father Macelwane had many good things to say about the graduate program at John Carroll and felt that it should continue.[77] His report on certain other Jesuit institutions, such as Marquette and St. Louis University, was not so flattering, and Father Samuel K. Wilson, president of Loyola University, Chicago, criticized him for being severe on those programs which had shown considerable development; Father Macelwane, he said, wanted a first-class institution overnight.[78] The basic difference between the two men seemed to be their difference over whether a limited or an unlimited number of graduate schools should be permitted to develop. Father Macelwane would have preferred to develop at least one department wherever it was possible in each Jesuit college.[79] Father Wilson would have limited the number of colleges offering graduate work so as to have the quality in one or two graduate schools as high as possible.

Between 1935 and 1940 there was very slow growth in graduate work at John Carroll. In 1940 Father Frederick E. Welfle, who held a doctorate in history from The Ohio State University, became head of the department of history and also director of what was now called the Graduate Division. When Father Welfle became president of the university in 1946, Dr. Hugh Graham assumed the position of acting director of the Graduate Division. In 1949 Father Henry F. Birkenhauer, seismologist and mathematician, succeeded Graham. In 1950 he issued the first *Graduate Bulletin* and in 1952 the first graduate student handbook. Master's degrees were now approved in eight departments: biology, chemistry, education, English, history, mathematics, physics, and religion. Total yearly enrollment at this time was generally around 75; 197 degrees had been granted by 1955.

One of the results of the intensive self-study, "The Decisive Years," was the establishment of the Graduate School in 1956 with Father Birkenhauer as its first dean. The growth of the school from 1956 to 1981 is evidenced by the granting of almost 3,500 degrees during that period. The issue of doctoral work did not come up until the self-study leading to the Blueprint Report of 1958, which saw "no cogent reasons for offering doctoral work."[80] Nine departments offered programs leading to master's degrees at that time with the addition of classical languages. At one time biology was forced to suspend its program because of few students, insufficient space, and inadequate facilities. Yet there was agreement that more graduate work could be offered at the master's level if the financial problems involved in hiring graduate assistants could be solved. Several departments, including modern languages, philosophy, sociology, and psychology, were then thinking of offering graduate work.

At the time the Decade of Progress Plan was prepared in 1963, the need for graduate work was still strong; graduate enrollment was expected to rise from 590 at the beginning of the period of the plan to 690 at the end of the ten-year period. The Cleveland Commission on Higher Education's forecasts of the greater need for graduate study encouraged John Carroll to anticipate more graduate offerings. One characteristic of the Graduate

School that was not expected to change was that the vast majority of its students were part-time.

The issue of doctoral work arose when the department of physics in 1967 sought to inaugurate a doctoral program. The department had been awarded a research grant under the Department of Defense's Themis Project, but it was conditional on a university commitment to a doctoral program. Consultants from the North Central Association agreed that this approach to inaugurating doctoral programs put the cart before the horse; the approach had been made without full study of its implication for the university. The Decade of Progress plan did not envision doctoral programs and the North Central Report stated that, "Only a well-documented extraordinary opportunity should be permitted to precede the conclusion of the current ten-year planning study";[81] under the circumstances, "one cannot determine whether the Themis grant is an outstanding opportunity and whether the university has the resources to handle it."[82] On 6 December 1967 the department proposal was presented in the Academic Senate and voted down by a wide margin.[83]

The Academic Guidelines of 1970 encouraged graduate programs where they could be justified, and where they did not detract from the undergraduate program; all programs were to be limited to the master's level. The idea of discontinuing graduate work was rejected; at the current level of offerings; graduate work was thought to have no measurable impact on faculty costs. To discontinue graduate work would, moreover, be bad for morale and public relations.[84] Among new programs offered were the Master of Arts in Elementary Teaching, which replaced a very successful MAT program for secondary teachers, and an MED and an MBA program beginning in 1974.

The closing of St. John College in 1974 created an opportunity for the Graduate School to provide for St. John students who had already begun their graduate programs. A rumor had circulated in 1972 that John Carroll would take over St. John College. It was without foundation, arising probably from an offer Father Birkenhauer had made to assist St. John in any way possible. When it was clear that the college was to close as of August 1975, Father Birkenhauer offered to pick up the St. John graduate students wherever they were in their programs and see them through to completion at John Carroll.[85] Father Joseph Nearon, S.S.S., chairman of the John Carroll department of religious studies, announced a master's program in religious studies in February 1975; it was the result of six years of work by the department. The announcement was timely because it was a means of serving the graduate students from St. John. Because of the nature of the program in religious education at St. John, it was, however, more practical that students already well along in their program enroll in the new master of arts in religious education which was later approved both by the diocese and John Carroll in 1976. The latter program was designed with the cooperation of the department of religious studies and diocesan directors of religious education. The nursing program at St. John College went to Ursuline College; the undergraduate programs were available at all of the local Catholic colleges. At John Carroll, diocesan elementary teachers were now given the same reduction in tuition enjoyed by diocesan secondary teachers. Another master's program introduced at John Carroll in 1976 was the Human Services program, the first interdepartmental program at the graduate level.

THE STUDENT OUTSIDE THE CLASSROOM

The student's introduction to the university as a freshman underwent further change in 1974 with the inauguration of the new summer orientation program. From the days in the 1940s when no formal attempt was made to introduce freshmen to the college, through the 1950s with an attempt to emphasize academic and psychological testing in addition to a week of Kangaroo Court known as Hell Week, to a modification in 1965 known as Hello Week, to further modification in favor of a counseling and testing program in 1970, to the new program in 1974, was a slow and sometimes painful evolution. The freshman together with his family now came to the campus during the summer and spent a few days getting his schedule and counseling in order to begin in the fall without the usual confusion of freshman registration. The program worked well under the direction of Dr. William O'Hearn, assistant dean of arts and sciences.

John Carroll in the late 1970s also became a more residential school so far as undergraduates were concerned. The number of dormitories increased from four to six and the number of residents from a little over 1,000 in 1970 to approximately 1,446 in 1981. Of this number a third or more were from the Greater Cleveland area, and over half of the full-time undergraduate enrollment lived on campus in 1981. A number of reasons might be assigned for the trend. Students still wished to go away to college, but reflecting a national trend, they didn't want to go so far that they could not easily get home on weekends to meet old friends. Off-campus apartment rent rates were becoming prohibitive; formerly available rooms in nearby homes were becoming scarce as the houses were now being purchased by growing young families who needed the space themselves. Local zoning regulations in University Heights also restricted occupancy of such rooms by students.

On campus the activism of the early 1970s declined and took on a more moderate tone; energies seem to be directed toward personal interests and development. Informal groups often replaced the volunteer activities of the earlier days; ethnic ties were important. A good illustration of the change from the earlier period can be found in the history of the Student Community Action Program (SCAP) which afforded the students a first-hand experience in a community project on the near West Side of Cleveland in the vicinity of the original location of the university. The program, which began in 1967 in an effort to channel student energies into social service, was not necessarily confined to the West Side Puerto-Rican and Appalachian community. Tutoring was done in some parishes serving black communities; Project Reach in St. Aloysius parish was the first large-scale tutoring program. The organization tended to focus later on social action, participating in boycotts and the peace movement. In 1976 the failure of the university to renew the contract of SCAP's director caused considerable misunderstanding. As both the director and the students viewed the matter it was a case of hiring the director, who was "considered radical," after the Kent State shootings to "help counteract unrest among the students" and then, in the belief "that the student body has returned to liberal and conservative views," letting him go, since he was no longer needed.[86] The actual situation was more involved, centering on the director's lack of necessary credentials to receive tenure and on fundamentally different views—the director's and the university's—of the university's purpose.

Other campus activity included Freedom University, sponsored in the early 1970s by the Student Union to provide access for the students to what some thought were courses more relevant than those offered in the regular schedule. There were antiwar demonstrations, one of which coincided with the twentieth anniversary of the establishment of the ROTC at John Carroll. A poll in 1971, when the morality of the presence of the ROTC on campus was questioned by the students, showed student resistance to it had declined since it had become voluntary. Eighty-seven percent of the students had no objection to the program and 59 percent of the students either had or were taking courses in the program.[87] In 1972 there was a student protest "involving symbolic blood throwing, (cow's blood) resulting in a cancellation of the ROTC Awards Banquet."[88] About twenty students marched into the ROTC building, sat in the hall, and sang for several hours after the cow's blood was spilled on the stairs. Some of the protest was against the university's holding of certain stocks and doing research for the Navy.

The protest may have provided an outlet for frustrations about the VietNam war, but it also had a strong negative effect, particularly since those who made the mess did not clean it up. That service was provided by the Christian Life Community, the new name for the former Sodality, and members of the Charismatic Prayer Community, which was active on campus. Both of these groups assisted the maintenance crews. The *Carroll News* commented that the incident had "increased polarization on campus. In terms of community, then, it cannot be termed a success."[89]

Other incidents in the early part of the decade included a drug raid on Bernet Hall by federal drug agents in 1972.[90] The Orientation program the following summer included a seminar on drugs as well as one on careers. A motion picture called "Return to Campus" was filmed on campus in 1973; it was a "Walter-Mitty-like fantasie" of a former football star who returned to his alma mater, made the football team, and became a hero.[91] The picture caused no great rush at the box office. Social integration of blacks and whites on campus was slow. Efforts of blacks to instruct whites on proper social behavior brought considerable criticism, if one judges by letters to the *Carroll News*.[92] Father Birkenhauer suspended Stunt Night in 1977 because scripts were changed after they had been approved. "This irresponsibility on the part of the student body," said Father Birkenhauer, "cannot be ignored."[93]

By 1978 the *Carroll News* was complaining about the decline of activism. " 'Who cares?' 'What difference does it make?' More people asking these questions and similar questions these days—few are showing interest in policy issues unless it affects their pocketbooks."[94] The editor attributed the change to disillusionment with the aftermath of the Great Society, the Viet-Nam war, and government scandals and corruption. Yet, it was not always quiet on campus. There were shouting matches such as the one in May 1980, apparently started by an exchange of pleasantries by students in Dolan Hall and New Hall. According to the *Carroll News*, "The JCU campus was a scene of a rare display of boisterosity as residents of Dolan, Murphy, and the New Dorm competed with one another in raising a din that shook the campus."[95] The *Carroll News* approved. "This is great," "we need more of this"; the shouting match was praised as a means of relieving tension, the "first indication of quality school spirit," and "a response to the school's authoritarian atmosphere." The melee, which lasted several hours, was cited by one student as meaning "We're asserting ourselves as adults."[96] Hopefully he was not representative.

INTERCOLLEGIATE COMPETITION

Intercollegiate competition is for the most part generally associated with athletics. At John Carroll, debating teams also had a long tradition of intercollegiate activity, winning a great number of competitions. The Carroll debate team had a most successful year in 1975 under the coaching of Dr. Austin Freeley, director of forensics since 1957. First place trophies were won in major tournaments at the University of Notre Dame, Southern

Connecticut State University, the University of Missouri, and Youngstown State University. The Carroll team was ranked among the nation's best in debating teams, and in 1979 won sixteen trophies in six intercollegiate debates.[97]

In football, after a miserable season in 1970, the 1971 Blue Streaks won their sixth PAC title in sixteen years; a seventh title came in 1973, and the Blue Streaks were co-champions in 1974 with a 7–2 record. This was also the year when a new individual record for yardage gained was set by Tim Barrett. His 1,410 yards surpassed the former record set by Carl Tasef. The tennis and rifle teams had their first wins in the PAC since 1968. After taking the PAC title in 1970–1971 season, the basketball team did not fare so well in succeeding years.

The wrestling teams of the 1970s supplied the measure of both local and national glory lacking in the other sports. In 1979 the wrestling team, under Coach Tony DeCarlo, won its thirteenth consecutive PAC title and also won in the National Catholic Invitational Tournament, beating rivals Marquette and Notre Dame. The Carroll team in 1975 also won the first national title for Cleveland area colleges in Division III of the NCAA.

One major change in the intercollegiate athletic program was the introduction of women's teams. Intramural programs for women had been operating since the institution officially went coeducational in 1968, with basketball and volleyball the principal sports. Success in intercollegiate competition in these sports was modest at first. Under the guidance of Kathleen Manning, coordinator of women's athletics, the teams gradually improved. Swimming, when competition was first introduced in 1975, gave the women further opportunity to demonstrate their skills as did the admission of women in 1973 to ROTC, when they joined the rifle teams. Rugby, baseball, and soccer remained male sport activities. All were originally club teams, but baseball again became a varsity sport in 1973.

The 1970s saw the culmination of efforts to establish a major program in physical education. The period also saw the development of the Belvoir property into the Bracken Athletic Complex with fields for baseball and other sports, and the Wasmer Field for track and football. Neighbors' fears dating back to the 1950s when a sign on the property said it was to be the home of a future football stadium were now quieted; residents of University Heights now had a recreational area for summer use. On the whole the period ended on a more positive note than it began.

XVI

Transition to the Second Century
1975–1980

As John Carroll University approached the end of its first hundred years and began looking toward its second century, at least one development was rather obvious. That was the increased number of students living on campus. In the face of a somewhat stable enrollment the increase of almost fifty percent of the number on campus in 1970 indicated a shift towards a residential school, which brought some changes in itself. Large waiting lists for dormitory space each fall had led to the construction of a new dormitory which opened in the fall of 1978; another dormitory was opened in 1981. The former was named after Walter S. Sutowski, prominent Cleveland businessman, the latter after Father William J. Millor, headmaster of residence halls for many years.

The William H. Johnson Memorial Swimming Pool became a reality in 1975. Perhaps no other addition to the campus had been anticipated for so long. Father John Weber, who recruited students for many years, had always promised that the pool would be awaiting freshmen when they enrolled. So persistent had been the promise and its lack of fulfillment that the name "Father Fibber" was often used to describe him. During the dedication ceremonies on 19 October 1975, a ripple developed on the surface of the pool's water and spread across the pool. Father Birkenhauer was said to observe that perhaps the spirit of Father Weber rising from the depths caused the motion.

The Religious Center, which in 1969 had risen on the foundation of the unfinished Bishop's Memorial Chapel of 1929, replaced the old gymnasium and former home of the School of Business. It was named after Allan Fritzsche, whose father, Alfred, had been vice-chairman of the sponsoring committee that began the work of moving the university to the East Side in 1923. Allan Fritzsche had been a long-time trustee of the university. As Father Birkenhauer said, "it was appropriate that our Religious Center should bear the name of one of our leading Catholic families, and that it completed a plan that the Fritzsche family helped develop so many years ago."[1] A general purpose room, an annex to the chapel, was part of the Center and named after Miriam Mackin Jardine, who, together with her late husband Frank, had been long-time friends of Father Benedict Rodman. The Rathskeller was already established in the basement below the Center.

Campus renovation projects were aimed more at functional rather than beautification objectives. Kulas Auditorium underwent a major face-lifting in the late 1970s. Improvement of the stage facilities was intended to provide an opportunity to schedule more cultural programs as the home of "Cleveland on Stage." The students were not forgotten in campus renovation projects. A perceptive superintendent of buildings and grounds, John Reali, found room for benches along the corridors where students had a tendency to congregate; the benches helped keep the students off the floor and permitted a better flow of traffic. A former men's lavatory was converted into a student lounge, appropriately named the Harry Gauzman Lounge. Harry's commentaries on life at John Carroll continued through the 1970s and there was every likelihood that they would continue into the second century. A patio dedicated to the memory of Jim Davis, a freshman who had died in the spring of 1974, was intended to provide a "quiet and serene area where students can converse and study."[2]

A student survey in early 1979 sought to discover what the university's value to its local community was in dollars and cents. Constant bickering with the residents over university parking plans and other issues had in part prompted the question of the economic impact of the university on property values in the local community. It may also have been inspired in part by a proposed more general study of the economic impact of higher education conducted by the Institute of Urban Studies at Cleveland State University. What the students found was that "there is an inherent prestige value of the University which carries a very pretty price tag indeed."[3] On a strictly cash basis the services provided by the city—police and fire protection, traffic control, and fire and building code inspection,—did not produce an annual surplus in the city's favor. On the other hand, university employees paid a sizeable amount of city income tax. Mayor Beryl Rothschild was quoted as considering the financial deficit "relatively unimportant. What is important is that having a college in the community is an asset in other ways. Housewives can go back to school; the architecture is elegant, and more importantly, there is an immeasurable prestige value in the community."[4] The *Carroll News* report tried to put a price on the intangible. Increased market value of homes and the resultant stabilizing effect on property value created a tax revenue from the areas that offset any actual financial loss.[5]

PLANNING FOR CHANGE

The Committee on University Planning had since 1972 made some headway on the agenda of that year, but it had not come up with any comprehensive plan or mechanism for implementing planning. In the midst of this activity the Academy for Educational Development based in Washington, D.C. devised a project to help selected colleges and universities prepare for society's changing expectations. Dr. John D. Millett, a former trustee of John Carroll, had moved to Washington with the Academy and was chairman of the new project. In 1976 John Carroll was one of the schools selected to participate in the planning project.

After a fall meeting between members of the John Carroll planning committee and the AED project team, a memorandum was circulated among the members of the planning committee asking three questions: What are the major planning problems? What are some possible solutions? What are the obstacles to solutions? The members supplied written answers which were then summarized, ranked in importance, and discussed by the planning committee. Problems most frequently listed were the need for a better Mission Statement, the changing educational and demographic environment, the need for accurate enrollment projections, and the need for effective Jesuit presence on campus.[6] Tentative solutions were varied and the obstacles cited were inertia, unwillingness to change, poor communication, and lack of recognition by some administrators of any real need for the type of planning envisioned by the Project.[7] Discussion of a rewriting of the Mission Statement occupied the next few meetings of the University Planning Committee. Father Lavelle, then dean of the School of Business, urged the strongest statement possible in terms of the Catholic and Jesuit character of the institution.[8]

A member of the AED Project, Sherman Jones, visited the campus in March 1977, was supplied with copies of planning efforts, conducted interviews, and then presented his report in April. This report, which came to be known as the Jones Report, recommended the retention of the current planning committee, more extensive use of task forces, consideration of program implications of the Mission Statement, clarification of the roles of the Academic Senate and Faculty Service Committee, multi-year forecasting of revenues for planning purposes, a revision of the university By-Laws to correspond to existing practice, clarification of the purpose of University College, and greater involvement of the faculty in the planning and decision-making process.[9]

It was unfortunate that the author of the Report severely damaged his own credibility by his reference to making practice correspond with the university By-Laws. Jones later admitted never having seen the By-Laws, which at John Carroll are called Regulations. Even though some of his observations had merit, his reference to By-Laws, the seeming lack of any knowledge of the *Faculty Handbook*, and what was perceived as an almost total lack of knowledge of Catholic institutions of higher education did not impress members of the Planning Committee.[10] In a letter to Millett regarding the Jones Report, Father Birkenhauer described the results of John Carroll's participation in the AED Project as "considerably short of what was hoped for."[11] The visit

> provided no basis for progress toward the fulfillment of our earlier expectations. Neither in his interviews nor in his report did Mr. Jones discuss the problem of obstacles to planning at John Carroll. Yet, this was one of the three issues which he had said in his letter he wished to discuss. In general, therefore, what negativism toward formal planning existed prior to participation in the AED project continues to exist, perhaps even in a confirmed state.[12]

Millet expressed his regret that the AED Project was "so unproductive."[13]

Future planning faced a number of issues, as Father Birkenhauer saw it. One was the need for institutionalizing the planning and decision-making process with proper participation of all concerned. Another issue was the recognition on the part of the Planning Committee of the value of "an integrated, comprehensive plan centrally surpervised. There should be a clear and explicit charge to a planning office to coordinate efforts to provide data, appropriate faculty participation in the process, and alternative plans for decision-making."[14] It was hoped that the Planning Committee would overcome a certain antipathy to integrated and centralized planning and devote itself to these issues in 1977–1978.

MISSION RESTATED

Although the Planning Committee was in the process of reviewing the Mission Statement for greater clarity and appropriateness when participation in the AED Project began, such participation did tend to make the need for clarification of the university's mission a little more urgent. The Planning Committee decided to publish a revised draft of a mission statement in the September 1977 issue of *Notes from the President's Desk* and use it as a basis for university-wide discussion. A further revised draft was then submitted to the University Council for its recommendation.[15] This process involved separating the Educational Philosophy section from the University Council Report of 1970 as it was revised in 1975.[16] The remaining sections, containing priorities and guidelines, were later discussed in a faculty meeting and the University Council. The final revision of the Mission Statement was approved by the Board of Trustees on 15 December 1977.

Criticism of the revised Mission Statement did not obscure a consensus on its content and expression. As a way of bringing out what was new and what was traditional in the statement, it might be interesting to speculate on what the founding Jesuit Fathers of 1886 might have thought of the new statement had they been able to comment on it. There certainly would have been some puzzlement over the omission of reference to the *Ratio Studiorum* which was so prominent in early statements about the university's educational philosophy. They would not have been surprised, as some later Jesuits were, that the *Spiritual Exercises* were directly related to educational activity. They undoubtedly would have been horrified at the use of the word "co-educational," but they would have approved of the commitment to excellence. The use of the term "liberal arts" in place of "classics" would have been acceptable, since they identified the two. The final paragraph, which described the kind of educational experience which the student was expected to acquire, would have met with substantial approval even though it was broader than the early Jesuits envisioned. The role of the layman and the openness to non-Catholics both as students and faculty would have caused concern; the impact of Vatican II would have been hard to understand. So also might the work of the Jesuits on Project One, their effort in the American Assistancy in the mid-1970s to explore options in the educational apostolate, and the Thirty-Second General Congregation of the Society of Jesus, which also had examined the role of Jesuits in higher education.

What the 1886 vintage Jesuit might have found particularly difficult was the concept of John Carroll as a university with the "autonomy and freedom appropriate to a University";[17] the founders of St. Ignatius College thought of their institution as a preparation for the university within the context of the traditional Jesuit college. The separation of the offices of rector and president also would have been difficult to understand, as would the addition of laymen to the Board of Trustees. They would have agreed that the Jesuits in the United States had lost control of their colleges and universities.

The 1880s were not an era willing to accept Catholics as part of the pluralistic society that was America; a defensive attitude by Catholics contributed to their unwillingness to be part of that society. This country puzzled the immigrant German Jesuits; they had difficulty coping with what they considered libertarian attitudes. Nevertheless, the fact that they could come to this country, face numerous obstacles including unfamiliarity with the language, and still accomplish what they did, would indicate that the early Jesuits could adjust to changing circumstances without thinking they had compromised their basic mission.

SPIRITUAL AND MORAL TRAINING

The earliest *Catalogues* of St. Ignatius College made it clear that the spiritual and moral training of the students was part of the educational enterprise. For that reason students were required to be present at daily Mass, make the annual retreat, and receive the Sacraments at least once a month. These requirements were stated in every *Catalogue* through the mid-1960s. The wording might change but the requirements were the same. In the 1940s and 1950s, the chaplain's office under Father Clifford LeMay became a very important part of this structure. Regularly scheduled conferences with each student gave the chaplain an opportunity to know almost every student in the college personally. The Sodality under the direction of Father James J. McQuade and Father Joseph O. Schell was also a very significant part of the commitment to spiritual and moral values.

The 1960s presented a vigorous challenge to this structured approach. The impact of Vatican II, changing attitudes of Catholics, the recommendations of the Los Angeles Workshop in the areas of philosophy and theology, and campus unrest over political and social issues made adjustment necessary. The wording in the 1966–1968 *Catalogue* recognized the problem and put the commitment to spiritual and moral training in words that seemed more an invitation than a requirement:

> In keeping with the tradition of the Society of Jesus, John Carroll University stresses the spiritual and moral formation of its students. For this reason, every effort is made to provide an atmosphere conducive to spiritual and moral growth and the means by which this growth can be effectively achieved. The university endeavors to make these means easily accessible to students. Mass is celebrated daily in each of the residence hall chapels. Holy Communion is available every fifteen minutes until noon. Full-time chaplains, aided by other priests on the faculty, serve the students, administer the Sacraments, and provide personal, spiritual, and moral guidance. Facilities for the annual retreat are provided on campus, at North Perry, and at other off-campus retreat houses. The Sodality, the Apostleship of Prayer, and the Confraternity of Christian Doctrine provide opportunities to embrace a special apostolic way of life.
>
> The Department of Theology offers to all students courses through which their growth in theological knowledge can be kept commensurate with academic de-

velopment and maturity. A minimum of three of these courses forms a part of the required liberal core for all Catholics seeking an undergraduate degree.[18]

The open dorm issue raised questions of student independence and responsibility that led to the formation of the Committee on Community. At the same time the Jesuit Community through Father Birkenhauer as president of the university requested Father Schell to provide the organization of a Campus Ministry Team. The concept of community made demands on all segments of the university and it was hoped that the Campus Ministry Team would play a crucial role in the revitalization and renewal of the spiritual life of the university.[19] Father Birkenhauer declared in his *Annual Report*, 1971–1972,

> A "Catholic presence" attesting to Christian spiritual and moral values will exist as long as the Jesuit Fathers and dedicated Christian laymen and women compose the John Carroll faculty. But a Jesuit university should not limit its role to presence alone. Rather it should use its resources to extend to the university community a variety of services within the realm of religious affairs.[20]

The goal was the establishment of a genuinely Christian academic community. Thus the Fritzsche Religious Center became the headquarters of the newly formed Campus Ministry Team and the focal point of the renewal.

In the fall of 1971 Father Schell, as coordinator of religious affairs, organized the Campus Ministry Team. Ten Jesuit Fathers and one Scholastic composed the Team. The purpose was, as Father Schell put it, "an effort to utilize fully the university resources to extend the services offered in the area of religious affairs for the benefit of the students and the faculty."[21] To enhance the position of the Campus Ministry within the university, the Coordinator of Religious Affairs was given vice-presidential rank. In recruiting members of the Team every effort was made to secure those who would also be eligible to participate in the academic life of the university.

The team concept was intended to provide the students with a wide variety of opportunities for spiritual and moral growth. The former structured organization of spiritual life on the campus of a Catholic institution under a single chaplain requiring student attendance at Mass, the making of an annual retreat, and a regularly scheduled appointment with the chaplain, was "no longer feasible, whatever its merits originally were," commented Father Peter Fennessy, a member of the campus Ministry Team.[22] It was now necessary to reach out to the students and to provide opportunities for them to react. The Campus Ministry was to be available to students on a twenty-four-hour basis, to provide liturgies as well as opportunities for making retreats, to build community, and to offer counseling for spiritual and moral growth. A "needed and welcome dimension to the Campus Ministry Team" was the addition of Sister Mary Ellen Greeley, R.S.M., who joined the Team in 1974.[23]

For those who sought a deeper commitment to the spiritual life, the Community for Charismatic Renewal was organized in the fall of 1970 with about twenty-five students.[24] In 1972 this group numbered about eighty with the majority of them John Carroll students. The group met weekly under the guidance of Father William H. Nichols, professor of physics and then Rector of the Jesuit Community. The Christian Life Community provided still other opportunities for students to manifest their Christian commitment.

The annual report of the Campus Ministry in 1981–1982 gave evidence of success for the new approach.[25] The eight-day retreats, which had been popular as early as the 1950s, now involved twenty-six students. About two hundred students worked with the Campus Ministry Team, which was composed of three Jesuits full-time, one Sister full-time, one lay woman full-time, a Dominican Sister part-time, and one Jesuit part-time. Twelve volunteer Jesuits assisted the Team. There was also the assistance of fifty Eucharistic Ministers trained through a diocesan program. Numerous retreats, reflective weekends, and discussions were provided. The work of building community continued.

ENROLLMENT

Following the adoption of the revised Mission Statement, the University Planning Committee took up the question of how to improve enrollment in the face of forecasts that the pool of high school graduates was declining. A report, commissioned by the Planning Committee, prepared by Raymond J. Reilly, and entitled "To Extend the Boundaries," was presented to the committee in the fall of 1978.[26] The report examined the current situation, considered future needs, and recommended a broad positive program of expanded recruitment.

One of the recommendations of the report was to expand program offerings that were in high demand. Others included using alumni in recruiting, placing the admissions office under the vice-president for business, and considering increasing dormitory space. Implementation of the publicity recommendations brought comment from the *Carroll News* that John Carroll was selling itself short in its recruiting promotion. An editorial objected to the type of radio appeal being broadcast and related it to a number of student dropouts who had responded to the radio appeal. The editorial claimed that:

It appears that John Carroll is selling itself short. Many members of the school faculty are nationally recognized and respected while the University has produced numerous community leaders in business and government. This article was written out of concern and not snobbery. I became concerned when an institution which has promoted academic excellence for nearly a centennial feels forced to rely on the merits of a four-year-old swimming pool.[27]

PRIORITIES AND GUIDELINES

The appearance of the approved Mission Statement in *Notes from the President's Desk* in December 1977 set the stage for the further revision of the original University Council Report of 1970. In January 1978 the local chapter of the AAUP brought a motion to the faculty through the Faculty Service Committee for the purpose of recommending new priorities and guidelines that would carry the university into the 1980s. On 15 February the faculty met to discuss the creation of a committee for this purpose. After a long meeting, during which many left before the final vote was taken, it was agreed to appoint a committee of the faculty with university-wide representation to propose new priorities and guidelines. The vote was twenty-six to twenty-three with three abstentions.[28] Father Birkenhauer said he would cooperate with the committee. Father Paul Woelfl was chosen chairman of the Committee on Priorities and Guidelines, which was to make its final report to the faculty.

On 6 April 1979 the committee made its final report under the title, "Design for a Second Spring." The report listed four major priority areas—student population, educational function, institutional image, and planning and governance. The report stated:

> The committee is convinced that, if constructive means can be found for meeting the need in these areas, the university will be able successfully to move into the '80s and, then, into the second century of its existence with a promise of new vitality, growth and productivity.[29]

Recommendations on how to achieve the desired state composed the rest of the report.

A faculty meeting on 19 April provided an opportunity for discussion of the report and its recommendations; the specific recommendation for future planning and governance provoked the sharpest differences of opinion. A vote conducted by the Faculty Service Committee resulted in an eighty-five to forty-nine vote of the faculty to accept the report as presented.[30]

Father Birkenhauer called a meeting of the University Planning Committee for 29 June. Selected faculty members were also invited to attend and to discuss reaction to the final report of the Priorities and Guidelines Committee. Father Birkenhauer spoke of the faculty comments on the ballots which indicated some serious criticism of the report. Many voted approval without supporting the report in its entirety; the specific recommendation on governance was looked upon by many as "divisive."[31] Several objected to the failure to emphasize value orientation and to make a firm commitment to liberal arts. Some thought that the report was simplistic and unrealistic and that there should have been a minority report.

When asked to express his own view of the report, Father Birkenhauer responded by pointing out the failure of the report to provide a "clear linkage" to the Mission Statement, the lack of any reference to the Jesuit traditions of the university, the omission of values and "somewhat skimpy treatment of religious affairs, religious formation, and campus ministry, and the omission of the development function of the University."[32] He saw difficulty in accepting the report exactly as it was presented, but felt that with additional information and clarification it could be improved.

In August 1979 the *Notes from the President*'s *Desk* carried a "President's Report on Planning." It reviewed planning activities since 1976, incorporated the substance of the report of the faculty on goals and objectives, but left open the development of operational guidelines; although not accepting the specific recommendation on governance, the report did promise a review of the current governance process to see how well it achieved the goal of a "rational and effective structure of governance which allows for broad participation of the faculty in the planning and decision-making process."[33] The president's Planning Report together with "Design for a Second Spring" were presented to the Board of Trustees in October 1979.

A committee of administrators in each division of the university together with faculty representatives worked on operational guidelines for each division through the spring of 1980. These guidelines were the subject of discussion at two faculty meetings. In May recommendations emerging from these meetings were incorporated in what was called a "Completed Report on Planning" and published in a special May issue of the *Notes from the President*'s *Desk*. This report included sections on the Jesuit tradition at John Carroll, the mission statement, goals and objectives, and a new set of guidelines. It remained to be seen whether this was an exercise in paperwork or whether the report would be taken seriously.

Before the presentation of the "Completed Report on Planning," Father Birkenhauer announced in February 1980 that he planned to retire at the end of the academic year in May. The Board of Trustees praised his achievements, openness and concern for students; the Board said it found him "refreshing to deal with and hard to replace."[34] Among Father Birkenhauer's accomplishments were a degree of success in maintaining enrollment levels in spite of tuition increases and a dwindling market, operating without budget deficits, giving personal attention to students and their problems, inaugurating master's programs in business, religious education, and human services, and constructing the swimming pool and the fifth dormitory. Father Birkenhauer also succeeded in striking a balance during his tenure between reaction to change and the maintenance of the Jesuit tradition at John Carroll; he still saw the graduate as one who fostered growth, ideas, and principles, the product of a distinctive education that justified the cost.[35]

Just before he officially turned over the presidency to his successor, Father Thomas P. O'Malley, former dean of arts and sciences at Boston College, Father Birkenhauer lost the services of Lillian Thomey, whom he called "the perfect secretary and the perfect student." During the last year of her life she had fought a losing battle with cancer and yet remained on the job as long as she could, "always cheerful, and always ready to give far more than she was paid for, more than anyone had a right to expect." Thomey joined the university in 1956 when she began her career as a secretary to Father Birkenhauer when he was director of the seismological observatory and dean of the Graduate School. She worked on her undergraduate degree while she fulfilled her duties as secretary, and graduating *summa cum laude* in 1963. She was given a standing ovation from those present at the commencement exercises. She was Father Schell's secretary from 1964 to 1967 when he was dean of the college of arts and sciences; she followed Father Schell into the president's office as his secretary. The author had many an occasion to benefit from her efficiency, accuracy, and knowledge of the people in the university, students as well as faculty.

At the university commencement in May 1980, Father Birkenhauer handed over the symbol of office to Father O'Malley, who became the twentieth president of John Carroll University. The new president, the first from a Province outside of the one in which the school was located, gave an interview to the *Carroll News* in which he described his goals.[36] While he praised the School of Business as one of the best, he stressed the importance of a liberal education. He pointed out the need for fund-raising and the involvement of the student in extracurricular activities. With respect to the local community, he saw the university playing an important role "in conjunction with the Church's role—we should remain what we are, but we can't fence ourselves from the community. We should find the needs and address ourselves to them."[37] He also said, "We must plan for the future, but we have to react to changes. Circumstances of the future may change, and we must react to the new situations."[38]

In the fall of 1980, as part of the *Annual Report* of the president, Father O'Malley discussed under the title "Liberal Education of the World of Work" what he had "long regarded as the single most important matter before the higher education establishment in our nation, the declining admiration and understanding of the role played in a person's life by an undergraduate liberal arts and sciences education."[39] There was need, therefore, "to restore confidence in liberal education."[40] Arguing that the most successful businessmen are not always in careers or posts for which they were originally prepared as undergraduates, Father O'Malley stressed the need to "Learn how to live," and proposed what he called a "Mentorship program" as a possible way to combine learning how to live with learning how to make a living. The Mentor, selected from the "world of work," conceived as broadly as possible, would work with small groups of students during a regular semester. Four years of this activity could help blend the best of both worlds in a way that would be helpful to the student and become a distinguishing feature of the undergraduate program at John Carroll.

THE CHANGING OF THE GUARD

Between 1967 and 1983 John Carroll lost twenty-one faculty members through death. Most of them had had a strong influence on the life of the university since its move to University Heights. Eight Jesuits and thirteen laymen made up the list.

Doctor George E. Grauel, who died of a heart attack in 1967, had joined the faculty in 1936 in the Department of English. His career was interrupted by a period of service in the Navy during World War II after which he returned to John Carroll as chairman of the department in 1946. He became dean of the Evening College and director of Institutional Planning in 1962; the latter post he held at the time of his death. Grauel was a very sensitive and serious person who frequently assumed other people's burdens, often to his disadvantage. This was particularly true during the latter part of Father Dunn's regime, when Grauel felt a personal responsibility for some of the criticism which led to Father Dunn's removal as rector and president in 1967.

In 1968 Bernard R. Campbell, who had joined the faculty in 1947 as a member of the Department of English, died after a relatively short illness. From 1947 to 1954 he was responsible for all university publications and moderator of the *Carroll News*. His addition to the faculty in 1947 enabled the university to offer a minor in journalism for the first time in response to a persistent student demand. He was also responsible for starting the *Carroll Quarterly* in 1947, a student literary magazine which was intended to carry on the tradition of the *Lumina*, which had been discontinued in 1919.

Top left, Bernard R. Campbell, English, 1947–67; *right,* Nicholas Predovich, S.J., Religious Studies, 1956–76; *Middle,* Jospeh Cotter, English, 1947–82; *Bottom left,* Vincent Klein, Communications, 1946–71; *right,* Robert Pingstock, S.J., 1965–78

Top left, Frank Devlin, Business, 1947–69; *right,* D'Alte Welch, Biology, 1942, 1970; *Middle,* Edwin F. Gilchrist, Biology, 1937–69; *Bottom left,* Philip H. Vogel, S.J., Biology, 1956–70; *right,* Terrence Ahearn, S.J., Biology, 1936–60

Top left, Terrence Kane, S.J., Theology, 1945–67; *right,* Edmund Thomas, Chemistry, 1936–75; *Middle,* Edward C. Reilley, History, Business, 1935–75; *Bottom left,* James J. Peirolo, Languages, 1946–66; *right,* James A. Mackin, S.J., History, Library, 1946–77

Campbell also drew up the original stylebook for the *Carroll News*, which with minor revisions was in use at the time of his death. Campbell was a tireless worker who attracted little attention while he carried out his responsibilities. He was a kind of invisible man whose influence was felt in all the university publications.

Between 1969 and 1971 there were six deaths, three of them in the Department of Biology. Dr. d'Alte Welch, who joined the department in 1942, was easily one of the more colorful members of the faculty. Enthusiastic, spirited, and sincere, with a love of life and learning, the tall man with the booming voice was a respected scholar not only in the field of biology but also in the highly specialized area of children's books, where he had an international reputation as a collector and codifier. An avid researcher, he was friendly and loved by all who knew him and could tell stories even on himself in his own inimitable style.

Father Philip Vogel, chairman of the Department of Biology, died of a heart attack in January 1969. Father Vogel had carried on the tradition of Father Ahearn's leadership in the department. In June 1971 Dr. Edwin Gilchrist, who had joined the faculty in 1937, died after an extended illness. Gilchrist had taught pre-medical biology courses and did research in microscopic anatomy. Father Terrence Kane, who had joined the faculty in theology in 1956, died in December 1969. He was famous for his rigorous discipline, Irish wit, and sharp remarks to students that earned him the nickname "Killer" Kane. The month of August in 1971 claimed the lives of two men who had given service above and beyond the call of duty. Frank Devlin as assistant dean of the School of Business and editor of the *Carroll Business Bulletin* had been on the faculty since 1947. Vincent S. Klein was the founding chairman of the Communications Department and coached the students in theater and debate during his early years. He was known for his enthusiasm in the classroom and his patience with students outside of it. He was intensely interested in students and their careers—"my kids," he called them.

John Carroll's "Mr. Chips," Professor Al Bungart, died in 1972. He had retired in 1959 after thirty-four years of teaching; he was given an honorary degree by the university and the title *professor emeritus*. His lively teaching of literature was interspersed with a homespun philosophy. He was described by one Jesuit as possessing "the body of a blacksmith and the soul of a poet."[41] One of his colleagues, Eugene Mittinger, once remarked, "He always wore black and I thought he was the funniest Scholastic I had ever met. He smoked a corn cob pipe and lit it with stick matches. I didn't know he wasn't a Jesuit until one day he told me about having a date."[42] Bungart acquired additional fame as an excavator and collector of Indian relics. He also discovered a species of grasshopper which was named after him, *Ocrididia bungartis.*

Although separated from Al Bungard by a generation of students, Joseph Cotter, who joined the facuty in the Department of English in 1947 and died in 1982, was in many respects a bearer of the Bungart tradition in the department. He had the same love of life and of students. His lively classes on Shakespeare and Milton influenced a generation of students, who for the most part felt it was a privilege to get into his classes even though they might get low grades in spite of their best efforts. The Distinguished Faculty Award given to Professor Cotter in 1970 is eloquent testimony of the esteem in which he was held by his colleagues and students. Cotter was more shy and retiring than the effervescent Bungart, but each in his own way typified the best in the John Carroll teaching tradition.

Another death was that of Father James A. Mackin, who joined the faculty in 1946. He taught history and was director of the library until 1977, when he resigned that post. In 1978 he went to Casa Scrittori, the Jesuit writers' house in Rome, where his linguistic ability was of great value in helping prepare a dictionary of the Society of Jesus. He returned to this country in 1981 because of ill health and spent the next two years at Columbiere, Michigan, where he died in August 1983. Father Mackin played an important role in the design of Grasselli Library and began the organization of the archives of John Carroll University. One of his many projects was a considerable amount of research into the thorny question of the financial agreements between the Buffalo Mission and St. Ignatius College.

John Carroll's "Music Man," Jack Hearns, died in January 1976. When he retired in 1972 he had given forty-one years of loyal, dedicated service to the university as director of the Band and Glee Club. In 1956 his Glee Club was given national recognition on Dave Garroway's program, "Monitor."

In 1976 and 1977 four Jesuits, two in each year, ended their earthly labors—Fathers Nicholas Predovich and Charles Castellano in 1976, and Fathers Robert Pingstock and William J. Millor in 1977. Father Predovich first came to John Carroll in 1956 as chairman of the Department of Theology. He left in 1960 for further studies at Woodstock, became director of Novices at Colombiere College, 1963–1969, and then returned to John Carroll. Father William Millor described Father Predovich as a consistently forward-looking theologian whose "impatience with older Jesuits earned him and a few others of his era the title, 'The Young Turks.' "[43] Father Predovich was exceptionally popular with the students. Father Charles Castellano was the last surviving member of the original Jesuits who opened the University Heights campus in 1935. He taught Latin and Greek; his methods and notes became a model for many Latin instructors. His pre-seminary Latin classes were often attended by many who were not actually in the classroom. These classes, taught during the summer with classroom windows open, allowed Father Castellano's booming voice to be heard for a considerable distance from the Administration Building where he was drilling the declensions and conjugations. His lifetime hobby was horticulture; when he was gardening he could be easily recognized at a distance by his trademark, a cassock and baseball cap.

Father Robert Pingstock, director of Alumni Relations, had been at John Carroll since 1964. One of his accomplishments was the transformation of the alumni organization from primarily a social one to one devoted to service to the university and to its students as well as to the alumni. Student recruitment, job placement, and continuing education for alumni were some of its services. Father Millor was a unique man with a varied career and interests. He had held nearly every administrative post in the Jesuit Order except that of Provincial and General. He was a scholar, editing commentaries and the text of John of Salisbury, by his own admission a kindred spirit with H. L. Mencken, head of the Classics Department, and for twenty years headmaster of the dormitories. He had also been dean of the Graduate School, executive dean, and academic vice-president. There are a number of stories as to why he was called "The Duke." One of them attributed the title to his "affinity for good clothes and Homburg hats and his iron administrative manner."[44]

Perhaps the most delightful and penetrating analysis of Father Millor was given by Father Joseph Schell, who was "the tall, slender man in the black suit," on the occasion of the celebration of Father Millor's fifty years in the Society.

> I have a few notes here. I'd be afraid to forget anything that Father Millor told me to say. . . . I do admit that one of the few joyful experiences to which I looked forward when I became president was the reversal of roles between Father Millor and myself. For many years he had spoken and I had obeyed. I thought it would be enjoyable to give him orders for a while. But after three years in office, I was unable to find any significant change in our previous relationship.[45]

Father Schell spoke of his first meeting with Father Millor and his fear of "The Duke," which had not abated in thirty years. Father Schell said he learned "that beneath that tough and aggressive exterior beats a heart that is even tougher and more aggressive."[46] Nevertheless, Father Schell admired Millor's "wise counsel," the "incredible retentiveness of his memory," and his "uncanny ability to know most of what is going on in Bernet, and everywhere else, it seems, and to guess at the rest. And I've observed the accuracy of his guesses, and the supreme confidence that enables him to act with equal assurance on knowledge or opinion."[47] In his concluding remarks about the man who was always given a standing ovation when he was introduced, Father Schell said,

> If Father Millor leaves John Carroll some day, it will be the end of tradition. No one else will ever again deal with students (and for that matter, with anyone else) in quite his way, with his unique combination of firmness and flexibility, sternness and concern. . . . Life is a challenge which Father Millor meets with aggressive assurance.[48]

Edmund B. Thomas, who died in 1978, had been recruited to join the faculty in 1936 by Father George Pickel. Until his retirement in 1975 he was a valuable member of the Department of Chemistry. From 1958 to 1959 he served first as acting director and then as director of the department. His interests were in instrumentation and he became quite a collector of electronic gear. The 1963 *Carillon* was dedicated to Thomas. He was always approachable and always had time for students. He was one of the better story tellers on the faculty.

Professor Edward C. Reilley joined the faculty in 1935 as a member of the first faculty on the University Heights campus. He retired in 1975 and died on 19 August 1980 after forty years of service divided between the Department of History and the School of Business. He was chairman of the Department of Business Administration for nine years. A good scholar, he made rigorous demands on students. Professor Reilley was a member of Father Winter's famous St. Ignatius College orchestra of 1927.

The death of Father Laurence Britt in November 1980 came as a great shock to the John Carroll family. He had joined the faculty in 1966 as coordinator of academic counseling after serving six years as president of the University of Detroit. He also had served as dean of the college of arts and sciences at Loyola University, Chicago, 1945 to 1956, and at the University of Detroit, 1956 to 1960. He was dean of the college of arts and sciences at John Carroll from 1967 to his retirement in 1977. After that he was Minister of the Jesuit Community and a counselor in the School of Business. As dean of the college of arts and sciences at John Carroll, Father Britt was often considered a bit hard to approach. After he left office, many faculty discovered that he was more open and fair in his dealings with them than they had suspected. His influence in guiding the fortunes of the institution was considerable. A man of a thousand stories and deep concerns, he was also a perfectionist.

One of the reasons John Carroll was able to operate without a deficit for many years was the skill and ingenuity of Vice-President for Business Francis A. Jones. Jones's motto was, "black ink's the only way." Jones himself attributed the black ink to a "great deal of continuity and understanding within the administration and good cooperation from the academic departments in budget control and other fiscal areas."[49] Father Birkenhauer paid tribute to Jones's skill during twenty-four years of service when he said, "at a time when higher education has faced severe financial problems, John Carroll has been fortunate to have a Frank Jones."[50] Jones resigned in 1972 and died of a heart attack in 1981.

Also in 1981, one of John Carroll's most beloved professors passed from the scene. Dr. James Peirolo, who joined the faculty in 1946 as a member of the Department of Modern Languages, was a warm and friendly person who took a sincere personal interest in all of his students. An experienced cabinet maker and a devoted opera lover, he had a personal dedication to his own intellectual growth and a personality that radiated warmth and affection.

A CENTURY OF GROWTH

We will end the story of the first century of the history of John Carroll in 1980 for both practical and theoretical reasons. On the practical side, preparing a manuscript for publication for the centennial year of 1986 precludes bringing the story up to that date; the years between 1980 and 1986 must be left for the writer of the account of the second century. On the theoretical side, the first agreement between the Buffalo Mission and Bishop Gilmour to establish a college was signed in 1880; the next six years were very much a part of John Carroll's history. One could argue, therefore, that the years 1880 to 1980 cover the first hundred years.

The history of John Carroll University is the history of a Jesuit college of the nineteenth century attempting to retain its traditional Jesuit character and at the same time react to its American environment. Often ignored by the community with which it shared its history, John Carroll survived the privations and hardships of those early years to begin breaking into the mainstream of American higher education in the period following World War I. An abortive attempt to achieve a measure of recognition in 1923 was forgotten when Father Rodman and Father Fox accomplished in the 1930s what had long been the goal of the Cleveland Jesuits, an East Side University. Unfortunately, the Corporate College experiment of the 1930s left a negative image of John Carroll that contributed to the failure of future attempts at cooperation of the Catholic colleges of Cleveland in the 1960s. The bitterness of the controversy of the 1930s, occuring as it did during the move to the East Side, was always subtley present in subsequent interinstitutional relations of the Catholic colleges.

Not until the presidency of Father Dunn, who built on the foundation laid by Father Welfle, did the university begin to take its place in the main-

John Carroll University

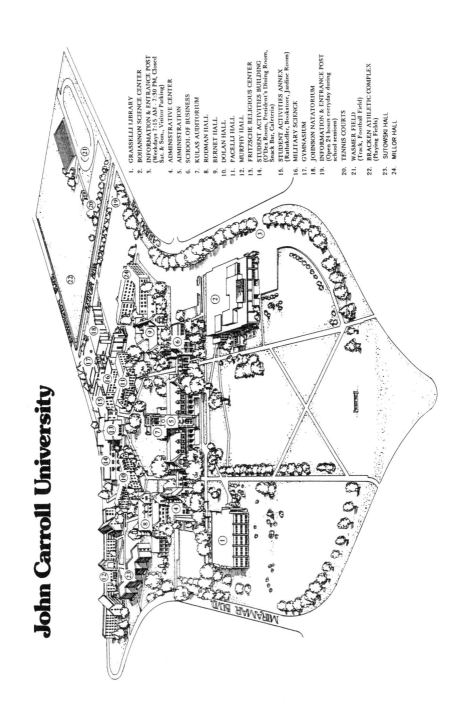

1. GRASSELLI LIBRARY
2. BOHANNON SCIENCE CENTER
3. INFORMATION & ENTRANCE POST (Weekdays 7:15 AM - 7:30 PM, Closed Sat. & Sun., Visitor Parking)
4. ADMINISTRATIVE CENTER
5. ADMINISTRATION
6. SCHOOL OF BUSINESS
7. KULAS AUDITORIUM
8. RODMAN HALL
9. BERNET HALL
10. DOLAN HALL
11. PACELLI HALL
12. MURPHY HALL
13. FRITZSCHE RELIGIOUS CENTER
14. STUDENT ACTIVITIES BUILDING (O'Dea Room, President's Dining Room, Snack Bar, Cafeteria)
15. STUDENT ACTIVITIES ANNEX (Rathskeller, Bookstore, Jardine Room)
16. MILITARY SCIENCE
17. GYMNASIUM
18. JOHNSON NATATORIUM
19. INFORMATION & ENTRANCE POST (Open 24 hours everyday during school sessions)
20. TENNIS COURTS
21. WASMER FIELD (Track, Football Field)
22. BRACKEN ATHLETIC COMPLEX (Playing Fields)
23. SUTOWSKI HALL
24. MILLOR HALL

MIRAMAR BLVD.

stream of Catholic and American higher education. The process was a painful one and left its mark on the university and the Jesuit Community. The presidencies of Fathers Schell and Birkenhauer were of necessity devoted to restoring a sense of community and dedication after the impact of student unrest and Vatican II. The interruption of the plans of Father Dunn left a long agenda of academic and internal governance issues to be attended to. A great deal of effort has been expended in an attempt to work out some of the items of this agenda, but there has probably not been a full commitment to centralized and integrated planning.

In spite of all that had been accomplished over the years, it was possible for the chairman of the Board of Trustees in 1977 to complain of a lack of recognition of these accomplishments. William H. Bricker saw the university's greatest strength in its "Commitment (and proven record for that matter) . . . to educate our students as capable and sensible people."[51] Other schools, he said, proclaimed this, but

> John Carroll actually lives it out daily. This fact of the university's life, I find, is not *sufficiently* appreciated in Cleveland and elsewhere. It is not enough to say John Carroll is "doing a good job," or is "a fine school."
> For the fact is, John Carroll is a superb school. It is superb, primarily because of the Jesuit educational philosophy to develop the "whole man" in a harmony which includes the intellectual, moral, emotional, and physical faculties.[52]

The challenge for the second century is clear; the problem of recognition remains as a legacy of the first century. But there are at least two new problems. One is the internal development of the institution as a university, the other, perhaps even more significant, the problem of the Jesuit community's relationship to the university, a problem arising from the administrative structural changes of the late 1960s. The latter is a situation not faced by the founding Buffalo Mission Jesuits, nor any other Jesuits of that era. But this would not be the first time Jesuits were placed in circumstances for which there was not much precedent.

Appendix A
The Buffalo Mission

Who were these Jesuits in Buffalo who were willing to come to Cleveland? Jesuits from the New York-Canada Mission of the Province of France had served in Buffalo since the creation of the diocese of Buffalo in 1847. Two Jesuits, Fathers Bernard Fritsch and Lucas Caveng, were from the Canadian part of the French Mission and had come to Buffalo at the request of its first Bishop, John Timon, C.M. Bishop Timon had sought their help because the trustees of the local church, St. Louis, had been particularly troublesome in not wishing the bishop to exercise control over the parish. After a drawn-out battle between the bishop and the trustees, the bishop created a new parish, St. Michael's, and gave it to the Jesuits, hoping to draw off the German Catholics to the new parish. The bishop met with some success and insisted that the Jesuits continue their parish work and establish a college in Buffalo. The need for Jesuits to work among the Germans of Buffalo was greater than the manpower supply of the New York-Canada Mission could handle. Yet, in spite of many difficulties, a new church was built at St. Michael's; part of the money that was needed came from European missionary societies. Manpower to serve the large German element in the diocese remained a problem; the illness or death of German-speaking priests only aggravated the situation.

Father James Perron, Superior of the New York-Canada Mission in 1868, was besieged with requests from various American bishops for German-speaking clergy. Father Perron thought that the German Province of the Society should establish a mission in the United States, and suggested to Father General that Buffalo would be a proper headquarters. Father Perron also tried to enlist the support of the Missouri Province Provincial, Father Ferdinand Coosemans, who at first was not sympathetic; his earlier experience with Swiss German Jesuits had not been reassuring. Many of them tended to return to Europe when trouble there subsided. The gathering clouds in Germany, foreshadowing Bismarck's Kulturkampf in the early 1870s, probably convinced Father Coosemans that the anti-Jesuit feeling in Europe would be longer lasting this time. Pressure from American bishops was also a very strong factor.

Father General Peter Beckx sent a Visitor to investigate and report. Father Peter Spicher made a tour of inspection which included Cleveland, where Bishop Rappe offered a parish in his diocese, a church in Toledo. After a visit to the midwest, Father Spicher made his report at the end of October 1868. Whatever problems there were in effecting the transfer of the Buffalo Mission from the New York-

Canada Mission to the German Province were soon overcome and the transfer was made official on 23 January 1869.

Father Spicher became Superior of the new Buffalo Mission and by 1870, the Jesuits had residences in Buffalo and Toledo with territorial rights in other areas of large concentrations of German population. These areas included, in addition to the dioceses of Buffalo and Cleveland, those of Erie, Fort Wayne, Rochester, Detroit, Marquette (Michigan), St. Paul, LaCrosse, Green Bay, and Racine or Madison. Milwaukee and Chicago were exceptions to the sweep along the American shores of the Great Lakes because the Missouri Province was already established in those cities. There were some in the New York-Canada Mission who questioned the advisability of setting up a province on the basis of a language.[1]

By mid-year in 1869, the German Jesuits began to arrive in Buffalo; one year later the last of the New York-Canada Mission Jesuits had departed except Fathers Joseph Durthaller and John Blettner, who remained for a while as pastors. In the fall of 1870 the German Jesuits began classes in the newly founded Canisius College; the number of Jesuits had increased to thirteen priests and five brothers.[2] Since these Jesuits were to play significant roles in the establishment of St. Ignatius College in Cleveland, a brief look at some of them will show the high calibre of these German exiles.

One of them, Father Henry Behrens, became Superior of the Buffalo Mission and rector of Canisius College in 1872. In 1876 he was succeeded by John Lessmann, who in turn was succeeded by Behrens in 1886. Father Behrens, born in 1815, had entered the Society in 1832. He spent some of his early years at the Jesuit College in Freiburg, Switzerland where he was prefect of discipline and taught mathematics. It was at Freiburg that the legend of Father Behrens' heroic exploits began. In 1847, during an attack of anti-clerical forces on the university for the purpose of vandalizing it, the story is told that Father Behrens, who had no difficulty assuming a military manner, donned a uniform that he must have secured in advance, took charge of the attackers and directed them to take the contents of the college (books, etc.), which he had placed in trunks, to a neutral place where he could later retrieve them. It is further claimed that when he was discovered he fled and returned later to assume charge of fresh replacement troops who did not know him. Shortly thereafter he made his first trip to the United States as an exile. Returning to Europe he served as a German chaplain in two wars, the Danish and Austrian. At the onset of the Franco-Prussian War, with the support of some influential German nobles, he again became a chaplain, over the objections of both Bismarck and the Kaiser. His ministrations during the major battles of the war played a considerable part in keeping up the morale of the Catholic soldiers in the German Army. For his work he was awarded the Iron Cross and a ride back to Berlin in the train with Bismarck. Not too long after, the Reichstag decree of 4 July 1872 forbade the Jesuits to exercise any of their priestly or educational functions in the newly united Germany. With a number of his fellow exiled Jesuits he arrived in Buffalo in December 1872, where his first task was to learn English. This in itself was a departure from the practice of his predecessor and some of his associates who used only the German language. After two terms as Superior and one as rector-president of Canisius College, Father Behrens then devoted his efforts to ministering to the Sioux Indians in South Dakota. He later resumed his ministry in Buffalo, where he died at age eighty in 1895.[3]

Father John Lessmann, of somewhat less legendary fame, is the second Jesuit of the Buffalo Mission who was intimately associated with the negotiations for the establishment of St. Ignatius College in Cleveland. He was born in 1825 and entered the Society in 1851 from the diocesan priesthood. Father Lessmann served as Provincial of the Bombay Mission and Superior and Visitor of the Madura Mission before he came to Buffalo. Even before Bishop Gilmour's "Curicular Letter" Father Lessmann had thoughts of a college in Cleveland. The early years of Canisius College were not as promising as the Jesuits had hoped. Fear that the college would not grow prompted Father Lessmann to approach the General of the Society, Father Beckx, about moving the college to Cleveland or to Rochester.[4] The General was not about to sanction such a change and so negotiations between the Buffalo Jesuits and Bishop Gilmour were not resumed until just before the appearance of the "Circular Letter." At that point the conditions in Buffalo were more favorable to Canisius, so a college in Cleveland would be a totally new venture.[5] At the time of resumption of the negotiations between Bishop Gilmour and the Buffalo Jesuits the supply of manpower was not a problem. Some 124 Jesuits were assigned to the Mission including sixty-three priests, fourteen scholastics, and forty-seven brothers.[6]

Appendix B
The Buffalo Mission Debt

Father Neustich always claimed that the money provided by the Buffalo Mission to finance construction of the original buildings and the purchase of property on the West Side was a gift from the Buffalo Mission and not a loan. He based his claim on the fact that benefactors in Germany provided the Buffalo Mission with funds for such purposes and on his recollection of Father Behrens's instructions that he (Father Neustich) was to go to Cleveland and that Father Behrens promised to bear the expenses.

When the Buffalo Mission was dissolved in 1907, the amount of money provided to St. Ignatius College was listed among the assets of the Buffalo Mission. The amount was, therefore, considered a debt and transferred to the Missouri Province as collectable. Father General Wernz at the time of the dissolution of the Buffalo Mission had sanctioned such a transfer.

In 1925 the debt was transferred to the new Ohio Vice-Province (which became the Chicago Province in 1928), to which John Carroll University was now attached. The tradition in the Jesuit Community in Cleveland, based on Father Neustich's understanding, was that the debt was an unjust one. Father Rodman, who joined the Community in 1928, was shocked to learn that someone had now raised the question of payment. He therefore was quick to defend the traditional position when he received word from the Chicago provincial, Father O'Callaghan, that the question had been brought up in Rome and Father General was ordering an investigation.

"Our troubles in Cleveland are not yet solved," wrote Father O'Callaghan, "a short time ago I got a letter from the General in which he had the following paragraph."[1] The long paragraph in Latin asked that Father O'Callaghan reexamine the debt of the Cleveland college to the Buffalo Mission and report to the Father General:

> More than once Father Kowald [who succeeded Father Neustich as treasurer in 1922] tried to get me interested in this question and I took the matter up with Father Wallace at St. Louis who told me that the question had been definitely settled by F. General (Wernz) after a lot of wrangling and correspondence. Now it seems, someone has started up the old question again, and we have orders from Rome to investigate it once more.[2]

Father O'Callaghan asked Father Rodman to get the facts ready and make a report. "As a matter of fact," continued Father O'Callaghan, "I don't think that the college has ever removed one cent of the debt . . . of course we don't want to be guilty of a thing like injustice to John Carroll, but justice is justice, and if the college owes the debt, I think that it should shoulder it manfully."[3]

Father Rodman sent a sharp reply to Father O'Callaghan expressing "surprise at the tone" of Father O'Callaghan's letter and pointing out that it is "strange" that such an issue is now being raised when all the consultors at John Carroll and Father Rodman himself agreed this debt was unjust and unfair.[4] All at John Carroll also agreed that "this House has been arbitrarily discriminated against, and that Father Wallace takes the other side. We have only the facts left here by Father Neustich to judge from. One of the first things Fr. Boylan told me was of the unfairness of that debt."[5] Father Rodman's solution was a "face to face" conference which he felt was necessary because "writing gets us nowhere." Such a conference, he thought, could settle the matter without going to Father General.[6] In an explanation of the injustice of the debt, Father Rodman said, "I cannot see for the life of me, nor can any of the seven others see why this House—the poorest of all—should carry a burden from which Toledo, and Prairie du Chien were released, when the Buffalo Mission was joined to the Mo. Province. There are lots of elements entering into this and I would rather talk to you for a few minutes than try to write."[7] It is not clear who had brought the subject of the debt question to Father General. Father Mattern, the American assistant in Rome, wrote to Father Rodman suggesting that the matter be brought to Father General; Father Rodman told Father O'Callaghan, "I do not want to do that if we can settle it together. There is one sure thing, that you and the province should be with us who have the objective facts."[8]

Father O'Callaghan quickly responded that he regretted that his words came across as unfair. He had always understood that the question had been settled by Father General, who had weighed all the arguments and gave a "definite decision"; there seemed to be no need to look further into the matter.[9]

Father O'Callaghan had never seen the reasons given by John Carroll as to why the debt was unjust; he would agree that if any injustice had been done, the debt should be cancelled. "In fact," he said, "I would be most willing to go farther, and agree to cancel the debt if it proved to be a just one. This I could not do on my own responsibility."[10] Meanwhile the matter had been referred to Fathers Germing and Wallace of the Missouri Province for their opinion.

Father O'Callaghan soon discovered that the Missouri Provincial, Father Germing, felt that he had conclusive evidence that the debt was a just one, which Father O'Callaghan then reported to Father Rodman. Father Germing listed his reasons for believing the debt was just: the Buffalo Mission claimed it as a debt; there was no proof this was an error; Father General Wernz had decreed that the *Arca Missionis* of the Buffalo Mission belonged to the Missouri Province, including debts owed by St. Ignatius College and Campion; among the assets of the Buffalo Mission in 1907 was a $92,000 debt owed by St. Ignatius College on which they had paid $13,000, thus acknowledging it; and finally, Father Neustich's word could hardly be taken as proof that Father General agreed that the debt was unjust, "as he took no step to rectify a mistake which he himself had made—if it was an error."[11]

Father Neustich's "mistake" seems to have involved the gift of a large sum of money from some benefactors in Germany to the Buffalo Mission. When St. Ignatius College built its permanent building, approximately $100,000 of this gift was given to the college. Father Neustich claimed this was a donation; the Superiors of the Mission thought otherwise and listed it as an asset when the Mission was dissolved.[12] Payments on the debt had reduced it to $79,000. Father Germing was unwilling to have a meeting with Father Rodman or anyone else on the matter. A financial report by Father Neustich to the Missouri Province in 1909 lists the St. Ignatius College debt to the Province as $92,000 at 3 percent interest, along with some other debts of the college totalling $111,229.99.[13]

With the evidence so apparently clear-cut there would seem to be little reason for the dispute having arisen every so often and continuing as long as it did. Father James A. Mackin, former director of the library at John Carroll University, once researched the subject of the debt and, based on all of the available evidence, his report raises some questions about whether the matter was as clear-cut a case as it seemed to Father Neustich.[14] There is evidence that there were letters of protest written by the Jesuits in Cleveland in 1894 and 1895 over the money for the new college being listed as a debt. These letters have since disappeared. Some of the content of these protests can be inferred from letters of Father Lessmann, who was Superior of the Mission between Father Behrens's two terms. Letters of Father Hoganforst, who was procurator of the Mission from 1873 to 1896, also contain some clues. Apparently the fine distinctions within the Mission treasury of those funds used for mission purposes only and those for funding colleges were not always observed. It is clear also that the Superiors had the power to cancel a portion of the debts owed to the Mission by colleges, as was done in the case of Canisius and Prairie du Chien. Father Hogenforst's records for St. Ignatius College showed a debt to the Buffalo Mission of $137,000 in 1896. In 1907, that debt was $92,000, suggesting payment for reduction or partial cancellation. It was Father Hogenforst's recollection that Father Behrens when he was Superior of the Mission did not wish to use the *arca missionis* funds for St. Ignatius College, but there is no written record of Father Behrens's intention. Father Hogenforst argued that St. Ignatius College had no right to complain of the debt, which it appears had been reduced by means other than payment. Part of the complaint of St. Ignatius College seems based on resentment that in transferring the assets of the Buffalo Mission to the Missouri Province there was no *quid pro quo*. The German Province got nothing out of the transfer in return for all the Houses it gave up; the Cleveland Jesuits were still being hounded for the debt, a debt that by tradition was considered unjustified.[15] Justified or not, the obligation to liquidate the debt followed John Carroll into the Chicago Province and remained there until 1932, when permission to borrow $100,000 from a bank to discharge the debt was received from the Congregation of Religious in Rome through the Provincial, Father Charles Cloud.[16]

The university now owed a bank instead of the Province; there the matter might have rested except for the separation of St. Ignatius High School from John Carroll University and the high school's status as a distinct Jesuit Community in 1939. The question now became one of the relative responsibilities of the two toward the old debt; the High School disclaimed any responsibility for the bank debt, while the university felt that the debt should have been prorated as of the time the two formed a single Jesuit Community. Much ink was spilled in the years prior to the 1950s until Father Frederick E. Welfle, president of John Carroll University, 1946–1956, settled the matter shortly before his death. In a letter dated March 26, 1956 to Father Ara F. Walker, then rector of St. Ignatius High School, Father Welfle noted that the High School was still carrying on its books a debt of $67,648.20 to John Carroll University, a debt that was contested by the High School. Telling Father Walker that the Provincial, Father Joseph Egan, had called Father Welfle on the telephone and told him "Either you settle it or I'll settle it for you," Father Welfle said, "Ergo, this is the official notice that the amount of $67,648.20 which St. Ignatius High School owes John Carroll University according to the agreement entered by Father Garvey and Father Donnelly [former rectors of the High School and the University] is null and void, of no effect, erased, obliterated, and forever consigned to the limbo of forgotten things. Just make sure that those St. Ignatius graduates come to John Carroll and we shall call it a fair deal. N.B. This closes this file."[17] Thus, with a certain flair not untypical of Father Welfle, ended the saga of the Buffalo Mission debt.

Appendix C
The New East Side Parish: Gesu

Permission to proceed in establishing a new Jesuit parish on the East Side had been given to Father T. J. Smith in early January 1925, but the location and boundaries of the parish were not yet specified.[1] Not until August 1925 was a pastor, Francis J. Rudden, appointed.[2] Father Smith, as rector of the Jesuit Community, bore responsibility in settling among other things the problem of location of the parish. Facilities on Silsby Road had been used for a school and the Town Hall served as a church until 1927, when the Cleveland Heights Board of Education donated three portable buildings which were placed on the Carroll property near Washington and Miramar Boulevards. Two of the buildings served for classrooms, and the third was used as a chapel. A frame bungalow was built for the pastor's residence.

The problem created by the location of the parish buildings on Carroll property was not solved by the time Father Rodman became rector and president of the university; in fact it wasn't solved until after he became pastor of the parish in 1937. Property for the location of the parish church was offered by the Rapid Transit Land Sales Company (R.T.L.S. Co.) to the Diocese of Cleveland as early as the fall of 1924.[3] This offer of nine lots was made after conversations between Father Smith and the R.T.L.S. Co. The lots located near Warrensville Center Road in a triangle formed by Washington Boulevard, Silsby Road, and Traymore Road, became known as the "church triangle." There was some urgency to accept the offer because if not accepted immediately the lots were to be sold; "the time has passed when we could have derived the selling benefits of a Jesuit Church," said a representative of the R.T.L.S. Co.[4] When Father Rudden became the first pastor of Gesu, the property still had not been accepted.[5] Father Boylan had written to Monsignor Smith urging immediate action, saying that Father Rudden had not yet had an appointment with the bishop, and that Father Rudden was "an active man and anxious to get down to work. And I feel convinced, that you, Msgr. Smith, are as anxious as we are to get going on the Heights."[6] Bishop Schrembs finally accepted the property on 4 December 1925. In March 1926, Father Rudden received permission to buy the adjoining sublots necessary to round out the property within the triangle.[7] This particular transaction was accomplished in spite of what seems to have been a rift between Monsignor Smith and Father Rudden. Father Boylan wrote to Father McMenamy that Father Rudden's

victory with the bishop over Msgr. Smith's head is going the rounds of the priests. Msgr. Smith tried to balk Fr. Rudge [sic] getting to the bishop; he did it openly. But, as it happened, Fr. Rudden rode up in the elevator with the bishop, who consequently knew that

Father Rudden was waiting. Msgr. Smith openly sent other priests ahead of Father Rudden 'till the bishop enquired, called Msgr. Smith outside and there was thunder and lightning outside; the whole corridor knew of it and Father Rudden was called, received very graciously and given leave to choose his Catholic architect and given full power to get those other lots, etc. Father Rudden is delighted over the outcome.[8]

After almost a year in the city, Father Rudden had an opportunity to size up the situation with regard to the parish and the university. It was his idea to secure the ten acres on the east side of Belvoir for a high school. He preferred the church to be located nearer the university thus concentrating Jesuit activities in the East Side. It was after this proposal and discussion that Father Boylan had taken measure to acquire the Belvoir property.[9] But this action also increased the uncertainty of where the church was to be located and what was to become of the "church triangle" if it was not used. It was Father Haggeney's opinion that the agreement to purchase the Belvoir property included its use for Gesu Church.[10] Yet in 1927, as already noted, the donated parish buildings were put on Carroll property.

The church was not located on Carroll property without challenge. A long, unpleasant, and bitter correspondence ensued involving Bishop Schrembs, Father Boylan, Father Rodman, the Van Sweringens, and William A. Horky, clerk of University Heights; the result was the removal of Father Rudden as pastor of Gesu. Among his many activities, Father Rudden had arranged for the purchase of five lots in the vicinity of the university; two of them were located on Warrensville Center Road and three on Fairmount Boulevard. Taking a page out of the Van Sweringens' book, Father Rudden had formed five syndicates, one for each lot, each composed of himself and four or five others. He then entered into a trust agreement with the Union Trust Bank, which advanced the necessary funds.[11] Each member of the syndicates was bound to the extent of his predetermined share. It is difficult to ascertain the actual amount of money Father Rudden himself invested. He did pay out $3,500 on one of the lots; the source of the money is not definitely known but it is clear that no parish funds were involved. It is certain that the original architect hired by the university, Edward T. P. Graham, was a source of some of the funds.[12] Father Rudden probably engaged in this real estate activity because he was aware that the location of the parish buildings on Carroll property was not intended to be permanent and no payment was charged to the parish for rent.[13] Father Rudden was in the process of attempting to secure a piece of property for the parish from the Cleveland Heights School Board and hoped to arrange for a sale of the "church triangle," which he did not consider suitable for the church.

Before selling the "church triangle" property Father Rudden sought to get it rezoned for business use so that the sale price might be higher. Horky opposed any such rezoning and the result was a running battle of words involving everyone concerned except Father Rudden, who refused to be part of an avalanche of bitter correspondence. The Van Sweringens, whose consent would be needed if the land was to be rezoned, were also opposed to the idea.[14] Horky began to publish a newsletter wherein he explained his views to the public. One of Horky's reasons for not wanting to rezone the triangle was that if it were rezoned, how could the village justify its refusal of the request of the Jewish Orphanage to rezone its thirty acres on Fairmount Boulevard? The Village had already lost its case in the court of appeals;

another appeal was pending. Horky complained that, "The Jewish Orphanage Home is battling us on three very vital points; the Humanitarian, the Religious and the Racial; we are fighting because we do not want our zoning law violated."[15]

An election in University Heights which turned out those councilmen—all Catholics—opposed to the rezoning but saw Horky reelected, became the focal point of Horky's further attacks on Father Rudden; he was accused by Horky of manipulating the election. Horky was further incensed when, after calling off his slander suit against a Gesu parishoner at Father Rudden's request, he felt that Father Rudden had reneged on his promise to stay out of politics.[16] Horky's appeal to Father Boylan to keep his promise of arranging a meeting between Horky and Father Rudden was hardly couched in language that would persuade Boylan to follow through. Horky was convinced that Father Boylan approved of Father Rudden's "pernicious political meddling [which] has caused a malignant ulcer to grow here, that should be removed."[17] Horky claimed that Father Rudden had played politics to the detriment of Catholics who were now "looked upon as fools."[18] Further correspondence between Boylan and Horky did nothing to calm the latter, who became convinced that not only Boylan but the entire Jesuit Order approved of Father Rudden's activities; "I will fight this matter to Rome if necessary," said Horky.[19] He would not be satisfied until Father Rudden was removed not only as pastor but from the city as well.

Father Boylan could find no cause for such action. Two letters of Father Boylan to Horky in December 1927 made it clear that he thought that there was nothing at all to investigate in Horky's charges, saying, "Dear Mr. Horky there is nothing tangible in all that you bring up; nothing any court could take up and decide satisfactorily."[20] Since Horky was elected Father Boylan could not see what he was complaining about, "all you seem to intend is to keep a little peeve brewing. . . . you cannot prove motives on any man. . . . Don't create bugaboos."[21] In an earlier letter Father Boylan had described Father Rudden as "positively slaving for the parish" and defended Mayor Howard, who was a Mason, as a "broad-minded man" who "offered no opposition to Father Rudden's having church functions in the town hall. We shall always be grateful to him for that."[22] Horky's main complaint was that although he was elected in spite of what he saw as Father Rudden's political meddling all other Catholics were defeated and replaced by Masons.[23]

This was the situation that greeted Father Rodman when he succeeded Father Boylan as rector in 1928. Father Rodman now had the responsibility of trying to settle parish matters which by this time were occupying considerable time of diocesan officials. Horky, writing to Monsignor McFadden, had demanded a meeting with the bishop: "if you do not arrange this meeting before the bishop of these people and me, you will confirm in me the slowly growing opinion that you are shielding Rev. Rudden and that you do not care for fairness and justice."[24] In an earlier letter to Horky, Father McFadden objected to the inaccuracy of Horky's report of an interview with the bishop's secretary: "I told you distinctly that the protest about the change of sites was late in view of the fact that the change of site [temporarily on Carroll property] had met with the approval of the bishop. . . . there are plenty of people who do not agree with your stand, and who intimate that you are the disturber."[25]

Father Rodman soon began receiving his share of the voluminous correspondence. Horky sent a long recitation of complaints against Father Rudden to Father Rodman, letting him know that "because I would not do as your Rev. Rudden wanted me to do, I was to be CRUSHED, My reputation was to be ruined, the MASONS were to help him CRUSH me."[26] Horky continued, "my experience will make interesting reading when it is broadcast. . . . I cannot get a square deal from you."[27]

A move to have Father Rudden transferred from Gesu elicited strong support for Father Rudden and his work in the form of petitions and numerous letters. One petition was from University Heights officials who described Father Rudden as a great force in the development and growth of the community that could "be traced very materially to his splendid work. . . . transfer would be a great loss to the village."[28] This petition was signed by the mayor of University Heights and other village officials. A petition of Gesu parishoners, containing many names of those whom Horky had thought would support him, was also presented to the bishop and urged the retention of Father Rudden. The petition contained 237 signatures and noted that the petitioners were "aware of antagonistic methods used to bring the situation to a head and we also know it has been a specific one-sided complaint."[29]

By this time Bishop Schrembs had decided that the only solution was the removal of Father Rudden. The Provincial, Father O'Callaghan, when informed of the bishop's wish, wrote to Bishop Schrembs regretting that Father Rudden "has incurred the displeasure of your Lordship," and saying that if he had known that Father Rudden was not managing affairs "tactfully and efficiently" he would have removed him."[30] Father O'Callaghan thought that his contacts with Father Boylan indicated that Horky "was a sort of meddler," and that if it were serious enough, Bishop Schrembs would soon say so.[31] In any case the new pastor was to be Father Arthur A. Versavel, a "kindly, zealous man with a lot of experience in parish work."[32] Father O'Callaghan felt constrained to add a note of assurance:

> Dear Bishop, I wish to assure you that our Fathers in Cleveland will give you their heartiest cooperation in all the activities of the diocese. We have a new rector in charge of John Carroll University, Father Rodman, a man of high ideals and principles, a man keenly interested in the promotion of Catholic higher education. We fondly hope that under his administration our college will make considerable progress.[33]

Bishop Schrembs replied to Father O'Callaghan without delay:

> it is scarcely accurate to say that Father Rudden has incurred my displeasure. Personally, I have absolutely nothing against Father Rudden. As I see it, it is purely a question of mismanagement and incapacity to manage the affairs of the new Gesu Parish. There are plenty of elements to substantiate this fact, and it surely must have been known to you, for I take it for granted that your representatives keep you posted.
>
> I hate to be constantly placed in the position of seemingly finding fault with your Fathers. For this reason I laid the whole affair plainly before Father Rodman, whom I esteem very highly, and I asked him if the matter could not be settled without my intervention.
>
> It is very disagreeable to fasten the odium of a bishop's demand for a change upon any religious and I felt that once you knew the situation you certainly would not want to have it continued that way. . . . The present is certainly a very tangled situation.[34]

On 12 November 1928 there was a meeting of Father McFadden with Monsignor Smith and Fathers Rodman, Rudden, and Versavel to review the situation. The various transactions were studied beginning with the acceptance by the diocese on 4 December 1927 of the "church triangle" property from the Van Sweringens. The total debt of the parish was now $57,754.26, including $35,000 for the additional lots to complete the "triangle" property; only seven of the lots were actually purchased, at a cost of $30,000. The figure also included $13,000 for necessary repairs on the portable school that had been erected on the corner of the Carroll property. Father Rudden admitted that he had not followed diocesan procedure in building the small bungalow on the Carroll property as a pastoral residence. He claimed the people urged him to build rather than continue to live in a rented house on Silsby Road. Father Rudden also claimed that it was on Father Mattern's advice on his visit in 1926 not to use the "triangle" property, but to build on part of the university property. Monsignor McFadden felt that if the site was changed on the advice of superiors there should be no further discussions about returning to the "triangle."[35]

In a subsequent meeting between Father Versavel and Bishop Schrembs, Father Versavel was given his instructions by the bishop; a year had passed during which the bishop had tried to settle matters but the Jesuits kept changing their minds; therefore, Father Versavel was to go personally to the parish and tell people the Jesuits were the cause of all the trouble. The bishop did not favor the site on Carroll property; he preferred it on the triangle. Father Versavel was to report to the bishop through Monsignor McFadden.[36] Father Versavel complained that the meeting lasted only five minutes and he was given no chance to talk.

Father Versavel took charge of a parish that had about 125 families on record, an enormous debt, and no definitely agreed-upon location or boundaries. The question of location involved university affairs as well as parish matters. Father Versavel favored the site on the Carroll property; he also thought the people favored it because the "people feel that the parish should be one with the college."[37] Father Versavel thought it would be a generous gesture on the part of the university to give the land to the diocese; it would "take off the sharp edges of a good many past misunderstanding[s]."[38] Father O'Callaghan supported this move and informed Father Rodman that Father General had already given permission to Father Boylan to sell part of the Carroll property to the diocese for the parish.[39]

Father Rodman meanwhile had been corresponding with Bishop Schrembs, assuring him that he would prefer to leave the choice of the site of the parish to the Bishop; "whatever you choose will be acceptable to us, as I wish to do whatever you determine in the matter."[40] Father O'Callaghan, to whom Father Rodman had conveyed these same sentiments, said that Father Rodman was doing the right thing in wishing to put the church on a site chosen by the bishop and hoped that the site issue would be settled "definitely and very soon."[41] It was to be some time before the matter was finally settled; meanwhile the church and other buildings remained on Carroll property, in spite of the fact that the John Carroll Consultors "to a man do not want Gesu on Carroll property."[42] The issue remained unresolved while Father Rodman devoted his entire effort to fund-raising for the new buildings for the college.

Appendix D
A Jesuit High School
on the East Side

In marked contrast to Bishop Farrelly, who wanted neither Loyola High School nor the Jesuits on the East Side, Bishop Hoban urged the Jesuits to build a high school in the vicinity of the university. Even before Bishop Hoban made his proposal, Father Donnelly had informed his consultors that "Priests and people have had the matter in mind for some time."[1] Father Donnelly expected a proposal from the bishop very soon and felt that the Jesuits should be ready with a plan. As Father Donnelly said, "There is no objection to letting people know we are considering a high school. Perhaps a beginning could be made this September."[2]

By 1945 the bishop's proposal had been received. Bishop Hoban was amenable to a collection in the parishes for a high school, which he wanted in the vicinity of Carroll. Father Donnelly now felt that the John Carroll debt and the shortage of Jesuit manpower would preclude any action at the time. Bishop Hoban thought that there was a Province Fund for such contingencies and then suggested that Gesu could build a high school either alone or with the help of surrounding parishes. Father Donnelly mentioned the subject to Father Rodman, who "seemed interested."[3]

There was a lively discussion among John Carroll consultors about the possible use of university property on the east side of Belvoir for a high school. It was soon clear that Gesu property was not large enough and university plans for the use of the Belvoir property were not yet formulated. The subject of the proposed high school was dropped.

Appendix E
The Belvoir Property

If the university was unable to build on the new site in the Heights in the mid 1920s, it at least managed to add new property to it. The property in question involved lots on both sides of Belvoir Boulevard; the thirteen lots on the west side of Belvoir adjoined the Carroll property; those on the east side directly opposite the Carroll property were half of a large tract of land known as the Majeska property. A total of approximately ten acres was added to the Carroll property through the purchase of these lots in a very complicated arrangement. The explanation of the arrangement that Father Rodman sought when he became president in 1928 was provided by Joseph A. Schlitz, the university attorney. In August 1926 Father Boylan sought an opportunity to do two things—round out the Carroll property by adding the adjoining lots on the west side of Belvoir, and secure a piece of land large enough for a high school by adding lots on the east side. The property on the east side of Belvoir was the only unrestricted property in the area that could be used for a high school. Father Boylan said that the Jesuits had to vacate St. Mary's parish within eight years and that the West Side property now occupied by St. Ignatius High School would be valuable only for business. The high school was to be moved to the East Side but it could not be on university property.[1]

Problems arose when it was discovered that the Majeska property had to be purchased in its entirety. Since the university wanted only half the property, the Rapid Transit Land Sales Company (R.T.L.S. Co.) agreed to take the other half, but the company had no money to invest and owed a $22,000 balance on a previous voluntary subscription to the university. The purchase price of the entire Majeska property was $89,250 or $44,625 for each half. The university then paid $22,650 to the Majeskas through the R.T.L.S. Co. This together with the amount owed to the university by the R.T.L.S. Co. covered the university's purchase of its half of the property. The R.T.L.S. Co. agreed to pay the rest of the purchase price and take title to the entire track. The R.T.L.S. Co. then gave back to the university a mortgage in the amount of $22,625 secured by a mortgage deed covering the entire property. The mortgage held by the university was secondary to the unpaid balance on the purchase price, but actually it was a fourth mortgage since the Majeskas already had two separate mortgages. All the papers remained in escrow and were apparently never filed for the record.[2]

The reason that title to the entire tract was to be in the name of the R.T.L.S. Co. was that part of the arrangements involved the widening of Washington Boulevard to seventy feet for uniformity's sake; a north-south street was to be located at the center of the property (Elmdale, since closed). The university as a nonprofit corporation could not legally act in those matters.[3] The sale of the lots that the R.T.L.S. Co. held was very disappointing; it was thought that the failure of the university to build on its own property was a major drawback to the sales. By 1928, no progress had been made and foreclosure seemed quite likely. One thing the university did have to show for its investment was some new names on surrounding streets, as University Heights officials cooperated in renaming some of them. Pemberton Boulevard, which ran east past Milton to Green Road, was renamed Carroll Boulevard. A number of other Jesuits names appeared as street names, for example, Loyola, Lalemont, and Claver. Nevertheless, the university stood a good chance at this time of having its investment wiped out by foreclosure. By 1931, the total investment including taxes and interest would have amounted to $83,125 if the university was able to come up with $15,000 to acquire clear title.[4]

Not until the tenure of Father Donnelly was the situation cleared sufficiently to allow some speculation as to the possible use of the property. At that time the best guess was that it could be used as a site for a high school thus concentrating Jesuit activities in one area. A hospital was a remote possibility. In the 1950s more definite plans were forming for the site's use as a football stadium. Since the area was heavily wooded, Father Joliat thought that he could get exercise cutting down the trees. At the age of seventy he cut down almost 200 trees; Father Weber arranged for stump removal.

Appendix F
Mission Statement

John Carroll University, founded in 1886, is a privately controlled, coeducational, Catholic and Jesuit university. It provides liberal arts programs in the arts, sciences, and business at the undergraduate level, and in selected areas at the master's level. In addition, an Office of Continuing Education offers courses and programs as part of life-long learning. The university also offers its facilities and personnel to the Greater Cleveland community and provides a wide variety of special services.

As a university, John Carroll is committed to the transmission and extension of the treasury of human knowledge with the autonomy and freedom appropriate to a university. As a Catholic university, it is further committed to seek and synthesize all knowledge, including the wisdom of Christian revelation. In the search for this integration of knowledge, the university community is enriched by scholarship representing the pluralistic society in which we live. All can participate freely in the intellectual, moral, and spiritual dialog necessary to the search. Within this dialog, in which theological and philosophical questions play a crucial role, students have the opportunity to develop, synthesize, and live a value system based on respect for and critical evaluation of fact; on intellectual, moral, and spiritual principles which enable them to cope with new problems; and on the sensitivity and judgment that prepares them to engage in responsible social action.

In a Jesuit university, the presence of Jesuits and others who are inspired by the vision of St. Ignatius Loyola, founder of the Society of Jesus in 1540, is of paramount importance. This vision, which reflects the value system of the Gospels, is expressed in the *Spiritual Exercises*, the source of Jesuit life and activity. To education the Jesuit spirit brings a rationality appropriately balanced by human affection, an esteem for the individual as a unique person, training in discerning choice, openness to change, and a quest for God's greater glory in the use of this world's goods. Commitment to the values which inspired the *Exercises* promotes justice by affirming the equal dignity of all persons and seeks balance between reliance on divine assistance and natural capacities. The effort to combine faith and culture takes on different forms at different times in Jesuit colleges and universities. Innovation, experiment, and training for social leadership are essential to the Jesuit tradition.

John Carroll University welcomes students and faculty from different religious backgrounds and value systems, in the belief that the educational environment which the University provides is one which these students and faculty may find congenial, rewarding, and enriched by their presence. Within this environment there is concern for the human and spiritual developmental needs of the students and a deep respect for the freedom and dignity of the human person. A faculty not only professionally qualified, but also student oriented, considers excellence in interpersonal relationships as well as academic achievement among its primary goals.

The University places primary emphasis on instructional excellence. It recognizes the importance of research in teaching as well as in the development of the teacher. In keeping with its mission, the university especially encourages research that assists the various disciplines in offering solutions to the problems of faith in the modern world, social inequities, and human needs.

The commitment to excellence at John Carroll University does not imply limiting admissions to the extremely talented student only. Admission is open to all students who desire and have the potential to profit from an education suited to the student's needs as a person and talents as a member of society.

The educational experience at John Carroll University provides opportunities for the students to develop as total human persons. They should be well grounded in liberalizing, humanizing arts and sciences; proficient in the skills that lead to clear, persuasive expression; trained in the intellectual discipline necessary to pursue a subject in depth; aware of the interrelationship of all knowledge and the need for integration and synthesis; able to make a commitment to a tested scale of values and to demonstrate the self-discipline necessary to live by those values; alert to learning as a life-long process; open to change as they mature; respectful of their own culture and that of others; aware of the interdependence of all humanity; and sensitive to the need for social justice in response to current social pressures and problems.

Appendix G
Generals of the Society of Jesus

Ignatius of Loyola, 1541–1556
Diego Laynez, 1558–1565
Francis Borgia, 1565–1572
Everard Mercurian, 1573–1580
Claudio Aquaviva, 1581–1615
Muzio Vitelleschi, 1615–1645
Vincenzio Carafa, 1646–1649
Francesco Piccolomini, 1649–1651
Luigi Gottifredi, 1652 (Jan.–Mar.)
Goswin Nickel, 1652–1664
Giovanni Paolo Oliva, Vicar 1661–1664,
                    General 1664–1681
Charles de Noyelle, 1682–1686
Tirso Gonzalez, 1687–1705
Michaelangelo Tamburini, 1706–1730
Frantisek Retz, 1730–1750
Ignazio Visconti, 1751–1755
Luigi Centurione, 1755–1757
Lorenzo Ricci, 1758–1773
Tadeusz Brzozowski, 1814–1820
Luigi Fortis, 1820–1829
Jan Roothaan, 1829–1853
Pieter Beckx, 1853–1887
Anton Anderledy, Vicar 1883–1887
                    General 1887–1892
Luis Martin, 1892–1906
Franz Wernz, 1906–1914
Wlodmir Ledochowski, 1915–1942
John Baptist Janssens, 1946–1964
Pedro Arrupe, 1965–1983
Peter-Hans Kolvenbach, 1983–

Appendix H
The Jesuits and John Carroll University

THE RESTORED SOCIETY IN THE UNITED STATES: CHRONOLOGY OF INVOLVEMENT OF PROVINCES IN THE HISTORY OF JOHN CARROLL UNIVERSITY

1814 Maryland Mission
1823 Missouri Mission of the Maryland Mission
1831 Missouri Mission independent under the General
1840 Vice-Province of Missouri
1863 Province of Missouri
1869 New York-Canada Mission independent under the General: Buffalo Mission of the Province of Germany
1907 Buffalo Mission dissolved; New York Houses (85 members) to the New York-Maryland Province; remaining Houses (195 members) to the Missouri Province
1925 Vice-Province of Ohio
1928 Vice-Province of Ohio becomes the Chicago Province
1955 Detroit Province created out of the Chicago Province

PROVINCIALS OF THE PROVINCE OF UPPER GERMANY DURING THE TIME OF THE BUFFALO MISSION

Clement Faller, 1869
Augustine Oswald, 1872
Caspar Hoevel, 1872
John Lohmann, 1884
James Rathgeb, 1888
Henry Haan, 1894
Charles Schaffer, 1900
Ernest Thill, 1907

SUPERIORS OF THE BUFFALO MISSION

Peter Spicher, 1869
William Becker, 1870
Henry Behrens, 1872
John B. Lessmann, 1876

Henry Behrens, 1886
Theodore Van Rossum, 1892
James Rockliff, 1898
Rudolph Meyer, 1906; became Missouri Province Provincial, 1907

PROVINCIALS OF THE MISSOURI PROVINCE

Rudolph Meyer, 1907
Alexander Burrowes, 1913
Francis McMenamy, 1919
Matthew Germing, 1926

PROVINCIALS OF THE CHICAGO PROVINCE

Jeremias O'Callaghan, Ohio Vice-Province 1925–1928;
                        Chicago Province, 1928–1930
Charles H. Cloud, 1930–1937
William M. Magee, 1937–1943
Leo D. Sullivan, 1943–1949
Joseph M. Egan, 1949–1954
Leo D. Sullivan, 1954, Vice-Provincial of the Ohio-Michigan region

PROVINCIALS OF THE DETROIT PROVINCE

Leo D. Sullivan, 1955–1958
James A. McGrail, 1958–1965
Walter L. Farrell, 1965–1971
Paul Besanceney, 1971–1977
Michael J. Lavelle, 1977–1983
Howard Gray, 1983–

BISHOPS OF THE DIOCESE OF CLEVELAND

Amedeus Rappe, 1847–1870
Richard Gilmour, 1872–1891
Ignatius Horstman, 1892–1908
John P. Farrelly, 1909–1921
Joseph Schrembs, 1921–1945
Edward F. Hoban, 1945–1966
Clarence G. Issenman, 1966–1974
James A. Hickey, 1974–1980
Anthony M. Pilla, 1980–

RECTOR-PRESIDENTS ST. IGNATIUS COLLEGE/JOHN CARROLL UNIVERSITY

John B. Neustich, Vice-Rector, 1886–1888
Henry Knappmeyer, Vice-Rector, 1888–1893
Joseph P. LeHalle, 1893–1897

Godfrey Schulte, 1897–1902
John Zahm, 1902–1906
George J. Pickel, Acting Rector 1906; Rector, 1907–1910
John B. Furay, 1910–1915
William B. Sommerhauser, 1915–1919
Thomas J. Smith, 1919–1925
Murtha J. Boylan, 1925–1928
Benedict J. Rodman, 1928–1937
William M. Magee, 1937
George J. Pickel, Acting Rector, 1937
Edmund C. Horne, 1937–1942
Thomas J. Donnelly, 1942–1946
Frederick E. Welfle, 1946–1956
Hugh E. Dunn, 1956–1967
Joseph O. Schell, 1967–1969

PRESIDENTS OF THE UNIVERSITY

Joseph O. Schell, 1969–1970
Henry F. Birkenhauer, 1970–1980
Thomas P. O'Malley, 1980–

SUPERIORS / RECTORS OF THE JESUIT COMMUNITY

Douglas A. Pearl, Superior, 1956–1962
Ernest J. Seebaldt, Superior, 1962–1968
Charles J. Castellano, Superior, 1968–1971
William Nichols, Rector, 1971–1977
Joseph Zombor, Rector, 1977–1982
Frederick J. Benda, Rector, 1982–

Appendix I
Enrollment and Degree Statistics

ENROLLMENT–FALL SESSION
TOTAL UNIVERSITY

1886	*76	1912	62	1937	700	1960	4,028
1887	*97	1913	58	1938	878	1961	4,118
1888	*124	1914	65	1939	1,033	1962	3,855
1889	*142	1915	69	1940	940	1963	4,109
1890	*143	1916	97	1941	951	1964	4,157
1891	*178	1917	72	1942	895	1965	4,360
1892	*200	1918	84	1943	185	1966	4,353
1893	*184		+123		**389	1967	4,235
1894	*225	1919	116	1944	107	1968	4,237
1895	*228	1920	146		**387	1969	4,195
1896	*205	1921	184	1945	243	1970	4,062
1897	*194	1922	234		**153	1971	3,964
1898	*195	1923	283	1946	1,921	1972	3,785
1899	*211	1924	345	1947	2,246	1973	3,671
1900	*185	1925	498	1948	2,285	1974	3,771
1901	*181	1926	510	1949	2,342	1975	3,709
1902	*226	1927	470	1950	2,184	1976	3,711
1903	*262	1928	462	1951	2,117	1977	3,637
1904	*285	1929	468	1952	2,267	1978	3,850
1905	*277	1930	613	1953	2,433	1979	4,000
1906	*292	1931	641	1954	2,724	1980	3,994
1907	*292	1932	606	1955	3,080	1981	3,890
1908	*290	1933	712	1956	3,205	1982	3,767
1909	*209	1934	812	1957	3,471	1983	3,681
1910	58	1935	701	1958	3,509		
1911	64	1936	685	1959	3,896		

 * Combined high school and college enrollment
** Navy V-12 Program
 + S.A.T.C. Program

DEGREES AND CERTIFICATES

	Degrees				Degrees	
	Bachelors	Masters			Bachelors	Masters
1890				1937	75	3
1891				1938	66	1
1892				1939	67	5
1893				1940	85	5
1894	2			1941	74	3
1895	1	2		1942	79	4
1896		1		1943	92	1
1897				1944	10	0
1898				1945	6	0
1899				1946	28	2
1900				1947	55	1
1901	4			1948	113	6
1902				1949	227	14
1903				1950	299	15
1904				1951	297	23
1905				1952	236	12
1906	7			1953	205	27
1907	5			1954	198	31
1908	12	2		1955	269	24
1909	4	2		1956	240	36
1910	8	1		1957	326	37
1911	12	1		1958	276	49
1912	7	2		1959	366	50
1913	11	1		1960	272	23
1914	8	6		1961	286	60
1915	18			1962	351	66
1916	10			1963	388	85
1917	21			1964	458	93
1918	10			1965	452	100
1919	15			1966	421	132
1920	3			1967	503	140
1921	9			1968	524	171
1922	16			1969	616	172
1923	16			1970	684	182
1924	25			1971	562	207
1925	35			1972	536	174
1926	37			1973	590	227
1927	35			1974	546	154
1928	39			1975	595	157
1929	34			1976	495	148
1930	58			1977	500	170
1931	49	2		1978	433	192
1932	63	2		1979	505	180
1933	56	6		1980	431	175
1934	67	5		1981	505	153
1935	57	1		1982	501	100
1936	64	4		1983	452	93

| | Certificates | |
	Classical	Commercial
1890		12
1891		10
1892	8	7
1893	4	8
1894	4	8
1895	3	4
1896	5	6
1897	9	7
1898	9	0
1899	9	Course discon-
1900	10	tinued in 1895
1901	8	
1902	10	
1903	17	
1904	8	

HONORARY DEGREES

1935   George MacDonald, Papal Marquis

1936   Herman R. Neff
Most Reverend Joseph Schrembs

1943   Most Reverend James A. McFadden

1946   Thomas A. Burke
Most Reverend John R. Hagan
Most Reverend Edward F. Hoban
Edward F. McGrady

1947   William G. Bernet
Joseph A. Schlitz
Francis Cardinal Spellman

1948   John T. Feighan
Daniel B. Kirby

1949   Maurice J. Tobin
John A. Toomey
John A. Victoreen

1950   Charles F. McCahill
John P. Murphy
David Sarnoff

1951   Most Reverend Floyd L. Begin
John Kerwin Thompson

1952   Curtis E. LeMay

1953   George M. Humphrey
Hugh M. O'Neill
Arthur Hays Sulzberger
Robert E. Wood

1954   James C. Connell
T. Keith Glennan
Elton Hoyt II
Frank E. Joseph
Thomas F. Patton

1955   John A. Greene
Most Reverend John F. Kroll
Frederick C. Robbins
John Closey Virden

1956   Fritz W. Graff
Paul Martin
Right Reverend Monsignor O. A. Mazanec
Edgar L. Ostendorf
Irving H. Page
Armstrong A. Stanbaugh

1957   Robert E. Briscoe
Allan W. Fritzsche
Carlos P. Romulo
Charles M. White

1958   Benjamin F. Fairless
James T. Griffin
George Gund
John Sherwin

1959   Frances P. Bolton
Aloysius A. Bungart
Sidney B. Congdon
Most Reverend Clarence Elwell
A. Carlton Ernstene

1960   Robert Foger Black
Charles Edward McDermott
Right Reverend Monsignor Robert B. Navin
Fred Andrew Seaton

1961   Harold Terry Clark
Earle B. Kay
John Allen Krout
Josephine Grasselli
Reverend Paul C. Reinert

1962   Herbert H. Kennedy
Kurt VonSchuschnigg

1963   James M. Roche

1964   Kent H. Smith

1966   James Alvin Bohannon
Theodore A. Distler

1967   Edwin A. Hahn
William R. Daley
Abe Silverstein

1968   Glenn T. Seaborg

1969   Edmund S. Muskie

1970   Reverend Robert J. Henle

1971   William H. Taft III

1972   Fred R. Harris

1973   Donald F. Shula

1974   Lowell P. Weicker

1975   Most Reverend James A. Hickey

1976   Bob Hope

1978   Mother Theresa of Calcutta
Anthony J. Celebrezze
Reverend Walter J. Ong

1979   Sister Henrietta Gorres
Donald Carl Johanson
Arthur B. Modell
Reverend Karl Rahner
Robert J. White

1980   Reverend Henry F. Birkenhauer
E. Mandell deWindt

1981   Clarence M. Mitchell
Most Reverend Anthony M. Pilla

1982   John E. Wasmer, Sr.
Florence O'Donnell Wasmer
H. Chapman Rose

1983   Dorothy Gauchat
        William A. Kinnison
        William M. McVey

1984   Reverend Joseph O. Schell
        Dorothy Fuldheim

No honorary degrees were awarded in 1937–1942, 1944–1945, 1965, and 1977.

Appendix J
Faculty Awards

To encourage research and writing, the university annually awards one or more Faculty Fellowships providing leave to work on special projects. The Fellowships are named in memory of Dr. George E. Grauel, who served the university from 1933 until his death in 1967. Grauel was professor of English, dean of the Evening College, and director of institutional planning. Recipients of the fellowships to date have been:

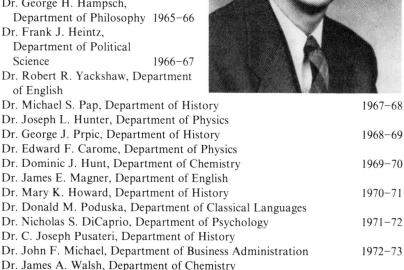

Dr. George H. Hampsch,
  Department of Philosophy 1965–66
Dr. Frank J. Heintz,
  Department of Political
  Science 1966–67
Dr. Robert R. Yackshaw, Department
  of English

Dr. Michael S. Pap, Department of History	1967–68
Dr. Joseph L. Hunter, Department of Physics	
Dr. George J. Prpic, Department of History	1968–69
Dr. Edward F. Carome, Department of Physics	
Dr. Dominic J. Hunt, Department of Chemistry	1969–70
Dr. James E. Magner, Department of English	
Dr. Mary K. Howard, Department of History	1970–71
Dr. Donald M. Poduska, Department of Classical Languages	
Dr. Nicholas S. DiCaprio, Department of Psychology	1971–72
Dr. C. Joseph Pusateri, Department of History	
Dr. John F. Michael, Department of Business Administration	1972–73
Dr. James A. Walsh, Department of Chemistry	
Dr. Margaret Berry, Department of English	1973–74
Dr. Joseph Trivisonno, Department of Physics	
Dr. Antonio Leal, Department of Modern Languages	1974–75

Mr. John R. Carpenter, Department of Sociology	1975–76
Dr. Andres C. Diaz, Department of Modern Languages	
Dr. Louis G. Pecek, Department of English	
Dr. Donald W. Smythe, S.J., Depart of History	1976–77
Dr. Max J. Keck, Department of Physics	
Dr. Verghese J. Chirayath, Department of Sociology	1977–78
Dr. Sonia S. Gold, Department of Economics	
Dr. David R. Mason, Department of Religious Studies	1978–79
Dr. Edward F. Carome, Department of Physics	
Dr. John R. Boatright, Department of Philosophy	1979–80
Dr. Klaus Fritsch, Department of Physics	
Dr. Joseph T. Bombelles, Department of Economics	1980–81
Dr. George A. Kanoti, Department of Religious Studies	
Dr. Harry C. Nash, Department of Physics	
Dr. Joseph R. Nearon, S.S.S., Department of Religious Studies	
Dr. Lynn Remly-Post, Department of English	
Dr. Kathleen L. Barber, Department of Political Science	1981–82
Dr. Kathleen Gatto, Department of Modern Languages	
Dr. James E. Magner, Department of English	
Dr. Robert D. Sweeney, Department of Philosophy	
Dr. Richard W. Clancey, Department of English	1982–83
Dr. Max J. Keck, Department of Physics	
Dr. Margaret Berry, Department of English	1983–84
Dr. Joseph Kelly, Department of Religious Studies	
Dr. Marian J. Morton, Department of History	
Dr. Frank J. Navratil, Department of Economics	
Dr. James A. Walsh, Department of Chemistry	
Dr. Gerald C. Hay, Jr., Department of Philosophy	1984–85
Rev. Francis J. Smith, S.J., Department of English	
Dr. John R. Spencer, Department of Religious Studies	
Dr. Thomas M. Tomasic, Department of Philosophy	

THE DISTINGUISHED FACULTY AWARD

The Distinguished Faculty Award is presented annually to a member of the faculty selected by the university community for excellence in classroom teaching, scholarship, advisement and leadership of students, and community concern.

The faculty member chosen to receive the award receives a $1,000 cash prize and an engraved plaque presented at Commencement ceremonies. Winners of the award to date have been:

Dr. Joseph L. Hunter, Department of Physics	1969
Mr. Joseph T. Cotter, Department of English	1970
Dr. Arther S. Trace, Department of English	1971
Dr. Michael S. Pap, Department of History	1972
Dr. Robert C. Bohinski, Department of Chemistry	1973
Dr. Robert S. More, Department of Business Administration	1974

Dr. Joseph P. Owens, S.J., Department of Education   1975
Dr. James A. Walsh, Department of Chemistry   1976
Dr. Walter S. Nosal, Department of Education   1977
Dr. Donald W. Smythe, S.J., Department of History   1978
Dr. Richard W. Clancey, Department of English   1979
Dr. Helen M. Murphy, Department of Psychology   1980
Dr. Casimir Bukala, S.J., Department of Philosophy   1981
Dr. Edward Walter, Department of Mathematics   1982
Dr. Joseph Miller, Department of Communications   1983
Dr. William H. Nichols, S.J., Department of Physics   1984

Appendix K
The Beaudry Award

For four years the Sodality at John Carroll had given an award to the student who had done the most for the University during that year. At the fifth annual Sodality dance in 1951 the award was changed in two ways. It was henceforth to be called the "Robert Beaudry Man of the Year Award" to commemorate the deceased Sodalist's memory. In the future only seniors were to be eligible as recipients.

The Beaudry Award is now given each year at graduation to the young man or woman voted most deserving of the honor by fellow students. As in the past, the Award recognizes outstanding service in the three areas of Christian leadership, academic achievement, and contributions to the university community.

Details of voting are given toward the end of the second semester. Voting is handled by the Christian Life Community (CLC), the contemporary form of the Sodality.

BEAUDRY AWARD WINNERS

1951	Lawrence Badar	1961	Edward Parks
1952	Jerome Miller	1962	John C. Wanamaker
1953	Thomas Dugan	1963	Gary J. Previts
1954	Nicholas DiCaprio	1964	James Bachmann
1955	George Sweeney	1965	Christopher Zegers
1956	Raymond Reilly	1966	R. John Fox
1957	Charles Novak	1967	Richard Tomc
1958	Gerald Porter	1968	Philip Giancinti
1959	J. Peter Fegen	1969	George Mackey
1960	Gerald Schweickert	1970	Donald Brown

1971	James H. Grendell	1978	Ara Bagdasarian
1972	Timothy Russert	1979	Maureen T. Rose
1973	Elias Naffah	1980	David T. Kusner
1974	M. Terence Dwyer	1981	Laura C. Lanza
1975	Lou DeMarco	1982	Mary Kay Merk
1976	Mary Jo Casserly	1983	Margaret Mary Mahon
1977	Patrick M. Cummings	1984	Peter Anthony Francel

Appendix L
John Carroll University Student Union Presidents

1920–1921	Walter J. Kiewel	1948–1949	Joseph DeGrandis
	Vincent Heffernan	1949–1950	James Conway
1921–1922	Vincent Heffernan	1950–1951	Richard Cusick
	James J. Corrigan	1951–1952	John Beringer
1922–1923	Aloysius Acker	1952–1953	John Beringer
	Carl A. Turk	1953–1954	Dave Schuler
1923–1924	John P. Rice	1954–1955	Kevin McDonough
	William F. Creadon	1955–1956	Frank Tesch
1924–1925	William J. Creadon	1956–1957	Richard Murphy
	Joseph T. Hodous	1957–1958	Patrick Doherty
1925–1926	Joseph T. Hodous	1958–1959	J. Peter Fegen
	Franklin J. Joyce	1960–1961	Kailish Bagaria
1926–1927	George P. Hausser	1961–1962	Thomas Fallon
	Hubert J. McCaffery	1962–1963	Charles T. Salem
1927–1928	Hubert J. McCaffery	1963–1964	James Bachmann
	Jack Sheehan	1964–1965	Richard J. Cermak
1928–1929	Jack Mulcahy	1965–1966	Louis P. Vitullo
1929–1930	Nicholas Sheehan	1966–1967	Thomas J. Murphy
1930–1931	Paul Carmody	1967–1968	George P. Maloney, III
1931–1932	Edmund Smolik	1968–1969	George G. Mackey
1932–1933	William McCarthy	1969–1970	James W. Laures
1933–1934	Joseph Fegen	1970–1971	Frank Chenette
1934–1935	J. Robert McCarty	1971–1972	Timothy J. Russert
1935–1936	Don Birmingham	1972–1973	John S. Kleshinski
1936–1937	William L. Peoples	1973–1974	Phillip A. Eichner
1937–1938	Edward Rambousek	1974–1975	James P. Eardly
1938–1939	Philip Lawton	1975–1976	Rob Cummings
1939–1940	Bernard J. Petty	1976–1977	Edward W. Rybka
1940–1941	William D. Joyce	1977–1978	Timothy Freeman
1941–1942	Robert Donnelly	1978–1979	Tracy Coyne
1942–1943	John V. Corrigan	1979–1980	Terry Heneghan
1943–1944	Albert Francesconi	1980–1981	Robert Hill
1944–1945	James L. Fullin	1981–1982	Edward Fay
1945–1946	John McCafferty	1982–1983	Christopher Miller
1946–1947	Leonard Schneeberger	1983–1984	Timothy Cavanagh
1947–1948	John J. Kilbane	1984–1985	David Pratt

Notes

Abbreviations used in notes:

ACC   Archives of Canisius College
ACWRU Archives of Case Western Reserve University
ADC   Archives of Diocese of Cleveland
AJC   Archives of John Carroll University
ALUC   Archives of Loyola University, Chicago
AMP   Archives of the Missouri Province
AMU   Archives of Marquette University
ARSI   Archivum Romanum Societatis Jesu
ASIH   Archives of St. Ignatius High School

<small>PREFACE</small>

Thomas O'Brien Hanley, S.J., ed., *The John Carroll Papers*, 1(1755–1791):301, Carroll to Leonardo Antonelli, April 19, 1788.

<small>CHAPTER I</small>

1. Robert J. Scollard, "Historical Notes on the Congregation of St. Basil," VII, 204, Father Dennis O'Connor to his Superior, 27 November 1867, a second postscript in the letter. Archives of the College of St. Michael, Toronto, Ontario, Canada.

2. Ibid.

3. Scollard, "Notes," Vincent to Soulerin, 2 April 1873, VIII, 185–87.

4. In the 15 May 1890, issue of the *Catholic Universe*, Bishop Gilmour wrote at length to the "Clergy and Laity of the Diocese of Cleveland" in an effort to explain a number of issues earlier in his career. The financial circumstances of St. Louis College were among the things the bishop discussed. Msgr. George Houck, Chancellor of the Diocese, in a letter to Father Hoffer written 7 April 1883, pointed out that the bishop had supported the college at a loss and the clergy did not want that situation to continue. In fact, just before the closing of the college, Bishop Gilmour had paid most of the interest due on the debt. The correspondence between Father Hoffer and Bishop Gilmour and Msgr. Houck is referred to in the "Notes" of Msgr. Michael Hynes made in preparation for his writing of *The History of the Diocese of Cleveland* (1956). Much of the material in the "Notes" was not used in the history. Father Hoffer felt that the diocesan administration gave up on the college which he considered a success because some ninety priests of the Cleveland diocese had begun their studies at St. Louis College during the seven years of its existence. Hoffer to Houck, 28 September 1822. "Notes" of Msgr. Hynes, *ADC*.

5. Gilbert J. Garraghan, S.J., *The Jesuits of the Middle United States*, III, 116.

6. See Appendix A on the Buffalo Mission for the story of the establishment of the Mission.

7. *Diarium* of the Jesuits of the Buffalo Mission, 17 September 1868; 1 October 1868 to 2 January 1869, *ACC.*

8. Francis X. Curran, S.J., *The Return of the Jesuits*, 137. The following letters in the Roman Archives of the Society of Jesus are cited: Behrens to Beckx, 13 February, 25 April, 11 July 1873.

9. Ibid., Behrens to Beckx, 26 June 1873.

10. "*Acta Consultationum Superioris Missionis Americae Septentrionalis*," cited hereafter as "*Acta*," 29 August 1876; 17 August 1877, *ACC.*

11. Edward T. Dunn, "A History of Canisius College, 1870–1907." An unpublished Master's thesis at Canisius College, 1964, 18.

12. Ibid., 53; Lessmann to Beckx, 27 November 1876, " 'There do not seem to be such difficulties as we suspected. . . . Behrens always and only wrote about problems and terrible difficulties, which, often enough, turned out on inspection to be ordinary ones.' "

13. Lessmann to Beckx, 8 March 1880, in ibid.

14. "*Acta*," 12 November 1877.

15. Ibid., 3 January 1878.

16. "Circular Letter" of Bishop Gilmour, 20 January 1878, *ADC.*

17. Ibid.

18. Ibid.

19. Lessmann to Gilmour, 20 March 1878, *ADC.* The Buffalo Jesuits had at this time offers to open a college in St. Paul and LaCrosse.

20. Gilmour to Lessmann, 20 March 1878, *ADC.*

21. Gilmour to Tappert, 29 January 1890, *ADC.* See also Paul J. Hallinan, "Richard Gilmour, Second Bishop of Cleveland," unpublished dissertation, Western Reserve University, 1963.

22. Gilmour to Weninger, 20 November 1878, *ADC.*

23. Lessmann to Gilmour, 26 March 1878, *ADC.*

24. Ibid.

25. Ibid. Father Lessmann did not go into any lengthy explanation of the Buffalo situation, which had seen the Jesuits rather deeply involved with a German parish there at the request of the bishop of Buffalo, John Timon, C.M., in the later 1850s. The Jesuits had become identified with the difficulties there. It was this identification with the German language that probably convinced Bishop Gilmour that the Buffalo Jesuits should be identified with a German parish in Cleveland. Bishop Gilmour, however, hoped for speedy Americanization; he wanted no repetition of the Canisius College experience where there were many complaints of the poor English of the German Jesuits. (Curran, *Return of the Jesuits*, 136.)

26. Lessmann to Gilmour, 26 March 1878, *ADC.*

27. "*Acta*," 2 April 1878, *ACC.*

28. Gilmour to Lessmann, 12 November 1879, *ADC.* According to the "Notes" of Msgr. Hynes, the only available source on the original proposal (*ADC*), Father Lessmann asked only the "patronage of the diocese," but expected that the Jesuits would be given charge of a parish "now existing or to be formed." Bishop Gilmour proposed a congregation of the West Side (St. Mary's) and the bishop's Council agreed and suggested that negotiations be opened.

29. Lessmann to Gilmour, 4 March 1880, *ADC.*

30. Ibid.

31. Gilmour to Lessmann, 27 March 1880, *ADC.*

32. Lessmann to Gilmour, 4 March 1880, *ADC.*

33. Gilmour to Lessmann, 27 March 1880, *ADC.*

34. Gilmour to Lessmann, 12 June 1880, *ADC.*

35. Ibid.

36. *Notice*, "To whom it may Concern," 10 July 1880, *ADC.*

37. "*Acta*," 29 January, 28 October 1880; 8 February, 14 March, 20 April 1881.
38. Gilmour to Lessmann, 29 May 1881, *ADC*.
39. Ibid., 30 August 1881, *ADC*.
40. Ibid., 9 November 1881, *ADC*.
41. Ibid.
42. Ibid.
43. Ibid.
44. Lessmann to Gilmour, 13 February 1882, *ADC*.
45. Ibid.
46. Ibid.
47. Ibid.
48. Ibid.
49. Gilmour to Lessmann, 27 February 1882, *ADC*.
50. Ibid.
51. Ibid.
52. Ibid.
53. Lessmann to Gilmour, 10 March 1883, *ADC*; Gilmour to Lessmann, 7 April 1883, *ADC*.
54. "*Acta*," 8 February 1881, "pro parte orientali, quae est major et potior."
55. *Litterae Annuae*, St. Ignatius College, 1882–83, *ASIH*.
56. *Litterae Annuae, Residentiae Clevelandensis* 1883–84, *ASIH*.
57. Ibid.
58. Zoeller to Gilmour, 24 April 1883, *ADC*; *Litterae Annuae*, 1882–83, *ASIH*; Houck to Zoeller, 30 April 1883, *ADC*.
59. Gilmour to Kocherols, 3 July 1883, *ADC*.
60. *Litterae Annuae*, 1882–83, *ASIH*.
61. Gilmour to Sorin, 4 August 1883, *ADC*.
62. Ibid.
63. Ibid.
64. Sorin to Gilmour, 5 August 1883, *ADC*.
65. Gilmour to Lessmann, 19 November 1883, *ADC*.
66. Lessmann to Gilmour, 12 July 1884, *ADC*.
67. Gilmour to Sorin, 10 November 1885, *ADC*.
68. Ibid.
69. Gilmour to Lessmann, 30 January 1886, *ADC*.
70. "*Acta*," 2 February 1886, *ACC*.
71. Ibid., 12 February 1886.
72. Gilmour to Behrens, 19 April 1886, *ADC*.
73. Gilmour diary, 19 April 1886, *ADC*.
74. Behrens to Gilmour, 26 April 1886, *ADC*.
75. Ibid.
76. Behrens to Gilmour, 5 June 1886, *ADC*.
77. Anderledy to Behrens, 10 July 1887, *ARSI*, on microfilm in *AJC*.
78. Father Neustich's description of the beginning of St. Ignatius College, probably prepared in connection with the Buffalo Mission Debt question, *ASIH*.
79. House Diary, St. Igantius College, 1886–93, *AJC*.
80. *Catholic Universe*, 3 June 1886, *ADC*.
81. Deeds and other documents pertaining to the purchase are in the Archives of the Buffalo Mission of the Society of Jesus. Microfilm copies in *AJC*. A dispute arose later as to whether the money was a loan or a gift. See Appendix B on Buffalo Mission Debt.
82. Ibid.

83. Ibid.

84. *Litterae Annuae*, 1886–1887, *ASIH*.

85. Ibid.

86. Ibid.

87. House Diary, 1886–91, *AJC*.

88. *Litterae Annuae*, 1886–87, *ASIH*.

89. Ibid. The reference may have been to a German newspaper but none has been found in available German papers.

90. Student Register—1886–96, St. Ignatius College, *AJC*.

91. *Cleveland Plain Dealer*, 8 September 1886.

92. *St. Ignatius College Catalogue*, 1886–87. Hereafter cited *Catalogue*.

93. House Diary, 1886–93, *AJC*.

94. Neustich to Rudolph Meyer (Missouri Province Provincial), 1 January 1909, *AMP*.

95. Charles A. Brady, *Canisius College: The First Hundred Years, 1870–1970*, 50–51.

96. John LaFarge, S.J., *The Manner is Ordinary*, 140.

97. Ibid., 141.

98. Ibid., 38.

99. *Litterae Annuae*, 1886–87, *ASIH*.

100. Ibid.

101. Ibid. This quote is from an alternate version; parts dealing with the Irish and their learning of German were omitted from the version sent to Rome. *ASIH*.

102. *Catholic Universe*, 23 August 1889. The article was aimed at Mr. Mueller, editor of the *Stimme der Wahrheit*, who later said he agreed with the bishop and invited everyone to the convention regardless of language or nationality.

103. *Litterae Annuae*, 1889–90, *ASIH*.

104. Father William B. Sommerhauser (rector 1915–19) to Father Thomas Gannon (American Assistant in Rome), 10 April 1916, *AJC*.

105. *Catalogue*, 1886–87, *AJC*.

106. Ibid.

107. Ibid.

108. Ibid.

109. John W. Donohue, S.J., *Jesuit Education*, 129.

110. *Catalogue*, 1904–05, *AJC*.

111. *Catalogue*, 1886–87, *AJC*.

112. *Litterae Annuae*, 1886–87, *ASIH*.

113. Garraghan, *Jesuits of the Middle United States*, III, 428, 505–08.

114. Ibid., 510.

115. Ibid., 511.

116. "Memorial of Visitation," of Father Behrens, 1884–85, 1886, 1887, *AJC*.

117. *Litterae Annuae*, 1887–88, *ASIH*.

118. Ibid.

119. *Catalogus Sociorum et Officiorum Dispersae Provinciae Germaniae*, 1886. 20, *AJC*.

120. Anderledy to Neustich, 2 May 1888, *ARSI*, on microfilm in *AJC*.

121. Bishop Horstmann's sermon quoted in the *Catholic Universe*, 21 July 1894.

122. *Woodstock Letters* (Woodstock, Md., 1872–1969) XXVI, 341.

123. Ibid.

124. *Historical Review of St. Ignatius College*, 1886–1917, Anon., 11, *AJC*.

125. House Diary, 1886–93, entry for 5 November 1888, *AJC*.

126. Minutes of Consultors' Meetings, St. Ignatius College, 1888–1917, 6 November 1888, *AJC*.

127. Ibid., 12 March 1890.

128. *Litterae Annuae*, 1888–89, *AJC*.

129. Anderledy to Knappmeyer, 23 April 1889, *ARSI*, on microfilm in *AJC*.

130. "Articles of Incorporation of St. Ignatius College," 1890, *AJC*. Recorded in volume 53, page 85 of the Records of Incorporations of the State of Ohio.

CHAPTER II

1. Chester A. Burns, S.J., "John Carroll University of Cleveland," unpublished manuscript, 3–4 (n.d.), *AJC*.

2. Ibid.

3. Garraghan, *Jesuits of the Middle United States*, III, 122–23.

4. Power, *Catholic Higher Education*, 124.

5. *Cleveland Plain Dealer*, 20 May 1900.

6. Power, *Catholic Higher Education*, 247–48.

7. John S. Brubacher, and Willis Rudy, *Higher Education in Transition*, 114.

8. *Catalogue*, 1888–1889.

9. Ibid., 1910.

10. Power, *Catholic Higher Education*, 127.

11. Lessmann's "Memorial," 17 March 1887, *AJC*.

12. Behrens's "Memorial," January (n.d.), 1890, *AJC*.

13. Van Rossum's "Memorial," 15 February 1896, *AJC*.

14. Rockliff to Martin, 12 January 1899, cited in Dunn, "History of Canisius," 75–76.

15. Theis to Martin, 31 January 1899; Zahm to Martin, 18 January 1892; both cited in ibid.

16. Charles A. Brady, *Canisius College, The First Hundred Years*, 1870–1970, p. 72.

17. Ibid., 114.

18. Power, *Catholic Higher Education*, 241.

19. *Catalogue*, 1886–87.

20. Ibid.

21. Ibid., 1915–16.

22. *Litterae Annuae*, 1886–87, *ASIH*. Boarders could be sent to Canisius. A check of the *Catalogues* of Canisius College will indicate that from 1870 on many students from the Cleveland diocesan area attended Canisius College as boarders. Aloysius Pfeil, who later became a Jesuit, Nicholas Pfeil, later a diocesan priest, and many others attended Canisius College as boarders. In 1886 boarders from Cleveland and the surrounding area at Canisius numbered 36, more than one third of the total number of boarders. Father Charles H. Metzger, S.J., from Shelby, Ohio, was one of these boarders. He became a noted historian and was chairman of the department of history at John Carroll University, 1929–33.

23. *Catalogue*, 1893–94.

24. *The Ignatian*, 10 April 1923, editorial, "The fact that there will be housing facilities for out-of-town students will strike a responsive chord in many a lad's heart, ..."

25. Power, *Catholic Higher Education*, 271.

26. *Litterae Annuae*, 1892–93, *ASIH*.

27. Power, *Catholic Higher Education*, 238, 272–73.

28. *Litterae Annuae*, 1892–93, *ASIH*.

29. "Memorial" of Rudolph Meyer, 16 April 1910; "Memorial" of Alexander Burrowes, 5 April 1913, *AJC*.

30. *Litterae Annuae*, 1889–90, *AJC*.

31. Alexander Burrowes's "Memorial," 18 December, 1915, *AJC*.

32. James A. Rockliff's "Memorial," 28 November 1898, *AJC*.

33. Minutes of Consultors' Meetings, 1888–1917, 141, *AJC*.

34. *Litterae Annuae,* 1889–90, *ASIH*.

35. *Carroll News,* 12 November 1925, a reporter's interview with Father Betten. Minutes of Consultors' Meetings, 1888–1917, 13 September, 21 October 1914, *AJC*.

36. William J. McGucken, S.J., *The Jesuits and Education,* 164–65.

37. Michael J. Hynes, "Notes" for his *History of the Diocese of Cleveland.*

38. *Catalogue,* 1910–11.

39. Power, *Catholic Higher Education,* 250.

40. "Memorial," Rudolph Meyer, 30 January 1908, *AJC*.

41. Anonymous, *Historical Review of St. Ignatius College,* 1886–1917; 11.

42. Father Van Rossum's "Memorial," 22 December 1893, *AJC*.

43. Ibid., 10 February 1895, *AJC*.

44. *Catalogue,* 1895–96.

45. Ibid.

46. Ibid.

47. Father Van Rossum's "Memorial," 18 February, 1897, *AJC*. Father Van Rossum referred to the statement in the 1891 Memorial of Father Rathgeb to the effect that, "Pueri ne corporaliter castigentur, nisi ex speciali commissione et licentia P. Rectoris," 27 June, 1891, *AJC*.

48. William G. Rose *Cleveland, The Making of a City,* 477, 535.

49. The occasion for the organization of an orchestra seems to have been the first visit of Bishop Horstmann to the college on 25 March 1892. Someone suggested that a reception be given and a musical program arranged. Members of the faculty who could play an instrument along with some students furnished the nucleus of the orchestra under the direction of Father Schulte. Father Pickel was one of the faculty members; he played the cornet. Father Hubert Gruender, a composer of some note, became a member of the faculty and of the orchestra in 1895. "John Carroll University Orchestra Scrap Book," 1927, *AJC*.

50. *Catalogue,* 1915–16.

51. Ibid., 1898–99.

52. Ibid., 1914–15.

53. Ibid.

54. Ibid. In the *Litterae Annuae* of 1883–84, *ASIH*, the pastor of St. Mary's Church had already discovered that American youth "prefer clubs, secular ones, in which they will more readily get a freer mode of living and acting."

55. Ibid.

56. *Woodstock Letters,* XXIX, 3, 521.

57. Student Register, 1886–96, *AJC*.

58. Anderledy to Neustich, 8 April 1887, *ARSI*, on microfilm in *AJC*.

59. Reminiscences of John T. Feighan, '91, *Carroll News,* XXXIII, 7, 15 February, 1952.

60. *Litterae Annuae,* 1892–93, *ASIH*.

61. *The Ignatian,* 4 November 1920. Father Haggeney had been interviewed on the history of the early days of the college.

62. *Litterae Annuae,* 1892–93, *ASIH*.

63. Ibid., 1894–95, *ASIH*. Copies of the awards in the 1893–94 and 1895–96 *Catalogues.*

64. Scrapbook, St. Ignatius College Athletic Association, *AJC*.

65. *Cleveland Plain Dealer,* 11 June 1907.

66. Ibid.

67. Ibid.

68. Ibid., 24 January 1905.

69. Scrapbook, St. Ignatius College Athletic Association, *AJC*.

70. Ibid.

71. Minutes of Consultors' Meetings, 1888–1917, 30 March 1915, 15 August 1915.

72. *Carroll News*, VIII, 8, 29 February 1927.

73. *Lumina*, I, 4, April 1916, 218.

74. *Litterae Annuae*, 1891–92, *ASIH*.

75. Interview with Hubert Borling (Borlinghausen), 17 February, 1891. Mr. Borling died 18 February 1984 just prior to his 107th birthday.

76. *Litterae Annuae*, 1891–92, *ASIH*.

77. *Carroll News*, 24 March 1927, an article on Father Rockliff who had died 4 December 1926 at Missoula, Montana. The author was probably Father Francis Haggeney, who joined the faculty at about the same time as Father Rockliff.

78. Ibid.

79. Ibid.

80. Ibid.

81. *Catholic Universe*, 9 September 1898.

82. Ibid.

83. *Carroll News*, 9 October 1931, an article on Father Odenbach on the occasion of his Golden Jubilee in the Society.

84. *Litterae Annuae*, 1895–96, *ASIH*.

85. *Carroll News*, 9 October 1931.

86. Ibid., 29 April 1932.

87. Pickel to Burrowes, 7 June 1910, *AJC* microfilm of original in Missouri Province Archives.

88. Ibid.

89. Pickel to Meyer, 7 June 1910, *AJC* microfilm, in *AJC*, original in Missouri Province Archives.

90. Pickel to Burrowes, 7 October 1909, on microfilm in *AJC*, original in Missouri Province Archives. James L. Farragher, one of the students involved in this incident, had received a letter from Frederick C. Waite, Secretary of the Medical Department of Western Reserve. This letter, dated 14 August 1909 *AJC*, criticized St. Louis University Medical School for poorly prepared students and poor facilities. The applicant sent Waite's letter to Father Haggeney who in turn sent the correspondence to Father John C. Burke, S.J., Regent of the St. Louis University Medical School. Father Burke's reply to Father Haggeney 10 September 1909, *AJC*, pointed out that Waite was less than an impartial judge in the matter. According to Father Burke, Waite was on a committee examining St. Louis University's Medical School for a chapter of the Medical Fraternity, Alpha Omega Alpha. The committee was favorable to establishing a chapter at St. Louis until Waite, after visiting Washington University, also in St. Louis, discovered that St. Louis University was a Jesuit university. The basis of Waite's comparative statistics of St. Louis and Western Reserve's medical schools was questioned by Father Burke along with the sincerity of Dr. Waite, whom Father Burke accused of injecting the religious issue into the matter. St. Ignatius College students were in demand at Western Reserve, but it was recommended that there be an even greater emphasis on biology and chemistry in their undergraduate program. Such a recommendation came from the president of Western Reserve, Charles F. Thwing, in a letter to Bishop Farrelly dated 8 October 1914 (*AJC*). Pointing out that Dr. Waite would be anxious to do whatever he could by conferring with the officials of St. Ignatius College to improve the students' transition to medical school, President Thwing also offered his assistance in the matter. What is most interesting is the fact that the attempt to deal with St. Ignatius College was made through the bishop and not directly with college officials.

91. Michael J. Hynes, *History of the Diocese of Cleveland*, 351, footnote.

92. Knappmeyer to Gilmour, 27 May 1890, *ADC*.

93. Brady, *Canisius*, 102–3, 124.

94. Scrapbook, General, St. Ignatius College, 26 August 1910 to 30 August 1919, *AJC*.

95. Ibid.

96. *The Ignatian*, VI, 14, 16 June 1925.

CHAPTER III

1. George E. Condon, *Cleveland, The Best Kept Secret* (New York: Doubleday, 1967). On pp. 8–11 is a humorous but perceptive description of East and West Side differences.

2. "Antecedents and the Beginnings of St. Ignatius College," unpublished manuscript (1916), 1–2, *AJC*. Probable author could be Father William B. Sommerhauser, S.J. or Father Francis Haggeney, S.J.

3. Ibid., 2.

4. Minutes of the Board of Trustees, 1906–32, 7 January 1907, 60, *AJC*. In May there was further discussion on whether to retain the present college and then begin to plan for a new college "in partibus urbis orientalibus."

5. Pickel to Horstmann, 1 July 1907, *ADC*.

6. Ibid.

7. Ibid., 2.

8. Ibid., 3.

9. Ibid., 4.

10. Ibid., 5.

11. Ibid.

12. Ibid.

13. Ibid.

14. Ibid., 6.

15. Ibid.

16. Pickel to Horstmann, 29 July 1907, *ADC*.

17. Houck to Pickel, 3 September 1907, *ADC*. The agreement was dated 31 August.

18. Copies of the contract dated 31 August 1907 are in both *ADC* and *AJC*.

19. Bishop Farrelly's explanation of his position in his response to questions from the Congregation for Religious on 12 October 1917, 7–10, *ADC*. Referred to later as Farrelly's "Response."

20. Pickel to Horstmann, 29 July 1907, *ADC*.

21. Farrelly's "Response," 12, *ADC*.

22. Minutes of the Board of Trustees, 12 August 1907, *AJC*.

23. Ibid.

24. Van Rossum to Horstmann, 16 June 1897, *ADC*. The Superior of the Buffalo Mission made this comment in the course of his efforts to set up a temporary Novitiate at what was then called Brighton. The first year (1897) that scholastics were not to be sent to Holland caused some shifting of personnel resulting in plans for a Novitiate in Cleveland.

25. Horstmann to Van Rossum, 19 June 1897, *AMP* on microfilm in *AJC*.

26. Sommerhauser to Burrowes, 13 September 1916, *AMP* on microfilm in *AJC*.

27. Minutes of the Board of Trustees, 1 December 1908, *AJC*.

28. Farrelly's "Response," 12 October 1917, 12, *ADC*.

29. Minutes of the Board of Trustees, January (n.d.) 1909, *AJC*.

30. Ibid.

31. Neustich to Bushart, 1 January 1909, *AMP*, on microfilm in *AJC*.

32. Ibid.

33. Ibid.

34. Ibid.

35. Ibid.

36. Neustich to Meyer, 6 January 1909, *AMP*, on microfilm in *AJC*.

37. Ibid.

38. Ibid.

39. Ibid.

40. Minutes of the Board of Trustees, February, (n.d.) 1909, *AJC*.

41. Meyer to Pickel, 7 May 1909, *AJC*.

42. Ibid.

43. Copy of the permission in *AJC*.

44. O'Neill to Sommerhauser, 12 February 1916, *AMP*. In this letter Father Michael O'Neill, Socius to the Provincial, says, "of my own knowledge, . . . the grant to Cleveland was *not* to buy and *build* Loyola High on the 'East Side of Cleveland', (as you put it) i.e., of a specific nature, but in a *general* way to purchase and build and then incur debt. I am sure that neither Father Pickel nor the Provincial (with his consultors) had at that time any desire to purchase the present Loyola High site. Rather we all desired to procure property and build towards the Western Reserve University."

45. Pickel to Farrelly 10 July 1909, *AJC*.

46. Ibid.

47. Ibid.

48. Ibid.

49. Ibid.

50. Ibid.

51. Ibid.

52. Ibid.

53. Ibid.

54. Pickel to Farrelly 12 July 1909, *AJC* copy with the heading "Memorial" sent to Rt. Rev. J. P. Farrelly, 12 July 1909.

55. Ibid.

56. Pickel to Meyer, 26 July 1909, *AJC*.

57. Ibid.

58. Ibid.

59. Ibid.

60. Ibid.

61. Ibid.

62. Meyer to Pickel, 27 July 1909, *AJC*.

63. Ibid.

64. Ibid.

65. Pickel to Meyer, 7 October 1909, *AMP*, on microfilm in *AJC*.

66. Ibid.

67. Sommerhauser to Burrowes, 4 August 1916, postscript on letter, *AMP*, on microfilm in *AJC*. This was apparently just rumor; Dominican sources reveal no attempt to locate a college in Cleveland at that time.

68. Pickel to Meyer, 7 October 1909, *AMP*, on microfilm in *AJC*.

69. Ibid.

70. Meyer to Pickel, 2 January 1910, *AJC*.

71. Grasselli to Pickel, 4 January 1910, *AJC*.

72. Pickel to Grasselli, 16 January 1910, rough draft in *AJC*.

73. Ibid.

74. Grasselli to Pickel, 3 March 1910, *AJC*.

75. Meyer to Pickel, 24 July 1910, *AJC*.

76. *Woodstock Letters*, V., 81, p. 380, obituary of Father John B. Furay, S.J.

77. Ibid., 380–381.

78. Farrelly's "Response," 12 *ADC*.

79. Ibid., 13.

80. Minutes of Consultors' Meetings, 8 September 1910, *AJC*.

81. Ibid.

82. Furay to Meyer, 19 September 1910, *AMP*, on microfilm in *AJC*.

83. Ibid.

84. Ibid., 27 September 1910.

85. Ibid.

86. Ibid.

87. Ibid., 12 October 1910.

88. Ibid.

89. Ibid.

90. Ibid.

91. Ibid.

92. Heiermann to Meyer, 17 October 1910, *AMP*, on microfilm in *AJC*. Reference to the consultor's opinion that did not count was probably to Father Neustich.

93. Furay to Heiermann, 15 October 1910, *AMP*, on microfilm in *AJC*.

94. Furay to Meyer, 1 November 1910, *AMP*, on microfilm in *AJC*.

95. Ibid.

96. Ibid.

97. Ibid.

98. Furay to Meyer, 15 November 1910, *AMP*, on microfilm in the *AJC*. Although apparently not discussed at his meeting with the bishop, another matter of grave concern bothered Father Furay and he included it in this letter to Father Meyer. Father Thomas C. O'Reily, chancellor of the Diocese of Cleveland, had informed Father Furay that it was the bishop's request that he serve on the diocesan committee required by order of Pope Pius X on 1 September 1910 to oversee the doctrinal orthodoxy of the clergy of the diocese. Father Furay was aware that the Jesuit General did not want the Jesuits to participate in these vigilante committees which had resulted from the Papacy's attack on "modernism" in philosophy, theology, science, biblical criticism, and politics. Father Furay feared that if he refused to serve on the committee the bishop would not take it well and if he did serve it could complicate the Jesuits' contacts with the priests of the diocese. Father Meyer at first advised Father Furay to avoid any association with such a committee. Meyer to Furay, 17 November 1910, *AJC*. Later, Father Meyer conceded the necessity of complying with the bishop's request and was thanked by the bishop for giving his approval for Father Furay to serve on the committee. O'Reily to Meyer, 9 December 1910, *ADC*.

99. Ibid.

100. Ibid.

101. Minutes of Consultors' Meetings, 14 November 1910, *AJC*.

102. Ibid., 15 December 1910, *AJC*.

103. Ibid.

104. Minutes of Consultors' Meetings, 1888–1917, 2 April 1911, 117, *AJC*.

105. Furay to Sommerhauser, 11 February 1916, *AJC*.

106. Ibid.

107. Furay to Farrelly, 26 January 1911, *AJC*. The date on the letter should be 1912 but internal evidences indicate that Father Furay had not changed his calendar after the beginning of the new year.

108. Ibid.

109. Farrelly's "Response," 11–12, *ADC*.

110. Minutes of Consultors' Meetings, 26 February 1912, *AJC*.

111. R. D. Stephen to Burrowes (n.d.), *AMP*, on microfilm in *AJC*.

112. Ibid.

113. Ibid.

114. Ibid.

115. Sommerhauser to Burrowes, 10 November 1915, *AMP*, on microfilm in *AJC*. The consultors had already agreed upon the desirability of remaining on the present Loyola site, St. Ignatius College, Minutes of Consultors' meetings, 1886–1917, 7 November 1915, *AJC*.

116. Ibid.

117. Ibid.

118. Ibid.

119. Sommerhauser to Burrowes, 11 November 1915, *AMP*, in *AJC* on microfilm.

120. *Cleveland Leader*, 5 January 1916.

121. *Cleveland Plain Dealer*, 5 January 1916.

122. Ibid.

CHAPTER IV

1. Farrelly's "Response," 8, *ADC*.

2. Sommerhauser to Farrelly, 4 January 1916, *ADC*.

3. Farrelly's "Response," 8, *ADC*.

4. Papi to Sommerhauser, 11 March 1919, *AJC*.

5. Farrelly to Sommerhauser, 23 January 1916, *ADC*.

6. Ibid.

7. Sommerhauser to Farrelly, 22 January 1916, *ADC*. The College consultors had considered the street car company's offer at a meeting, 10 January 1916.

8. Sommerhauser to Farrelly, 26 January 1916, *ADC*. The letter is not dated, but "Tuesday is used in place of the date which is as given above.

9. Scullen to Sommerhauser, 22 March 1916, *AJC*.

10. Sommerhauser to Farrelly, 23 March 1916, *ADC*.

11. Ibid.

12. Farrelly to Sommerhauser, 4 August 1916, *ADC*.

13. Ibid.

14. Ibid. What Bishop Farrelly is referring to is the Constitution *Romanos Pontifices* of Leo XIII issued in 1881. This Constitution was issued after a controversy arising in 1874 in England over the right of the Jesuits to establish colleges without the consent of the Ordinary. The Jesuit Provincial, a "holy but impetuous Irishman" named Peter Galwey, acted on the strength of papal permissions to erect such colleges. Cardinal Manning and the English bishops sought changes in ecclesiastical law which would give the bishops authority in such cases. The Constitution of 1881 settled such matters in favor of the bishop. Bishop Farrelly's long experience in Rome made him familiar with the issue.

15. Sommerhauser to Farrelly, 7 August 1916, *ADC*.

16. Farrelly's "Response," 9, *ADC*.

17. Pickel to Sommerhauser, 5 February 1916, *AJC*. There was formal approval by Bishop Gilmour's Council for the Jesuits coming to Cleveland.

18. Ibid.

19. Farrelly's "Response," *ADC*.

20. Pickel to Sommerhauser, 5 February 1916, *AJC*.

21. Ibid.

22. Farrelly to Sommerhauser, 4 August 1916, *ADC*.

23. Furay to Sommerhauser, 11 February 1916, *AJC*.

24. Ibid.

25. Farrelly's "Response," pp. 9–10, *ADC*.

26. Ibid.

27. Pickel to Sommerhauser, 5 February 1916, *AJC*.

28. Ibid.

29. Furay to Sommerhauser, 11 February 1916, *AJC*.

30. Ibid.

31. Pickel to Sommerhauser, 5 February 1916, *AJC*.

32. Artist's sketch in the Archives of the Diocese of Cleveland.

33. "Notes," Loyola Controversy, *ADC*.

34. *The Catholic Universe*, 31 August 1917.

35. Hynes, *History of the Diocese of Cleveland*, 286.

36. Ibid., 285.

37. Burrowes to Sommerhauser, 21 March 1916, *AJC*.

38. Ibid.

39. Ibid. Father Papi had stated that the bishop had the right to forbid making Loyola a permanent foundation with a residence.

40. Burrowes to Sommerhauser, 17 January 1916, *AJC*.

41. Ibid.

42. Ibid.

43. Ibid.

44. Furay to Sommerhauser, 2 February 1916, *AJC*. A letter from Father Sommerhauser to Father Donovan, 1 April 1916, discussed the question of the canonical status of Loyola High School. "Our canonical status seems under attack—I found a document left by previous rector—agreement between Horstmann and Pickel allowing us to locate anywhere on East Side as long as chapel is confined to students. Msgr. Geo. F. Houck, Chancellor and Vicar General under the late bishop tells me that this was only a 'friendly agreement,' for which the *Beneplacitum Apostolicum* was not obtained. Both the Bishop and Fr. Meyer [Provincial] thought that for such an extension it was unnecessary. The present bishop in one of the first interviews Fr. Pickel had with him demanded the authorization we had for the High School and declared his predecessor's permission invalid on account of the *Beneplacitum Apostolicum* not having been obtained. Bishop requested to apply for it (since only the bishop could) said, 'he could not do it without jeopardizing his popularity among the priests which he couldn't risk at the very beginning of his administration'—asked whether we could purchase property on East Side—never answered more than, 'The Society will do so at its own risk.' " Father Sommerhauser went on to say, "Bishop Farrelly wanted everything in the status quo and later always gave him other reasons than the lack of the *Beneplacitum Apostolicum* for refusing permission to buy other property on the East Side. The future of the college would hang in the balance and the Jesuits would continue to have the opposition, suffering, and privation they have always suffered in Cleveland." *AMP*.

45. Sommerhauser to Gannon, 1 April 1916, an explanation to the American Assistant to Father General of the situation in Cleveland, *AJC*.

46. Sommerhauser to Gannon, 10 April 1916. This was a follow-up letter to the first, adding information on the opening of Cathedral Latin and rejoicing over Cardinal Falconio's appointment as Prefect of the Congregation of Bishops and Regulars, *AJC*.

47. Ibid.

48. Ibid.

49. Sommerhauser to Gannon, 1 April 1916, *AJC*.

50. Ibid.

51. Sommerhauser to Bonzano, 12 July 1916, *AJC*.

52. Sommerhauser to Bonzano, 14 July 1916, *AJC*. In a letter to the Provincial after visiting the Apostolic Delegate, Father Sommerhauser reported that the Apostolic Delegate was not sure about the *Beneplacitum Apostolicum* or the permission of Bishop Horstmann, but "stated it was clear that all the laws of equity and human justice are in our favor." He offered to forward the case personally to Cardinal Falconio in Rome. Father Sommerhauser also reported that the canonist of the Apostolic Delegate, Dr. Phillip Bernardini said that, "Our good Bishop lost out in two cases against two priests of the diocese lately, and I am told that he has a holy fear of the Apostolic Delegate, (John Bonzano). The latter with his canonist are eager to get a case against our Ordinary as I gathered from his Excellency's own remarks to me personally. I do not feel as though want of charity or respect prompts this remark to your Reverence; the propaganda of the Free (?) High School being waged here now, and the almost brutal way we are being ignored and descried [*sic*], make me less scrupulous in the manner of defending our cause, as long as it is just. . . . I shall bear up under the strain if you [Provincial] are with me; indeed the petty persecution on the part of Diocesan Powers that Be are telling on me heavily; but I have resolved not to worry more than is becoming, and take a firm stand against the petty onslaughts made on us here." Sommerhauser to Provincial, 4 July 1916, *AJC*.

53. Sommerhauser to Bonzano, 2 August 1916, *AJC*.

54. Gannon to Sommerhauser, 24 October 1916, copy in *AJC*.

55. Ibid.

56. Bonzano to Sommerhauser, 10 September 1917, *AJC*.

57. *Catholic Universe*, 24 March 1916.

58. Minutes of Consultors' Meetings, 1888–1917, 3 December 1916, *AJC*.

59. Decree of Congregation of Religious, 10 December 1918, also letter of Father Alfred Maertens, Procurator General of the Society of Jesus, to Sommerhauser, 19 December 1918, *AJC*.

60. Sommerhauser to Farrelly, 27 January 1918; Scullen to Sommerhauser, 29 January 1919, *AJC*.

61. Papi to Sommerhauser, 11 March 1919, *AJC*.

62. Farrelly's "Response," *ADC*.

63. Ibid., 4.

64. Papi to Sommerhauser, 11 March 1919, *AJC*.

65. Sommerhauser to Hanselman, 22 March 1919, *AJC*.

66. Ibid.

67. Copy of letter in *AJC*.

68. Letter on microfilm in *AJC* from *AMP*.

69. Minute Book, Consultors of John Carroll Univ., 1917–49, 23 March, 1919, *AJC*.

70. Ibid.

71. Sommerhauser to Father General, 3 April 1919, *AJC*.

72. Hanselman to Sommerhauser, 4 May 1919, *AJC*.

73. Sommerhauser to Hanselman, 12 June 1919, *AJC*.

74. T. J. Smith's notes on the move to the East Side, *AJC*.

75. Sommerhauser to Smith, 3 July 1919, *AJC*.

76. Hanselman to Sommerhauser, 19 July 1919, *AJC*.

77. Papi to Sommerhauser, 5 July 1919, *AJC*.

78. Ledochowski to Sommerhauser, 6 August 1919, *AJC*.

79. Minutes of Diocesan Consultors, v. 2, p. 51, 19 January, 1918, *ADC*.

80. Ibid.

81. Consultors' notes in T. J. Smith's papers, *AJC*.

82. Ibid.

83. Minutes of Diocesan Consultors, v. 2, p. 76–77, 13 April 1922, *ADC*.

84. T. J. Smith Papers, *AJC*.

85. Ibid.

86. Ibid.

87. Hynes, *History of the Diocese*, 299.

88. T. J. Smith Papers, *AJC*.

89. McMenamy to Smith, 19 May 1921, *AJC*.

90. McMenamy to Smith, 23 May 1921, *AJC*.

91. In the effort to keep Loyola open, Father Smith had asked his consultors' opinions and had then drawn up a list of pros and cons on the problem, *AJC*.

92. Ibid.

CHAPTER V

1. *The Ignatian*, 26 November 1919, *AJC*.

2. T. J. Smith, "Notes on the founding of John Carroll," *AJC*. Father Smith says that it was on the occasion of the Mass of the Holy Ghost that this occurred. The Mass of the Holy Ghost that year was not until 27 September. On 11 September the Board of Trustees already was referring to the bishop's permission to locate on the East Side and had started the search for a site. Since the "Notes" were made in his later years he probably confused the two dates. It was not, however, until early 1922 that the matter was officially settled. Bishop Schrembs had come to administer the Sacrament of Confirmation at St. Mary Parish. "While he was with us he said to Father rector that the matter of a new college for us was settled in our favor. He wished to know where we desired the college and whether we wished to have a parish near the new college or at some other place in the city." Minutes Book, Consultors of John Carroll Univ., 1917–49, 5 March 1922, *AJC*.

3. Minutes of the Board of Trustees, 11 September 1921, *AJC*.

4. *The Ignatian*, 4 October 1921, *AJC*.

5. Minutes of Diocesan Consultors, v. 2, 3 March 1922, *ADC*.

6. Ibid. 26 November 1924.

7. Bernet to Arnold (Van Sweringen, General Manager), 25 May 1922, *AJC*.

8. Ian S. Haberman, *The Van Sweringens of Cleveland*, (Cleveland: Western Reserve Historical Society, 1979), 8–9.

9. Ibid., 10–15.

10. T. J. Smith, "Notes," *AJC*.

11. Arnold to T. J. Smith, 10 July 1922, *AJC*.

12. Ibid.

13. T. J. Smith to Arnold, 9 October 1922, *AJC*.

14. Agreement between St. Ignatius College and the Van Sweringen Company, 18 October 1922, *AJC*.

15. T. J. Smith to O. P. Van Sweringen, 12 December 1922, *AJC*. The consultors had met on 4 December and after discussion of a new site known as the "Davey" property, location not identified, thought that Father Smith should contact the Provincial and lay the matter before him. There is no written evidence that Father Smith did contact the Provincial but his firm action on 12 December suggests that he probably did. Minute Book, Consultors of John Carroll, 1917–49, 4 December 1922, *AJC*.

16. T. J. Smith, "Notes," *AJC*.

17. Ibid. Before the Jesuits decided definitely on the "Wain Farm" they had considered the

"Davey" property seriously enough to put down a $2,000 option on 8 January 1923 only to discover a month later that the restrictions were the same as had already been rejected. On 4 February the decision to look elsewhere was made, and on 19 March the "Davey" property was definitely rejected in favor of the "Wain Farm." Minute Book, Consultors John Carroll, 1917–49, 8 January, 4 February, 19 March 1923, *AJC.*

18. Arnold to Union Trust Company, 8 July 1924, *AJC.*

19. T. J. Smith, "Notes." According to Father Smith the Vans had originally said there were no restrictions but later told Joseph Schlitz, Father Smith's attorney, that they were ashamed to face the president when they found this was not so. The change was agreed to by the Consultors on 25 February 1924 because it was "to our advantage." Minute Book, Consultors of John Carroll Univ., 1917–49, *AJC.*

20. *The Ignatian,* 10 April 1923, *AJC.* Another article in the same issue noted that "It has long been the dream and hope of everyone interested in Ignatius, that someday the college would be housed in more commodious quarters, with sufficient facilities to meet the ever increasing tide of collegiate enrollment, and with ample athletic advantages, to enable the teams representing the institution to compete with other institutions of higher education. . . . The fact that there will be housing will strike a responsive chord in many a lad's heart."

21. *Cleveland Plain Dealer,* 4 April 1923. See also *The Province News Letter,* Missouri Province, June 1923.

22. *Litterae Annuae,* 1923, *AJC.* The name change had been approved by the consultors 11 May 1923, Minute Book, Consultors of John Carroll Univ., 1917–49, 11 May 1923, *AJC.*

23. *The Ignatian,* 10 April 1923, *AJC.*

24. *Cleveland Plain Dealer,* 21 March 1923.

25. William W. Walter to Bishop Schrembs, 29 May 1939, *ADC.*

26. Minutes of Diocesan Consultors, v. 2, p. 123, 11 June 1923, *ADC.*

27. Ibid., 11 July 1923.

28. It had been agreed by the bishop and his consultors in order to put aside "all wild rumors" to sell or preferably lease the old cathedral property. Ibid., 3 May 1923. The Wade Park property was selected as the new cathedral site on 7 January 1924. Ibid. However, in June 1926 the tract was sold to Western Reserve University for approximately $750,000, about twice what was paid for it in 1917. By this time it was clear that the old cathedral property would not bring in the amount expected.

29. *Catholic Universe,* 27 July 1923. In May, the Ward Systems of Chicago had been hired by the university to manage the campaign. Minute Book, Consultors of John Carroll, 1917–49, 20 May 1923, *AJC.*

30. Preliminary Report on St. Ignatius College," 21 May 1923, *AJC.*

31. Ibid.

32. *A Child's Birthright,* 7, *AJC.*

33. Unsigned and undated memorandum to T. J. Smith, *AJC.*

34. Ibid.

35. Ibid.

36. Schrembs to T. J. Smith, 29 June 1923, *AJC.*

37. MacGrath to Monsignor Smith, no date, *AJC.*

38. MacGrath to Tuttle, 14 July 1923, *AJC.*

39. Haggeney to Boylan, 19 April 1928, *AJC.* Until the publication by Father James Brodrick, S.J., of *Saint Ignatius Loyola* the common explanation for the shield's wolves, pot, and red and gold bars interpreted the name of Loyola as a derivation of *lobo y olla,* Spanish for wolves and kettle or pot. Father Broderick pointed out that the Basque name, Loyola, had quite a different origin. "*Loi* is Basque for loam, *ol* is a suffix meaning abundance or profusion, and *a* is the definite article, the abundance of loam. That is the lowly, earthy, unromantic derivation of a name so celebrated as any in history" (p. 12). Father Brodrick points out that

the "two wolves rampant on either side of a hanging cauldron . . . was the adopted escutcheon of the Loyolas, and has given rise to fanciful interpretation of their name, based on Spanish for volves and pot—*lobos* and *olla*. But the Basque name for volves is *otsoak*, and there is no reason why a Basque family should have regarded the beasts as something peculiarly and horribly Castilian. They were much more common in the forests of the Guipuzcoa than in Castile and the farmers kept up with them a relentless battle. Some exploit or other in the fight may account for the Loyola wolves, which anyhow were an accepted emblem in the heraldry of the period. The boiling cauldron or pot symbolized hospitality, a virtue for which the Basques have always been justly celebrated. The full blazon of the Loyolas included the seven gold bars of the Onaz family which possibly commemorated the seven paladins of Beotibar [seven brothers of Onaz and Loyola family, defenders against Castile in 1321]. There is no certain record of a royal grant of arms to either house, and they may simply have been appropriated, as has happened thousands of times in all national histories" (pp. 18–20). It has been customary for most Jesuit colleges and universities to use the basic shield as their emblem or seal adding only some particular designation such as school colors. Some, including John Carroll, still retain the Spanish words for wolves and kettle.

40. Monsignor Smith to All Pastors, 25 July 1923, *AJC.*
41. Collection responses to Monsignor Smith's circular letter of 4 August 1923, *AJC.*
42. Frank A. Scott to Monsignor Smith, 16 August 1923, *AJC, ACWRU.*
43. Ibid.
44. Henry Turner Bailey to Monsignor Smith, 31 August 1923, AJC.
45. Ibid.
46. Ibid.
47. Ibid.
48. Monsignor Smith to the newspaper editors and publishers, 14 August 1923, *AJC.*
49. Notes of B. E. Bettinges, staff of MacGrath, 18 August 1923, *AJC.*
50. D. J. Kennedy to MacGrath, 10 August 1923, *AJC.*
51. MacGrath to J. J. Kelly, 13 August 1923, *AJC.*
52. Monsignor Smith's remarks (stenographic report), 29 August 1923 luncheon, *AJC.*
53. Ibid.
54. Ibid., 2–3.
55. Ibid., 5.
56. T. J. Smith's remarks, ibid., 6.
57. Ibid., 7–8.
58. MacGrath's remarks, ibid., 9.
59. MacGrath to All the Staff, 29 August 1923, *AJC.*
60. Ibid.
61. *Cleveland Plain Dealer*, 5 September 1923.
62. MacGrath to Staff, 29 August 1923, *AJC.*
63. Ibid.
64. Ibid.
65. Memorandum to Frank S. Whitcomb and Harold T. Clark, 26 October 1923, *ACWRU.* In April there had been inquiries by Newton D. Baker, who had apparently heard some rumor to the effect that one of the local colleges had acquired the name of Cleveland in its title. He apparently understood it to be "University of Cleveland" and wrote to J. D. Williamson of Western Reserve to find out whether Baldwin-Wallace College had acquired a new name, Baker to Williamson, 14 April 1923, *ACWRU.* Baker wanted to know if Baldwin-Wallace still needed the name in view of the "recent amalgamation of Baldwin and the German-Wallace College. If they did not need it would they be willing to release it to us." Baker had written earlier to the president of Baldwin-Wallace and received a reply that the president "had never heard any discussion of the name, University of Cleveland, for the insti-

tution here at Berea whether for the original Baldwin University or for the institution since the merger, now called Baldwin-Wallace," A. B. Storms to Baker, 13 April 1923, *ACWRU*. Baker then wrote to Wiliamson again: "Apparently the official people at the Baldwin-Wallace are not responsible for the taking out of the Charter at Columbus. Perhaps all I can do under these circumstances is to find out who are recorded in Columbus as Trustees or organizers of the institution chartered there," Baker to Williamson, 16 April 1923, *ACWRU*. Dr. Robert Vinson, president of Western Reserve University, wrote to Newton Baker thanking him for "all the trouble you have taken to find out about the existence of a corporation entitled 'University of Cleveland.' " Vinson then informed Baker that he had learned from his secretary that Charles Thwing, Vinson's predecessor, had gone into this matter in 1919, Vinson to Baker, 17 April 1923. The confusion of titles University of Cleveland and Cleveland University had thrown them off the track. When Newton Baker did find out that it was St. Ignatius College that had acquired the title Cleveland University, he is reported to have said, "that it was too bad that Western-Reserve had not the activity and the prevision necessary to have acquired the name in some form in proper season," J. F. MacGrath to John Dwan, 6 September 1923, *AJC*.

66. Original copy of the "Understanding" in the Archives of Case Western Reserve University. The document is dated 29 August 1923. There is no copy in the Archives of John Carroll University.

67. T. J. Smith to Boylan, 10 December 1925, *AJC*.

68. Boylan to Provincial, 28 March 1926, *AMP*, on microfilm in *AJC*. Father Boylan wrote to the Provincial a short time after receiving Father Smith's letter. "Msgr. Smith is on the rampage. I received a curt note about not sending bill he spoke of, in your presence, for printing incidental [*sic*] to change of name. Consultors advise me not to send the bill as nothing, or at least very little would come of it. He seems to be playing politics some way or other in this matter." The Jesuits had come to question Msgr. Smith's activities after his confusing role in the acquisition and loss of the name "Cleveland University."

69. Monsignor Smith to Frank A. Scott, 18 October 1928, *ACWRU*.

70. Ibid.

71. Ibid.

72. Scott to Monsignor Smith, 13 November 1928, *ACWRU*.

73. Ibid.

74. Scott to Monsignor Smith, 30 August 1923, *AJC*.

75. Scott to Andrew Squire, Esq., 30 August 1923, *AJC*.

76. Ibid.

77. Scott to Vinson, 30 August 1923, *AJC*.

78. Monsignor Smith to Rodman, 14 November 1928, *AJC*.

79. Monsignor Smith to Scott, 14 November 1928, *AJC*.

80. *The Province News Letter*, Missouri Province of the Society of Jesus, v. 4, December 1923.

81. T. J. Smith to Rodman, 5 December 1928, *AJC*.

82. Joseph A. Schlitz to Rodman, 9 October 1928, *AJC*.

83. Ibid., "I have exhausted all sources of information that occur to me as likely to be productive of results in connection with occurrances [*sic*] surrounding change of name of your University several years ago. Of the attorneys with whom I have spoken, Mr. Richard Moriarty, while having nothing to do with the amendment creating change of name, comes nearer than anyone to knowing about the situation. While he cannot state so definitely, it is Mr. Moriarty's impression that the University authorities, acting perhaps with the advice and assistance of the campaign manager in the fund campaign, [James MacGrath] then about to get underway, affected the change of name directly. [This was the change from St. Ignatius College to Cleveland University.] Very shortly after the name had been first changed, Father

Smith, then President of your University, called on Mr. Moriarty stating that Mr. Grant, then President of the Chamber of Commerce and who as such would naturally be one of the influences whose support for the fund would be solicited, had protested against the use of the new name, and in this talk between Father Smith and Mr. Grant the name Mr. Samuel Mather was used. Mr. Moriarty is not very clear, after the lapse of these many years, as to the details of the conversation, and remembers only that Father Smith sought his advice as to the best thing to do in view of this protest. I am very much inclined to think, although please understand that I am just guessing, that the manager of the fund campaign produced the idea relative to original change of name, and it is quite likely that he caused the certificate of amendment to be drawn up, no doubt on his own account getting some outside legal advice as to just how to go about it. Whether this assumption be right or wrong, there is no doubt that very effective protest was made by powerful local interests, with the result that the name was again changed to the present name. If this assumption be correct, I am very much inclined to think that perhaps no one outside of Father Smith and Mr. McGrath [*sic*], the manager of the fund campaign knows any substantial part of the whole story. In any event, those who in the past had done legal work for the college, so far as I know of the attorneys who acted in that capacity, had nothing to do with the matter."

84. Harold T. Clark to Sidney S. Wilson, 23 May 1927, *ACWRU*.

85. Harold T. Clark to Robert D. Fisher, Vice-President of Western Reserve University, 5 October 1942, *ACWRU*.

86. Minutes of the Board of Trustees of Cleveland University, 19 April 1943, *ACWRU*.

87. T. J. Smith to Boylan, 10 March 1926, *AJC*.

88. Father James A. Mackin, former archivist at John Carroll, in a letter to the author, 8 August 1980. Frank Jones, former Vice President for Business at John Carroll University, also recalls that there were Cleveland-Cliffs stock certificates, presumably a gift of Mather, held by the University; they were of no value; conversation with author, 21 April 1981.

89. G. Y. Anderson [Mather's secretary] to Schrembs, 6 February 1930, *ADC*.

90. *The Ignatian*, VI, 2, 22 October 1924.

91. *Litterae Annuae* to Father General, July 1923 to July 1924, *AJC*.

92. MacGrath to Dwan, 31 August 1923, *AJC*.

93. *Catholic Universe*, 7 September 1923.

94. Minute Book, Consultors of John Carroll Univ. 1917–49, 20 August 1923, *AJC*. "Two consultors and three other fathers present. Change of name from Cleveland to John Carroll University discussed. This was caused by prominent men in the city who were displeased because we took the name Cleveland. All fathers except one agreed that it was better to change the name—all agreed to the name John Carroll." On 13 September the consultors met again and discussed the reaction to the name John Carroll after it had been announced. "It was agreed that it was favorable."

95. *The Province News Letter*, Missouri Province, V., 4, December 1923.

96. Bailey to Monsignor Smith, 15 September 1923, *AJC*.

97. MacGrath to Bailey, 18 September 1923, *AJC*.

98. MacGrath to Dwan, 6 September 1923, *AJC*.

99. D. J. Kennedy to MacGrath, 5 October 1923, *AJC*. Kennedy was regional director of the campaign in Youngstown.

100. *The Ignatian*, 9 October 1923.

101. Ibid.

102. Ibid.

103. Ibid., 26 October 1923.

104. Ibid., 10 April 1923.

105. Ibid.

106. Ibid., 26 October 1923.

107. MacGrath to T. J. Smith, 12 September 1923, *AJC*.

108. T. J. Smith to Boylan, 10 March 1926, *AJC*. The Diocesan letter of 18 September 1923, stated that, "it is my wish that each year during the entire month [October], no other demand for money (except pew rent and ordinary Sunday Collection) be made upon the people, so that the combining effort of pastors and people shall be devoted to the success of the collection for the support of ecclesiastical students of this Diocese."*ADC*.

109. MacGrath to T. J. Smith, 12 September 1923, *AJC*.

110. MacGrath to T. J. Smith, 20 October 1923, *AJC*.

111. T. J. Smith to members of the Executive Committee, 25 October 1923, *AJC*.

112. MacGrath to T. J. Smith, 20 October 1923, *AJC*.

113. *Litterae Annuae*, from July 1923 to July 1924, *AJC*.

114. *Cleveland Plain Dealer*, 19 October 1931, editorial on death of Samuel Mather.

115. Mather to Vinson, 23 February 1923, *ACWRU*. This remark is in a letter regretting the newspaper leak over Vinson's appointment, but it was in character with his preference for privacy.

116. MacGrath to Scott, 6 September 1923, *AJC*. Both Mather and Baker were on their way to Europe.

117. Haggeney to Boylan, 5 May 1927, *AJC*.

118. Form letter to parish chairmen from John A. Dwan, campaign director, 1 November 1923, *AJC*.

119. *The Ignatian*, 6 February 1924.

120. Ibid.

121. Undated and unsigned memorandum intended as a press release, probably late February 1924, *AJC*.

122. T. J. Smith to McMenamy, 14 July 1925, *AJC*. Also Minute Book, Consultors of John Carroll Univ., 1917–49, 30 June 1924, *AJC*,.

123. T. J. Smith to McMenamy, 14 July 1925, *AJC*. Apparently the Provincial had mentioned Father Anthony Wilwerding as a possible choice for the first pastor of Gesu, the new parish. Father Smith recounts his experience with Father Wilwerding as a member of the faculty committee (Fathers Bracken, Wilwerding, and Charles M. Ryan) appointed to carry on the drive. Father Bracken accepted Father Wilwerding on the committee because the Jesuit Community thought he knew so many wealthy Catholics on the East Side. Father Wilwerding was to work with Monsignor Smith but "very bluntly and to the consternation of all in the meeting, said, 'I resign as a member of the committee.' As far as I know he never gave any assistance in the 'drive' thereafter . . . if appointed pastor he might be lacking in similar loyalty to the Jesuit cause in Cleveland and rather follow the suggestions and wishes of the bishop and Monsignor Smith in preference to the wishes of his superiors. . . . In my opinion much of the success of the new college as well as our new parish depends on the father that is appointed pastor."

124. Boylan to Provincial, 11 September 1925, *AMP*.

125. Ibid.

126. Ibid. Also Minute Book, Consultors of John Carroll Univ., 1917–49, 11 September 1925, *AJC*. Ibid., 27 October 1925 it was the Provincial's desire that some building be started.

127. *Carroll News*, 3 December 1925.

128. Ibid.

CHAPTER VI

1. *Lumina*, II, 5, June 1917, 313.

2. Ibid., III, 2, Christmas 1917, 85.

3. Ibid.

4. Ibid., 88–89.

5. Ibid., 93.

6. *The Ignatian*, I, 6, May/June, 1920.

7. *Lumina*, III, 3, February 1918, 141.

8. Sommerhauser, "Notes on SATC," 15 April 1918, *AJC*.

9. Ibid.

10. Ibid.

11. Ibid.

12. *Lumina*, III, 4, April 1918, 183–188.

13. Ibid., III, 5, June 1918, 249–250.

14. Sommerhauser to War Department, Committee on Education and Special Training, 26 July 1918, *AJC*.

15. War Department to Sommerhauser, 1 July 1918, *AJC*.

16. *Lumina*, IV, 5, June 1919, 49.

17. Minute Book, Consultors of John Carroll Univ., 1917–49, 18 November 1918, *AJC*.

18. Ibid.

19. Sommerhauser to Dr. R. M. Hughes, District Education Director, 6th District, Ohio, Indiana, West Virginia, 22 November 1918, *AJC*.

20. Report of Sommerhauser to the War Department, December [?] 1918, *AJC*. The report was received and acknowledged by the War Department, 8 January 1919, *AJC*.

21. Minute Book, Consultors of John Carroll Univ., 1917–49, 2 October 1920, *AJC*.

22. Ibid., 14 January 1919, *AJC*.

23. *The Ignatian*, 23 December 1919, *AJC*.

24. Ibid., 20 October 1920.

25. *Carroll News*, IX, 1, 6 October 1927.

26. *The Ignatian*, I, 2, 23 December 1919.

27. Ibid., I, 6, May/June, 1920.

28. Minutes of Consultors' Meetings, 1888–1917, *AJC*. At a meeting 18 February 1918, the consultors agreed that "the unanimous opinion was that the rector should not allow ours to witness even Shakespearean plays in public theaters."

29. Samuel K. Wilson, S.J., "Catholic College Education, 1900–1950," *Catholic School Journal*, 51:3, 121.

30. Ibid.

31. Brubacher and Rudy, *Higher Education in Transition*, 244–250.

32. Ibid.

33. McGucken, *Jesuits and Education*, 136.

34. Ibid., 144. Father John F. Bannon, S.J., "Notes on the History of St. Louis University," n.d. In Father Bannon's possession.

35. Bannon, "Notes on the History of St. Louis University."

36. Ibid.

37. Ibid.

38. Ibid.

39. Garraghan, *Jesuits of the Middle United States*, III, 511.

40. "Father Fox's Papers," Box 1, File A 1.3, Series 3, *AMU*. See also Raphael N. Hamilton, S.J., *The Story of Marquette University*, 186–191.

41. Talk at a convocation at Marquette University, 16 October 1924, A 4.5, File 247, *AMU*.

42. *The Province News Letter*, Missouri Province, XIII, 31, January 1928. Also, Father Hamilton points out that Father Fox was so successful in creating a favorable public image for Marquette during his tenure there that some of his fellow Jesuits "criticised him as going too far in his concessions to public opinion. He once printed an advertisement stating that

Marquette was a non-sectarian university. His critics saw this as typical of a 'blind spot' in his character. Since he was contemporaneously publishing the University's creed as standing 'firmly and undeniably for God, home, and country,' it seems fairer to think that he took it for granted that people would realize that he was conducting a school based on Catholic principles; and that he was only making the non-Catholic understand, in language that was plain to them that there would be no proselytizing of students who were of divergent faiths." Hamilton, *Marquette*, 190. One of Father Fox's most frequently heard statements was, "the soul of education is the education of the soul."

43. *The Ignatian*, I, 6, May/June 1920.

44. Ibid.

45. *Catalogue*, 1919–1920.

46. *The Ignatian*, II, 4, 26 November 1919.

47. Ibid., 20 October 1920.

48. St. Ignatius College Diary, 1909–28, 4 April 1928. *AJC.*

49. *The Ignatian*, II, 1, 20 October 1919.

50. St. Ignatius College Diary, 1909–28, 28 May 1928, *AJC.*

51. *The Ignatian*, II, 1, 20 October 1920.

52. Ibid.

53. Ibid.

54. Ibid., II, 14, 8 June 1921, a front-page, two-column, length of page article.

55. Ibid.

56. Ibid., II, 7, 11 February 1921.

57. Ibid., III, 11, 22 April 1922. An attempt to secure the original report brought the following response from Dr. Charles M. Cook, Assistant Director, to the author 10 February 1981: "I am sorry to inform you that the Commission [on Institutions of Higher Education] a number of years ago destroyed documents related to individual institutions prior to a certain date. As a result, the earliest records we have for the university date from 1955. As a professional historian by training, speaking personally, I lament this self-inflicted historical amnesia, but there is little I can do about it."

58. *The Ignatian*, III, 11, 22 April 1922.

59. St. Ignatius College Diary 1909–28, 29 March 1928, *AJC.*

60. *The Ignatian*, VI, 7, 4, February 1925.

61. Haggeney to Boylan, 3 May 1927, *AJC.*

62. St. Ignatius College Diary 1909–28, 18 January 1928, *AJC.*

63. Ibid.

64. Ibid., 7 April 1928.

65. Ibid., 18 January 1928.

66. *Carroll News*, VIII, 2, 28 October 1926.

67. Ibid.

68. Ibid., VIII, 1, 7 October 1926.

69. Ibid.

70. Ibid., VIII, 6, 13 January 1927.

71. St. Ignatius College Diary, 1909–28, [?] February 1928.

72. Ibid. In one incident fourteen students were barred from registration for the second semester in February 1928. Ten of these had dropped out because of absences. The problem the parents saw was that a student with three E's might take the examination and pass. By this time he had missed a month of class. Father Boylan wanted no injustice; to placate the parents and priests who complained he allowed another chance for all. Father Degleman was convinced that "new regulations have to be thought out and duly promulgated" (Ibid). As a result a temporary rule that three F's would prevent a student from registering was established.

73. Ibid., 7 February 1928.

74. Ibid.

75. *The Ignatian*, 28 February 1928.

76. *Litterae Annuae*, 1926–27, *AJC*.

77. St. Ignatius College Diary, 1909–28, 9 February 1928.

78. Ibid., 16 April 1928.

79. Ibid., 1 June 1928. Commencement on 17 June 1920 was the first time there was an academic procession and the faculty wore cap and gown.

80. Ibid., 4 June 1928.

81. Ibid., 3 May 1928.

82. Pickel to Meyer, 7 June 1910, *AJC*.

83. Minute Book, Consultors of John Carroll Univ., 1917–49, speaks of a discussion of the problem of sufficient numbers of Jesuits. "Efforts to secure extern teachers was advocated." 7 September 1919, *AJC*,.

84. *Carroll News*, 7 October 1926.

85. Minute Book, Consultors of John Carroll Univ., 1917–49, 2 May 1919, *AJC*. This figure did not change for some years.

86. Bannon, "Notes on History of St. Louis University."

87. Haggeney to Boylan, 14 May 1926, *AJC*.

88. Ibid.

89. C. H. Cramer, *Case Western Reserve, A History of the University 1826–1976*, 234. Also C. H. Cramer, *Case Institute of Technology, A Centennial History, 1880–1980*, (Cleveland: Case Western Reserve University, 1980), 75–80.

90. *Lumina*, II, 4, April 1917.

91. *The Ignatian*, I, 6, May/June 1920.

92. Ibid.

93. Ibid., II, 2, 4 November 1920.

94. Ibid.

95. Ibid., III, 7, 20 January 1922.

96. Ibid., II, 4, 10 December 1920. The searchlight had been used by the French government during World War I. Father Odenbach secured it through the National Carbide Co., which had purchased it from France.

97. Ibid., II, 13, 17 May 1921; IV, 12, 16 May 1923.

98. *Carroll News*, X, 11, 19 April 1229 [*sic*], should be 1929.

99. *The Ignatian*, I, 6, May/June 1920.

100. *Lumina*, I, V, June, 1916, quoted from *Catholic Universe*.

101. *Lumina*, 2, Christmas, 1916.

102. Minutes of Consultors' Meetings, 1888–1917, 18 February 1917, *AJC*.

103. *Lumina*, III, 5, June 1918.

104. *The Ignatian*, III, 14, 14 June 1922; *Sunday News Leader*, 5 February 1922; *Cleveland Plain Dealer*, 11 February 1922.

105. Quoted in *The Ignatian*, V, 13, 4 June 1924.

106. Cramer, *Case Western Reserve*, 235–38.

107. *Cleveland Plain Dealer*, 6 December 1920.

108. Ibid., 27 May 1924.

109. *Cleveland Times*, 1 November 1924.

110. Address of Robert Vinson to Cleveland Chamber of Commerce, 25 November 1924, *ACWRU*.

111. *Cleveland Plain Dealer*, 1 November 1924.

112. The Cleveland Foundation Commission, *Survey of Higher Education in Cleveland* (Cleveland, 1925), 470.

113. *Cleveland Plain Dealer*, 19 October 1925.

114. *Yale Alumni Weekly*, October, 1925, *ACWRU IFH*.

115. *Cleveland Plain Dealer*, 25 November 1925.

116. Ibid., 19 February 1926.

117. Ibid., 22 February 1926.

118. T. J. Smith to McMenamy, 5 August 1923, *AJC*.

119. Same to same, 17 February 1925, *AJC*.

120. Ibid.

121. McMenamy to Smith, 27 November 1924, as quoted in Smith to McMenamy, 17 February 1925, *AJC*.

122. Ibid.

123. There is a letter in the Archives of the Diocese of Cleveland, which the author was permitted to see only in paraphrased form; the explanation given was the strong language used in the letter. No salutation or signature was on the copy the author was given. The date was 11 December 1929 and the contents dealt in a very unflattering way with what the author of the letter considered the totally inadequate qualifications of the faculty of John Carroll University including its new dean, Father Albert C. Fox. The letter was written at the time of Father Fox's proposal to establish the Corporate Colleges of John Carroll University. From internal evidence the letter was most probably written by Father John R. Hagan to the seminary rector, Monsignor James McDonough. It refers also to events of 1922 and 1923.

124. Smith to McMenamy, 17 February 1925, *AJC*.

125. Minute Book, Consultors of John Carroll Univ., 1917–49, 11 September 1925, 21 January 1926, *AJC*.

126. Ibid., 13 August 1925.

127. Smith to Boylan, 10 March 1926, *AJC*.

128. Garraghan, *Jesuits of the Middle United States*, III, 597.

129. Haggeney to Boylan, 5 May 1927, *AJC*.

130. Ibid.

131. Haggeney to Boylan, 4 October 1927, *AJC*.

132. Ibid.

133. Haggeney to Boylan, 14 May 1926, *AJC*.

134. Unsigned and undated memorandum which was most probably prepared by Father Boylan about 1927, *AJC*.

135. St. Ignatius College Diary 1913–29, 13 and 18 July 1926, *AJC*.

136. Monsignor Smith to Mattern, 26 July 1926, *ADC*. This letter was sent to Mattern with a copy to Bishop Schrembs.

137. Ibid.

138. Ibid.

139. Mattern to J. F. Smith, 15 September 1926, *ADC*.

140. Fox to Blakely, 9 January 1929, *AJC*. The year should be 1930 as is evident from the full context of the letter.

CHAPTER VII

1. Brubacher and Rudy, *Higher Education in Transition*, 120–122.

2. *Carroll News*, 24 March 1927. The survey also showed that 94, or almost one-third of the students, worked during the entire year. Practically every student worked at some time or other. The average earnings amounted to $38 a month with one student earning $140 a month.

3. Minutes of Consultors' Meetings, 1888–1917, 2 October 1915, *AJC*.

4. St. Ignatius College Diary, 1909–28, 2 April 1928, *AJC*.

5. *The Ignatian*, II, 4, 10 December 1920.

6. Ibid.

7. Minutes of Consultors' Meetings, 1888–1917, 30 April 1916, *AJC.*

8. *Lumina*, II, 4, April 1917, 248.

9. Ibid.

10. *The Ignatian*, II, 3, 18 November 1920.

11. Minutes of Consultors' Meetings, 1888–1917, 12 September 1915, *AJC.* In February under Father Furay the consultors had said, "A college periodical is not favored." Ibid., February 1912.

12. Ibid., 11 November 1917; *Lumina*, III, 3, February 1918.

13. Minutes of Consultors' Meetings, 1888–1917, 18 February 1917, *AJC.*

14. Ibid., 16 September 1917; permission to sell arrived 30 January 1918. The property, however, was not sold.

15. Cleveland Diocesan Accounts, 1918, 230, *ADC.*

16. *Carroll News*, XII, 1, 3 October 1930.

17. *Lumina*, I, 3, February 1916.

18. *The Ignatian*, 23 December 1919.

19. Ibid.

20. St. Ignatius College Diary 1919–28, 3 May 1928, *AJC.*

21. Ibid., 31 May 1928.

22. *Carroll News*, X, 4, 22 November 1928.

23. Ibid.

24. *The Ignatian*, I, 6, May/June, 1920.

25. *Carroll News*, XI, 2, 18 October 1929.

26. Ibid., VIII, 1, 7 October 1926. The two statues, Ora and Labora, were brought from the West Side where they had been since 1916 and placed in an alcove on the second floor of the Administration building. They seem not to have been noticed very much until some of the students in the late 1940s grew curious about their origin. An article in the *Carroll News*, 21 November 1947, explored the question but had little success in finding any solid answers. Father Weber volunteered the information that they were old classmates of his; Labora was the serious type, but Ora often enjoyed a quiet smoke dressed in a derby and yellow jacket. Father Murphy, in a more serious vein, said their purpose was to simulate the ideals of the typical Catholic student and "not to be hat racks or ash trays." While Carroll students did not always limit their activities to those represented by the statues the graduates did acquire an enviable reputation as providing the best advertising the university had. During his visitation, 19–25 November 1951, Father Maline reported he had heard this when he visited other cities, particularly Chicago.

27. St. Ignatius College Diary, 1909–28, 9 May 1928, *AJC.*

28. Ibid., 28 March 1928, *AJC.*

29. Ibid., 8 February 1928.

30. One student of the post–World War I era when asked by the author about the library said he didn't know where it was; he never used it.

31. Minutes Book, Consultors of John Carroll Univ., 1917–49, 4 November 1931, *AJC.*

32. *Lumina*, III, 3, February 1918.

33. *Carroll News*, XIII, 7, 17 February 1933.

34. Ibid., 19 December 1934.

35. Author's interview with a former Loyola student.

36. *The Ignatian*, I, 3, 31 January 1920.

37. *Lumina*, II, 1, October, 1916.

38. Ibid., III, 3, February, 1918.

39. Ibid., III, 2, Christmas 1917.

40. Ibid.

41. Ibid., II, 1, October 1916.

42. Ibid.

43. Ibid.

44. *Carroll News*, VII, 1, 8 October 1925.

45. Ibid., also author's observation as a bystander.

46. *Lumina*, III, 2, Christmas 1917.

47. *Carroll News*, VIII, 2, 28 October 1926.

48. *Carroll News*, VII, 1, 8 October 1925.

49. *Lumina*, I, 4, April 1916, statement of ownership management and circulation required by an Act of Congress, 24 August 1912.

50. Ibid., II, 2, Christmas 1916.

51. *The Ignatian*, I, 1, 26 November 1919.

52. Minute Book, Consultors of John Carroll Univ., 1917–49, 20 October 1918, *AJC*.

53. *The Ignatian*, I, 1, 26 November 1919.

54. Ibid.

55. Ibid., 23 December 1919.

56. Ibid., 31 January 1920.

57. Ibid.

58. Ibid., III, 1, 4 October 1921.

59. Ibid., IV, 4, 28 November 1922.

60. *Carroll News*, VII, 1, 8 October 1925.

61. Hynes, *History of the Diocese*, 351.

62. Boylan to McFadden, 20 March 1927, *ADC*.

63. McFadden to Boylan, 1 April 1927, *ADC*.

64. Ibid.

65. Boylan to McFadden, 6 April 1927, *ADC*.

66. *The Ignatian*, I, 2, 23 December 1919.

67. Ibid.

68. Ibid., I, 3, 31 January 1920.

69. Ibid., I, 4, 28 February 1920.

70. Ibid., II, 1, 20 October 1920.

71. Ibid., II, 3, 18 November 1920.

72. Ibid., I, 6, May/June 1920.

73. *Carroll News*, VII, 7, 18 February 1926.

74. Ibid., 11 March 1926.

75. *The Ignatian*, V, 10, 9 April 1924.

76. *Carroll News*, VII, 5, 21 December 1925.

77. Ibid., XII, 3, 31 October 1930.

78. *Lumina*, I, 4, April 1916, and I, 5, June 1916.

79. Ibid., I, 3, February 1916.

80. Ibid., II, 3, February 1917.

81. Ibid., III, 3, February 1918.

82. *The Ignatian*, I, 1, 26 November 1919.

83. St Ignatius College Diary, 1909–28, 18 May 1928, *AJC*.

84. *Carroll News*, X, 4, 22 November 1928.

85. Minute Book, Consultors of John Carroll Univ., 1917–49, 15 October 1935, *AJC*.

86. *Carroll News*, VIII, 9, 10 March 1927.

87. McFadden to all Pastors in the Diocese of Cleveland, 2 May 1928, *ADC*.

88. *Carroll News*, IX, 14, 24 May 1928.

89. Ibid., XI, 4, 15 November 1929.
90. Ibid., XII, 1, 3 October 1930.
91. Ibid., VII, 8, 11 March 1926.
92. *The Ignatian*, II, 4, 10 December 1920.
93. Ibid.
94. Ibid.
95. Ibid., IV, 7, 29 January 1923.
96. *Carroll News*, VII, 1, 8 October 1925.
97. Ibid., IX, 7, 18 January 1928.
98. Ibid., XI, 4, 15 November 1929.
99. Ibid., XII, 14, 22 May 1931.
100. Minute Book, Consultors of John Carroll Univ., 1917–49, 30 September 1930, *AJC*.
101. *Carroll News*, XII, 1, 9 October 1931.
102. *Lumina*, I, 3, February 1916.
103. Ibid., I, 6, June 1916.
104. Ibid., II, 5, June 1917.
105. *The Ignatian*, I, 2, 23 December 1919.
106. Ibid., I, 3, 31 January 1920.
107. Ibid., I, 4, 28 February 1920.
108. Ibid., II, 2, 4 November 1920.
109. Ibid., IV, 2, 18 October 1922.
110. Ibid., IV, II, 30 April 1923.
111. *Carroll News*, IXXX, 9, 20 April 1933.
112. *Lumina*, I, 5, June 1916.
113. Ibid., II, 5, June 1917.
114. *The Ignatian*, II, 14, 8 June 1921.
115. *Lumina*, II, 5, June 1917.
116. *The Ignatian*, II, 4, 10 December 1920.
117. Ibid.
118. Ibid., V, 9, 9 April 1924.
119. *Carroll News*, VII, 2, 29 October 1925.
120. Schrembs to Boylan, 24 March 1926, *ADC*.
121. Ibid.
122. Ibid.
123. Ibid.
124. Boylan to McMenamy, 26 March 1926, *AJC*.
125. Boylan to Schrembs, 1 April 1926, *ADC*.
126. Ibid.
127. *Carroll News*, VII, 8, 11 March 1926.
128. Ibid., VII, 10, 29 April 1926.
129. Ibid., VII, 11, 20 May 1926.
130. Ibid.
131. Ibid.
132. Schrembs to Rodman, 3 February 1936, *ADC*.
133. Rodman to Schrembs, 6 February 1936, *ADC*.
134. Minute Book Consultors John Carroll, 1917–49, 10 February 1926, *AJC*.
135. Ibid., 3 March 1936.
136. *Carroll News*, XVI, 10, 25 March 1936.
137. Ibid., XVI, 11, 1 April 1936.
138. *The Ignatian*, II, 4, 10 December 1920.

139. Ibid., II, 13, 17 May 1921.
140. *Carroll News*, IX, 5, 1 December 1927.
141. *Lumina*, II, 3, February 1917.
142. *The Ignatian*, III, 3, 16 November 1921.
143. *Carroll News*, XII, 2, 17 October 1930.
144. Ibid.
145. Ibid., 9 October 1931.
146. Ibid., XIV, 1, 6 October 1933.
147. Ibid., XIV, 10, 16 March 1934.

CHAPTER VIII

1. Father Meyer to the Rectors of the Missouri Province, undated, probably 1909 or 1910. Campion College Archives, Box 9, Father Meyer's letters, 1908–12, now in the Archives of Marquette University.

2. Ibid.

3. Ibid.

4. A. J. Burrowes, Provincial of the Missouri Province, 1912–19, to Missouri Province Rectors, 7 April 1918, Campion College Archives, Letters of Father Burrowes, 1913–18, now in Marquette University Archives.

5. "Regulations prescribed by Father General Ledochowski for the conduct of Athletics in all colleges and universities of the American Assistancy," in the Papers of Father Matthew Germing, Campion College Archives, now in the Archives of Marquette University.

6. Brady, *Canisius*, 187.

7. Furay to Burrowes, 9 June 1913, *AMP* on microfilm at *AJC*. The Trustees debated the need and prospects for building a gymnasium during the summer of 1912. The decision to build was made definite on 14 September. The cost was to be betwen $8,000 and $10,000.

8. Minutes of Consultors' Meetings, 1888–1917, 7 August 1912, *AJC*.

9. Ibid., 14 September 1912.

10. Furay to Burrowes, 9 June 1913, *AMP* microfilm in *AJC*.

11. Minutes of Consultors' Meetings, 1888–1917, 12 November 1914. *AJC*.

12. Ibid., 2 October 1915.

13. Ibid., 30 April 1916; the removal of the burned-down grocery store on Lorain gave still more space in the yard, ibid., 21 January 1917.

14. *Lumina*, I, 15, October 1915.

15. Ibid.

16. Ibid., I, 4, April 1916.

17. Minutes of Consultors' Meetings, 1888–1917, 21 January 1917 *AJC*.

18. *Lumina*, III, 3, February 1918.

19. *The Ignatian*, II, 1, 20 October 1920.

20. Ibid.

21. *Cleveland Plain Dealer*, 2 March 1923.

22. Ibid.

23. Ibid., 11 March 1923.

24. Ibid., 18 May 1917.

25. Ibid., 19 May 1917.

26. Ibid.

27. *Lumina*, IV, 5, June 1919.

28. *The Ignatian*, V, 11, 7 May 1924.

29. *Lumina*, II, 1, October 1916.

30. *Cleveland Plain Dealer*, 1 October 1918.
31. *The Ignatian*, I, 1, 26 November 1919.
32. Ibid., I, 3, 28 February 1920.
33. Ibid., I, 6, May/June, 1920.
34. Ibid.
35. Ibid.
36. Ibid.
37. Ibid., II, 1, 20 October 1920.
38. Ibid.
39. Ibid.
40. Ibid.
41. Ibid., II, 2, 4 November 1920.
42. Ibid., II, 3, 18 November 1920.
43. Ibid.
44. *Cleveland Plain Dealer*, 23 November 1920.
45. *The Ignatian*, II, 4, 10 December 1920.
46. Ibid., II, 6, 25 January 1921.
47. *Cleveland News*, 17 February 1922.
48. *The Ignatian*, III, 9, 24 February, 1922.
49. Ibid., IV, 2, 18 October 1922.
50. Ibid., IV, 3, 31 October 1922.
51. Ibid., IV, 4, 28 November 1922.
52. Ibid., IV, 5, 12 December 1922.
53. Ibid., V, 1, 9 October 1923.
54. Ibid., V, 5, 11 December 1923.
55. Ibid., V, 9, 4 April 1924.
56. Ibid., V, 12, 21 May 1924.
57. Ibid., V, 14, 13 June 1924.
58. Ibid.
59. *Cleveland News Leader*, 14 September 1924.
60. *The Ignatian*, V, 12, 21 May 1924.
61. *Cleveland News*, 6 December 1924.
62. *The Ignatian*, VI, 3, 5 December 1924.
63. *Carroll News*, VII, 2, 29 October 1925.
64. *Cleveland News*, 6 November 1924.
65. Ibid., 23 November 1924.
66. *Carroll News*, 1, 8 October 1925.
67. *The Ignatian*, VI, 9, 4 March 1925.
68. *Carroll News*, VII, 5, 21 December 1925.
69. Ibid., VIII, 1, 7 October 1926.
70. Ibid., VIII, 4, 24 November 1926.
71. Ibid., VII, 8, 11 March 1926.
72. Ibid.
73. Ibid., VIII, 5, 13 December 1926.
74. Ibid.
75. *Cleveland Plain Dealer*, 2 April 1927; *Cleveland Press*, 1 April 1927.
76. *Carroll News*, X, 1, 11 October 1928.
77. Ibid., V, 5, 11 December 1923.
78. *Case Tech*, 4 April 1928. Also in *Carroll News*, IX, 12, 26 April 1928.
79. *Carroll News*, X, 3, 8 November 1928; X, 4, 22 November 1928.

80. Ibid., XI, 4, 15 November 1929.

81. Ibid., X, 6, 18 January 1929.

82. Ibid.

83. Ibid., XII, 5, 5 December 1930.

84. Ibid.

85. Ibid.

86. Ibid., XII, 1, 3 October 1930.

87. Cramer, *Case Institute of Technology,* 149–50.

88. John Carroll, General and Sports Scrapbook, 1923–1930, *AJC; Cleveland Press,* 11 September 1929.

89. *Cleveland Press,* 11 September 1929; also 12 September 1929.

90. Ibid., 18 September 1929; also John Carroll Scrapbook, 1923–1930.

91. Rodman to O'Callaghan, 13 September 1929, *AJC.*

92. A reprint of an editorial from the University of Dayton *Exponent* in *The Ignatian,* II, 12, 2 May 1921, deals at length with these issues.

93. *Carroll News,* VII, 2, 29 October 1925.

94. Minute Book, Consultors of John Carroll Univ., 1917–49, 11 September 1925, and 4 December 1925.

95. Minute Book, Consultors of John Carroll Univ., 1917–49, 5 February 1934. *AJC.*

96. Ibid., 8 February 1934.

97. Ibid., 29 October 1934.

98. Ibid.; the remark about Father Fox's intervention was attributed to Father Allan Farrell, S.J.

99. Ibid.

100. Ibid., 19 March 1935.

101. Calvin Olin Davis, *A History of the North Central Association of Colleges and Secondary Schools,* 141.

102. *Carroll News,* XVI, 12, 16 April 1936.

103. Louis G. Geiger, *A History of the North Central Association, 1945–1970,* 38.

CHAPTER IX

1. *Carroll News,* X, 1, 11 October 1928.

2. Ibid.

3. Minute Book, Consultors of John Carroll Univ. 1917–49, 7 September 1928, *AJC.*

4. *Carroll News,* X, i, 11 October 1928.

5. Ibid., XI, 8, 14 February 1930.

6. *Carroll Alumni Magazine,* 4:1, Winter, 1966.

7. *Carroll News,* XIII, 8, 3 March 1933. Caption under the pictures in local newspapers made it clear that John Carroll students were not involved.

8. *Carroll News,* X, 10, 27 March 1929.

9. Rodman to O'Callaghan, 15 December 1928, *AJC.*

10. Ibid.

11. Ibid.

12. Ibid.

13. Ibid.

14. Rodman to Rhode, 15 June 1930, *AJC.*

15. Haggeney to Boylan, 14 May 1926, *AJC.*

16. Witnessed by the author who was also present a few lengths behind Aloysius Bungart, 1935. Father Bracken had returned to John Carroll and replaced Father Ralph Gallagher as

dean in September 1934. On another occasion a faculty member was in Father Bracken's office discussing the problem of a student who had failed, when another student burst in and demanded immediate attention to his problem. Father Bracken threw the student out verbally in no uncertain language. When the student had gone, Father Bracken turned to the faculty member and said, "I must see what I can do for that fellow."

17. Rodman to O'Callaghan, 15 May 1929, *AJC*.

18. Author as witness.

19. Rodman to Mattern, 30 October 1930, *AJC*.

20. Boylan to Rodman, 9 June 1929, *AJC*. Father Rodman had received a request from McDonnell asking for the return of the frame drawings made for Father T. J. Smith. Father Rodman had written to Father Smith saying, "I have never seen them. Could you give me any clues as to their whereabouts?" Rodman to T. J. Smith, 28 May 1929, *AJC*.

21. Ibid.

22. Minutes Book, Consultors of John Carroll Univ., 1917–49, 7 February 1929, *AJC*, Rodman Hall.

23. Ibid.

24. Rodman to Graham, 23 February 1929, *AJC*.

25. Dougherty's Report in *Carroll News*, X, 10, 27 March 1929.

26. Graham to Rodman, 25 March 1930, *AJC*.

27. *Carroll News*, X, 16, 27 March 1929.

28. Ibid.

29. Ibid.

30. Rodman to O'Callaghan, 13 September 1929, *AJC*. Father Rodman had erected a classroom building at St. Mary's College, Kansas, where he had been before coming to Cleveland.

31. "The John Carroll Campaigner," 18 October 1929, *AJC*.

32. *Carroll News*, XI, 4, 15 November 1929. Dougherty had written to the *Carroll News* when the student subscription had been announced, "You fellows have helped make history for John Carroll," *Carroll News*, XI, 2, 18 October 1929.

33. Schrembs to Rodman, 24 April 1929, *ADC*.

34. "Letter of Bishop Schrembs to Laity of the Diocese," 20 April 1923, *ADC*.

35. "Letter of Bishop Schrembs to the Clergy of the Diocese," 20 April 1929, *ADC*.

36. A copy of a speech of Bishop Schrembs, no date, no place, *AJC*.

37. Ibid.

38. Dougherty to Schrembs, 26 September 1929, *ADC*. Dougherty said that he was "greatly concerned over the continous failure of many parishes to appoint Parish Chairmen."

39. Unsigned "Memorandum" concerning the Parish campaign, 5 December 1929, *ADC*.

40. Ibid.

41. Jennings to Dougherty, 27 December 1929, *AJC*.

42. Ibid.

43. Rodman to O'Callaghan, 15 May 1929, *AJC*.

44. Ibid.

45. Rodman to O'Callaghan, 24 October 1929, *AJC*.

46. Ibid.

47. O'Callaghan to Rodman, 13 May 1929, *AJC*.

48. Rodman to O'Callaghan, 15 May 1929, *AJC*.

49. Rodman to O'Callaghan, 24 October 1929, *AJC*. Father Rodman had also been told of the qualities of Bernet by Charles Adams. Adams had been Father Rodman's first choice to call a meeting of prominent men to plan for the campaign. Adams had refused because he was so completely involved in the Community Fund, and wrote to Father Rodman suggesting J. J. Bernet, president of the Erie Railroad, as "one of the outstanding men in town, the type of

man that can draw around him as strong a group of men as any man in Cleveland and I would be glad to recommend him to see you next." Adams to Rodman, 18 March 1929, *AJC.*

50. Ibid.

51. Ibid.

52. Pastoral Letter VIII, 23, 12 December 1929, *ADC.*

53. Ibid.

54. *Carroll News,* XI, 3, 4 November 1929.

55. Rodman to O'Callaghan, 31 October 1929, *AJC.*

56. Ibid.

57. Ibid.

58. O'Callaghan to Schrembs, 5 November 1929, *ADC.*

59. O'Callaghan to Schrembs, 11 December 1929.

60. O'Callaghan to Rodman, 6 November 1929, *AJC.* The reference to Bernet's language arose from his extraordinary vocabulary of expressive words and his willingness to use all of them graphically.

61. Rodman to O'Callaghan, 9 November 1929, *AJC.*

62. *Carroll News,* XI, 4, 15 November 1929.

63. Letter of Monsignor Smith to priests of the diocese explaining the purpose of the subscription campaign, 28 May 1929, *ADC.* The total cost was not to exceed $300,000, each priest was to give a certain amount, the pledges were to be given in writing by 15 June. A payment schedule was arranged so that 20 percent was due at the time of the beginning of construction, 20 percent at the cornerstone laying, 20 percent when the walls were up and 20 percent on the completion and dedication; these payments were after the initial payment of 20 percent.

64. Monsignor W. A. Scullen to Monsignor Smith, 5 June 1929, *AJD.*

65. Ibid.

66. Monsignor Smith to Pietro Fumasoni Bondi, 6 June 1929, *ADC.*

67. Bondi to Smith, 18 June 1929, *ADC.*

68. Schrembs to Rodman, 23 August 1929, *AJC.*

69. Rodman to O'Callaghan, 13 September 1929, *AJC.*

70. Ibid.

71. "The Man with the Answer," no date or author, a campaign brochure, *AJC.*

72. Ibid.

73. Dougherty to Kenneth Sturges, 7 November 1929, *AJC.*

74. *Cleveland Plain Dealer,* 19 May 1929.

75. O'Callaghan to Rodman, 21 May 1929, *AJC.*

76. Rodman to O'Callaghan, 26 May 1929, *AJC.*

77. *Cleveland Plain Dealer,* 19 May 1929, *AJC.*

78. Rodman to O'Callaghan, 24 May 1929, *AJC.* The explanation for the statement in the article given by Father Rodman was that in a press conference one of the non-Catholic reporters raised the question of what Carroll did in regard to teaching religion that differed from other colleges and how it fitted into the program. Father Rodman said that religion was taught once or twice a week but non-Catholics need not take the course. Another reporter, a non-Catholic who had gone to Marquette, said the Jesuits do not proselytize. Father Fox then said that he had heard many remarks at Marquette from non-Catholic students saying they were not hounded as they were at state schools by the YMCA. The subject of nonsectarianism came up in the 1923 campaign but it caused no discussion. Father Smith was quoted as saying "entrance into the University is not to be conditioned on religious belief or nationality, but will be open to all students seeking a moral education, whose keynote is American citizenship." Monsignor Smith, Vicar General of the Diocese of Cleveland, was also quoted as saying, "This university, while under the management of the Jesuit Fathers will be conducted along non-sectarian lines. No proselytizing is ever permitted in Jesuit colleges. What they seek is a

proper system of morals which every creed assents to." Both of these quotations were in the *Jewish Independent*, 31 August 1923.

79. Rodman to O'Callaghan, 26 May 1929, *AJC*. Father Rodman added at the end of his letter, "The man who wrote might have come in first and talked the matter over and asked if we had any such fanciful ideas to erect a $700,000 gymnasium, but we do not do things that way. But enough of this."

80. Bannon, S.J., "Notes on the History of [St. Louis] the University," summary of points in questionnaire and letter of Father General Ledochowski.

81. Ledochwoski to the Superiors of the American Assistancy, 7 June 1928, *ACC*.

82. Ibid.

83. Ibid. The General also condemned "Coeducation," and revoked any permissions already given or presumed, as well as giving only tolerance for the time being for summer schools and extension courses for religious.

84. Ibid.

85. O'Callaghan to Rodman, 12 September 1929, *AJC*.

86. John H. Johnson to Rodman, 16 January 1930, *AJC*.

87. Dougherty to Schrembs, 8 April 1931, *ADC*.

88. Schrembs to Dougherty, 13 April 1931, *ADC*.

89. *Carroll News*, XI, 7, 17 January 1930.

90. *Catholic Universe Bulletin*, 24 January 1930.

91. Rodman's reply contained in a letter from Dougherty to Thomas S. Grasselli, 15 January 1930, *AJC*.

92. *Carroll News*, XI, 8, 14 February 1930.

93. Ibid.

94. Ibid.

95. Ibid.

96. Rodman to Schrembs, 3 February 1930, *ADC*.

97. *Carroll News*, 14 February 1930.

98. Schrembs to Dougherty, 5 February 1930, *ADC*.

99. Schrembs to C. Adams, 8 February 1930, *ADC*.

100. Schrembs to the Grassdelli's—Thomas E., Ida, Josephine, and Aloise (Mrs. W. T. Cashman)—5 February 1930, *ADC*.

101. Schrembs to O. P. and M. J. Van Sweringen, 5 February 1930, *ADC*.

102. Schrembs to Sam Mather, 5 February 1930, *ADC*.

103. Schrembs to Alexander C. Brown, 5 February 1930, *ADC*.

104. Rodman to Schrembs, 15 February 1930, *ADC*.

105. Schrembs to Rodman, 6 March 1930, *ADC*.

106. *Carroll News*, 14 February 1930.

107. Ibid.

108. Ibid.

109. Bernet to McFadden, 6 February 1930, *ADC*.

110. Recounted to the author by Father Bannon, S.J. of St. Louis University, who says the story was circulated among the Jesuits.

111. L. A. Lux, "A Tribute from the Four Hundred to the Speakers' Table John Carroll Drive," 1 February 1930, *AJC*.

112. Ibid.

113. Dougherty to Rodman, 11 February 1930, *AJC*.

114. *Carroll News*, 14 February 1930, quoted a speech Dudley Bloosom had given on the success of the fund-raising campaign to which he contributed a substantial amount; he had been disinterested in the 1923 campaign.

115. Donald C. Dougherty, Manager's Report, John Carroll University Building Fund Campaign, 20 February 1930, *AJC.*

116. Ibid.

117. Ibid.

118. Ibid.

CHAPTER X

1. Minutes of Diocesan Consultors, II, 13 April 1922, *ADC.*

2. Ibid.

3. Louthian to Sister Mary Agnes, Notre Dame College, 9 February 1928, *ADC*; Louthian to Sister Mercedes, Ursuline College, 9 February 1928, *ADC.*

4. Annual Report of the Diocese of Cleveland, 1927–1928, John R. Hagan, *ADC.*

5. Ibid.

6. Ibid.

7. John R. Hagan, *The Diocesan Teachers College*, 6.

8. Ibid., 171.

9. Hagan to Schrembs, (n.d.) *ADC.*

10. Ibid.

11. Memorandum on Present Sisters' College Situation, 14 June 1926, *ADC.*

12. Louthian to Hagan, 11 February 1928, *ADC.*

13. Ibid.

14. Ibid.

15. Louthian to Hagan, 14 February 1928, *ADC.*

16. Report of Commission on Coeducation, 1939, 6, Commission appointed by Father General Ledochowski, *ALUC.*

17. William B. Faherty, S.J., *Dream by the River, Two Centuries of St. Louis Catholicism, 1766–1967*, 163–164.

18. *Carroll News*, VII, 7, 18 February 1926.

19. Ledochowski to American Jesuit Superiors, 7 June 1928, *ACC.*

20. Ibid.

21. Report of Commission on Coeducation, section on "The Problem of Coeducation in American Colleges." *ALUC.*

22. Wilson to Edward B. Rooney, S.J., 4 March 1942, *ALUC.*

23. Rodman to O'Callaghan, 15 May 1929, *AJC.*

24. Minute Book, Consultors of John Carroll Univ., 1917–49, 25 May 1929, *AJC.*

25. O'Callaghan to Rodman, 3 June 1929, *AJC.*

26. Ibid.

27. Ibid.

28. Ibid.

29. Ledowchowski to American Jesuit Superiors, 7 June 1928, *ACC.*

30. Ibid.

31. Baker to Rodman, 4 March 1930, *AJC, Current History*, January 1928, 527 ff.

32. Baker to Rodman, 4 March 1930, *AJC.*

33. Rodman to Baker, 18 March 1930, *AJC.*

34. Louthian to Hagan, n.d., probably January or February 1929, *ADC.*

35. John R. Hagan, "Conflict between Sisters' College and JCU," memorandum prepared by Hagan for the case of the four bishops of Ohio against Father Fox. Undated, probably November 1933, *ADC.*

36. Louthian to Hagan, undated, probably January or February, 1929, *ADC.*

37. P. J. McCormick to Hagan, 1 August 1928, *ADC*. McCormick was dean of the Catholic Sisters' College of Catholic University.

38. Fox to Hagan, 28 February 1929, *ADC*.

39. Ibid.

40. This information is contained in a lengthy account by Hagan called "Conflict between Sisters' College and JCU" (Letter P) defending his position in the later controversy.

41. Hagan to Fox, 4 March 1929, *ADC*.

42. Hagan to Fox, 14 March 1929, *ADC*.

43. Ibid.

44. Hagan, "Conflict between Sisters' College and JCU."

45. Jordan to Hagan, 13 April 1929, *ADC*. Edward P. Jordan was secretary at the Catholic Sisters' College of Catholic University.

46. Ibid.

47. Hagan to Schrembs, 25 September 1929, *ADC*.

48. Ibid.

49. Ibid.

50. Memorandum, "Corporate Colleges," (n.d.) Father Fox's Papers, *AJC*.

51. Ibid.

52. Ibid. In a letter to Father Paul Blakely of the Jesuit magazine, *America*, Father Fox gave an account of the development of the idea of the Corporate Colleges. Shortly after he had come to Cleveland in 1928 he was approached by Notre Dame and Ursuline colleges for help. "I encouraged the Sisters but proceeded very deliberately because I did not want them to wake up and find themselves married to a corpse. However, as soon as the campaign gave signs of success I reopened the question of incorporation and encouraged it." It was at this point the bishop raised the question of degrees for seminarians which led to the conference with the bishop. Father Fox also noted the difference between the earlier St. Louis plan and the Cleveland plan. In the St. Louis plan Archbishop John Glennan took no part, in Cleveland Bishop Schrembs cooperated "from first to last." The St. Louis plan did not include the major diocesan seminary where the Cleveland experiment did. The term "incorporation in a non-legal sense" was meant to exclude "a full and legal incorporation, which . . . would include financial matters, a thing I did not want to touch." Fox to Blakely, 9 January 1929, *AJC*. The year should be 1930 as is clear from the contents of the letter.

53. Fox to Schrembs, 3 October 1929, *ADC*.

54. Ibid.

55. Schrembs to Fox, 17 October 1929, *ADC*.

56. Navin to Louthian, 21 November 1929, *ADC*.

57. Ibid.

58. Abstracted letter referred to in Chapter VI, footnote 123, *ADC*.

59. All of the preceding paragraphs are from the abstracted letter of 11 December 1929, *ADC*.

60. Fox, "Corporate Colleges," *AJC*. This is a collection of various letters, affidavits, and comments by Father Fox, *AJC*.

61. Schrembs to Fox, 10 January 1930, *AJC*. Typical of articles which appeared in the papers praising the plan was one in the WARREN [Ohio] *Tribune* for 21 December 1929 which pointed out that, "The new arrangement is the fruition of a plan that has long been entertained by Bishop Schrembs to unify and strengthen all Catholic institutions of higher learning in Cleveland under the leadership of John Carroll University.

While in other dioceses some schools have been incorporated in this manner, this is the first time in the history of the church in this country that all diocesan institutions including the diocesan seminary, have been made part of a university. The wisdom of the restoration of the diocesan seminary to its original rank of a major seminary is vindicated for it now gives the divinity department to the new university."

62. Fox, "Corporate Colleges."

63. *Diocesan Letters, Communications and Pastorals*, IX, 9, 27 May 1930, *ADC.*

64. Fox, "Corporate Colleges."

65. "An Agreement Between John Carroll University and the Corporate Colleges of John Carroll University, Cleveland, Ohio," 14 December 1929, *AJC* and *ADC.*

66. Fox to Louthian, 25 April 1930, *AJC.*

67. Louthian to Fox, 29 April 1930, *ADC.*

68. Fox to Louthian, 30 April 1930, *ADC.*

69. Hagan to Schrembs, 9 May 1930, *ADC.*

70. Ibid.

71. Ibid.

72. Ibid.

73. Ibid.

74. Fox, "Corporate Colleges."

75. Ibid., and Schrembs to Deans, Heads of Departments, and Members of the Faculty of the Corporate Colleges and Schools of the Diocese of Cleveland, 11 July 1930, *AJC.*

76. Fox to Navin, 9 July 1930, *ADC.*

77. Rodman to Rhode, 17 June 1930, *AJC.*

78. Minutes, Second Quarterly Meeting of the Corporate Colleges, 8 October 1930, *ADC.* Father Fox acted as chairman at this meeting. Also at this meeting Hagan made his first appearance since going to Washington and "without a word of explanation, took his place among the representatives of the various colleges. Before the meeting began, Father Joseph Walsh somehow felt constrained to come to Father Fox and say that Dr. Hagan came to represent the Seminary because he taught some courses in Education there! From the first, amenities were to be served in the breach." Father Fox's account of the meeting in Fox, "Corporate Colleges."

79. Fox to T. H. Winters, 8 December 1930, *AJC.* Winters was assistant director of the department.

80. Fox, "Corporate Colleges."

81. Ibid., the statement was reported by one of the Sisters.

82. Ibid.

83. Schrembs to Fox, 3 March 1931, *AJC.*

84. Hagan, "Conflict between Sisters' College and JCU."

85. Minutes of a Meeting of Sister Superiors of various Communities of the Diocese of Cleveland, 16 September 1931, *ADC.*

86. Ibid., Also Minutes of Diocesan Consultors, II, 23 September 1931, *ADC.*

87. Hagan, "Conflict between Sisters' College and JCU."

88. Ibid.

89. Fox to Rodman, 29 September 1931, *AJC.*

90. Navin to Schrembs, 6 October 1931, *ADC.*

91. Schrembs to Fox, 3 October 1931, *ADC.*

92. Schlitz to Rodman, 9 February 1933, *AJC.* The seminary would be excluded from granting degrees because it was not yet incorporated as a separate entity and Auxiliary Bishop McFadden argued against incorporation at the time. This information is included in a letter of 12 December 1939 from Father Joseph E. Walsh of the seminary to Eugene R. Mittinger, registrar at John Carroll, *AJC.* The letter leaves the impression that Hagan played no role and is not mentioned as making the trip to Columbus with Monsignor McDonough. The state

department of education saw no difficulty in John Carroll University's granting degrees to seminarians. A communication from T. Howard Winters, assistant director, to Father Fox said, "It is our opinion that John Carroll University can grant degrees to graduates of the Diocesan Seminary of Our Lady of the Lake who have completed practically the same work." Winters to Father Fox, 27 December 1930, *AJC*. In 1932 when Father Fox was asked by the registrar of Western Reserve University about the relationship of John Carroll and the seminary in the matter of degrees, he referred to the seminary as the divinity school of John Carroll and said that, "Students who satisfactorily complete lower division work in the Liberal Arts College may transfer to the Seminary at the end of two years, according to this arrangement for a combined course may receive the degree of B.A. at John Carroll University." Fox to Hunter, 3 March 1932, *AJC*.

93. Report of the Committee on Constitution, 6 January 1933, *ADC*. This was a committee appointed by the bishop to review the Corporate College Agreement. Father Fox was absent from this meeting because of illness. Also, Schlitz to M. P. Mooney, 7 January 1933, *ADC*. Mooney was the diocesan attorney. Schrembs to Mother Evarista, 17 January 1933, *AJC*, the bishop said that the "so-called Corporate Colleges arrangement has no legal value and that any diplomas issued under the name of the Corporate Colleges prove invalid. Under the circumstances there is nothing to do but to issue diplomas under the authority of your own college. I still hope that we may find a formula for some unification of our colleges which will prove valid in law, but until this is done, we will have to move along individually." Also memorandum of M. P. Mooney on "Validity of Corporate College Degrees," 11 February 1933, *ADC*. The attorney general's written opinion supporting the validity of the degrees was in the hands of the bishop and also of the other colleges. The claim that the degrees granted by the Corporate Colleges were invalid made no reference to this written opinion.

94. Hagan, "Conflict between Sisters' College and JCU."

95. Ibid.

96. Hagan, "Conflict between Sisters' College and JCU," also Fox, "Corporate Colleges." Father Fox relates that when Hagan discovered that the charge against Fox had been proved manifestly wrong, Hagan then "turned the blame on Dr. Graham, whom he lashed unmercifully and with a venom that revealed a long, pent up hatred that have gave vent to its fury in language as vile as it was violent. Throughout this recital, Bishop Schrembs nooded assentively and encouragingly plainly showing that his mind had been poisoned by Dr. Hagan against Dr. Graham."

The teaching certificates that were withheld did arrive in time for commencement but only through a mistake in the State Department office. The state director of education informed Father Fox that a clerical error of "a certain Mr. Wilson had permitted the certificates to be sent. It was thought wiser not to recall them than to admit the blunder of Mr. Wilson's staff." Fox, "Corporate Colleges."

At the meeting referred to above, Hagan also challenged Father Fox on the continuous discussions of the Administrative Board about Sisters' College, which Hagan said the minutes would prove. When the minutes of the meetings were produced to substantiate the charge they were never opened by Hagan. Father Fox described this as a clear case of "bullying." In Hagan's account of this meeting none of these details are supplied. It was Father Fox's opinion that both Bishop Schrembs and Monsignor McFadden "were vexed. They were unmistakeably disappointed. Once [*sic*] could readily see that the stage had been set to implicate the Jesuits hopelessly; but Dr. Hagan's series of assertions were silenced one after the other, and the whole meeting was a disgraceful anticlimax of its intended purpose."

97. Affidavit of W. W. Boyd, 19 July 133, *AJC*. This affidavit was made as part of the testimony that Father Fox had no part whatsoever in the loss of accreditation by Sisters' College. In Boyd's judgment there were "many improvements" that were needed before ac-

creditation could be given. There is also an affidavit of Skinner to the same effect 24 July 1933, *AJC.*

98. Hagan, *The Diocesan Teachers College,* 173.

99. Ibid., 27.

100. Ibid., 48.

101. "The Diocesan Normal School," editorial, *Catholic School Journal,* June 1933.

102. Affidavit of Edward A. Fitzpatrick, 13 July 1933, *AJC.*

103. Bruce to Hagan, 13 June 1933, *ADC.*

104. *Catholic Universe Bulletin,* 16 June 1933.

105. Ibid.

106. McNicholas to Schrembs, 29 May 133, *ADC.* The same Mr. Boyd who was being accused of bigotry had previously visited the seminary and was "delighted with the scholastic as well as the physical condition of the Seminary." If the seminary were incorporated, it could have granted degrees on its own. Walsh to Mittinger, 12 December 1939, *AJC.*

107. Ibid.

108. Memorandum of the Administration of Catholic Education in Ohio, 2 June 1933, *ADC.*

109. Ibid.

110. Ibid.

111. Ibid.

112. Ibid.

113. Skinner to Schrembs, 3 June 1933, *ADC.*

114. Schrembs to Skinner, 15 June 1933, *ADC.*

115. Skinner to Schrembs, 23 June 1933, *ADC*; Schrembs to Skinner, 3 July 1933, *ADC.*

116. Memorandum of Father Rodman, conversation with Bishop Schrembs on 3 July 1933, at 2:00 P.M. in the bishop's office, *AJC.*

117. Ibid.

118. Ibid.

119. Ibid.

120. Ibid. Throughout the memorandum, Father Rodman notes that in all cases of accusations the bishop used the word "feel" and that no specific charges were made. Father Rodman also noted that Father Fox was given no opportunity to respond to the accusations. Father Rodman's "personal opinion" was that the bishops "realize that Father Fox is too well informed, has too well established a reputation as an educator with the State Department and consequently is an obstacle that must be gotten out of the way by fair means or foul." Father Rodman changed the subject during the course of the discussion to question the bishop on whether he really wanted any affiliation of the local colleges. "Oh! Father," replied the bishop, "I always did want some kind of an affiliation." Father Rodman concluded that what the bishop wanted was an affiliation "in which he is everything and the Jesuits are merely one of his non-authoritative aggregations." Father Rodman admits his account is from memory and represents "only the kernel of the conversation; but it is accurate in substance."

121. Affidavit of Father Fox, 17 July 1933, *AJC.*

122. Father Rodman, Report of conversation with Bishop Schrembs on 22 July 1933 at his office, *AJC.*

123. Ibid. After the meeting with the bishop, Father Rodman went again to see Monsignor Smith, who suggested that Rodman see Archbishop McNicholas. Father Rodman thought this was not appropriate. Monsignor Smith's advice then was "to drop the matter for at least a month and let Bishop Schrembs sweat." Monsignor Smith also said that the bishop "had not advised with his consultors lately" and that "he had been unduly influenced by three young men in his close retinue."

124. Ibid.

125. Report of Father Rodman's conversation with Bishop Schrembs on August 19th at his office and again at St. John Hospital on 20 August, *AJC.*

126. Ibid.

127 Ibid. It was at this time that Graham heard that the bishop had asked for the transfer of Father Fox and understood that his dismissal had also been requested. Graham wrote to Bishop Schrembs on 2 August 1933, *AJC,* and said he was unable to get any clarification of what the charges were. He had become convinced that he was the "victim of an unparalleled campaign of calumny." In the letter Graham said that he had been told more than a year before that a "vicious attack" had been made on him in the bishop's presence. He said he knew of nothing that he had done that merited such an attack and was ready to answer any charges that the bishop might make. In reply, Bishop Schrembs told Graham that he had not demanded Graham's removal and added that, nevertheless, Graham's "attitude toward Diocesan Education Problems has not always been above reproach" and reminded him that "the bishop is the lawful head of the Diocese," Schrembs to Graham, 19 August 1933, *ADC.*

128. Schrembs to McNicholas, 17 October 1933, *ADC.* The Provincial obviously confused the graduation exercises with the "opening of Sisters' College."

129. This account bears no date and no signature but the date would be sometime in early November and it is clearly Hagan's work, *ADC.* Copies were sent to the bishops on 21 November 1922.

130. Ibid.

131. Alter to Schrembs 23 November 1933; Hartley to Schrembs, 24 November 1933.

132. McNicholas to Schrembs, 24 November 1933, *ADC.*

133. Schrembs to Cloud, 29 November 1933, *ADC.* Under the date of 29 November 1933, Bishop Schrembs issued a *Diocesan Letter,* XII, 19, which barred all conferences to Sisters by visiting priests, Sisters or lay lecturers without written permission of the bishop. Nor could any of these groups address students in high schools, academies, colleges, or seminaries without written permission. The ban also included conventions or general gatherings of religious organizations "in any place in the Diocese without written permission from the bishop."

134. Report of the conversation between Bishop Schrembs and Father Rodman held at St. John's Hospital, Cleveland, 3 December 1933, *ADC.*

135. Ibid.

136. Cloud to Schrembs, 3 December 1933, *ADC.*

137. Schrembs to Cloud, 7 December 1933, *ADC.*

138. Cloud to Schrembs, 11 January 1934, *ADC.*

139. Evarista to Schrembs, 11 January 1934, *ADC.*

140. Report on the private conference of Mother Mary Evarista and Sister Agnes with Bishop Schrembs, 21 March 1934, *AJC.*

141. Ibid. The other colleges of the corporate group all had copies of the attorney general's opinion.

142. Report of Father Rodman's conversation with Bishop Schrembs on 28 April and 5 May concerning a united graduation of the Cleveland Diocesan Colleges, *AJC.*

143. Ibid.

144. *Cleveland Plain Dealer,* 9 September 1934.

145. Wickenden to Rodman, 3 September 1934; Bradley to Rodman, 8 September 1934; Moore to Rodman, 3 September 1934; Thomas to Rodman, 8 September 1934; Baker to Rodman, 8 September 1934; Boyd to Rodman, 10 September 1934; Stradley to Rodman, 12 September 1934; Skinner to Rodman, 12 September 1934; Zook to *Catholic Universe Bulletin,* telegram, 10 September 1934. All in *AJC.*

146. *Cleveland News,* 10 September 1933.

147. Memorial Address of Father Rodman, 13 September 1934, *AJC.*

148. Quoted in Obituary of Father Fox, typewritten copy in *AJC.* Obituary later appeared in *The Province Newsletter*, Missouri Province, January 1935.

149. Ibid.

150. Memorial Address of Father Rodman.

151. Hynes, *History of the Diocese of Cleveland*, quoted from *Catholic Universe Bulletin*, 4, 25 October 1946.

CHAPTER XI

1. Bernet to Rodman, 30 July 1930, *AJC.*

2. Bernet to Rodman, 10 July 1930, *AJC.*

3. Ibid.

4. Memorandum of a Conference on a Dormitory, 1 July 1930, *AJC.* Another memorandum dated 10 July 1930 indicated the abadonment of the idea of a separate gymnasium after the conference between Father Rodman and Bernet.

5. Bernet to Rodman, 10 July 1930, *AJC.*

6. Memorandum of a meeting of Bishop Schrembs, Father Rodman and F. K. Draz (architect partner of Small), 3 November 1930, *AJC.*

7. *Cleveland News*, 7 April 1931.

8. Ibid.

9. Philip L. Small to Hunkin-Conkey Construction Company, 27 January 1932, *AJC.*

10. *Carroll News*, XII, 8, 12 February 1932.

11. Ibid.

12. Minute Book, Consultors of John Carroll Univ. 1917–49. 18 April 1932, *AJC.*

13. General Scrapbook, John Carroll University, January 1932 to December 1938.

14. *Cleveland Press*, 14 March 1933.

15. Ibid.

16. Ibid.

17. *Catholic Universe Bulletin*, 24 March 1933.

18. Minute Book, Consultors of John Carroll Univ., 1917–49, 22 April 1932; 4 June 1932; *AJC,*. See Appendix B for the story of the Buffalo Mission Debt.

19. Ibid., 11 March 1932.

20. Ibid., 13 March 1932.

21. Rodman to Schrembs, 11 May 1932, *ADC.* See chapter 10, p. 260 for a discussion of other reasons for the cancellation of the 1932 Summer School.

22. *Cleveland News*, 22 December 1932; also, *Carroll News*, XIV, 6, 20 December 1933.

23. Minute Book, Consultors of John Carroll Univ., 1917–49, 15 February 1933, *AJC.*

24. *Carroll News*, XIII, 7, 17 February 1933.

25. Ibid.

26. The Memorandum, "Urgent Reasons Why the Jesuits Should Complete the New College Building," is to be found in both *AJC* and *ADC.* It is probably the product of some lengthy discussion by the Consultors toward the middle of 1933.

27. Schrembs to Ledochowski, 11 August 1933, *ADC.*

28. Ibid.

29. Ledochowski to Schrembs, 5 September 1933, *ADC.*

30. Ibid.

31. Ibid.

32. Ibid.

33. Ibid.

34. Ibid.
35. Minute Book, Consultors of John Carroll Univ., 1917–49, *AJC*, 20 October 1933.
36. Ibid.
37. Ibid., 11 November 1933.
38. Ibid. 22 January, also 30 January 1934.
39. Ibid., 16 August 1934.
40. Ibid.
41. Rodman to Schrembs, 12 June 1931, *ADC*.
42. Monsignor Smith to Clergy of the Diocese, 27 July 1931, *ADC*.
43. Minute Book, Consultors of John Carroll Univ., 1917–49, 15 October 1931, *AJC*.
44. Bernet to Schrembs, 5 December 1931, *ADC*.
45. Schrembs to Bernet, 19 December 1931.
46. Ibid.
47. Ibid.
48. Ibid., 31 December 1931; both versions in *ADC*.
49. Ibid.
50. Ibid.
51. Bernet to Schrembs, 5 January 1932, *ADC*.
52. Ibid.
53. Ibid.
54. Schrembs to Bernet, 25 January 1932, *ADC*.
55. Ibid.
56. Ibid., 5 February 1932, *ADC*.
57. Rodman to O'Callaghan, 13 September 1929, *AJC*.
58. McFadden to Rodman, 18 November 1929, *ADC*.
59. Ibid. Another part of the problem was the dissatisfaction of many parishoners with Father Rudden's successor, Father Versavel. The bishop had complained to Father Rodman about Father Versavel's decidedly foreign accent although he praised Father Versavel as a priest. In his letter to Father O'Callaghan, n. 57, Father Rodman reported that the bishop did not see why there was not a "more up-to-date purely American priest," in charge of the parish. Father Rodman agreed that perhaps a mistake had been made in that appointment. See Appendix C for the story on the parish problems.
60. Minute Book, Consultors of John Carroll Univ., 1917–49, 25 March 1930, *AJC*.
61. Schlitz to McFadden, 25 March 1930, *ADC*.
62. Ibid.
63. Mooney to McFadden, 5 April 1930, *ADC*.
64. Cloud to Rodman, 19 August 1930, *AJC*.
65. Minute Book, Consultors of John Carroll Univ., 1917–49, 15 October 1931, *AJC*. The order was first given orally.
66. Schrembs to Rodman, 26 October 1931, *ADC*. The bishop added that his consultors agreed with this action.
67. Rodman to Milet, 27 April 1932, *AJC*.
68. There is in Father Rodman's papers a five-page undated (probably 1937) memorandum of reasons for not revoking the permission of 1931 to exchange the "triangle" property for the Board of Education site. The memorandum makes a strong case for the exchange as the only possible solution to parish problems.
69. "Faculty Reflector," I, 1, 10 February 1931, *AJC*.
70. Ibid., II, 2, 14 December 1931.
71. "Certificate of Amendment to Articles of Incorporation of The John Carroll University." Filed 18 November 1932. Corp. No. 7849. The document was approved by the Board of

Trustees on 17 November 1932. It is recorded in the office of the secretary of the State of Ohio. Volume 410, page 74 of the Record of Incorporations.

72. Ibid.

73. "What was officially called an amendment to the charter of John Carroll University, . . . is in reality a total recasting of the former charter. . . . when opposition to the legal rights of the school's power is to grant degrees was at its height, Father rector (Rodman) had the lawyers put this through to safeguard the University in the future." *The Province News Letter*, Missouri Province, XIII, 13 January 1933. See chapter 10 for the full story.

74. Minute Book, Consultors of John Carroll Univ., 1917–49, 3 March 1935, *AJC*.

75. Ibid., 19 March 1935.

76. Report of the Board of Review on Higher Education of the North Central Association, 15 March 1934, *AJC*.

77. Ibid.

78. Ibid.

79. Ibid.

80. The North Central complaint about the difficulty in understanding the financial reporting of Jesuit institutions, indeed those of all Catholic institutions, was the result of the lack of professional preparation of those reports. For the most part the reports were prepared by procurators or treasurers who had little or no preparation in accounting practices and were generally unsympathetic to the idea of reporting to the North Central. The manner of accounting for the contributed services of Jesuits, whose salaries were considered to be paid out of interest on what would normally have been a monetary fund, had become a complicated matter. The practice was originally sanctioned by the North Central in 1921. Indebtedness incurred by the expansion of the colleges and universities since that time raised questions as to how to cover the mounting indebtedness. Fearful that an institution's indebtedness was not covered by the amount computed as the "endowment of men," the North Central in 1933 conducted a survey among some of the Jesuit colleges to determine their exact financial situation.

The Provincials of the Missouri and Chicago Provinces in 1934 called a meeting of the college and university presidents to determine what response should be made. This meeting on 24 February coincided with the North Central visitation at John Carroll, but Fathers Rodman and Fox both attended the meeting. Father Fox was unanimously elected chairman. Father Fox in his role of leadership made it abundantly clear that what the Jesuits needed to do was to introduce proper accounting procedures in their institutions. This meant the hiring of professional accountants. The scope of the discussions was quite broad and included the question of whether the Jesuit colleges and universities should pull out of the North Central. Father Fox was adamant on their remaining in it.

A direct outcome of this meeting was Father Rodman's search for ways and means to bring John Carroll's accounting up to standards. Father Fox felt that the addition of a school of business would be a desirable step. The hiring of Fritz W. Graff to begin a department of business administration and ultimately a school of business was Father Rodman's solution. The department was established in the fall of 1934. Meeting of the Bi-Province Committee on Outside Standardizing Agencies, Loyola University, Chicago, 24 February 1934. *ALUC*.

81. North Central Report, 1934.

82. Hunkin-Conkey to Neff, 24 May 1934, *AJC*.

83. Minute Book, Consultors of John Carroll Univ., 1917–49, 21 October 1934. *AJC*.

84. Ibid.

85. Phillips to Rodman, 21 January 1935, *AJC*.

86. Ibid.

87. Phillips to Schrembs, 4 February 1935, *ADC*.

88. Phillips to Rodman, 4 February 1935, *AJC*.
89. "A Memorandum of Conclusions and Suggestions of the Report of Fr. Phillips," an insert in Minute Book, Consultors of John Carroll Univ. 1917–49, n.d. *AJC*.
90. Ibid., Also a letter of Father Phillips to Father Rodman, 22 February 135, *AJC*.
91. Ibid.
92. Rodman to Phillips, 25 March 1935, *AJC*.
93. Ibid.
94. Story related to author by Mr. Mittinger.
95. Minute Book, Consultors of John Carroll Univ., 1917–49, Meeting of the Special Committee, 17 April 1935, *AJC*.
96. Cigonani to Schrembs, 11 May 1935, *ADC*.
97. Schrembs to Cigonani, 21 May 1935, *ADC*.
98. *Carroll News*, XV, 15, 22 May 1935.
99. Ibid.
100. Minute Book, Consultors of John Carroll Univ., 1917–49, 5 September 1935, *AJC*.
101. Cloud to Rodman, 8 July 1935, *AJC*.
102. Neff to Schrembs, 22 July 135, *ADC*.
103. *Carroll News*, XVI, 1, 16 October 1935.
104. Ibid.
105. Minute Book, Consultors of John Carroll Univ., 1917–49, 15 October 1935, *AJC*.
106. *Carroll News*, XVI, 2, 30 October 1935. Mittinger's recreation room in his home near the college was the temporary editorial office of the *Carroll News*.
107. Minute Book, Consultors of John Carroll Univ., 1917–49, 13 November 1935, *AJC*.
108. Ibid.
109. Rodman to Wilson, 23 July 1936, *AJC*.
110. Rodman to Maher, 8 January 1937, *AJC*. Father Maher had been president of Santa Clara University from 1921 to 1926 and faced with similar building problems. Father Rodman undoubtedly thought he would understand the situation. Father Rodman finished his letter by saying, "I have not mentioned this to the Consultors of the Province except one, Father McKernan."
111. Rodman to Ledochowski, 7 January 1937, *AJC*. The choice Father Rodman referred to was Father Jerome Jacobsen who had a degree in Latin American history, having studied under Herbert Bolton at the University of California.
112. Ibid.
113. *Cleveland Plain Dealer*, 7 March 1937.
114. Ibid.
115. Rodman to Schrembs, 9 August 1942, *ADC*.
116. Schrembs to Rodman, 20 August 1942, *ADC*.

CHAPTER XII

1. Rodman to Schrembs, 15 May 1936, *ADC*.
2. Minsiter's Diary, 1935–1939, 7 June 1936, *AJC*.
3. Minute Book, Consultors of John Carroll Univ., 1917–49, 10 February 1936, 3 March 1936, *AJC*.
4. Since the first honorary degree awarded by the university went to George MacDonald in 1935, it is hard to understand why there should have been a question about awarding honorary degrees in 1936, yet such such was the case. MacDonald was a leading Catholic layman, president of the Newman School in Lakewood, New Jersey, chairman of the Federal Loan Bank of Newark, New Jersey and a Papal Marquis. No question seems to have been

raised at the time he was awarded the degree. The award was duly noted in the *New York Times* of 7 July 135. The question of whether the University should award degrees at the Jubilee commencement was discussed by the consultors at two separate meetings, 14 April 1936 and 14 May 1936, (Minute Book, Consultors, John Carroll 1917–1949.). Father Bracken seemed to be under the impression that the Province Prefect of Studies had frowned on such awards.

    5. Ledochowski to Schrembs, 13 June 1936, *ADC.*

    6. Schrembs to Ledochowski, 29 June 1936, *ADC.*

    7. *Cleveland Press*, 3 November 1936.

    8. This particular quote seemed to have very wide circulation. It appeared in a number of newspapers outside of Cleveland. *Pittsburgh Press*, 17 October 1938, *West Chester* [Pa.] *News*, 17 October 1938, *Latrobe* [Pa.] *Bulletin*, 17 October 1938, and many others.

    9. Minute Book, Consultors of John Carroll Univ., 1917–49, 4 September 1940; 30 September 1940.

    10. Ibid., 29 October 1942; 6 December 1942.

    11. Ibid., 14 July 1941; 17 July 1941; 28 July 1941.

    12. Ibid., 4 January 1937; 12 February 1937.

    13. Ibid., 30 October 1942; 9 October 1942.

    14. Ibid., 14 July 1941.

    15. *Carroll News*, XXIV, 1 September 1943.

    16. Minister's Diary, 4 December 1941, *AJC.*

    17. *Carroll News.* XVII, 12, 21 April 1937.

    18. On a number of occasions the authorities at the city hall would call and say that there was a report of someone with a rifle in the area in front of the school. Mittinger, the registrar, was the one who usually received the calls and was able to defuse the situation by rounding up the "suspects." The author once bagged a pheasant on the windshield of his automobile while driving on the street to the rear of the property. Discussions between the author and Mittinger, 10 April 1980.

    19. Rector's Diary [Father Donnelly], 1942–1946, October 1943, *AJC*; Minute Book, Consultors, John Carroll, 1917–1949, 6 October 1943, *AJC.*

    20. *Carroll News*, XVII, 9, 10 March 1937.

    21. Ibid., 16 April 1936.

    22. Ibid.

    23. Pickel to Schrembs, 3 October 1937, *(ADC)*. Shortly after he had finished his second appointment to the office of president, Father Pickel celebrated his Golden Jubilee in the Society with a testimonial dinner in the new cafeteria. It was a gala affair attended by 150 priest alumni of John Carroll and the largest assembly of clergy at the new institution. Father Thomas E. Walsh, pastor of St. Aloysius Church in East Liverpool, Ohio, and a member of the first class Father Pickel taught as a scholastic at St. Ignatius College was among those present. Present also were Monsignors John R. Hagan and James McDonough, as well as Bishop McFadden. Father Pickel's response to the various words of praise heaped upon him was to say, "There is one thing I want to ask, and that is this, I want you to help us fill our new John Carroll to capacity. It is your university. Your great Bishop Gilmour brought us here. Your Bishop Horstmann and Bishop Farrelly kept us here. Your zealous Bishop Schrembs has called us to greater service by inaugurating the present enlarged school." *Catholic Universe Bulletin*, 2 April 1938.

    24. *Catholic Universe Bulletin*, 4 September 1942.

    25. *Cleveland Press*, 2 September 1942.

    26. *Cleveland Plain Dealer*, 31 August 1934; *Cleveland News*, 31 August 1934. Both professors Graff and March had considerable experience in the field of business. Graff had been

professor of business administration at the University of Texas and was a member of the Texas bar. For nine years he had been in charge of the department of accounting. March taught accounting at Cleveland College and was an investigator for the Ohio Tax Commission. It was rumored that the dispute with Ellis was over a new emphasis on social sciences and a question of standards.

27. Minute Book, Consultors of John Carroll Univ., 1917–49, 19 December 1945, *AJC.*

28. Ibid.

29. *Carroll News*, XX 13, 12 April 1938.

30. Minute Book, Consultors of John Carroll Univ., 1917–49, 9 October 1942, *AJC.*

31. Wilson to O'Connell, 6 January 1936, *ALUC.*

32. Minute Book, Consultors of John Carroll Univ., 1917–49, 3 March 1935. See also chapter XI, footnote 80.

33. Ibid., 19 March 1935.

34. Ibid., 7 September 1935; 19 September 1935.

35. Ibid., 28 April 1936.

36. Ibid., 17 September 1936. The situation was serious enough for the matter to be put before the entire Jesuit Community.

37. Ibid., 27 October 1936; 3 March 1936. A board had been set up to review each tuition reduction and an *advocatus diaboli* appointed to show why the reduction should not be granted.

38. Ibid., 10 December 1936.

39. Ibid.

40. Ibid., 4 September 1942.

41. Ibid.

42. Ibid., 21 August 1944, 6 October 1944, 15 November 1944.

43. Ibid., 18 April 1939.

44. Horne to Schrembs, 29 November 1939, *ADC.*

45. Minute Book, Consultors of John Carroll Univ., 1917–49, 27 March 1945, *AJC,*. For a more detailed account of the debt question see Appendix B.

46. Ibid. See also Appendix B for the story of the debt.

47. Ibid.

48. Rector's Diary, 1942–1946, 22 June 1946, *AJC.*

49. Ibid., 19 July 1946.

50. Ibid., 31 July 1946.

51. Minute Book, Consultors of John Carroll Univ., 1917–49, 28 April 1936. Father Haggerty brought the matter up at the consultors' meeting but there was no discussion recorded.

52. Ibid., 27 October 1936.

53. Author was present when Father Rodman made the point that the laymen were tolerated until they could be replaced by Jesuits.

54. Minute Book, Consultors of John Carroll Univ., 1917–49, 15 September 1939. Shortly after classes began each layman received what amounted to a unilateral contract. Almost without exception the laymen saw no advantage in signing and returning it. Most of the contracts were torn up and put in the wastebasket.

55. Ibid., 18 November 1941.

56. *Cleveland Plain Dealer*, 3 April 1937.

57. Minute Book, Consultors of John Carroll Univ., 1917–49, 23 December 1937.

58. Rector's Diary, 1942–1946, 24 May 1943.

59. Minute Book, Consultors of John Carroll Univ., 1917–49, 19 June 1940.

60. Ibid., 30 September 1940.

61. Ibid., 30 January 1942.

62. Ibid.

63. Ibid., 4 March 1943.

64. Ibid.

65. Ibid.

66. Rector's Diary, 1942–1946, 22 April 1943.

67. Ibid., 26 May 1943.

68. Ibid., 1 June 1943.

69. Minute Book Consultors of John Carroll Univ., 1917–49, 2 June 1943.

70. *Carroll News*, XXIV, 3, November, 1943.

71. Minute Book, Consultors of John Carroll Univ., 1917–49, 21 August 1944; also 11 May 1946; 18 June 1946.

72. Ibid., 11 May 1946.

73. *Carroll News*, XXIV, 1, 1 September 1943.

74. Ibid., June 1944.

75. Minute Book, Consultors of John Carroll Univ., 1917–49, 22 January 1944.

76. *Carroll News*, XXVI, 3, November 1945.

77. *Ibid.*, XXI, 13, 2 May 1941. Ted Saker, the writer, may have had in mind the action of 500 students who in 1936 sought to "fight disloyal pacifism" when most all the other colleges were going in the opposite direction, *Cleveland News*, 22 April 1936.

78. *Ibid.*

79. *Ibid.*, XVI, 6, 15 January 1936.

80. *Ibid.*, XXI, 12, 20 March 1941.

81. *Ibid.*, XVI, 6, 15 January 1936.

82. *Ibid.* In the *Carroll News* of 7 February 1941, a column written by Jack Cooper was called "Screwball Haul" and it contained personal items about students and goings at the University.

83. *Ibid.*, 19 November 1941, 16 December 1941.

84. *Ibid.*, XXIV, 2 October 1943.

85. *Ibid.*, XXVI, 6, February 1946.

86. *Ibid.*, XVI, 6, 15 January 1936.

87. Minute Book, Consultors of John Carroll Univ., 1917–49, 10 February 1936.

88. *Plain Dealer*, 17 November 1937; *Carroll News*, 24 November 1937; Ministers' Diary, 1939–49, 17 November 1937.

89. Minute Book, Consultors of John Carroll Univ., 1917–49, 7 March 1940.

90. *Catholic Universe Bulletin*, 13 January 1939.

91. Minute Book, Consultors of John Carroll Univ., 1917–49, 16 March 1936.

92. *Carroll News*, XXI, 3, 3 November 1939.

93. Ibid., XXI, 10, 1 March 1940.

94. Ibid., XXIX, 6, 17 December 1948.

95. Rodman to Schrembs, 5 February 1936, *ADC*.

96. Schrembs to LeMay, 24 March 1936, *ADC*.

97. McFadden to Father Hartford P. Brucker, S.J., 11 February 1937. Father Brucker was in charge of the symposium.

98. Begin to Horne, 25 February 1938, *ADC*.

99. Minute Book, Consultors of John Carroll Univ., 1917–49, 10 June 1939.

100. Ibid.

101. Ibid.

102. Schrembs to Joseph Wilson, 31 May 1939, *ADC*.

103. *Carroll News*, XIX, 12, 5 May 1939. The officials of the University of Detroit chapter installed the charter members, Carl Burlage, Tom Corrigan, Jim Smith, John Zeleznik, and

Bob Marchand. The first members picked by the charter members were Nick Ronan, Ray McGorray, Vince LaMaida, Bill Duffin, and Justin Noetzel.

104. Minister's Diary, 1939–1949, 17 January 1939.

105. *Carroll News*, XIX, 12, 5 May 1939.

106. *Catholic Universe Bulletin*, 26 May 1939.

107. *Carroll News*, XVIII, 6, 19 January 1938.

108. Ibid., XXV, 4, December 1944.

109. Ibid., November 1944.

110. Ibid., XXII, 11, 6 March 1942.

111. Ibid.

112. "Report of the Inspection of John Carroll University, 24–25 February 1936, J. R. Sage to Board of Review of North Central," *AJC.*

113. W. S. Robb to J. R. Sage, 25 February 1936, *AJC.*

114. North Central Report, 1936.

115. Wilson to O'Connell, 8 February 1936, *ALUC.*

116. Ibid., also 10 February 1936, *ALUC.*

117. Ibid., 10 February 1936, *ALUC.*

118. Ibid.

119. Wilson to Rodman, 10 February 1936. *ALUC.*

120. Ibid.

121. Rodman to Wilson, 12 February 1936, *AJC.*

122. Wilson to the Provincial, Father Charles Cloud, 18 February 1936; also Wilson to Rodman, 18 February 1936, *ALUC.*

123. *Carroll News*, XVI, 10, 25 March 1936.

124. Ibid. XX, 1939. Success was determined by the won and lost record. The schedule in 1939 was a local schedule. The 1924 schedule was a national schedule in which there was one more loss than in 1939. There are those who consider the 1924 schedule a more difficult one.

125. Ibid., XX, 3, 3 November 1939.

126. Ibid., XXII, 4, 7 November 1941.

127. Father Eckman, "Recommendations re: Football," 4 November 1942, *AJC.*

128. Ibid.

129. *Carroll News*, XXIV, 1, September 1943. The Navy later said that it had not intended to exclude football. It was agreed to permit intramural football. Carroll would not be a member of any league nor have paid coaches, Minute Book, Consultors of John Carroll Univ., 1917–49, 7 July 1943.

130. Ibid., XXIV, 4, December 1943.

131. Ibid., XX, 10, 1 March 1940.

132. Donnelly to Conley, 8 October 1942, *AJC.*

133. Minute Book, Consultors of John Carroll Univ., 1917–49, 28 April 1944.

134. Ibid., 19 December 1945.

135. Ibid. Discussion of subsidization had taken place as early as October 1945 and the general consensus was opposed to it then, ibid., 19 October 1945.

136. Ibid., 29 January 1946.

137. Ibid., 16 March 1936.

138. Ibid., 27 March 1945.

139. Ibid., 29 May 1945.

140. Rector's Diary, 1942–1946, 15 February 1946; also Minute Book, Consultors of John Carroll Univ., 1917–49, 29 January 1946.

141. Minute Book, Consultors of John Carroll Univ., 1917–49, 18 June 1946; see also 2 May 1948.

142. "Form of Statutes For Institutions of Complex Organization," Jesuit Educational Association Recommendations, 23 February 1935, *ALUC.*

143. Wilson to O'Connell, 13 May 1935, *ALUC.*

144. Minute Book, Consultors of John Carroll Univ., 1917–49, 21 August 1944, *AJC.*

145. Ibid.

146. Ibid., 5 January 1945.

147. Ibid., 19 October 1945; 19 December 1945.

148. Ibid., 15 November 1945; 19 October 1945; 11 May 1946.

149. Father Rodman was no stranger to difference of opinion with local bishops. In this instance he was less than enamoured of Bishop Hoban's building program and said so publicly. The Provincial, Father Sullivan, wrote to Bishop Hoban, 29 July 1946, saying "Since I wish to withdraw Father Benedict J. Rodman from Gesu Church, I should like to propose Father S. Walker as pastor of the Church," Sullivan to Hoban, 29 July 1946, *ADC.* The Bishop gladly accepted the proposal. A letter of thanks was sent 6 August 1946; Sullivan to Hoban, 6 August 1946, *ADC.*

150. *Carroll News,* XXV, 1, September 1944.

151. Ibid.

152. Ibid., XXVI 3, November 1945.

CHAPTER XIII

1. Minute Book, Consultors of John Carroll Univ., 1917–49, 12 March 1949, *AJC.*

2. Ibid.

3. Minister's Diary 1956–73, 17 August 1956, *AJC.*

4. *Carroll News,* XXVII, 1, 25 October 1946.

5. "Semi annual Report of the president of the University to the Members of the Advisory Board of Lay Trustees, 14 November 1956," *AJC.*

6. Author's interview with some of the members of the Advisory Board of Lay Trustees who served during Father Welfle's regime, 15 June 1981. One trustee was amazed to find this view still held by some Jesuits in 1970.

7. Minute Book, Consultors of John Carroll Univ., 1917–49, 18 November 1946.

8. Minutes of the Academic Council, 3 May 1947, *AJC.*

9. Minute Book, Consultors of John Carroll Univ., 1917–49, 17 November 1947, *AJC.*

10. Ibid.

11. Ibid., 13 July 1949, 23 September 1949.

12. Ibid., 23 February 1949.

13. The first members of the Advisory Board of Lay Trustees were: W. G. Bernet, Tom Dolan, Charles McCahill, John Murphy, Edgar Ostendorf, John Rice, Joseph Schlitz, John K. Thompson. Within a year Frank Joseph, Allan Fritzsche, and Walter Daly were added.

14. Minute Book, Consultors of John Carroll Univ., 1917–49, 27 October 1948, *AJC.*

15. Ibid., 23 December 1948. At this Consultors' meeting there occurs the first use of the name Rodman Hall in place of Faculty Building.

16. Ibid., 12 March 1949.

17. Ibid., 11 April 1949.

18. Ibid., 29 November 1949.

19. Ibid., 25 March 1949.

20. House Diary 1948–55, 31 March 1949, *AJC.*

21. *Carroll News,* XXX, 1, 23 September 1949.

22. Consultors' Meetings, 1950–65, 24 January 1952, *AJC.*

23. Ibid.

24. *Carroll News,* XXVII, 2, 1 November 1946.

25. Minute Book, Consultors of John Carroll Univ., 1917–49, 21 February 1948, *AJC.* Three hundred nineteen lineal feet (5,000 square feet) of quonset huts had been offered to the university after they had been rejected by Youngstown College. In spite of the need for office space it was agreed that these huts would spoil the appearance of the campus.

26. *Carroll News,* XXVII, 6, 17 January 1947. Father Raymond Mooney, S.J., was instrumental in the acquisition.

27. Consultors' Meetings, 1950–55, 19 May 1960, *AJC.*

28. Minutes of Academic Council, 7 October 1953.

29. Ibid., 16 December 1946.

30. Ibid., 4 December 1946.

31. Ibid., 16 December 1946.

32. Ibid., 27 January 1947.

33. Ibid., 1 March 1950.

34. Ibid., 23 April 1952.

35. Ibid., 17 October 1951.

36. Ibid., 23 April 1952.

37. Ibid.

38. Ibid., 30 April 1952.

39. Ibid., 18 November 1953.

40. Ibid., 23 February 1955.

41. Ibid.

42. Ibid., 7 February 1958.

43. Ibid.

44. Minute Book, Consultors of John Carroll Univ., 1917–49, 13 May 1949, *AJC.*

45. *Carroll News,* XXX, 13, 21 April 1950.

46. Consultors' Meetings, 1950–65, 8 May 1950, *AJC.*

47. Ibid., 24 May 1950.

48. "Father Maline's Report on Visitation, 19–25 November, 1951" attached to Minutes of Academic Council, 1951–52, *AJC.*

49. Ibid.

50. Minutes of Academic Council, 13 December 1950, *AJC.*

51. Ibid., 7 March 1951.

52. Deters to Welfle, 4 December 1950, *AJC.*

53. Minutes of Academic Council, 22 February 1950, *AJC.*

54. "Father Maline's Report on Visitation."

55. Minutes of Academic Council, 12 March 1952, *AJC.*

56. Consultors' Meetings 1950–65, 28 April 1953, *AJC.*

57. "Positions and Procedures Regarding Expansion of Jesuit Institutions, Jesuit Educational Association Statement, 1955," *AJC.* See also George E. Ganss, S.J., "St. Ignatius and Jesuit Education," *Jesuit Educational Quarterly* 18 (June 1955), pp. 17–31.

58. Minutes of Academic Council, 2 November 1953, *AJC.*

59. Ibid.

60. Welfle to each faculty member, 26 October 1955, in Minutes of Academic Council, 26 October 1955, *AJC.*

61. "The Decisive Years, University Self-Study 1955–1956," 12 June 1956, *AJC.*

62. Consultors' Meetings 1950–65, 16 October 1951, *AJC.*

63. Deters to Welfle, 14 October 1953, *AJC.* In this letter Father Deters pointed out his problems in trying to handle 880 undergraduates, 100 graduates, and nearly 100 day students. Responsibility for promotional literature was a large order, and he was practically functioning as dean of men and women and also as superintendent of buildings and grounds at night.

Father Deters needed help, an office of his own, and asked that definite plans for the future of the Evening College be drawn up. The substance of this letter was repeated in another letter of Father Deters to Father Welfle, 12 October 1955. *AJC.*

64. *The Alumni Carroll News*, 4:9, September, 1952.

65. *Carroll News*, XXVIII, 6, 19 December 1947.

66. Ibid., XXVIII, 12, 16 April 1958.

67. Minute Book, Consultors of John Carroll Univ., 1917–49, 10 September 1948, *AJC.*

68. *Carroll News*, XXXVIII, 14, 14 May 1948.

69. Consultors' Meetings, 1950–65, 24 September 1953, *AJC.*

70. Ibid., 20 October 1954.

71. Ibid., 22 November 1954.

72. House Diary, 1948–55, 21 May 1949; also *Carroll News* XXIX, 20 May 1949.

73. House Diary 1948–55, 24, 25, 26 November 1950, *AJC.*

74. Ibid.

75. *Carroll News*, XXVII, 1, 25 October 1946.

76. Ibid., XXIX, 12, 3 May 1957; XLI, 6, 12 December 1958.

77. Ibid., XXXII, 1, 28 September 1951.

78. Ibid.

79. Ibid., XL, 5, 22 November 1957.

80. Ibid.

81. Ibid., 12 December 1958; 15 November 1959.

82. Ibid., XLII, 13, 26 February 1960.

83. Ibid., XLII, 17, 29 April 1960.

84. Cooney to Welfle, 16 August 1946, *AJC.*

85. Cooney to Welfle, 9 September 1946, *AJC.*

86. Welfle to Hugh Rodman, 16 September 1946, *AJC.*

87. *Carroll News*, XXVII, 6, 20 November 1946.

88. Welfle's "Memorandum," 8 December 1946, *AJC.*

89. Mooney to Welfle, 10 December 1946. *AJC.*

90. *Carroll News*, XXVII, 26 April 1947; 23 May 1947. Of the 100 students responding to a poll on the name Blue Streaks, 89 voted to retain the nickname, ibid. XXVLLL, 9 May 1947.

91. Ibid., 23 May 1947.

92. Ibid., 10 October 1947.

93. Ibid., XXVIII, 2, 24 October 1947.

94. Ibid., XXIX, 1, 8 October 1948.

95. *Cleveland News*, 9 November 1950.

96. *Cleveland News*, 14 November 1950.

97. Ibid.

98. Welfle's speech at football banquet 15 January 1951, *AJC.*

99. Englum, "Football as we have it at John Carroll University," 4 December 1951.

100. Ibid.

101. Ibid.

102. "Estimated Budget Report for Football" as of 12 February 1952.

103. Minutes of Academic Council, 23 April 1952.

104. Consultors' Meetings, 1950–65, 6 February 1953.

105. *Cleveland Plain Dealer*, 19 March 1951.

106. Ibid., 19 March 1954.

107. *Carroll News*, XXXV, 12, 9 April 1954.

108. Ibid., XLI, 15, 1 May 1959.

109. *Cleveland News*, 20 April 1949.

110. Ibid.

111. Ibid.

112. "Playing in the Arena," notes of a meeting between Father Welfle, Cooney, Eisele, and George, 6 August 1951, *AJC*.

113. Welfle to George, 16 August 1951, *AJC*.

114. Minutes of Academic Council, an undated spring meeting in 1947; Father Poetker's article is attached to the minutes. *AJC*.

115. Ibid.

116. Minute Book Consultors of John Carroll Univ., 1917–49, 10 September 1947, *AJC*.

117. Ibid.

118. Ibid., 18 November 1946.

119. Such problems as to the manner and for what purposes Jesuit expenses were to be collected from the university and other similar items remained to be clarified.

120. Consultors' Meetings, 1950–65, 12 November 1951.

121. Ibid.

122. Ibid., 20 December 1951.

123. Ibid., 18 February 1952.

124. House Diary, 23 April 1952; 10 May 1952; Consultors' Meetings, 1950–65. 23 April 1952, *AJC*.

125. "Father Maline's Report of Visitation."

126. Minutes of Academic Council, 28 April 1954, *AJC*.

127. Ibid.

128. "Prexy Talks it Over," *Faculty Notes*, X, 4, 2 March 1956, *AJC*.

129. Ibid.

130. Ibid.

131. Welfle to Sullivan, 18 May 1956 announced the approval of the Consultors on May 10 to the Provincial who then gave his approval to Father Welfle. Sullivan to Welfle, 22 May 1956, *AJC*.

132. After Father Welfle's death on 17 August 1956, Father William J. Millor, who had become executive dean and acting president, dealt with an interim committee for the Lay Faculty Association, which had a membership of 65 laymen. Edward Eggl became the first president until his death in December 1956. The Association continued to exist until 1962, when it was replaced by a Faculty Service Committee with somewhat different purposes. Father Dunn did not like the distinction between lay and Jesuit faculty and thought that the Lay Faculty Association had served its purpose by 1962.

133. Minutes of the meeting of 17 February 1961 of the Department of English. In Department of English files.

134. Consultors' Meetings 1950–56, 24 February 1961, *AJC*.

135. Whealon to Krol, 13 January 1954, *ADC*.

136. Hoban to Welfle, 2 September 1954, *ADC*. In Father Welfle's letter to Bishop Krol, in which he confirmed the arrangements, Father Welfle said, "In view of His Excellency's great kindness to John Carroll University, I feel that he should not be asked to pay for the man whom he sends to us for further education." Welfle to Krol, 1 September 1954, *ADC*.

137. Memorandum, Welfle to Faculty Members, 8 August 1956.

138. House Diary, 1956–73, 17 August 1956; 22 August 1956, *AJC*.

139. *Carroll News*, XXXIX, 1, 28 September 1956.

140. Blueprint steering committee meeting, 11 December 1956, *AJC*.

141. Ibid., 14 November 1956.

142. *Carroll News*, XXXIX, 5, 14 December 1956.

143. Minutes of the Blueprint Committee, 22 February 1957, *AJC*.

144. Ibid.

145. Ibid.

146. Spath to Dunn, 24 March 1957, *AJC*. Dr. Richard Spath, chairman of department of Classical Languages was informing Father Dunn of the existence of the sheet.

147. Minutes of Academic Council, 7 February 1958, *AJC*.

148. *Ibid.*

149. "Blueprint Report," 1959, *AJC*.

CHAPTER XIV

1. *Carroll News*, XLIII, 12, 14 April 1961.

2. Ibid., XLIV, 8, 16 February 1962.

3. Ibid., XLV, 1, 28 September 1962.

4. "Blueprint Report," 50, *AJC*.

5. McGucken to Wilson, 8 April 1935; Wilson to McGucken, 18 April 1935, *ALUC*.

6. "Blueprint Report," 4.

7. Minutes of Academic Council, 13 January 1961, 10 February 1961. There were marked differences of opinion between the dean of the College of Arts and Sciences and the Academic Council; Father Millor, as chairman of the Council, was the arbitrator.

8. For more on the material in the preceding paragraphs, see Philip Gleason, "In Search of Unity; American Catholic Thought, 1920–1960," *The Catholic Historical Review*, LXV, 2, April 1979, 185–205.

9. *Carroll News*, XLV, 5, 30 November 1962.

10. Ibid.

11. Downey to Gerken, 8 May 1961, *AJC*.

12. "Final Report of the Workshop on the Role of Philosophy and Theology as Academic Disciplines and their Integration with the Moral, Religious and Spiritual Life of the Jesuit College Student," Jesuit Educational Workshop, Volume V, 6–14 August, 1962, 413–414.

13. Ibid., 414.

14. Ibid., 416.

15. Ibid., 419.

16. Ibid.

17. Ibid.

18. "Alumni Description of the Department of Philosophy," based on Alumni Questionnaire, 26 December 1963, *AJC*.

19. Minutes of Academic Council, 4 October 1964.

20. Ibid., also, Report of Father Gerken to Academic Council, 9 January 1963, *AJC*.

21. *Carroll News*, XLVIII, 5, 10 December 1965. The new requirements were approved in a letter from Father Dunn to the deans and departmental chairmen, 8 November 1965 *AJC*. The reduction of the hours in the philosophy requirement had been opposed by the chairman of the department, W. Edmund Thirlkel. To give less, he said, would weaken the program and to go to twelve hours would be a "tragedy," Thirlkel to Conry, 1 October 1965. Father Gerken felt that the department of theology would have faculty with the necessary training for the new program. Gerken to Conry, 4 October 1965, *AJC*.

22. Minutes of Academic Council, Father Dunn's report on the North Central Review, 8 May 1964.

23. Report of the North Central Visitation to John Carroll University, 3–5 May, 1964. *AJC*.

24. Executive Committee Report, #F-5, Ground Rules for Curricular Reform, 8 September 1964.

25. *Carroll News*, LII, 8, 12 December 1969.

26. Ibid.

27. Consultors' Meetings 1950–65, 16 February 1963.

28. "Principal Features of the Proposed Shorter Contract," 4 March 1963, *AJC*.

29. Minutes of Academic Council, 6 November 1965.

30. Ibid., 30 September 1966.

31. *Carroll News*, XLIII, 31, 28 April 1961.

32. Ibid., XLIII, 14, 12 May 1961.

33. Yackshaw to Dunn, 19 June 1961, *AJC*.

34. Ibid.

35. Yackshaw to Dunn, 12 July 1961, *AJC*.

36. Yackshaw to Lay Faculty Association, 15 September 1961, *AJC*.

37. Ibid.

38. Ibid.

39. Ibid.

40. Ibid.

41. Minutes, the Lay Faculty Association Meeting, 16 October 1961, *AJC*.

42. Ibid.

43. Author was present at this meeting with Father Dunn. Others present were Dr. George Grauel, Dr. Richard Spath, Dr. Edward Walter.

44. Dunn to Yackshaw, 14 May 1962, *AJC*.

45. Ibid.

46. Ibid.

47. Minutes, Faculty Service Committee, 1962−1966, 21 May 1962, *AJC*.

48. Consultors Meetings, 1950−65, 27 October 1962, *AJC*.

49. *Carroll News*, XLIV, 1, 29 September 1961.

50. Ibid.

51. Ibid., XLIII, 2, October 1960.

52. Ibid.

53. Ibid.

54. Ibid.

55. Ibid., XLV, 1, 28 September 1962.

56. Ibid., XLVI, 2, 11 October 1963.

57. Minutes of Academic Council, 1961−62, Evaluation Report of JCU, 1962, *AJC*.

58. Consultors Meetings 1950−65, 30 January 1962, *AJC*.

59. Minutes of Academic Council, 1961−62, Evaluation Report in preparation for the North Central, *AJC*.

60. Ibíd., Appendix 16.

61. Ibid., "Report on Spiritual Activities," 12 February 1962, *AJC*.

62. Ibid.

63. Ibid.

64. *Carroll News*, XLIV, 10, 2 March 1962.

65. Ibid.

66. Ibid., 16 March 1962.

67. Ibid., XLVII, 10, 26 March 1965.

68. Ibid.

69. North Central Report, 1964, *AJC*.

70. *Carroll News*, VI, 4, 18 October 1968.

71. Minutes, Faculty Meeting, 30 January 1967, *AJC*.

72. *Carroll News*, LI, 8, 31 January 1969.

73. Ibid.

74. Ibid., LII, 13, 20 March 1970.

75. Ibid.

76. Ibid., 6 March 1970.

77. Ibid., LI, 9, 19 February 1969.

78. Ibid., LI, 12, 14 March 1969.

79. An undated, unidentified article in a Scrapbook. The year is 1941, probably September and possibly the *Catholic Universe Bulletin, AJC.*

80. Minute Book, Consultors of John Carroll Univ., 1917–49, 11 May 1943, *AJC.*

81. Ibid., 2 September 1943.

82. Ibid.

83. Ibid.

84. Ibid., 31 October 1946.

85. The increasing number of women in the Evening College had been due to a deliberate policy of promoting the Evening College as coeducational.

86. "Blueprint Report," 24–26, *AJC.*

87. Ibid.

88. *The Cleveland Press,* 14 September 1962.

89. *Carroll News,* XLV, 2, 12 October 1962.

90. George E. Grauel, "Stabilization of Evening Enrollment: A Proposal." 15 October 1962, *AJC.* Father Dunn approved the proposal 29 October 1962. Also, Minutes of Academic Council, 19 October 1962, *AJC.*

91. Ibid.

92. *The Cleveland Press,* 13 November 1962.

93. Ibid.

94. *Carroll News,* XLV, 5, 30 November 1962.

95. Ibid.

96. Ibid.

97. Minutes of Academic Council, 10 May 1963.

98. Owens to Dunn, 31 July 1963, *AJC.* Copies of this letter were sent to a number of faculty and administrators. The letter cited the insignificant numbers of female enrollment; 2 percent of full-time and 12 percent of total enrollment.

99. North Central Report, 3–9 May, 1964, *AJC.*

100. Various facets of the subject received attention. The women's honor fraternity, Gamma Pi Epsilon, counterpart of Alpha Sigma Nu, had a rough time. The editor of the *Carroll News,* changed his mind on that one, *Carroll News,* 6 November 1964, 20 November 1964. There was also an article by a coed who pointed out that if the coeds were to be accused of looking for husbands, there were cheaper ways than paying tuition at Carroll, *Carroll News,* 10, 26 March 1965.

101. *Carroll News,* XLVII, 11, 9 April 1965.

102. Ibid., XLVIII, 5, 10 December 1965.

103. Ibid., XLVIII, 5 11 February 1966.

104. Ibid., XLVIII, 11, 13 May 1966.

105. Ibid., LI, 2 September 1967.

106. Minutes, Jesuit Board of Trustees, 16 November 1967, *AJC.*

107. Ibid., 12 December 1967.

108. Ibid., 9 January 1968.

109. Conry to Academic Senate, Memorandum, 15 January 1968; 31 January 1968, *AJC.*

110. Minutes of Academic Council, 1962–63, various discussions, *AJC.*

111. Dunn to Auxilary Bishop Clarence E. Elwell, 20 September 1963, *ADC.*

112. Minutes, Liaison Committee, 15 July 1963, *AJC.*

113. Ibid., 6 December 1966.

114. "Feasibility Study Report—Cleveland Catholic Colleges and Seminaries, 4 December 1967," *AJC.*

115. Novicky to Grauel, 3 March 1965, *AJC.*

116. Ibid.

117. Neil G. McCluskey, S.J., ed., *The Catholic University, A Modern Appraisal,*" Chapter on "Governance" by Neil G. McCluskey, 150.

118. Ibid.

119. John J. McGrath, *Catholic Institutions in the United States.*

120. Ibid.

121. *Carroll, IV,* 4, Fall, 1966.

122. *Carroll News,* XLIX, 6, 11 November 1966.

123. Ibid., LII, 7, 21 November 1969.

124. *Time,* 20 January 1967, 66; also *National Catholic Reporter,* 18 January 1967.

125. *Cleveland Press,* 16 January 1967.

126. *Carroll News,* XLIX, 8, 27 January 1967.

127. Minutes, Faculty Meeting, 30 January 1967.

128. *Carroll Alumni Magazine,* V, 3, Summer 1967.

129. Ibid.

130. In an interview by the author with some of the Advisory Lay Board of Trustees in June 1981, the opinion seemed to be that they were surprised by the change and unaware that it was impending. They had invited the Provincial to meet with them to explain the change since it came just as the second phase of the Decade of Progress was about to get underway. The advisory Lay Board was given to understand that university considerations played no part in the change, nor was the Provincial thought to have given consideration to the impact of the change on the university.

131. *Carroll,* (Alumni Magazine), V, 3, 4 August 1967.

132. Ibid., No. 4, October-December, 1967.

133. *Carroll News,* L, 1, 2 September 1967.

134. Minutes, Jesuit Board of Trustees, 16 November 1967, *AJC.*

135. Ibid., 9 January 1968.

136. Ibid.

137. Ibid.

138. Minutes, Joint Council, 12 February 1968, *AJC.*

139. Ibid.

140. Ibid.

141. Ibid.

142. Ibid.

143. "John Carroll University Meeting of the Jesuit Community," 15 September 1968, *AJC.*

144. Ibid.

145. Ibid.

146. Minutes, Special Meeting of the Board of Trustees, 4 October 1968, *AJC.*

147. Ibid., also 11 November 1968.

148. Ibid., 14 October 1968.

149. Minutes, Special Meeting of the Board of Trustees, 7 January 1969, *AJC.*

150. Minutes, Meeting of the Joint Council, 21 April 1969, *AJC.*

151. Ibid., 15 September 1969.

152. Ibid., 20 January 1969.

153. Ibid., 1 March 1968.

CHAPTER XV

1. Reported to the author at a meeting with members of the Board of Trustees of 1970. Interview, June 1981.

2. "Computation of Instructional Expense per Credit Hour for years ending 30 June 1963 thru 31 May 1971," *AJC*.

3. Francis A. Jones, "Comments on the Financial Operation of the University for the year ended 31 May 1971," *AJC*.

4. *Carroll News*, LIII, 1, 4 September 1970.

5. Ibid.

6. Ibid.

7. Ibid.

8. Birkenhauer to Members of the Budget Council, 12 February 1971, *AJC*.

9. *Carroll News*, LIII, 8, 11 December 1970.

10. Ibid., LIII, 9, 29 January 1971.

11. Report of the President, 1971–1972, "President's Message," *AJC*.

12. Report of the President, 1973–1974, *AJC*.

13. Ibid.

14. Report of the President, 1975, *AJC*.

15. Report of the President, 1972–1973, *AJC*.

16. Report of the President, 1970–1971, *AJC*.

17. *Carroll News*, LIII, 4, 16 October 1970.

18. Ibid., 30 October 1970.

19. Ibid.

20. Ibid., LIII, 6, 13 November 1970.

21. Ibid.

22. Ibid.

23. Ibid., LIII, 7, 20 November 1970.

24. Ibid., LIII, 6, 13 November 1970.

25. Ibid.

26. Ibid., LIII, 8, 11 December 1970.

27. Ibid., During the discussions on extending parietal hours in the spring of 1970, many Jesuits expressed strong opposition to any extension of these hours. Several put their objections in writing, sending their letters to the Student Affairs Committee. Running through these letters was a common theme that any extension of these hours would compromise the position of the University's claim to certain basic moral convictions and Christian ideals. The writers said they would be obligated, if hours were extended, to warn parents not to send their sons and daughters to John Carroll. (Student Affairs Committee Correspondence, *AJC*.)

28. Ibid.

29. Ibid., LIII, 9, 29 January 1971.

30. Ibid., LIII, 10, 12 February 1971.

31. Ibid., LIII, 14, 12 March 1971.

32. Ibid.

33. Ibid. Father Birkenhauer was also quoted as saying that because of the obvious moral issue involved he sought recourse to prayer during which when he considered how God trusted His people; he was not being "particularly Christian" if he didn't "trust the students." Father Birkenhauer said, "As I prayed it seemed to me that the crucial point was to trust the students to the extent of their maturity. I talked to the students, I listened to them and felt that they had a claim to be trusted." *Carroll*, Alumni News, 9:3, Summer, 1971.

34. *Carroll News*, LIII, 17, 8 April 1971.

35. Ibid.

36. Ibid., LIII, 15, 26 March 1971.

37. Ibid.

38. Ibid., LIII, 18, 23 April 1971.

39. Ibid., LVII, 15, 14 March 1975.

40. Ibid.

41. Memorandum, Birkenhauer to Members of the University Council, 14 September 1970. *AJC.*

42. *Carroll News,* LIV, 11, 3 December 1971.

43. Minutes of the University Council, 9 February 1972.

44. Ibid., 10 February 1972; also *Carroll News* LIV, 15, 25 February 1972.

45. *Carroll News,* LIV, 17, 17 March 1972.

46. Ibid.

47. Ibid.

48. Ibid., LV, 10, 17 November 1972.

48. "The Decade of Progress Plan, 1963," *AJC.*

50. Ibid.

51. Ibid.

52. Ibid.

53. *Carroll,* Spring, 1970.

54. *Carroll News,* LV, 9, 10 November 1972.

55. "Recommendation of the Curriculum Committee on the Core Curriculum," May, 1972. *AJC.*

56. Britt to Birkenhauer, 4 December 1972.

57. Report of the President, 1973–1974.

58. Gavin to Birkenhauer, 5 February 1971, *AJC.*

59. Minutes, Cleveland Catholic Colleges Meeting of Presidents with Consultants, 14–15 November 1969, *AJC.*

60. Cahill to Gavin, 18 December 1969, *AJC.* Father Lawrence Cahill was president of St. John College.

61. Cahill to Presidents, Cleveland Catholic Colleges, 23 January 1970, *AJC.*

62. Ibid.

63. Ibid.

64. Ibid.

65. Regulations of the Associated Colleges, 14 August 1970, *AJC.*

66. Gavin to Birkenhauer, 28 January 1971, *AJC.*

67. Gavin to Thompson, 16 July 1971.

68. Britt to Noetzel, 31 January 1974, *AJC.*

69. Minutes of the Meeting of the Associated Colleges, 19 September 1975, *AJC;* also Gavin to Birkenhauer, 7 October 1975, *AJC.*

70. Minutes of the Associated Colleges of Cleveland, 15 March 1976, *AJC.*

71. Report of the President, 1971–72 and 1972–73, *AJC.*

72. *Carroll News,* LVII, 2, 27 September 1974.

73. Ibid., 20 September 1974.

74. Ibid., LVIII, 2, 19 September 1975.

75. Committee on University Planning, Meeting, 27 October 1976, *AJC.*

76. Report of the Interprovince Committee, 20 June 1922, *ALUC.*

77. Wilson to Francis J. Gerst, S.J., (dean of graduate school at Loyola University, Chicago.) 2 October 1935.

78. Ibid.

79. Wilson to O'Connell, 29 January 1935, *ALUC.*

80. "Blueprint Report."

81. Report to the North Central Association of a Consulting Visit to John Carroll University, Sherman K. Haynes and Martin Stevens, 1 November 1967, *AJC.*

82. Ibid.
83. Minutes Academic Senate, 6 December 1967.
84. "F-2 of Planning Agenda, 5 April 1972," *AJC.*
85. Birkenhauer to James A. McManamon, O.F.M., (president of St. John College), 14 April 1975, *AJC.*
86. *Carroll News*, LVIII, 15, 13 February 1976.
87. Ibid., LIII, 9, 29 January 1971.
88. Ibid., LIV, 20, 5 May 1972.
89. Ibid.
90. Ibid., LV, 11, 8 December 1972.
91. Ibid., LVI, 3, 28 September 1973.
92. Ibid., LVIII, 19, 2 April 1976.
93. Ibid., 59, 18, 6 May 1977.
94. Ibid., 62, 2, 22 September 1978.
95. Ibid., 63, 20, 2 May 1980.
96. Ibid.
97. Ibid., 62, 12, 9 February 1979.

CHAPTER XVI

1. *Carroll*, 10:1, Winter 1972.
2. Ibid., 12:2., Spring 1974.
3. *Carroll News*, v. 62, p. 17, 6 April 1979.
4. Ibid.
5. Ibid.
6. "Summary of Responses to Long-Range Planning Question for Academy for Educational Development Project," 4 February 1977, *AJC.*
7. Ibid.
8. Minutes of the University Planning Committee, 21 February 1977, *AJC.*
9. The Jones Report was the name given to the memorandum submitted by Sherman Jones, who made the visitation for the AED. It is undated and without title, *AJC.*
10. Gavin to Birkenhauer, 26 April 1977; Britt to Birkenhauer, 23 June 1977; Schell to Birkenhauer, 22 June 1977; Pecek to Birkenhauer, 23 June 1977; Schaefer to Birkenhauer, 27 June 1977, *AJC.*
11. Birkenhauer to Millett, 29 June 1977, *AJC.*
12. Ibid.
13. Millett to Birkenhauer, 9 August 1977, *AJC.*
14. Birkenhauer to Millett, 29 June 1977, *AJC.*
15. Meeting of the Planning Committee, 18 July 1977, *AJC.*
16. Ibid.
17. From the Mission Statement, which can be found in Appendix E.
18. *John Carroll University Undergraduate Bulletin, 1966–1968.*
19. Report of the President, 1971–1972, John Carroll University.
20. Ibid.
21. *Carroll News*, v. LIV, p. 5, 1 October 1971.
22. Ibid., v. 60, p. 17, 7 April 1978.
23. Ibid., v. LVII, 11 October 1974.
24. Ibid., v. LIII, p. 14, 12 March 1971.
25. Report of the Campus Ministry at John Carroll, 1981–1982. Submitted by Father Joseph O. Schell.

26. Meeting of the Planning Committee, 2 November 1978, *AJC*. Raymond J. Reilly was an alumnus of John Carroll and a consultant for Ernst and Ernst (Ernst and Whinney) for the previous eleven years. The study took four months.

27. *Carroll News*, v. 52, p. 3, 16 February 1979.

28. Minutes of the Faculty Meeting, 15 February 1978, *AJC*.

29. "Design for a Second Spring," 6 April 1979, *AJC*.

30. Memorandum of the Faculty Service Committee, 9 May 1979, *AJC*.

31. Information Meeting on Priorities and Guidelines Report, 29 June 1979, *AJC*.

32. Ibid.

33. Notes from the President's Desk, Special Issue, August 1979.

34. *Carroll News*, v. 62, p. 13, 16 February 1979.

35. Ibid., interview.

36. Ibid., 63:14, 22 February 1980.

37. Ibid.

38. Ibid.

39. "*Liberal Education and the World of Work*, Report of the President, 1980, *AJC*.

40. Ibid.

41. *Carroll*, 10:4, Fall 1972.

42. Ibid.

43. *Carroll News*, LVIII, 18, 26 March 1976.

44. Ibid., LX, 5, 28 October 1977.

45. *Carroll*, Fall-Winter, 1975–76, Remarks of Father Schell in the occasion of Father Millor's fiftieth anniversary in the Society of Jesus.

46. Ibid.

47. Ibid.

48. Ibid.

49. Ibid., 10:7, Spring 1972.

50. Ibid.

51. William H. Bricker in Report of the President, 1977.

52. Ibid.

APPENDIX A

1. Garraghan, *The Jesuits of the Middle United States*, I, 583–87. Also Garraghan, I, 524–41 for the story of the refugees. Also Curran, *The Return of the Jesuits*, 108–34.

2. Curran, 119.

3. There is a good account of Behrens' character in Brady, *Canisius College, The First Hundred Years*, 76, ff. Father Behrens's obituary is in *Woodstock Letters*, XXV.

4. Curran, *Return of the Jesuits* 136–38. There was an attempt to set up a college in Toledo at the beginning of Bishop Gilmour's episcopate in 1872 but the bishop was somewhat intractable. When the Jesuit who had been teaching in the Cleveland seminary was recalled by his superiors, Bishop Gilmour became even more irritable.

5. Father Behrens had been admonished by the General in 1872 not to attempt too much in the way of expansion and warned that one could not do everything in this "boundless land." The large German populations in Cleveland and elsewhere were too tempting and the original purpose of the Mission was to serve these German people, Brady, *Canisius*, 115, ff. Father Lessmann either had not seen the General's admonition to Father Behrens or he simply ignored it. At the time of Bishop Gilmour's "Circular Letter" the Buffalo Jesuits were considering several possibilities of opening colleges in the area which had been assigned to them.

6. *Catalogus Sociorum et Officiorum Dispersae Provinciae Germaniae Societas Jesu,* 1886, *AJC.*

APPENDIX B

1. O'Callaghan to Rodman, 9 December 1928, *AJC.*
2. Ibid.
3. Ibid.
4. Rodman to O'Callaghan, 15 December 1928, *AJC.*
5. Ibid.
6. Ibid.
7. Ibid.
8. Ibid.
9. O'Callaghan to Rodman, 16 December 1928, *AJC.*
10. Ibid.
11. O'Callaghan to Rodman, 27 December 1928, *AJC.*
12. Ibid.
13. Neustich to Bushart, 1 January 1909, *AJC.*
14. James A. Mackin, Report on the Buffalo Mission debt, 1886–1907, *AJC.*
15. This account is a brief summary of Father Mackin's Report. An additional point of resentment that seems to go back to Father Neustich's time was the feeling that when Brother Wipfler was sent to design the new building that Father Neustich had already designed, the building became more elaborate and the cost greater. What Father Neustich felt he could have built for $60,000 now cost $150,000; the Buffalo Mission should bear the difference in cost. On the other hand, Father Neustich did not stop Brother Wipfler when he exceeded the cost but gave tacit approval; it was assumed, however, by the Consultors that Father Neustich, a vice-rector, had no funds. Minutes of Consultors' Meetings, 1888–1917, 13 January, 7 July, 12 November, 18 November, 20 November, 1890; 4, 5 February, 24, 27 March, 1891, *AJC.* Father Behrens never made clear the terms of the task; he simply ordered Father Neustich to go, build a college and he would pay. As late as 1894, Father LeHalle understood that the funds were collected for St. Ignatius College by Father Behrens and that the College was in legitimate possession of them, Minutes of Consultors' Meetings, 1888–1917, 12 October 1894, *AJC.*
16. Cloud to Rodman, 3 August 1932, *AJC.* The permission from the Congregation of Religious was dated 11 July 1932 with Father General Ledochowski's permission dated 16 July 1932, *AJC.*
17. Welfle to Walker, 26 March 1956, *AJC* and *ASIH.*

APPENDIX C

1. Minute Book, Consultors of John Carroll Univ., 1917–49, 6 January 1925, *AJC.*
2. Some Jesuits felt that Father Anthony Wilwerding should have been made pastor of Gesu. Monsignor Joseph F. Smith opposed such an appointment because he wanted a younger man who was enthusiastic and a good preacher; Father Wilwerding's age and rather high-pitched voice did not meet those qualifications. Father Thomas J. Smith was equally opposed to the appointment but for quite different reasons. Father Wilwerding had apparently told Father T. J Smith that he (Wilwerding) did not think that information about the Jesuits should be withheld from Monsignor Smith. Father T. J. Smith wrote Father Mc-Menamy that Father Wilwerding had given information to Monsignor Smith "and that is why

I have withheld information from the Community concerning my dealing with Real Estate Companies in choosing the new site." T. J. Smith to McMenamy, 14 July 1925, *AMP*.

3. Ford (president of R.T.L.S. Co.) to Schrembs, 5 November 1924, *ADC*.

4. Komlos to T. J. Smith, 19 November 1924, *ADC*. This letter was sent to Bishop Schrembs by Father Smith, who said he was not aware of the offer already made; he did not wish to act without Schrembs's advice, T. J. Smith to Schrembs, 21 November 1924, *ADC*.

5. Boylan to McFadden, 20 August 1925, *ADC*. Boylan was urging the bishop to make a formal request in writing for the deed to the "church triangle" property.

6. Boylan to Monsignor Smith, 26 August 1925, *ADC*.

7. McFadden to Rudden, 26 March 1926, *ADC*.

8. Boylan to McMenamy, 26 March 1926, *AJC*.

9. Minute Book, Consultors of John Carroll Univ., 1917–49, 14 July 1926, *AJC*.

10. Haggeney to Boylan, 3 May 1927, *AJC*.

11. An unsigned and undated memorandum, probably by Father Boylan, called "Report Concerning Some Land Deals in University Heights Village," probably 1928, *AJC*. Its contents are supported by legal papers on each of the properties; also in *AJC*.

12. There is a note (*AJC*) given by Father Rudden, February 15, 1926, to Edward T. P. Graham, in the amount of $5,000 for "development of the parish." Graham was a member of the syndicate formed to buy one of the lots. In 1931 Graham was still seeking repayment, Graham to McFadden, 22 December 1931, *AJC*.

13. Minute Book Consultors of John Carroll Univ., 1917–49, 6 September 1927, *AJC*.

14. B. L. Jenks (for the Van Sweringens) to Horky, October 10, 1927, *ADC*. Jenks explained to Horky that in the original zoning the "triangle" could be used for a church and was subsequently given to the diocese of Cleveland. The zoning map of University Heights shows business districts on both sides of Warrensville Center Road south of Cedar. Therefore, there seemed no need for further business districts. Jenks asked that the University Heights Council take no action.

15. Horky, newsletter attached to letter from Van Sweringens to Horky, 10 October 1927, *ADC*.

16. Horky to Boylan, 30 November 1927, *ADC*.

17. Ibid.

18. Ibid.

19. Horky to Boylan, 4 December 1927, 12 December 1927, *ADC*.

20. Boylan to Horky, 16 December 1927, *ADC*.

21. Ibid.

22. Boylan to Horky, 7 December 1927, *ADC*.

23. Horky to Rodman, 15 October 1928, *AJC*.

24. Horky to McFadden, 29 April 1928, *ADC*.

25. McFadden to Horky, 26 April 1928, *ADC*. A long list of complaints had been sent to Bishop Schrembs by Horky in March. The letter ended with a diatribe against Jesuits in general, "I wonder if the Jesuits are soul-savers and educators or political meddlers, history tells us that they were banished away from Catholic Countries in the past centuries, we have always been made to believe that the old so called Jesuit 'The end justifies the means' is a slur on our Church and on the . . . ."; the next page of this letter is missing. Horky to Schrembs, 27 March 1981, *ADC*.

26. Horky to Rodman, 15 October 1928, *AJC*.

27. Ibid.

28. "Petition of University Heights Citizens," signed by Mayor Howard, six councilmen, the clerk, assistant clerk, solicitor, and building supervisor. October 29, 1928, *ADC*.

29. "Petition of Committees of Gesu Parish" to Bishop Schrembs, no date but from contents it might have been presented after Father Rudden's removal in November, *ADC.*
30. O'Callaghan to Schrembs, 11 November 1928, *ADC.*
31. Ibid.
32. Ibid.
33. Ibid.
34. Schrembs to O'Callaghan, 16 November 1928, *ADC.*
35. Report, McFadden to Schrembs, 13 November 1928, *ADC.*
36. Versavel's Memorandum on meeting with Bishop Schrembs, no date, *AJC.*
37. Versavel to Rodman, 7 December 1928, *AJC.*
38. Ibid.
39. O'Callaghan to Rodman, 12 December 1928, *AJC.*
40. Rodman to Schrembs, 14 December 1928, *ADC.*
41. O'Callaghan to Rodman, 16 December 1928, *AJC.*
42. Rodman to O'Callaghan, 15 December 1928, *AJC.*

APPENDIX D

1. Minute Book, Consultors of John Carroll Univ., 1917–49, 11 May 1943.
2. Ibid.
3. Ibid., 13 June 1946.

APPENDIX E

1. Boylan to O'Callaghan, 22 September 1926, *AJC.*
2. Schlitz to Treasurer (F. X. Kowald), August 31, 1928, *AJC.*
3. Ibid.
4. George J. Arnold (R.T.L.S. Co.) to Herman Neff, 31 January 1931, *AJC.* At this time there was a possibility for the university to rescue its investment; but it would have cost an additional $15,000. In February, Father Rodman decided to "drop out of the picture" (Schlitz to Rodman, 24 February 1931, *AJC*). Schlitz informed Father Rodman that the decision had been communicated to all concerned. A memorandum two months later indicated that there was further investigation into the matter. The new treasurer of the university, Father Wilfred Robb, did not think that John Carroll should give up its rights without permission from Rome; in any case to do so would jeopardize further claims against R.T.L.S. Co. Father Robb felt that the company had "utterly failed to fulfill its contract with J.C.U." (Memorandum of Father Robb, 13 April 1931, *AJC.*) Father Robb recommended that although the mortgage that the university had was only a fourth mortgage, it should be recorded and claim should not be relinquished.

Notes on the Sources

Except for a few sketchy accounts that tend to repeat each other, there are no previously published histories of John Carroll University. The *Catalogue* of 1895–1896 included a very brief account of the first ten years. At the celebration of the Silver Jubilee in 1911, the *Catholic Universe*, the local diocesan newspaper, devoted a considerable amount of space to the growth of the college during its first twenty-five years. In 1917 a *Historical* Review of St. Ignatius College was published. Although no author was listed probably either Father Francis Betten or Father Francis Haggeney prepared it. The Golden Jubilee, 1936, saw the publication of a small memorial volume, *John Carroll University, The Golden Jubilee, 1936*, which repeated much of what had appeared in the 1917 account. In 1962 Father Edmund Te Pas, S.J., wrote a master's essay for his degree from Loyola University, Chicago. The essay brings the account to 1923 but devotes a disproportionate amount of space to the formation of the Diocese of Cleveland, the Buffalo Mission, and the problems of Loyola High School. The unpublished essay does have some value in its limited use of archival material at John Carroll University and in interviews the author had with some of the early Jesuits who were still living at the time, particularly Father Henry Brockman and Louis Puhl.

The archives of John Carroll University and St. Ignatius High School contain much of the material necessary for a history of the institutions. There are, of course, large gaps in the material, particularly in the correspondence of the early rectors, but a fair amount has been preserved. Nearly all of the *Litterae Annuae* are available. These yearly communications to Rome are not always as useful as they might be because they tend to omit a great deal, but they do reflect the opinion of the writer, who is generally not the rector.

Also available are: *Catalogus Sociorum et Officiorum Dispersae Provincial Germaniae*; the "House Diaries" usually kept by Father Minister; a "Rector's Diary" for the years 1942 to 1946; a diary kept by the dean and entitled, "St. Ignatius College Diary," in which Father George Degleman's years are recorded; the Minutes of the Consultors' Meetings; the Minutes of the Board of Trustees; Provincial "Memorials"; and the St. Ignatius College Register for the years 1886 to 1896. There is also a House Announcement Book for the years 1886 to 1897. The *Woodstock Letters* (1872–1969), a record of events connected with the colleges and missions of the Society of Jesus in the United States, is a useful source as are also the *Provincial Newsletters* of the Missouri and Chicago provinces. The Archives of the Diocese of Cleveland are important because of the very close relationship between the university and the diocese during the first half of the century. The Archives of Case Western Reserve University contain material concerning the name change of

St. Ignatius College in 1923 which is not available in the Archives of John Carroll University.

Microfilm copies of the material in the Archives of Canisius College pertaining to the Buffalo Mission of the German Province and the establishment of St. Ignatius College are to be found in the Archives of John Carroll University. Some letters from Father General to Fathers Neustich and Knappmeyer in the Archives of the Society of Jesus in Rome are also on microfilm in the John Carroll Archives. Much material in the Archives of Canisius College pertaining to the early days of St. Ignatius College is available only at Canisius. There are also microfilm copies in the John Carroll Archives of much of the correspondence between the rectors of St. Ignatius College and the Missouri provincials; the originals are in the Archives of the Missouri Province in St. Louis. The Archives of the Chicago Province contain little relating to John Carroll University except for the period of Father Albert C. Fox's difficulties with the Diocese of Cleveland. The Archives of Marquette and those of Loyola University, Chicago contain important material concerning the activities at John Carroll in the 1920s and 1930s. The Campion College Archives, now at Marquette University, are also useful for John Carroll history.

The first student publication of the university was the *Lumina*, 1915–1919, succeeded by *The Ignatian*, 1919–1925, then the *Carroll News* since 1925. The diocesan newspaper was the *Catholic Universe*, begun in 1874; it later became the *Catholic Universe Bulletin*. Cleveland newspapers, the *Plain Dealer*, the *Press*, the *Leader*, and the *News*, are all available at the Cleveland Public Library.

The following selected list contains items which are helpful in rounding out the history of John Carroll University.

Andrica, Theodore. "Germans Came Early, Played a Vital Role." *The Cleveland Press*, 28 September 1950, p. 20.

Avery, Elroy McKendree. *A History of Cleveland, the Heart of New Connecticut*. 3 vols. Chicago: The Lewis Publishing Company, 1918.

Baker, Samuel J. "The Original Surveys of Cleveland." *Journal of the Association of Engineering Societies* III, 10 (August 1884): 218.

Bangert, William V., S.J. *A History of the Society of Jesus*. St. Louis: Institute of Jesuit Sources, 1972.

Bannon, John F., S.J. *The Missouri Province*. St. Louis: Missouri Province, 1977.

Barry, Colman J. *The Catholic Church and German Americans*. Milwaukee: The Bruce Publishing Company, 1953.

Brady, Charles A. *Canisius College, the First Hundred Years*. Buffalo: Holling Press, 1970.

Brodrick, James, S.J. *St. Ignatius Loyola*. London: Burns & Oates, 1956.

Brown, S. W. *The Secularization of American Education*. New York: Russell and Russell, 1912.

Brubacher, John S. and Willis Rudy. *Higher Education in Transition*. 3d edition. New York: Harper and Row, 1976.

Chapman, Edmund A. *Cleveland, Village to Metropolis, A Case Study of Problems of Urban Development in Nineteenth Century America*. Cleveland: The

Western Reserve Historical Society, The Press of Western Reserve University, 1964.

Cheit, Earl F. "The New Depression in Higher Education: Implications for Trustees." Association of Governing Boards of Universities and Colleges, Report of the Annual Business Meeting, 13, no. 8 (May–June 1971): 10–20.

Cleveland Commission on Higher Education. *The Future of Higher Education in Cleveland: A Report to the Community by the Cleveland Commission on Higher Education.* Prepared under the direction of Howard Whipple Green and Gale R. Ober, Jr., 1959.

Condon, George E. *Cleveland, The Best Kept Secret.* New York: Doubleday, 1967. Reprint, J. T. Zubal and P. J. Dole, 1981.

Cramer, C. H. *Case Western Reserve, A History of the University, 1826–1976.* Boston: Little, Brown and Company, 1976.

Curran, Francis X., S.J. *The Return of the Jesuits.* Chicago: Loyola University Press, 1966.

Davis, Calvin Olin. *A History of the North Central Association of Colleges and Secondary Schools.* Ann Arbor: The North Central Association of Colleges and Secondary Schools, 1945.

Donohue, John W., S.J. *Jesuit Education: An Essay on the Foundations of Its Idea.* New York: Fordham Univ. Press, 1963.

Eliot, Charles W. "Recent Changes in Secondary Education." *Atlantic Monthly* 84 (October 1899), pp. 433–44.

Ellis, John T. "American Catholics and the Intellectual Life." *Thought* 30 (Autumn 1955): 351–88.

Faherty, William B., S.J. *Dream by the River, Two Centuries of St. Louis Catholicism, 1766–1967.* St. Louis: Piraeus, 1973.

Garraghan, Gilbert J., S.J. *The Jesuits of the Middle United States.* 3 vols. New York: America Press, 1938.

Gawrysiak, Kenneth John. "The Administration of Albert C. Fox, A Portrait of Educational Leadership at Marquette University, 1922–1928." Unpublished Ph.D. dissertation, Marquette University, 1973.

Gleason, Phillip. "The Crisis in Catholic Universities, A Historical Perspective." *Catholic Mind* 64 (September 1966): 41–55.

Guilday, Peter. *The Life and Times of John Carroll, Archbishop of Baltimore, 1735–1815.* 2 vols. New York: Encyclopedia Press, 1922. Reprint, one vol., Westminster, Md.: Newman Press, 1954.

Hagan, John R. *The Diocesan Teachers College, A Study of its Basic Principles.* Washington D.C.: Catholic University of America Press, 1932.

Hamilton, Ralph N., S.J. *The Story of Marquette University.* Milwaukee: Marquette University Press, 1953.

Hanley, Thomas O'Brien, S.J. *The John Carroll Papers.* 3 vols. Notre Dame: University of Notre Dame Press, 1976.

Hassenger, R. N., ed. *The Shape of Catholic Higher Education.* New York: John C. Wiley, 1967.

Hennesey, James J., S.J. *American Catholics, A History of the Roman Catholic Community in the United States.* New York: Oxford University Press, 1981.

Hofstadter, Richard and Wilson Smith, eds. *American Higher Education, A Documentary History.* Chicago: University of Chicago Press, 1961.

Hynes, Michael J. *History of the Diocese of Cleveland.* Cleveland: World Publishing Company, 1953.

Kennedy, James Harrison. *A History of the City of Cleveland, Its Settlement, Rise and Progress, 1796–1896.* Cleveland: The Imperial Press, 1896.

LaFarge, John, S.J. *The Manner is Ordinary.* New York: Harcourt, Brace and Company, 1954.

McAvoy, Thomas T., C.S.C. *A History of the Catholic Church in the United States.* Notre Dame: University of Notre Dame Press, 1969.

McCluskey, Neil G., S.J., ed. *The Catholic University, A Modern Appraisal.* Notre Dame: University of Notre Dame Press, 1970.

McGrath, John J. *Catholic Universities in the United States; Canonical and Civil Law Statutes:* Washington, D.C.: Catholic University of American Press, 1968.

McGucken, William J., S.J. *The Jesuits and Education.* Milwaukee: The Bruce Publishing Co., 1932.

Muller, Herman, S.J. *The University of Detroit, 1877–1977, A Centennial History.* Detroit: University of Detroit, 1976.

Parsonage, Robert Rue, ed. *Church Related Higher Education in the United States.* Valley Forge: Judson Press, 1978.

Power, Edward J., S.J. *Catholic Higher Education in America, A History.* New York: Appleton Century Crofts, 1972.

Rose, William Ganson. *Cleveland, The Making of a City.* Cleveland: World Publishing Company, 1950.

Savage, Howard. *American College Athletics.* New York: Carnegie Foundation, 1929.

Thelin, John R. *The Cultivation of Ivy: A Saga of the College in America.* Cambridge: Schenkman Publishing Company, 1976.

Veysey, Lawrence. *The Emergence of the American University.* Chicago: University of Chicago Press, 1965.

Wheeler, Robert A. *Pleasantly Situated on the West Side.* Cleveland: The Western Reserve Historical Society, 1980.

Index

496n. 26

Orchestra, St. Ignatius College: organized, 47; interest declines, 181, 183; Winter as conductor, 157–58

O'Reilly, Thomas C. (bishop Scranton), first president of Alumni Association, 50

Otting, Rev. Leonard, S.J.: credits required for degree, 151; suspends classes, 172

Oxford-Cambridge debate, 315

Pacelli Hall, dedicated, 333

Pap, Michael S., Soviet Institute, 408

Papi, Rev. Hector, S.J.: Loyola High School decree, 97; Sommerhauser and, 88, 100

Parmadale Band, 184

Pearl, Rev. Douglas, S.J., superior of the Jesuit Community, 328

Peirolo, James, 333, 437

Pharmacy School, proposed, 331

Phillips, Rev. Edward C., S.J., financial report of, 289–90

Philosophy: added to curriculum, 43; alumni reaction to, 363; integrating factor, 360–61; Los Angeles Workshop, 363; oral examination discontinued, 170; requirement changed, 365

Physics, department of, Themis proposal and doctoral program, 413

Pickel, Rev. George, S.J.: biography, 58; boarding students, 78; borrowing money from Ursuline and Notre Dame Colleges, 76; Golden Jubilee celebration, 515n. 23; proposes lay advisory board, 78–79; East Side location search, 67–68, 72–73, 75; Jesuit contribution to education in Cleveland, 74–75; Loyola High School controversy, 92; medical school proposal, 59–60; replaces Magee as president, 296; rose garden, 301; secular colleges, 75; St. Mary Cemetery fund, 76; Scientific Academy, 187; sixteenth-century maps, 60; Sommerhauser and, 90–91; Western Reserve Medical School and, 60, 479n. 90

Pingstock, Rev. Robert, S.J., 435

"Pink Barn," 333

Pinochle majors, 314

Planning: Academy for Educational Development and, 420–21; Frank Jones on, 394; obstacles to, 421; committee formed, 398; Reilly Report, 425

Poetker, Rev. Albert M., S.J., role of lay-

men, 351

Predovich, Rev. Nicholas, S.J., 434

President's Athletic Conference (PAC), origin, 49

Priorities and Guidelines, report of committee on, 426–27

Professional Schools, and Cleveland University, 304

Project Vela Uniform, 409

Prpic, George, and Soviet Institute, 408

Public relations: academic council and, 334; coeducation and, 380; department added, 176; Odenbach and, 231–32

Quigley, Rev. Patrick, on quality of students, 42

Quinlan, Rev. James, S.J., appointed treasurer, 292

Race relations, campus integration, 416

Rapid Transit Land Sales Co.: original agreement rejected, 108; promotes education, 115

Rappe, Amedeus (bishop of Cleveland): Jesuit House in Toledo established, 3; seeks a college, 2

Rathskeller, opened in original chapel foundation, 375

Ratio Studiorum: described, 25–27; and rewritten Mission Statement, 422

Ray, John: football coach, 349; record, 376

Reali, John, Harry Gauzman lounge, 419

Reconstruction Finance Corporation, loan sought from, 279

Reilley, Edward C., 436

Reilly, Raymond J., report on enrollment, 425–26

Religion, role in curriculum, 43

Rice, Jack, tennis champion, 199

Ride, Ray, Case coach agrees to play Carroll, 214

Ripley, Elmer, basketball coach, 349, 351

Ritter, Emmerick, and Odenbach, 156

Robb, Rev. Wilfred, S.J., on boarding students, 281

Rockliff, Rev. James A., S.J.: German Jesuits and English competency, 36; biography, 54, 56

Rodman, Rev. Benedict J., S.J.: Bernet and, 228; Buffalo Mission debt, 444–45; civic welcome, 219; classes on Heights to open,

Donald P. Gavin has served John Carroll University as Chairman of the Department of History, Dean of the Evening College, Dean of the Graduate School, and Director of Institutional Planning. He is now University Historian.